GEOLOGICAL EXCURSIONS

around

GLASGOW & GIRVAN

Other guide books and pamphlets published by The Geological Society of Glasgow and obtainable from the Publications Officer at the address below:

An excursion guide to the GEOLOGY OF THE ISLE OF SKYE
by B.R. Bell and J.W.Harris.

Macgregor's excursion guide to the GEOLOGY OF ARRAN
edited by J.G. MacDonald and A. Herriot.

BUILDING STONES OF GLASGOW
by Judith Lawson.

An excursion guide to DOB's LINN
by S. Henry Williams

Excursion guide to the geology of the ISLE OF EIGG
by Judith Lawson.

Also, in association with the Edinburgh Geological Society:
An excursion guide to the MOINE GEOLOGY of the Scottish Highlands
edited by I. Allison, F. May and R.A. Strachan.

Geological Society of Glasgow
% Department of Geology & Applied Geology
Lilybank Gardens
University of Glasgow
GLASGOW G12 8QQ.

Cover picture:
View looking NNW up Loch Lomond from the hill of Duncryne (NS 435 859), near Gartocharn. To the left are the hills around Luss where slate was once extensively quarried. The distant jagged hill left of centre is Ben Arthur ("The Cobbler"): Ben Lomond is the snow-covered mountain right of centre. All these hills are part of the Dalradian block, eroded by ice and water from schistose greywackes, mica schists and slates.

On the right the village of Balmaha can be seen along the shore of the loch: the wooded ridge behind is the westerly continuation of Conic Hill, formed of steeply-dipping conglomerates of the Lower Old Red Sandstone. These rocks continue to the left as wooded islands across the loch. Between these ridges and the higher ground of Dalradian rocks to the north, lie the Highland Border Complex and the Highland Boundary Fault. This fault is a terrane boundary separating the Dalradian block from the Midland Valley block: in Ordovician times these two terranes had such entirely different histories that they could not then have been adjacent to one another.

The foreground is underlain by soft, easily eroded sandstones and mudstones of the Lower Old Red Sandstone. The hill of Duncryne, composed of agglomerate and basalt, is an eroded volcanic plug of Lower Carboniferous age.

GEOLOGICAL EXCURSIONS
around
GLASGOW & GIRVAN

Edited by

J.D. Lawson and D.S. Weedon

Published by

THE GEOLOGICAL SOCIETY OF GLASGOW

ISBN number 0 902892 09 6

British Library Cataloguing in Publications data

British Library Cataloguing-in-Publication Data
A catalogue record for this book is available
from the British Library.

Bibliographical Reference

Reference should be made to this publication as follows
Lawson, J.D. and Weedon, D.S. 1992. Geological Excursions around Glasgow and Girvan.
Geol. Soc. Glasgow. 1992 pp.496

Prepared for printing in the U.K. by Carnmor Print and Design, Preston

CONTENTS

Excursions

6

ACKNOWLEDGEMENT

The Geological Society of Glasgow is grateful to the following companies and organisations for their financial contributions towards the production of this excursion guide.

Clyde Petroleum plc

Lomond Associates

Reservoir Research Ltd

Thorburn plc

LIST OF CONTRIBUTORS

Bluck, B.J., Department of Geology & Applied Geology, University, Glasgow, G12 8QQ.

Bowes, D.R., Department of Geology & Applied Geology, University, Glasgow, G12 8QQ.

Bowes, G.E., Department of Geology & Applied Geology, University, Glasgow, G12 8QQ.

Burton, C.J., Department of Geology & Applied Geology, University, Glasgow, G12 8QQ.

Durant, G.P., Hunterian Museum, University, Glasgow, G12 8QQ.

Gribble, C.D., Department of Geology & Applied Geology, University, Glasgow, G12 8QQ.

Ingham, J.K., Hunterian Museum, The University, Glasgow, G12 8QQ.

Jardine, W.G., Department of Geology & Applied Geology, University, Glasgow, G12 8QQ.

Keen, M.C., Department of Geology & Applied Geology, University, Glasgow, G12 8QQ.

Lawson, J.D., 47 Southbrae Drive, Glasgow, G13 1PU.

Lawson, Judith A., 47 Southbrae Drive, Glasgow, G13 1PU.

MacDonald, J.G., Department of Adult and Continuing Education, University, Glasgow, G12 8LW.

Patterson, E.M., 25 Caldwell Road, West Kilbride, KA23 9LF.

Rolfe, W.D.I., Royal Museum of Scotland, Edinburgh, EH1 1JF.

Tanner, P.G.W., Department of Geology & Applied Geology, University, Glasgow, G12 8QQ.

Todd, J.G., "Eastfield", Tandlehill Road, Kilbarchan, PA10 2DQ.

Weedon, D.S., 9 Montgomerie Terrace, Skelmorlie, PA17 5DT.

Williams, S.H., Department of Earth Sciences, Memorial University of Newfoundland, St. Johns, Newfoundland, Canada.

Deceased
Mykura, W.
White, F.

FOREWORD

Scope of the guide

Glasgow can justly claim to have a greater variety of geology which can be visited on single day excursions than any other city in Britain. The first account of these excursions was published in 1958 in Dr D.A. Bassett's "Geological Excursion Guide to the Glasgow district". It was updated in 1973 by the guide edited by Dr B.J. Bluck. A projected guide to the Girvan area never reached fruition. The present guide-book makes good that deficiency by including seven excursions in the Girvan to Ballantrae areas together with illustrated discussions of the fundamental problems. The Dob's Linn locality may seem to be well outside Glasgow's province but it can easily be visited in a day and, indeed, has been a regular excursion for students from Glasgow University. The comparison with the Girvan rocks of similar age has long been a matter of great interest. It is also the nearest locality which yields abundant graptolites and contains the international stratotype for the Ordovician-Silurian boundary; the section has recently been redescribed by S. Henry Williams when a research student at Glasgow University and he is the main author of the excursion account. As for the Glasgow area itself, most of the excursions in the 1973 guide have been retained in revised forms. However the Lugton quarries are now flooded and the Boyleston Quarry has deteriorated considerably although a brief account is still included. The Great Cumbrae excursion has been simplified and Little Cumbrae omitted because of access difficulties. There are new excursions around the Rosneath peninsula, to Loanhead Quarry, on the Old Red Sandstone of the Clyde coast and the Building Stones of Glasgow.

Many of the excursions are suitable for beginners in the subject of geology but others are at a higher level. In these more complex excursions, however, an attempt is made to provide guidance for the amateur who wishes to advance his knowledge: there are extended explanations with helpful illustrations. For instance the Firth of Clyde Old Red Sandstone excursion explains the interpretation of some sedimentary structures, the Trearne excursion instructs in palaeoecology, the Balmaha excursion discusses terranes, the Rosneath excursion explains the interpretation of structures in metamorphic rocks and the Ballantrae excursions introduce plate tectonic concepts.

A glossary of all except the commonest technical terms is appended and the words listed appear in bold type at first mention in the text of an excursion. The definitions are, however, brief and without illustration. Fuller explanations will be found in the various dictionaries of geology. However it is strongly recommended that the reader should study some elementary texts in order to obtain an integrated picture of the subject. An indication of the standard of the various excursions is given in the subsequent Excursion Planner.

Additional geological excursions which can be undertaken in a day trip from Glasgow are included in Lothian Geology (Edinburgh Geological Society) and Fife and Angus Geology (St Andrews University - new edition in preparation).

Behaviour and Conservation

The rapid increase in geological field studies in recent years has often resulted in the deterioration or even destruction of important outcrops and has also caused considerable inconvenience (and even financial loss) to landowners. Visitors are therefore *exhorted* to follow both the **Country Code** and the Geologists' Association's "**A Code for Geological Field Work**" (copies free from the G.A., $^c/_o$ Burlington House, Piccadilly, London W1V 9AG). Some of the main points are highlighted below.

> **Ask permission to enter private land or quarries**
> **Park cars sensibly - not in front of field gates or obstructing narrow roads**
> **Close gates - unless they obviously need to be kept open**
> **Do not damage stone walls or fences**
> **Do not walk through crops - including meadow grass**
> **Do not interfere with machinery** *e.g.* **in quarries**
> **Do not hammer indiscriminately or unnecessarily**
> **Wear protective goggles when hammering**
> **Do not undermine hedges or walls**
> **Keep collecting to a minimum: collect from debris**
> **Do not litter fields or roads with rock debris**
> **Drop no litter - take it home if necessary**
> **Observe the Mountain Safety code**
> **Avoid loosening rock on steep slopes**
> **Do not enter old mine workings or cave systems**

Do not get cut off by the tide
Wear safety hats in quarries or below cliffs
Do not disfigure outcrops with paint or core-holes

Some of the localities recommended in this guide are **Sites of Special Scientific Interest** (SSSIs), designated by the Nature Conservancy Council. The function of this body is to conserve the scientific interest of these sites and for that reason their whereabouts are not widely publicised. Whilst the existence of these sites is public knowledge, most of them are in private ownership: designation as an SSSI does not confer any increased rights of access for the public. Some of the sites do not, at present, require prior permission but the usual courtesies should still be observed. The geological visitor is expected to respect their status and restrict hammering to a minimum. In some cases, however, (clearly indicated in the guide) a special permit is required from the NCC to cover access and limited collecting. Where relevant, the present landowner's name and address is provided in the appropriate excursion. If prior written permission is required it is advisable to write several months in advance as the landowner may have to consult the NCC. The local contact address for the Nature Conservancy Council is: The Castle, Balloch Castle Country Park, Balloch, Dunbartonshire, G83 8LX. Tel. (0389) 58511. At the time of writing there are proposals to reorganise and rename the NCC in Scotland, as part of Scottish Natural Heritage.

Transport and Accommodation

Most of the excursions assume the availability of a private car but it is possible to use public transport in some cases, as indicated in particular excursion accounts, albeit with some loss of convenience and time, plus extra walking distance.

Information on routes and time-tables can be obtained from the following:

Rail Service Enquiries:	(041) 204.2844
The Travel Centre, St Enoch Square, Glasgow	(041) 226.4826
Buchanan St Bus Station, Glasgow	(041) 332.9644
(for longer distance buses)	
The Tourist Information Office in St Vincent	
Place, Glasgow, can provide maps and advice	
on accommodation	(041) 204.4400

Acknowledgements: The editors wish firstly to thank the authors for their expert contributions and to their institutions for providing facilities. Special thanks are due to Professor B.E. Leake of the Department of Geology and Applied Geology at the University of Glasgow for providing expert secretarial assistance from Mrs Mary Fortune, Mrs Betty Mackenzie, Mrs Irene Wells and Miss Jeanette Wylie and draughting work by Mrs Sheila Hall. Drs. G.E.Bowes and C.Farrow deserve our gratitude for their unfailing help in solving "Word-processing" problems.

Dr. J.P. Burlison of the Nature Conservancy Council kindly took the time to advise us on the Sites of Special Scientific Interest, and their protection.

We are also indebted to the following for permission to reproduce figures from their publications:

Chapman and Hall Limited for Figures 21.2c, 22.1a
Linnaean Society for Figures 21.2 e,f
Schweitzerbart'sche Verlagsbuchhandlung for Figure 22.2
Dr. A. Ritchie for Figure 22.1h
Royal Society of Edinburgh for Figures 10.2 and 10.3, reproduced with permission from Curry *et al* in the Transactions of the Royal Society of Edinburgh vol. 75, pp. 113-133, Figures 7 and 8 (1984).

The commercial organisations who generously donated money to help in the production of this guide are acknowledged separately on page 8.

Finally, we would like to express our personal gratitude to Brian and Aileen Evans of Carnmor Print & Design for their patient and friendly advice during the preparation of this Guide.

J.D. Lawson
D.S. Weedon

Disclaimer

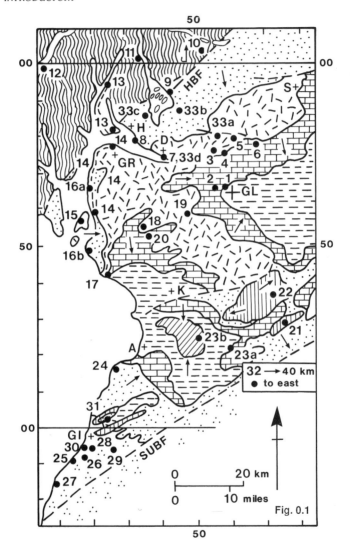

Fig. 0.1

STRATIGRAPHICAL SUMMARY

A summary of the stratigraphical succession of the region is presented in Table 0.1, with a simplified geological map in Figure 0.1; see also the section Figure 0.2. Relevant detail is given in the excursion accounts. Comprehensive and systematic coverage for the Glasgow area of this guide is mostly provided in the recent (1985) third edition of the British Geological Survey's Regional Geology handbook on "The Midland Valley" which contains numerous maps and photographs. The companion volume on "The South of Scotland" (3rd. edition, 1971) covers the Girvan and Ballantrae areas of this guide and has recently been supplemented and updated by B.G.S. booklets on Girvan (Cameron, Stone and Smellie 1986) and Ballantrae (Stone and Smellie 1988). "The Geology of Scotland" (third edition, Craig 1991)

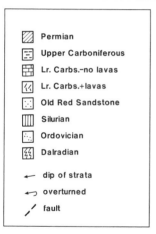

Permian
Upper Carboniferous
Lr. Carbs.-no lavas
Lr. Carbs.+lavas
Old Red Sandstone
Silurian
Ordovician
Dalradian

dip of strata
overturned
fault

Figure 0.1. Simplified geological map of the area covered by the guide: the locations of excursions are shown diagrammatically by numbered dots. A key to the numbers is provided in the Contents list and also (more briefly) on the inside back cover. HBF = Highland Boundary Fault, SUBF = Southern Upland Boundary Fault, H = Helensburgh, D = Dumbarton, GL = Glasgow, K = Kilmarnock, A = Ayr, Gl = Girvan, S = Stirling.

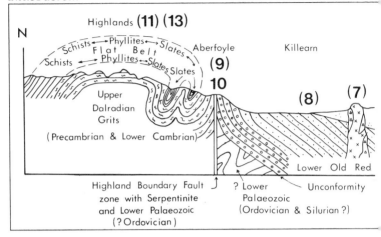

Figure 0.2. Diagrammatic section through the north-western part of the Midland Valley, showing the positions of relevant excursions: the numbers in brackets are of excursions which are not on the line of the section.

places the geology of the region in its wider context. A concise and simplified account of the succession and palaeography, together with descriptions of excursions at an elementary level, is contained in the book "Geology Explained........." by Lawson and Lawson (1976). Although now out of print, this book is available at most public libraries in the Glasgow area.

The above books do not, however, deal adequately with the difficult and controversial subject of the plate tectonic history of the region. It is for this reason that there follows an essay by Professor B.J.Bluck on "Terrane Accretion in Western Scotland".

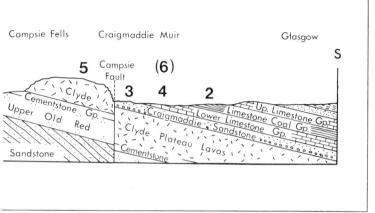

References

CAMERON, I.B. and STEPHENSON, D. 1985. *British Regional Geology: The Midland Valley of Scotland* (third edition). British Geological Survey (HMSO, London).

CAMERON, I.B., STONE, P. and SMELLIE, J. 1986. *Geology of the country around Girvan.* (Sheet 7). (HMSO, London).

CRAIG, G.Y. (editor), (Third edition), 1991. *Geology of Scotland.* Scottish Academic Press, Edinburgh.

GREIG, D.C. and others, 1971. *British Regional Geology: The South of Scotland.* British Geological Survey (HMSO, Edinburgh).

LAWSON, J.A. and LAWSON, J.D. 1976. *Geology explained around Glasgow and South West Scotland, including Arran.* David and Charles, Newton Abbot.

STONE, P. and SMELLIE, J.L. 1988. Classical areas of British geology: *The Ballantrae area* (Sheets NX 08, 18 and 19). British Geological Survey. (HMSO, London).

TABLE 0.1 Stratigraphical succession for the Glasgow and Girvan areas

AGE Ma	SYSTEM and PERIOD	MAJOR ROCK UNITS	MAIN ROCK TYPES and SELECTED FORMATIONS
2-	QUATERNARY		glacial deposits, alluvium, raised beach deposits, peat
65- 145- 205- 250-	TERTIARY CRETACEOUS JURASSIC TRIASSIC	not present in this area but represented on the Isle of Arran	
290-	PERMIAN	Mauchline Sandstone	red dune-bedded sandstones lavas and ashes
	CARBONIFEROUS	Coal Measures	mudstones, sandstones, coals Barren Red Measures at top
		Passage Group	coarse cross-bedded sandstones, fireclays: some lavas
		Up. Limestone Gp.	sandstones, shales, limestones (Giffnock Sdstn., Orchard Lstn.)
		Limestone Coal Gp.	sandstones, shales, coals
		Lr.Limestone Gp.	shales, limestones, sandstones (Hurlet & Blackhall Limestones)
360-		Calciferous Sdstn. Measures	lstns. & shales (Ballagan Beds) Clyde Plateau Lavas: sandstones
	DEVONIAN	Upper Old Red Sandstone	less coarse conglomerates redder sdstns., cornstones
410-		Lower Old Red Sandstone	coarse red conglomerates and sandstones: lavas in Ayrshire
	SILURIAN	Girvan & Midland Valley inliers	conglomerates, sdstns, shales passing up into red beds
440-		Southern Uplands	greywackes, black shales, mdstns. (Birkhill Shales)
	ORDOVICIAN U.O. = upper Ord. L.O. = lower Ord.	Highland Border Complex (L&U.O.)	spilites, black shales, cherts, serpentinite: sdstn. & lstn.
		Girvan Cover rocks (U.O.)	conglomerates, greywackes, shales, limestones
		Ballantrae Complex (L.O.)	black shales, cherts, spilites, serpentinite, gabbro etc.
510-		Southern Uplands (U.O.)	greywackes, black shales, cherts, (Hartfell Shales)
570-	CAMBRIAN	?	
	PRECAMBRIAN	Southern Highland Group	schistose grits (Ben Ledi Grits) slates, phyllites (Aberfoyle Slates)

18

TABLE 0.1 continued

FOSSIL GROUPS	ENVIRONMENT	EXCURSIONS (Shortened titles)	PALAEO LATITUDE
marine shells	glacial erosion & deposition changes of sea level	**33.** Quaternary **5.** Campsie	50°N
			40°N
			30°N
	sand deserts - wind from east: vulcanicity	**23.** Lugar etc	
non-marine bivalves plants	forested tropical swamps, rivers and lakes	**17.** Saltcoats	8°N
plants	large rivers and deltas	**17.** Saltcoats **24.** Heads of Ayr	
bivalves brachiopods	cyclical deposition of muds, deltaic sands		
bivalves, plants Lingula	swamp vegetation (to form coals) with	**2.** Fossil Grove	0°
brachiopods, corals, bivalves, crinoids	marine incursions (limestones)	**20.** Trearne, **4.** Blairskaith, **6.** Corrie Burn, **5.** Campsie	
rare ostracodes	lagoons and vulcanicity	**5.** Campsie, **3.** Milngavie **7.** Dumbarton, **18.** Loanhead	5°S
plants rare fish	alluvial sedimentation in a strike-slip fault regime	**16.** Clyde ORS, **15.** Cumbrae **14.** Greenock, **24.** H. of Ayr	
plants rare fish		**9.** Balmaha, **16.** Clyde ORS, **8.** Ardmore	10°S
brachiopods trilobites, fish	shallowing sea becoming non-marine	**30.** Girvan, **31.** Craighead **21.** Hagshaw, **22.** Lesmahagow	
graptolites	oceanic muds with turbidites	**32.** Dob's Linn	0°
brachiopods rare	oceanic muds, oozes: ophiolite evolution	**9.** Balmaha **10.** Aberfoyle	
trilobites graptolites	proximal fore-arc basin variable depth	**29.** Stinchar Valley **28.** Dow Hill, **30.** Girvan	15°N
rare graptolites rare radiolaria	volcanic arc and marginal basin	**27.** Bennane Hd. **25.** Pinbain **26.** Knocklaugh, **28.** Dow Hill	
graptolites	oceanic muds with turbidites	**32.** Dob's Linn	
			25°N
	oceanic muds with turbidites	**11.** L.Lomond, **13.** Rosneath **10.** Aberfoyle	

TERRANE ACCRETION IN WESTERN SCOTLAND

B.J.Bluck

Since the last edition of this guide our perception of geology in general and Scottish geology in particular has changed dramatically. New theories on the origin of continents and oceans have been postulated which are stimulating changes in the way we look at rocks and try to reconstruct their geological history. It is important therefore that the geology we study locally be no longer divorced from these all-embracing theories. Therefore, the orientation of parts of the new edition of this guide has been changed: particular observations and the explanations of them are now related to the wider geological regimes under which the rocks formed.

It is now generally accepted that oceanic plate is produced mainly at spreading ridges and that, after moving some distance from the ridge, it either descends back into the mantle or it is attached to a continental block without descending beneath it (Fig. 0.5). Where the oceanic plate descends (is subducted) into the mantle oceanic trenches are produced and as the plate moves deeper into the mantle the higher temperatures cause part of it and the surrounding crust to be melted. The ascending molten rocks form volcanoes, giant granitoid batholiths and a host of intrusive igneous rocks associated together as a volcanic and plutonic arc. However, if the ocean plate descends beneath pre-existing oceanic plate, (Fig 0.5A), then island arcs are produced which are dominated by basic igneous rocks, and do not normally have the great plutonic masses characteristic of the continental margins.

The region below such an arc, being hot and under compression (because of the convergence of the two plates), is often the site of regional metamorphism and accompanying polyphase deformation. The continental crust here is thickened and its surface is divided into a series of basins in which sediments accumulate, sediments domi-nated by volcanic and plutonic arc sources - the foundation upon which the arc was built.

We have become increasingly aware as we examine the surface of the earth, that it may be divided into various regimes, each typified by a group of rocks generated ultimately by the dominant influence of a single, albeit complex, process. The types of metamorphic, igneous and sedimentary rocks, the ways in which they are folded and faulted,

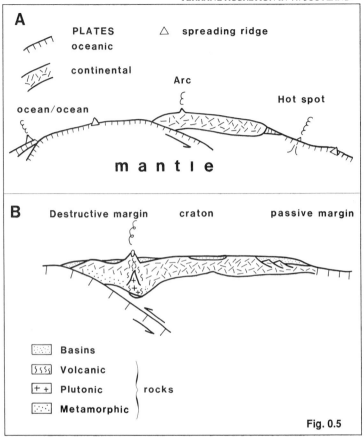

Figure 0.5. The disposition of plates and the tectonic environments associated with them. **A,** showing the various plate-tectonic domains with particular reference to oceanic crust, and **B,** the various tectonic elements associated with continental crust.

and the nature of their vertical and lateral associations are all typical of the major oceanic or continental regimes in which they are found. These various regions, or plate regimes, where distinctive rock associations are found are illustrated in Figures 0.5B and 0.6 together with a brief statement of their essential nature.

If we accept the concept of plate tectonics, the establishment of a plate regime involves looking at all rock types over a wide area. When examining the rock assemblages of any one region, for example western Scotland, it is appropriate that we should ask the question - where on the oceanic/or continental plate was the assemblage formed? Where was subduction taking place at this time? What was the plate tectonic regime? We are, by accepting the theory of plate tectonics also forced to think in a more global way. Probably for the first time, many

Figure 0.6. A, The detailed structural elements of a destructive margin, along with the spatial and vertical scales. In the accretionary prism the sequence **(i),(ii)** etc records the relative ages of the slices scraped off as the ocean plate descends beneath the continent. In the fore-arc basin **(i),(ii)** etc refers to the sequence of filling, which contrasts markedly with the accretion in the trench. **d,** the distance from the volcanic surface to the top of the descending plate, is normally 90 km. **B,** is a compilation of the distances between the arc and the trench taken from present-day systems.

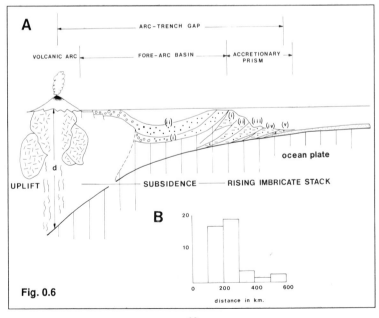

Fig. 0.6

excursions in this Guide are not seen in isolation, but as part of an integrated history which involves a great deal of Scotland and beyond. It is from such an integrated history for a given time span, the way in which the rocks are associated and the areal and vertical disposition of this rock association assessed, that we are able to identify the tectonic regime in which the rocks of a given region were generated.

A corollary of the comments listed above is that when the geology of an area is being summarised, rather than taking an entire, composite stratigraphical column for it, and explaining it as a sequence of geological events, it is now more appropriate to divide the area into regions which have similar rocks and have undergone a similar history. It then becomes important to examine the sequence of geological events within any one of these regions, to identify the types of process which could be responsible for creating the rocks and their history, and to relate the regions to each other to see if they can be assembled logically in terms of processes into the components of a plate tectonic regime as illustrated in Figure 0.5. This is now attempted for the west of Scotland.

Western Scotland in the Lower Palaeozoic

The geological divisions of western Scotland are set out in Figure 0.7. Each division is characterised by an area of rock with similar geological aspects; and each is divided from the others by major and well-known faults. The divisions are not new: they have been the traditional way of dividing Scotland geologically. It is their interpretation as individual blocks which is new. Each block will be briefly described and the relationships between them then discussed.

1. The Ballantrae Complex (Excursions 25, 26 and 27).

The Ballantrae Complex comprises black shales, **cherts**, pillow lavas, gabbros, minor granitoids, **serpentinite** and some metamorphic rocks. It appears a structurally dismembered **ophiolite** - a fragment of oceanic crust which is mainly of Arenig age(Barrett *et al* 1982; Bluck1985; Stone *et al* 1988). Oceanic crust of the type seen at Ballantrae can form in a number of different situations - at oceanic ridges, the most common way of creating ocean crust; at hot spots formed where the ocean crust moves over a fixed zone of magma rise; or at marginal basins where there is a complex relationship between arcs and ocean crust.

Fig. 0.7

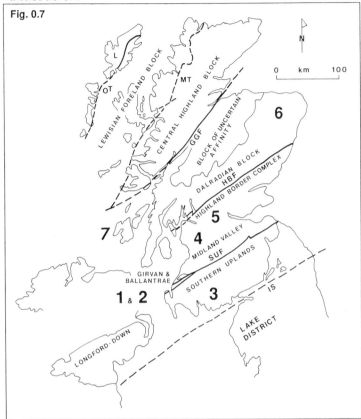

Figure 0.7. A map of the Palaeozoic tectono-stratigraphic blocks within Scotland. **1,** Ballantrae ophiolite, **2,** the Girvan cover sequence, **3,** the Southern Uplands, **4,** the Midland Valley, **5,** Highland Border Complex, **6,** the Dalradian Block, **7,** the Islay-Colonsay Terrane.
HBF=Highland Boundary Fault; SUF=Southern Uplands Fault; IS=Iapetus Suture; L= Isle of Lewis; OT=Outer Isles Thrust; MT=Moine Thrust; GGF=Great Glen Fault. Blocks to the north of the great Great Glen Fault are not numbered as they are not covered in this account.

The origin of the Ballantrae Complex is conjectural. The hypothesis favoured here is that it is arc related; but in any event its presence in southwestern Scotland is significant, for it implies that during Arenig times there was some interaction between oceanic and some other crust (oceanic or continental), which resulted in the oceanic crust rising up rather than descending into the mantle. From the age determinations made at Ballantrae and its relationship to the cover sequence it is now apparent that the ophiolite was created and destroyed within c. 20 million years, implying that it was created near the margin onto which it was finally thrust (obducted). Had it been created at a ridge some distance from the continent to which it finally accreted, there would be a substantial difference between the age of generation of the ophiolite and the time of its emplacement onto the continent—a difference proportional to the width of ocean traversed by the ocean crust after its generation.

Ophiolites are typical of destructive margins. They are commonly part of the process of arc development, and after obduction may form the floors to fore-arc basins, as can be seen around much of the Pacific area today.

2. The Girvan cover-rocks   (Excursions 28,29, 30 and31).

The Ordovician and Silurian rocks of the Girvan district are classical: they have been the studying ground for researcher and student for almost 100 years. To many, they are a geologist's Elysium where highly significant geological problems are abundant and never fully resolved. The Ordovician, and to a lesser extent the Silurian rocks are conglomerates, sandstones, shales and limestones which have been deposited in fault- bounded basins, and unconformably overlie the Ballantrae Complex (Williams 1962; Ingham 1978). The conglomerates are commonly mass flows or fan deltas which were deposited at the fault-margins of the basins and interfinger with deeper water sandstones laid down by turbidity currents. The tops of the fault blocks are coated with shallow water, often reefal, limestone.

Although the Ordovician rocks are divided from the Silurian by an unconformity, the lower part of the Silurian sequence was probably deposited in a regime similar to the Ordovician: coarse conglomerates being deposited near active faults but replaced by finer sediments away from the margins of the basin. Later Silurian rocks within the Midland Valley (including the sequence at Girvan) were deposited in shallow water conditions and finally become terrestrial, with the deposition of fluvial conglomerates. These terrestrial conditions which first appear in the Late Silurian become dominant in the Devonian, with a consequence that there is no clear lithological distinction between the two systems in the Midland Valley.

Within this stratigraphical framework several important observations can be made.

a. The conglomerates and sandstones are dominated by volcanic and ophiolitic rock fragments, which clearly indicate a provenance comprising ophiolitic rock and volcanic and plutonic rocks. The ophiolitic rocks will have come from the Ballantrae Complex, but the origin of the acid volcanic and plutonic rocks is far from clear. Age determinations made on the granitic clasts show that many of them are c.470 Ma (Llanvirn) in age (Longman *et al* 1979). As these clasts have a chemistry similar to some of the associated volcanic and hypabyssal rock fragments, they are thought to have come from a contemporary Ordovician igneous complex. We know that both ophiolites, volcanic and plutonic rocks typify destructive margins, so the discovery of the existence of an Ordovican igneous complex of this kind is clearly significant. But where was it?

b. The conglomerates are boulder-bearing and have palaeoflow indicators showing a flow towards the SE. In the reconstructions of the stratigraphy produced by Williams (1962) and Ingham (1978) the fault bounded basins deepened towards the SE. On these two lines of evidence a source block to the NW is indicated. But how far away was this source? The conglomerates contain boulders which are sometimes well over 2 m in diameter. Sailors and others are glad to know that boulders do not travel large distances by normal (i.e.non glacial) agents of transport, so that a source block a little way to the north, within the Midland Valley, is indicated.

c. Shallow water (neritic) faunas are strikingly Laurentian in aspect up to levels of late Caradoc age. Above this, such faunas become increasingly cosmopolitan.

3. The Southern Uplands   (Excursion 32).

The Southern Uplands comprises a thick sequence of **greywacke** deposited by turbidity currents overlying black shales and cherts which rest on remnants of an ocean crust foundation. This essentially greywacke pile, most of which is vertical or dipping at very steep angles almost invariably youngs to the NW. The Southern Upland sequence begins in the Llanvirn and ends in the Wenlock, but the age of the basal greywackes where they rest on the black shales and cherts gets younger to the SE. The oldest rocks are therefore found in the north (the northern belt) and the central and southern belts contain progressively younger rocks.

The greywacke and the conglomerates which interfinger with them contain abundant volcanic rock fragments. As with the sediments at Girvan, boulders within the Ordovician and Silurian conglomerates have been dated and some show Ordovician (Llanvirn; 470 Ma) ages, indicating a source partly in a contemporaneous volcanic-plutonic complex. The palaeoflow in the Southern Uplands is, however, far from clear. There is considerable evidence in the greywackes for flows from the NE and SW; the coarse conglomerates, however show evidence of having been derived from the NW, and there is a favoured view that the greywackes were deposited by turbidity currents travelling along the axis of a large, elongate trough. There were points of sediment input to this trough which were in the NW; and these include the conglomerates which are thought to occupy deep channel systems.

The origin of the Southern Uplands is a matter of controversy and there are some important additional points which have to be considered:

a. The vertical rock sequence in the Southern Uplands indicates that the base is towards the SE, so that the sequence should get younger to the NW. The description above (and see Fig. 0.6), shows the reverse to be true: the *oldest* rocks are found in the NW.

b. The whole sequence is cut by a series of strike faults, which also bring up to the level of erosion slices of the basement. This basement material is thought to be oceanic as it comprises black shale, chert and pillow lava (see Excursion 32 to Dob's Linn for black shales and cherts).

c. The conglomerates and turbiditic sandstones contain clasts of pre-existing shales which have already suffered some cleavage. No faunas have been collected from these shales but if they belong to older rocks of the Southern Upland pile, then it suggests that a recycling process is taking place in which older formations are being

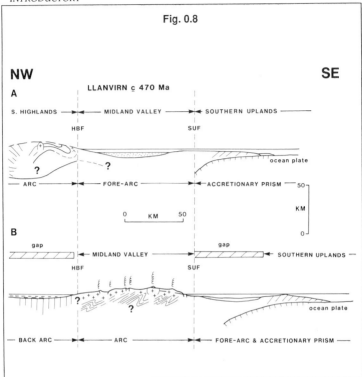

Figure 0.8. Cross sections through Scotland. **A** assumes that there are no tectonic elements missing, **B** assumes that there are tectonic elements missing and that the Caledonides is a collage of largely unrelated terranes. The positions of the Highland Boundary Fault (HBF) and Southern Uplands Fault (SUF) are as they are today, and are only positioned for reference; at the time of the sections, the positions of these faults is unknown.

eroded to supply sediment to younger ones.

    d. The age of the first turbidites to enter the basin i.e. the first turbidites to interfinger with the black shales as at Moffat, get younger as one goes south. This suggest that the greywacke pile grows towards the S or SE over a belt in which the black shale was accumulating.

On the basis of these observations McKerrow *et al* (1977) interpreted the Southern Uplands as an accretionary prism (see Figures 0.5, 0.6, 0.7). Since that time however, a number of points have been raised which challenge this model:

a. In middle Ordovician times there was also a source of sediment to the south or SE of the Northern Belt of the Southern Uplands, and this source supplied fresh volcanic sediment which has the characteristics of a volcanic arc (e.g. Stone *et al* 1987). This sediment, although fresh, nevertheless is older than the sediment in which it is included being *c. 550* Ma (Early Cambrian). An accretionary prism would not normally have a source outboard of it.

b. The sediments are possibly rather coarse to have formed in a trench. Most of the conglomeratic sediment is derived from an arc to the NW. and much of the greywacke in sharing this arc-type petrography presumably came from the same source. The sediment would have to have been yielded from the arc, dispersed over a fore-arc region and then into the trench— a distance which is usually well over 100 km. By that time it should have been fairly fine grained, perhaps finer than the grain size now seen in the Southern Uplands greywackes.

Two alternative views are, therefore, that the Southern Uplands formed either in a back-arc basin or a fore-arc basin (see McKerrow 1987 for many diverse views).

Whatever may be the interpretation of the Southern Uplands in general, it is clear that the Midland Valley, Ballantrae-Girvan and the Southern Uplands all resemble the tectonic elements of a destructive plate margin (Fig. 0.8) and if the Southern Uplands were to be an accretionary prism the whole areal sequence of tectonic blocks from there to the Midland Valley would be in the right order for being a destructive margin (cf. Fig.0.6 and Fig.0.8).

Destructive plate margins are often very extensive: some are tens of thousands of kilometres long. The destructive margin of which Scotland was a part was also long. Evidence used to determine that a destructive margin characterised this part of Scotland is also used to show that this margin extended from north of Florida through the Atlantic states, Newfoundland, NW Ireland-Scotland and out into east Greenland. The large landmass bordering this destructive margin was called Laurentia (Fig.0.9). Laurentia was bordered to the south by a wide ocean over which it was sliding, often obliquely, and it is as a result of this interaction, that the southeastern margin of Laurentia is seen to have been destructive.

4. The Midland Valley   (Excursions 5,6,7,8, 14, 16, 21, 22 and 24)

Upper Palaeozoic and minor outcrops of Mesozoic rocks dominate in the Midland Valley. However, although there are few Lower Palaeozoic outcrops here, evidence from flanking areas such as the Southern Uplands, zones such as the Highland Border Complex, xenoliths in Carboniferous igneous rocks within the Midland Valley and evidence from existing Palaeozoic outcrops gives some clues about the nature of its rocks and the role it may have played in Caledonian times.

Many Lower Palaeozoic boulder-bearing conglomerates and sandstones within the Southern Uplands, and also at Girvan, have been derived from the NW and contain abundant metamorphic and igneous clasts. Lower Palaeozoic rocks of the Highland Border Complex also contain igneous and metamorphic clasts, although the direction of transportation of these sediments is not known. Blocks of metamorphic and igneous rocks (other than obvious Carboniferous) are found as xenoliths in Carboniferous volcanic and associated rocks. All these observations imply there to have been a metamorphic-igneous complex within the region which is now the Midland Valley.

Age determinations for the granitic detritus (see last section) suggest the Midland Valley to be the site of an igneous complex in Ordovician-Silurian times, and this may have continued on into the Devonian as the Ochil-Sidlaw volcanic pile. Metamorphic clasts and detrital sedimentary micas in the sediments of the Southern Uplands have Cambrian-Silurian ages (Kelley and Bluck 1989), and some clasts found in the Highland Border Complex have ages *c.* 1800Ma. During the Caledonian cycle the Midland Valley was probably a magmatic arc founded on an old metamorphic basement.

The Silurian rocks of the southern Midland Valley also contain metamorphic and igneous detritus which may have been derived from the Midland Valley arc. This sequence shows a basin which began with marine turbidites and by gradual infilling was converted to a basin which became terrestrial.

5. The Highland Border Complex   (Excursions 9 and 10)

The Highland Border Complex, as its name implies, comprises a structural assemblage of rocks of differing ages and differing aspect. The rocks comprise pillow lavas, serpentinites, black shales and cherts, conglomerates and limestones, and various sandstones. The age and affinity of these rocks have always been problematical. They were once thought, on structural grounds, to belong to the Dalradian block against which they now lie. A Laurentian trilobite fauna in a limestone near Callander gives a Lower Cambrian age; a trilobite fauna in limestones at Dounan's Quarry, near Aberfoyle revealed a Lower Ordovician (Arenig) age (Curry *et al* 1982; Ingham *et al* 1985). As main Dalradian folding took place before 590 Ma (Rogers *et al* 1989), i.e. within the Late Precambrian, it is no longer possible to see the Highland Border Complex as part of this metamorphic terrane, but rather as a tectono-sedimentary unit of its own.

Further research has shown that there is a complicated stratigraphical and structural sequence within the Highland Border Complex. Bluck et al (1984) demonstrated the presence of an old ophiolitic assemblage which Dempster and Bluck (1991) showed was obducted at c 540 Ma (Lower Cambrian); on top of this were deposited shallow water carbonates and conglomerates (Arenig); these are structurally followed by shales, cherts and spilites (probably mainly Llanvirn), which in turn are finally unconformably overlain by sandstones and limestones. The sequence is thought to span most of the Ordovician.

The origin of this Complex is still not fully understood. Bluck *et al* (1984) believed it to resemble a collapsed back-arc basin sequence, but there is at the moment insufficient evidence for this or any other interpretation and the question must be regarded as open.

6. The Dalradian block (Excursions 10,11 and 13)

The Dalradian belt comprises a Late Proterozoic sequence of quartz-arenites and carbonates which formed on a continental shelf, a pile of lavas and associated volcanogenic sediments which may represent a phase of structural extension of the shelf, tillites from an ice sheet the location of which relative to the Dalradian basin is uncertain, and finally some turbidites which are found along the southern margin of the block (Anderton 1985).

This rock sequence was subsequently folded and metamorphosed in two stages, before and after the intrusion of the Ben Vuirich granite. Rogers *et al* (1989) showed this granite to have cooled at 590 Ma. (Late Proterozoic) and now divide the folding into an early phase (D1 and D2) and probably a local metamorphism which is precedes the intrusion of the granite; and a later phase, (D3 and D4) with substantial metamorphism which is post the intrusion. Although the first stage in the Dalradian structure and metamorphism produced the the big D1 overfold, the second was responsible for the main metamorphism and uplift of the block. These later events took place from c. 515 Ma- 430 Ma for the main part of the belt and continued down to 390 Ma in the northernmost Dalradian.

The origin of the Dalradian block is at present uncertain and will be discussed at a later stage when the concept of terranes has been considered.

Growth of continents by terrane accretion

Although there is convincing evidence for there being a destructive margin in Scotland during the Lower Palaeozoic, examination of present-day margins of this type show that there is another major process at work. Many of the tectonic elements such as accretionary prisms and fore-arc basins, are bounded by major faults and it is fairly clear that in some instances these elements are no longer in the position of their growth. Subsequently or even during their generation they have moved either towards the craton or laterally along the cratonic edge. Large blocks which have suffered this type of displacement are referred to as terranes. From these observations a new theory of the growth of continental masses has arisen.

The new theory is a corollary of plate tectonics and was developed to explain some anomalies in the geology of parts of western U.S.A. Here were blocks of ground, usually major tectonic elements (terranes), bounded by faults, which had very clearly undergone quite a different history from the blocks now adjacent to them and also a different history from the North American craton. Some have sedimentary rocks with faunas which are totally different from the faunas of the same age found on cratonic North America. Indeed, some of the faunas resemble more the faunas found in Asia. This evidence, together with the more soundly based palaeomagnetic evidence, has been integrated to chart the paths taken by these terranes relative to North America. It has become clear that "blocks" of oceanic or continental crust became attached to North America at low latitudes, then migrated northwards along the continental edge towards, and often reaching, Alaska.

This type of accretion was achieved by the movement of North America westwards over a Pacific plate which is moving roughly eastwards. Blocks of high-riding crust, continental or oceanic, instead of disappearing down a subduction zone became attached to the western edge of the North American craton. However if a continent rides obliquely over an oceanic plate then the blocks of accreted crust may be dragged along the continental edge. This has been (and still is) the case along western North America.

Since these early discoveries it has become clear that any destructive margin where the overriding continent converges obliquely onto the underriding oceanic plate is liable to be a zone where terranes may move laterally along the continental edge. The terranes may include seamounts or other topographic highs on the oceanic plate, or microcontinents originating in totally different continental masses. Terranes of this kind are exotic; they did not originate in the continent to which they are now attached. However there are other terranes which are generated at the continental margin, as for example the microcontinent of Japan, which are then moved along the margin to accrete to the same continent which spawned them, but in a position different from their origin. Japan became detached from Asia during the opening of the sea of Japan; it may subsequently be pushed back to Asia, and thus back to the continent of its origin. The early part of Japan's history is similar to that of Asia. Subsequently their differing histories will reflect terrane isolation, and eventually, on accretion their histories will unite.

Destructive plate margins generate many outboard volcanic arcs and fore-arc regions, as can be seen along the western Pacific. Such tectonic elements (arcs, etc) are particularly liable to be moved laterally if subduction changes from head-on (orthogonal) to oblique. So it is not uncommon to find that destructive margins comprise assemblages of tectonic elements which are not in the exact position where they were formed. How does one recognise that a destructive margin has been re-assembled in this way?

Evidence for terrane accretion in Scotland

There is now considerable evidence to suggest that much of Scotland has been assembled from displaced terranes, and we here emphasise those which are covered in this field guide. The origin of the Moine, Dalradian and Islay-Colonsay terranes will be discussed briefly later.

1. *The Ballantrae Complex*
Being a fragment of oceanic crust on land, this is evidently a terrane of either island arc, oceanic hot-spot or oceanic ridge which has been accreted onto the northern margin of Laurentia.

2. *The Southern Uplands*
There are several lines of evidence suggesting that the Southern Upland Fault is a terrane boundary:

a. It has already been postulated that the cover rocks at Girvan (Excursions 28,29,30 and 31) belong to the proximal (near to the arc) part of a fore-arc sequence, and that the Southern Uplands (Excursion 32) is possibly an accretionary prism or prisms. The distance between the trench (where the accretionary prism forms) and the arc is usually >90km. But the Southern Uplands Fault brings rocks of the accretionary prism into contact with rocks of similar age belonging to the proximal fore-arc sequence. There has been a loss of ground here (Fig.0.8, compare Fig.0.6).

Figure 0.9. A general view of the dispositions of the landmasses of the North Atlantic during the Palaeozoic. In Cambrian times the dispersed continental blocks we see today were assembled into the single large continent of Laurentia. The southern margin (i.e. south with respect to the present pole) was a large passive margin seqence (see Fig. 0.5) which included the Cambrian rocks of the NW Highlands. By Ordovician times this whole southern continental margin of Laurentia became destructive and took on the characteristics which resemble the present-day western Pacific. To the south of it lay the Iapetus Ocean, on the other side of which lay continents such as Baltica (roughly including Norway, Sweden, Finland and Denmark) and Gondwana (which also included southern Britain and central and southern Europe).

In Silurian-Devonian times the Iapetus Ocean to the south had closed and there were major continent-continent collisions such as in Scandinavia (Baltica-Greenland) and eastern North America. (America-Gondwana). Here fold-thrust mountain belts rose to yield vast quantities of sediment to very large river systems, much like the Himalayas do today. In the U.K.- Newfoundland region there was less fold-thrusting and a greater degree of strike-slip faulting.

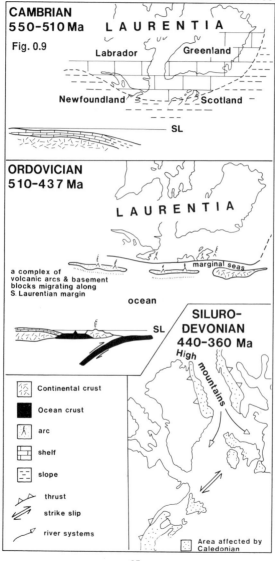

CAMBRIAN 550–510 Ma

Fig. 0.9

LAURENTIA

Labrador   Greenland

Newfoundland   Scotland

SL

ORDOVICIAN 510–437 Ma

LAURENTIA

marginal seas

a complex of volcanic arcs & basement blocks migrating along S. Laurentian margin

ocean

SL

SILURO-DEVONIAN 440–360 Ma

High mountains

Continental crust

Ocean crust

arc

shelf

slope

thrust

strike slip

river systems

Area affected by Caledonian

b. This evidence is corroborated by the rocks of the Silurian inliers running along the northern margin of the Fault. Some of the rocks in these inliers show a palaeoflow from the SE, in which direction now lies the Southern Uplands greywackes which should, therefore, supply the Silurian conglomerates with clasts. However, of the three conglomerates present in the Silurian inliers, only the upper one contains greywackes and even these do not have the characteristics of a Southern Uplands-type greywacke. The lower-most two have quartzite and igneous rock clasts, which are unlikely to have come from the Southern Uplands. The direct inference therefore is that the Southern Uplands were not in their present position when these conglomerates were laid down and that the source of the conglomerates has either shifted or has been replaced by the in-thrust Southern Uplands.

c. The foundation for an accretionary prism is clearly oceanic crust, but the crust beneath the Southern Uplands may now be continental (Hall *et al* 1988). If this is the case then the accretionary prism has to have been thrust onto continental crust.

3. The Highland Border Complex

The Highland Border Complex is composite, comprising at least two discrete rock units. The first is an ophiolite, the obduction of which occurred during the Cambrian; the second, an assemblage of sedimentary and igneous rocks, mainly of Ordovician age. The ophiolite is a terrane in its own right; it is a fragment of oceanic crust which has been obducted onto a continental landmass. The overlying sequence did not form adjacent to the Dalradian block, and is also part of a separate terrane.

During Ordovician times the Dalradian landmass was undergoing uplift with a substantial volume of sediment being removed almost to the level we now see. The volume removed was in the range of 10-30 cubic kilometres for every square kilometre of Dalradian surface. This sediment load would have been removed partly by erosion and, possibly, partly by tectonic sliding—but in either case any nearby basins would have been filled by the coarse debris from the rising landmass.

The now adjacent Highland Border basin was in existence at this time. It was accumulating black shales and cherts in fairly deep water conditions; had it been lying adjacent to the Dalradian block it would have received a good deal of the debris eroded from it. On this evidence it is fairly clear that the two blocks were far removed from each other for most of Ordovician time. On evidence seen in western Ireland, where sediment of Llandovery age rests on rocks which are lateral equivalents of both these units, they had clearly been brought together sometime before or during the earliest Silurian (Fig.0.9).

4. Basement blocks

North of the Highland Boundary Fault there is a variety of basement blocks, and to give an account of each of these is outside the scope of this discussion. Only the basements to the south of the Great Glen Fault are dealt with as these have interacted with the Caledonides or, as with the Dalradian, form part of the Excursions in the Guide.

Early workers trying to solve the provenance and assembling-history of terranes, made the assumption that the basement blocks (Dalradian, Islay-Colonsay, Moine and Lewisian) had been part of the southern Laurentian continental margin, some time before the opening of the Iapetus Ocean. Recently the possiblity has arisen that all blocks except the Lewisian have been moved into Laurentia after the development of the ocean.

The Dalradian block for example, bounded on the north by the Great Glen Fault and on the south by the Highland Boundary Fault has a history which is quite unlike the history of any other part of the Laurentian margin between c.600-650 Ma (Late Proterozoic). Whilst the Laurentian margin was typified by extensional tectonics and the development of a passive margin, the Dalradian block was undergoing compression, typically found on a destructive margin. In contrast, the African-European margin to Iapetus was destructive at this time, and was undergoing a geological history very similar to that of the Dalradian block. For this and other reasons Bluck and Dempster (1991) suggested that the Dalradian may have been part of the larger African craton, then moved into Laurentia in Cambrian times.

The parts of Scotland which have been discussed so far are now seen, at least as far as the Ordovician is concerned, as a group of terranes each with its own history and divided from each other by well known fractures along which there has been considerable movement. Each terrane has a history which is not compatible with its being adjacent to another during Ordovician time. The Cambrian-Ordovician history of Scotland in the context of the North Atlantic is illustrated in Figure 0.9.

The questions then arise, when was present-day Scotland assembled together, and what kinds of rocks formed while this process of assembling was taking place ?

Western Scotland in the Upper Palaeozoic, Mesozoic and Tertiary

Upper Palaeozoic rocks include the Devonian (Old Red Sandstone), Carboniferous and Permian (New Red Sandstone): rocks belonging to the former two periods are particularly well seen in the Glasgow district. Both these groups of rocks occur mainly within the Midland Valley of Scotland, but, significantly they also occur in the Lower Palaeozoic and pre-Palaeozoic terranes flanking it.

1. Lower Devonian

The base of the Devonian is not easily identified in midland Scotland: both Late Silurian and Early Devonian rocks lack fossils, are terrestrial and are often red in colour, so determining the boundary between them is difficult. These Silurian-Devonian (Lower Old Red Sandstone) rocks are found on the NW and SE margins of the Midland Valley, but it is the outcrops on the NE margin which are the most extensive, and where the sequence is thickest and the best exposed. Throughout the Midland Valley region rocks of this age and association are seen to comprise mainly red coloured conglomerates, sandstones and shales together with lavas. Most of the lavas form the Ochil-Sidlaw uplands; most of the conglomerates are found near the basement rocks which flank the Midland Valley and most of the finer rocks occur away from the flanks to dominate those outcrops removed from the NW and SE margins. This disposition of lithologies led many, including myself, to suggest that the flanking regions of the Southern Uplands and the Southern Highlands were the source of the Lower Old Red Sandstone sediment. This concept is now seen to be invalid, and there are now some considerable departures from former views about the source and sedimentation of the Lower Old Red Sandstone. The most critical of these changes are as follows:

a. On the northern margin of the Midland Valley the Lower Old Red Sandstone is not always faulted against the Dalradian basement or Highland Border Complex to the north. At many localities the basal Old Red Sandstone conglomerates rest unconformably on the Highland Border Complex. This fact has resulted in a number of important implications:

i. The Lower Old Red Sandstone is now seen to be not as thick as formerly thought.

ii. To the south of the Highland Boundary Fault, the basement to the Old Red Sandstone is the Highland Border Complex: to the north it is the Dalradian block.

iii. The great thickness difference between the Old Red Sandstone at Stonehaven and Lomondside is now explained stratigraphically rather than, structurally, where beds were thought to be faulted out in a SW direction.

b. The earlier views that the Old Red Sandstone sequence on the north margin of the Midland Valley was one of continuous lithostratigraphic units which extended from Stonehaven to Arran is not now supported by the evidence available. Detailed mapping along parts of the Highland Border is at present showing that the Old Red Sandstone conglomerates, at least for the NW Midland Valley, are a series of lenses, which may have been deposited in a series of basins, rather than a single one. The rock sequence for the southern Midland Valley appears to be more straightfoward, with a conglomerate characterized by greywacke clasts being overlain by sandstones and lavas and a conglomerate with lava clasts. These units appear to run as laterally continuous sheets from the Pentland Hills to the Clyde.

c. When the lenses of conglomerate are examined in the NW Midland Valley they overlap each other as they are traced towards the SW (Excursion 9, Balmaha). This type of overlapping is not diagnostic of but is certainly characteristic of fault basins. For that reason the Lower Old Red Sandstone sediments there are thought to have been deposited in a series of fault-bounded basins in which the faults were active at the time of deposition.

d. The conglomeratic sediments along the northern margin are dispersed in a range of directions, some from the south, the NE and north. It is clear that sedimentation along this northern margin was indifferent to the presence of the Dalradian block and the Highland Boundary Fault.

e. The sediments which occur away from the bounding faults i.e. towards the central parts of the Midland Valley are mainly sandstones rich in metamorphic and igneous detritus of non-Dalradian type and near the north margin of the Midland Valley very thick siltstones. The discovery of a large river bar >12m thick near Perth, prompted the notion that a very large river system, a little less extensive than the present-day Mississippi flowed into eastern Scotland and along the Strathmore area towards the Clyde. Large alluvial bars are also recorded in the sandstones which crop out in the southern Midland Valley. This river is thought to have drained the Norwegian-Greenland area. Laurentia, of which Greenland is a part, collided with Baltica during the Late-Silurian-Early Devonian and the result of this collision was a long series of mountains running to the present NE. These mountains would have yielded a great deal of sediment which Bluck (1990), Bluck *et al* (1989) thought was dispersed through central Scotland.

2. Upper Devonian

As with the base of the Lower Devonian there is a problem in identifying the base and top of the the Upper Devonian. Fossil fish and spores used to date the Lower Devonian, are even less common in the Upper, and the top of the Upper is often gradational into the Carboniferous. For this reason red rocks which unconformably overlie the Lower Devonian (Excursion 8) and grade up into the Carboniferous are referred to as the Upper Old Red Sandstone. Rocks of Middle Devonian age, which form such thick and important sequences north of the Highland Boundary Fault, are not known from the Midland Valley.

During the Middle or late Lower Devonian times the main known events in the Midland Valley were the development of the Strathmore Syncline in the north, and a number of more local folds and faults in the south. The Strathmore Syncline is a very extensive structure which runs parallel to the Highland Boundary Fault. Its NW limb is steeply dipping, occasionally overturned, and is terminated by the Highland Boundary Fault which, in places, is steeply dipping towards the NW. The Syncline probably formed as a consequence of a reverse movement along the Highland Boundary Fault and the convergence of the Dalradian block onto the Midland Valley.

A similar interpretation is made for the folds in the southern Midland Valley which have steep limbs on the SE flanks, although here they are not as extensive as those along the northern margin. In this instance the Southern Uplands block was probably thrust NW, so folding the sedimentary sequences NW of it. Clearly sometime during the Middle Old Red Sandstone interval there was a compression which resulted in both blocks flanking the Midland Valley converging on it.

The Upper Old Red Sandstone occurs as separated outcrops which are generally found more within the central part of the Midland Valley, but the most complete exposures and also the thickest and most informative sequences are found in the region around the Firth of Clyde (Excursion 16). In the Clyde region the thickness of the Upper Old Red Sandstone is difficult to estimate because of faulting and poor exposure, but it may be as much as 3-4 km in the region of Inverkip-Rosneath-Helensburgh. At its most complete, the Upper Old Red sequence begins with conglomerates which grade upwards into sandstones and finally quartz-rich sandstones, with caliche forming the top of the sequence. This whole succession then thins and becomes finer to the NE, south and SW, and it is the thinning to the SE which can be reasonably well documented in sections running from the Firth of Clyde to the Southern Uplands (see introduction to Excursion 16). As well as thinning to the south, the whole sequence is replaced by sandstones with very thick caliche beds. Caliche and the quartz arenites associated with them are produced by crustal stability, and in the Upper Old Red Sandstone there are grounds for seeing the early conglomerate beds as the product of much structural activity : as one goes upward in the sequence the evidence for structural control diminishes so that towards the top of the succession mature sandstones are produced on tectonically stable surfaces. The Carboniferous rocks then replace the red sandstones and caliches.

The Upper Old Red Sandstone rocks were thought to have formed in an extensional regime which may have been initiated by shearing along older Caledonian faults, the Highland Boundary and related faults in particular (Excursion 16). In the Firth of Clyde region the effect of contemporaneous faulting on the deposition of the Upper Old Red Sandstone is well illustrated with the generation of at least three fault-bounded basins (Bluck 1980).

3. Carboniferous

The stability which characterised the Upper Old Red Sandstone was short-lived, to be broken in the Carboniferous with the reactivation of older faults, the widespread occurrence of volcanic rocks, and the re-development of thick local basin sequences.

41

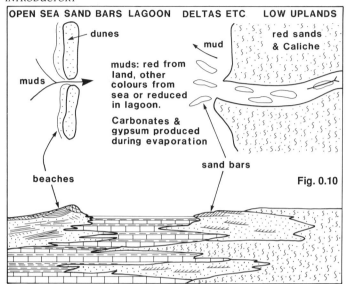

Figure 0.10 Diagram illustrating the origin of the Ballagan beds, and showing how the limestone-shale, sandstone and caliche can all be integrated into one environment of deposition.

The transition between the Old Red Sandstone and the Carboniferous is seen in Campsie Glen (Excursion 5), in the western Kilpatrick Hills east of Dumbarton, along the Clyde coast (Excursion 14), and on Great Cumbrae (Excursion 15). With the exception of the Cumbrae islands and parts of the Clyde coast, caliche-bearing Upper Old Red Sandstone is replaced upwards by white sandstones and also by alternations of carbonate and shale beds (the Ballagan Beds). These beds are not present on the Cumbraes and the nearby mainland; basaltic lavas and tuffs which normally rest on Ballagan beds are seen to rest directly on the white or red sandstones on Little Cumbrae and the adjacent mainland.

The Ballagan Beds are well exposed in the Dumbarton Muir-Campsie areas. At Murroch and Auchenreoch Glens, Overtoun and Ballagan Glens they are quite magnificently exposed. Critical to their understanding is that they comprise not only dolomites but also sandstones, caliche beds and evaporite minerals such as gypsum. The sandstones are often cross-stratified, but some contain long, low-angled cross strata which have on their surfaces rounded fragments of shark teeth. These sandstones were deposited in the upper foreshore of beaches and once this is recognised the interpretation of the origin of the Ballagan Beds becomes clear. A model of the types of sedimentation developed is given in Figure 0.10.

The Ballagan Beds were deposited in lagoonal areas trapped behind sand bars (Fig.0.10). These sand bars are now some of the sandstone sheets and wedges which occur within the sequence; the margins of the sand bars which faced the open sea developed upper foreshore low-angled cross strata with sedimentary lineations; the edges of the sand sheets which faced the lagoon are fine-grained, rippled, sometimes cross stratified and interfinger with the shales of the shale-carbonate facies. The caliche beds occur on the landward side of the lagoons. They are typical of the low-lying land fringe and are particularly common in the Cumbrae region, which appears to have been a low-lying upland area during deposition of these beds. When the water level in the lagoon rose, the carbonate-shale sequences of the lagoon spread over the peripheral caliches, but when the level fell the caliches prograded out over the lagoonal facies and the river deposits built into them, forming the cross stratified sandstone sheets.

This lagoonal episode was terminated in the west by the outpouring of a great number of basalt lava flows, now seen in the Campsie (Excursion 5), Kilpatrick and Renfrew Hills. Lava sequences are quite magnifiently exposed in many localities. They comprise tuffs and a red soil (**bole**) in alternation with vesicular and massive (although poorly jointed) basalt. This alternation of flow followed by weathering of its upper surface is common throughout the region and accounts for the 'trap topography' typical of these types of rocks. The lavas are variable in composition and texture and these two criteria have been used to divide the lava succession; they were probably extruded from fissures from which extensive flows spread widely.

Accompanying the lava extrusions are the volcanic plugs which have filled the conduits of volcanoes which originally covered a much wider area than the plugs themselves. These form small rounded hills all over the region and one is examined in detail at Dumbarton Rock (Excursion 7).

After a maximum of 900m of lavas had been extruded, the lava

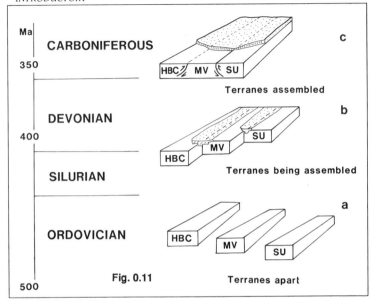

Figure 0.11 Showing the evolution of the main tectonic elements, Highland Border Complex, (HBC); Midland Valley (MV) and the Southern Uplands (SU) through time. In the Ordovician they were distinctive terranes which were being produced somewhere along the southern margin of Laurentia, and then progessively came together. By Devonian times these terranes were probably all overlapping each other, almost, but not quite, in the positions we now see them. During this time when the terranes were accreting, many basins developed along their margins forming the fault basins of the Old Red Sandstone. By Carboniferous times, but already beginning in the Devonian, sheets of sandstone produced from the erosion of the Caledonian mountains of Scandinavia and Greenland spread over the terranes, thus demonstrating them to be in postion at that time.

field was covered in places by fine grained, dark grey, coal-bearing sediments, and some of which are rich in fireclays, shales, and thin coals. The fireclays are the seat-earths upon which Carboniferous plants grew, so they formed in low ground not far above sea or river level. Such sediments are typical of the lower reaches of river systems and their associated coastal and deltaic deposits. In the regions of

Craigmaddie and Douglas Muir sheets of sands and gravels interrupted this phase of fluvial-deltaic sedimentation. These deposits, laid down by braided and meandering rivers are well developed in the west, and are succeeded by sandstones, shales, coals and limestones of the later Carboniferous. The deltas and alluvial coastal deposits which form much of the coal-bearing Carboniferous probably extended far into the Southern Highlands and Southern Uplands. The source for these sediments is probably to be sought in areas further to the north such as Scandinavia and Greenland where, on the basis of other evidence, the mountains, which reached their climactic uplift rates in the Devonian, are known to have been uplifting at a much diminished rate in the Carboniferous (Bluck 1990 and Fig.0.9). These sandstone sheets covered terrane boundaries which were later reactivated to show only minor displacements (Fig.0.11).

Whilst rivers from the north spread sheets of sand and mud over most of Scotland and northern England, there were numerous marine transgressions reaching far into this coastal plain. These transgressions originated from the sea which covered the southern part of Britain and made irregular incursions into the deltas and alluvial plains: in the Midland Valley, for instance marine transgressions probably came from the SW and NE margins, avoiding the higher ground of the Southern Uplands. One such transgression deposited a widespread limestone bed in central Scotland, the Hurlet Limestone which is seen on Excursions 6&20; this limestone in particular, but others like it, provide the Carboniferous with excellent marker beds to aid in the correlation of sections over the Midland Valley.

4. New Red Sandstone

Rocks of New Red Sandstone age are not abundant in the western Midland Valley, yet those exposures which are present are most instructive. The main areas of outcrops are in Arran in the west and Mauchline in the south, and these are both remnants of a sandstone sheet which, at one time, spread widely over central Scotland and beyond. In both these localities, and particularly in Arran, there is abundant evidence for deposition from aeolian activity. Not only are there large scale cross strata produced by dunes, but also the dune interbeds are preserved, making some of these sections classical ground for the study of aeolian sediments.

There is now mounting evidence that much of the basement rock of Scotland was being uplifted at this time. Alluvial sequences, some deposited in active fault controlled basins are found on the western and eastern seaboards, having their sources in the intervening ground of the basement uplift. This deposition of New Red Sandstone sediment on the western and eastern margins of Scotland may be related to the extensional basins which now form the North Sea, and in the Minch (and ground to the west of it).

5. Other Mesozoic and Tertiary rocks

Rocks of the Jurassic Period are not represented in central Scotland but, as with the Permian and Triassic, they are found on the western and eastern margins of northern Scotland where, once again they are the marginal deposits to a much larger basins sited to the east (North Sea) and west (Irish Sea and the continental edge beyond).

The Cretaceous Period is, however, represented by a block of chalk found within a Tertiary intrusion on Arran—suggesting that rocks of that period may have been deposited over central Scotland but have since been eroded away.

Dykes of Tertiary age are particularly abundant along the Ayrshire coast where they have a characteristic NW-SE or WNW-ESE trend. These are related to the big Tertiary centres of the western edge of Scotland.

References

ANDERTON, R. 1985 Sedimentation and tectonics in the Scottish Dalradian. *Scott. J. Geol.* **21** 407-36.

BARRETT, T.J., JENKYNS, H.C., LEGGETT, J.K. and ROBERTSON, A.H.F 1982 Comment and reply on 'Age and origin of the Ballantrae ophiolite and its significance to the Caledonian orogeny and the Ordovician time scale. *Geology* **9,** 331-3.

BLUCK, B.J. 1980 Evolution of a strike-slip fault controlled basin, Upper Old Red Sandstone. Scotland. *In* Ballance, P.F. and Reading R.G. (eds) Sedimentation in oblique-slip mobile zones. Spec.Publ.int.Ass. Sediment. **4,** 63-78.

————1985, The Scottish paratectonic Caledonides. *Scott. J. Geol.* **21,** 437-464.

————.1990, Terrane provenance and amalgamation: examples from the Caledonides. *Phil. Trans R. Soc. Lond.* **A 331,** 599-609.

————and DEMPSTER (in press). Exotic metamorphic terranes in the Caledonides: tectonic history of the Dalradian, Scotland. *Geology.*

————, INGHAM.J.K., CURRY,G.B. and WILLIAMS, A. 1984. Stratigraphy and tectonic setting of the Highland Border Complex. *Trans R. Soc. Edinb. Earth Sci.* **75,** 124-33.

————, HAUGHTON,P.D.W. HOUSE,M.R. SELWOOD,E.B. and TUNBRIDGE I,B. Devonian of England, Wales and Scotland in McMillan, M.J. Embry, A.F. and Glass, D.J. (eds) Devonian of the world. Canadian Society of Petroleum Geologists. 305-325.

CURRY, G.B. INGHAM, J.K., BLUCK, B.J. and WILLIAMS, A. 1982. The significance of a reliable age from some Highland Border Rocks in Central Scotland. *J.Geol. Soc. Lond.* **139,** 451-4.

DEMPSTER, T.J. and BLUCK,B.J. 1989. The age and origin of boulders in the Highland Border Complex: constraints of terrance movements. *J. Geol. Soc. Lond.* **146,** 377-379.

————1991. Age and tectonic significance of the Bute amphibolite, Highland Border Complex, Scotland. *Geol. Mag.* **128,** 77-80.

HALL, J.,POWELL, D. ANDESANYA, O.1982, Seismological evidence for shallow crystalline basement in the Southern Uplands of Scotland. *Nature* **305,** 418-20.

INGHAM, J.K. 1978. Geology of a continental margin 2: Middle and Late Ordovician transgression, *In* Bowes, D.R. and Leake,B.E. (eds) Crustal evolution in Northwestern Britain and adjacent regions. *Geol.J.* Special Issue **10.** 163-7.

INGHAM, J.K., CURRY, G.B. AND WILLIAMS, A. 1985. Early Ordovician

Dounans Limestone fauna, Highland Border Complex, Scotland. *Trans. R. Soc. Edinb. Earth Sci.* **76,** 481-513.

KELLEY, S. and BLUCK B.J. 1989. Detrital mineral ages from the Southern Uplands using ^{40}A-^{39}Ar laser probe. *J. Geol. Soc. Lond.* **146.** 401-403.

LONGMAN, C.D., BLUCK, B.J. and van BREEMEN, O. 1979. Ordovician conglomerates and the evolution of the Midland Valley. *Nature* **280,** 578-81.

MCKERROW, W.S. 1987. The Southern Uplands Controversy. *J. Geol. Soc.* **144,** 735-6.

———— , LEGGETT, J.K. and EALES, M.H. 1977. Imbricate thrust model of the Southern Uplands of Scotland. *Nature* **267,** 237-9.

ROGERS, G., DEMPSTER, T.J., BLUCK, B.J. and TANNER, P.W.G. 1989. A high precision U-Pb age for the Ben Vuirich granite: implications for the evolution of the Dalradian supergroup *J. Geol. Soc.* **146,** 789-98.

STONE, P. FLOYD, J.D. BARNES, R.P. and LINTERN,B.C. 1987. A sequential back-arc basin and foreland thrust duplex model for the Southern Uplands of Scotland. *J. Geol. Soc.* **144,** 753-64.

————-and SMELLIE, J.L. 1988. The Ballantrae Area. B.G.S. London.

WILLIAMS, A. 1962. The Barr and Lower Ardmillan Series (Caradoc) of the Girvan district, south-western Ayrshire. *Mem. Geol. Soc. London,* No **3,** 267pp.

EXCURSION PLANNER
List of Excursions (Fig. O. 3)
(with abbreviated titles)

1. Building Stones	12. S. Sluaigh	23. Lugar etc
2. Fossil Grove	13. Rosneath etc.	24. Heads of Ayr
3. Milngavie etc.	14. Greenock-Largs	25. Pinbane
4. Baldernock	15. Cumbrae	26. Knocklaugh
5. Campsie	16. Clyde ORS	27. Bennane Head etc.
6. Corrie Burn	17. Saltcoats	28. Dow Hill etc.
7. Dumbarton	18. Loanhead	29. Stinchar Valley etc.
8. Ardmore	19. Boyleston	30. Girvan Foreshore
9. Balmaha	20. Trearne	31. Craighead
10. Aberfoyle	21. Hagshaw	32. Dob's Linn
11. Lomondside	22. Lesmahagow	33. Quaternary

Standards of Excursions

a) Less advanced - but can provide advanced study as well:
1, 2, 3, 4, 5, 6, 7, 8, 14, 15, 17, 18, 19, 20, 21, 23, 24, 31, 33 (excursion) plus introductory itineraries for Girvan (25 to 30) and Dob's Linn (32).

b) More advanced - but with impressive exposures for all levels of knowledge and explanation of the more advanced features in most cases:

9 -	faulting and terrane development
10 -	cleavage and overfolding
11 -	polyphase deformation
12 -	a metamorphic aureole
13 -	Dalradian structures
16 -	alluvial palaeoenvironments in Old Red Sandstone
20 -	palaeoecology in the Carboniferous
22 -	arthropods and early fish (Silurian)
25 to 30 -	history of the Girvan area (plate tectonics)
32 -	graptolite succession
33 -	Quaternary (account)

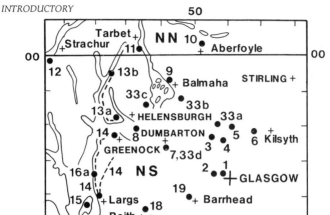

Figure 0.3. Map showing by the numbered dots the centres of location of the excursions: a key to the numbers is provided in the Contents list and on the back cover. The National Grid 100 km and 10 km lines are shown.

Topics in Excursions

The Stratigraphical Summary (Table O.1) indicates which excursions are most suitable for studying particular examples of the following:

1. **Stratigraphical systems**
2. **Rock groups or important formations**
3. **Sedimentary facies**
4. **Faunal associations**

More detailed information is given under the heading *Features* at the beginning of each excursion account.

The following topics are not adequately covered in Table 0.1.

1. **Igneous intrusions**
    a) **sills**: excursions **3, 17, 23**
    b) **dykes**: excursions **3, 14, 15, 17, 18, 24, 25, 30**
    c) **plugs and vents**: excursions **7, 12, 24**

2. **Metamorphism**
    Excursions **10, 11, 12, 13**

3. **Structural Features**
    a) **simple folds**: excursion **8**
    b) **complex folds**: excursions **10, 11, 13, 25**
    c) **minor faults** (visible): excursions **7, 8, 13, 14, 15, 24, 27, 28, 29, 30, 32**
    d) **major faults** (not usually visible):   excursions **5, 6, 9, 10**
    e) **cleavage**: excursions **10, 11, 13**

4. **Fossil Collecting**
    a) **Ordovician and Silurian shells**: excursions **28, 29, 30, 31**
    b) **Ordovician and Silurian graptolites**: excursion **32**
    c) **Devonian plants**: excursion **8**
    d) **Carboniferous shells**: excursions **4, 5, 6, 20**
    e) **Carboniferous plants**: excursion **2**

5. **Mineral Collecting**
    Excursions **18, 19, 20**

Timing of Excursions

Estimates of the time needed for each excursion are provided at the beginning of each account. In some cases a shortened itinerary is suggested.

1. **Suitable for half-day or summer evening**
   Excursions **1, 2, 3, 4, 5, 6, 7, 8, 9, 17, 18, 19, 20**

2. **Combinations of above geographically convenient for a day trip**
   Excursions **1** and **2: 3** and **4: 7** and **8: 18** and **19: 18** and **20**

3. **Week-end trip**
   Selected localities in the Girvan and Ballantrae area from Excursions **25** to **31**. See Introduction to Girvan - Ballantrae section.

Maps

The 1: 63 360 and 1 : 50 000 geological (BGS) maps which cover the area are shown on Figure 0.4.

The following O.S. 1 : 50 000 maps cover the excursion area:

56   Inveraray and Loch Lomond
57   Stirling and The Trossachs
63   Firth of Clyde
64   Glasgow
70   Ayr and Kilmarnock
71   Lanark and Upper Nithsdale
76   Girvan
79   Hawick and Eskdale

Figure 0.4. Map showing the present coverage of the area by British Geological Survey (B.G.S.) maps. The names in bold with the larger numbers indicate the older series of maps, some of which (with numbers in brackets) can no longer be purchased. The italicised names with smaller numbers are for recent maps: there are now separate sheets for the western and eastern parts and their boundaries are shown by broken lines. The Irvine map (22W) is as yet only in Drift edition. More of the new maps will be forthcoming. The National Grid squares are indicated.

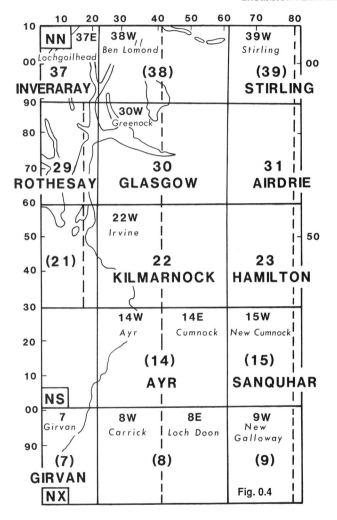

Fig. 0.4

GEOLOGY IN GLASGOW MUSEUMS

G.P.Durant
(after W.D.Ian Rolfe)

Large collections of geological specimens, featuring much local material, are housed in both the Hunterian Museum at Glasgow University (open to the public 9.30 - 5 pm. Monday to Friday, 9.30 - 1 pm. Saturday and Sunday) and the Glasgow Art Gallery and Museum, Kelvingrove (open to the public 10-5 pm. Monday to Saturday, late-night opening to 9 pm. on Thursdays, 12 noon- 6pm. Sunday). Each museum contains exhibits of general geological interest, as well as locally relevant displays and both mount temporary exhibitions which often feature geological subjects. They employ geological curators who can help visitors with specimen identification and geological information.

Only a small part of the collections is on exhibit at any one time, but access to the catalogues and large reserve collections in store can be organised by prior arrangement with the curators. Both museums are always anxious to see and record new geological finds in the region, even if the finder does not wish to present the specimens to either museum.

The Hunterian Museum collections are particularly rich in local Palaeozoic fossils especially from the Ordovician of the Girvan district (collected by J.Begg, A.Lamont, R.P.Tripp and J.K.Ingham) and the recently discovered Carboniferous fish and arthropods from Bearsden, including the Bearsden Shark (collected by S.P.Wood), fresh water mussels of the Coal Measures (collected by A.E.Trueman, J.Weir and their students) and Quaternary shells of the Clyde basin (H.W.Crosskey collection). It also houses the Kidston collection of thin-sections of fossil plants, including the famous Old Red Sandstone flora of the Rhynie Chert. Many thousands of the fossils are especially important in being "type-specimens", the ultimate name bearers and reference standards for comparison of one fossil with another.

The Hunterian Museum also possesses suites of major local rock types (a collection largely built up by G.W.Tyrrell) and large collections of rocks from around the world (including many specimens collected by J.W.Gregory). The petrological reference collection also includes many thousands of microscope thin-sections, which can be made available to *bona fide* research workers. The museum has important mineral collections including many connoisseur pieces from classic European localities assembled by William Hunter, the founder of the museum, as well as the Brown of Lanfine, Eck, Rutley and Clarke collections. There are excellent collections of zeolites from the local Carboniferous lavas, minerals from the Leadhills mining district and gemstones from a variety of sources. The meteorite collection includes the High Possil meteorite which landed in Glasgow in 1804. Several historically important geological collections include that of D.Ure, Lord Seymour and Playfair's collection of rocks from Glen Tilt illustrating Hutton's theories and Sir G. S. Mackenzie's 1810 Iceland collection. The museum has recently been designated as the Scottish Universities' Earth Sciences collections centre and regularly receives research collections from research students and academic staff.

Glasgow Art Gallery and Museum has fine collections of fossils from the West of Scotland including the John Young collection of local Carboniferous fossils, the Slimon collection of Silurian arthropods from Lesmahagow, the Dairon collection of graptolites from the Southern Uplands and the Lord Archibald 'Campbell collection of Tertiary plants from Ardtun, Mull, first described by Campbell's father the 8th Duke of Argyll. The relatively small mineral and rock collection includes the important D.C.Glen and J.Fleming collections. A collection of fossils was purchased by the Museum in 1899 from the Geological Society of Glasgow.

Excursion 1   BUILDING STONES of GLASGOW
Judith Lawson

Themes: Building stones and facing stones, and their sources.

Features: Various sandstones, granites, marbles, gneiss, oolitic and fossiliferous limestones, breccias, travertine etc.

Maps: Plans of central Glasgow available from Tourist Information Office, St Vincent Place (and see Fig. 1.1).

Distance and Time: About 1200m or 0.75 miles: allow two hours at least.

Access: City Chambers provides free guided tours at 10.30 am and 2.30 pm on Monday, Wednesday and Friday.

In the city of Glasgow it is possible to see a great variety of rocks used in many different ways. A walk through the centre can provide an introductory course in the identification of rocks - sedimentary, igneous and metamorphic - in hand specimen. Many of the facing stones have been imported from overseas and are beautifully polished to show their constituent minerals. This is a suitable winter excursion when the weather does not allow trips further afield. This account describes a 'starter' route with a range of typical examples. Numerous other walks can then be added and explored (Lawson 1981).

Start at the southern exit of Buchanan Street Underground station (Fig. 1.1). The old station was excavated in sandstone, with plaster and paint applied directly to the sandstone walls, and immediately to the north there was an extensive area of sandstone quarries which supplied much of the stone for building the older (pre-1835) parts of Glasgow (Lawson 1984). There is now no surface evidence of these quarries.

On the west side of Buchanan Street at the corner of Nelson Mandela Place is the former Royal Scottish Academy of Music & Drama (1908-9), whose red sandstone comes from the New Red Sandstone (Permian) of Locharbriggs in Dumfriesshire. It is a fairly even-grained sandstone with cross bedding on such a large scale that some blocks show parallel bedding. On either side of the main entrance, blocks can be seen which have been cut with "mirror image" bedding. Some blocks show good cross bedding (up-side-down!): the

Figure 1.1.   Sketch map of central Glasgow showing route of excursion.

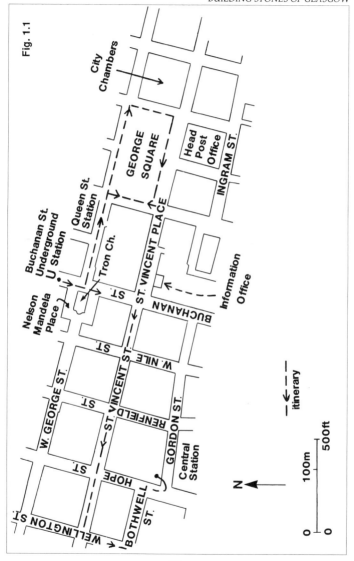

Fig. 1.1

intricate carving of the sandstone is impressive. Red sandstones like this were commonly used in Glasgow from the late 19th century onwards.

In the middle of Nelson Mandela Place the Tron Church (1807) is built of a contrasting cream sandstone of Carboniferous age. Numerous fine bedding planes are picked out with brown organic matter. The partings, up to a few centimetres thick, often show cross sections of ripple marks. This sandstone is very typical of the local sandstone and may even have come from the quarries farther up the road. The facade is of smooth ashlar, the rear and sides of tooled blocks. On the next corner is the Stock Exchange building (1875) built of a cream-coloured Carboniferous freestone, i.e. a sandstone without obvious bedding planes and which can therefore be cut evenly in all directions. It was quarried at Overwood in Lanarkshire. Thus, in three adjacent buildings, the three main types of sandstones used in the building of Glasgow can be studied. In other buildings throughout the city the same three types, from various quarries can be seen over and over again, sometimes alone, sometimes mixed. Although other materials, including brick, may have been used in the internal construction all these buildings appear outwardly as sandstone buildings.

On the opposite (east) side of the street, at the corner with West George Street, there is a modern building showing a completely different use of stone. The Clydesdale Bank is a concrete frame structure clad with thin slabs of granite used both for protection and decoration. The surface may be highly polished or be flame finished to a rough texture. The granite is coarse grained and largely made up of red feldspar and grey quartz with smaller amounts of biotite and hornblende. The texture can be well seen on the polished panels. This granite came from Sierra Chico in Argentina. Continuing along West George Street, the next building, Dale House, also uses a South American 'granite', one of the creamy-brown rocks which have become popular as facing stones in recent years. Although referred to in the trade as a granite, one of its most obvious features is conspicuous banding with large crystals of cream-coloured feldspars. This is a metamorphic rock, a gneiss, and not an igneous granite, although the minerals are similar. It comes from the Campo Grande region of Brazil. The upper storeys and columns near the entrance of the building are clad with a cream sandstone from Stainton in the north of England. Other rock types can be seen in the entrance, including a cream limestone (Serpeggiante "marble") on the floor, and a dark brown travertine on the walls, both rocks from Italy.

On the north side of this part of West George Street, the Connell building (nos 34-38), shows a typical combination of stone used in many of the older city centre buildings. The lower storeys, pillars, steps and balustrades have the flesh coloured Peterhead granite with its pink feldspars, clear quartz and dark mica. **Xenoliths** are common and may be quite large. The upper storeys are of the red Locharbriggs sandstone which has here been carved with fine detail into ships, locomotives and other engineering sculptures.

Moving eastwards into George Square note the browny pink Tranos granite from Finland at the Standard Chartered Bank on your left. George Square was largely rebuilt during the 19th century and there are many of the solid Victorian buildings for which Glasgow is so famous. These mainly have cream sandstone exteriors with some granite at lower levels. The City Chambers on the east side is clad with Dunmore and Polmaise Sandstone from the Carboniferous of Stirlingshire. It has pink Correnie granite from Aberdeenshire at ground level. The richly decorated interior is well worth a visit (free guided tours at 10.30 am and 2.30 pm on Monday, Wednesday and Friday). On the west side, the Merchants' House and the Bank of Scotland, also of Dunmore Sandstone, are quite typical. Stone from Stirlingshire was commonly used in the centre of Glasgow and was normally transported by rail. Generally it is a good quality stone which weathers well. Such stone may be used as ashlar with a rusticated or vermiculated finish. In the Head Post Office on the south side of the Square it was combined with stone from Giffnock (to the south of Glasgow) and from Hermand (near Linlithgow). On the north side of the square is a new office block clad in the rather yellowy green sandstone from Springwell in Co. Durham. Also on the north side is Queen Street Station which was built on the site of some of the old quarries. When the bulk of the good sandstone had been removed, the quarries provided convenient excavations for the railway companies which were seeking space for their new termini. In the centre of the square are various statues. Sir Walter Scott stands on a tall column of honey coloured sandstone from Eastwood quarry near Giffnock while most of the smaller statues and the war memorial are on plinths of granite, largely from Scotland, although that below James Watt in the SW corner, with its large white feldspar phenocrysts may be from Cornwall. Greggs Bakery on the south side is clad at ground level with green slate, a metamorphosed volcanic ash of Ordovician age, from Cumbria.

From the SW corner of George Square walk into St Vincent Place, a short street with a great variety of stone. On the north side are, in turn, the Dunmore Sandstone of the Bank of Scotland, the white tiles and green serpentinous marble pillars at nos 12-16 and red sandstone from Mauchline (in Ayrshire) at no. 24. This last is the former Citizen newspaper office whose name can still be seen carved in the sandstone at first floor level. The Clydesdale Bank at the corner has a balustrade of an unpolished granite whose very large pink feldspar phenocrysts make it easily recognizable as Shap granite from Cumbria. On the south side of St Vincent Place, near George Square, are several older (early 19th century) buildings of local ripple-marked sandstone. The office block at nos 19-29, is of Carboniferous Blackpasture Sandstone from Northumberland. The Tourist Office (at nos 31-39) is housed in another sandstone block: the pillars at the entrance are of a dark fine grained granite with small white feldspar phenocrysts, which may be the 'blue' Cairngall granite from Aberdeenshire: the balustrades are of the more typical Peterhead type.

Continue west along St Vincent Street to the junction with West Nile Street. On the SW corner Mappin and Webb has a facing of pink limestone which is full of fossils. There are algal structures, corals, gastropods and bivalves all veined with dark pink **stylolites**. Stylolites are irregular zig zag boundaries often developed in limestones which form by solution and re-deposition of the calcium carbonate at pressure points. They may cut across the fossils. This is probably Estoril 'marble' of Cretaceous age from Portugal. The banks at the NW and SE corners have grey granite near ground level and cream sandstone above, a very common combination. The canopy at the NE corner is of the coarse-grained feldspar rich rock from Norway called **larvikite**. Here it is the dark 'emerald' variety; there is also a pale blue variety which is often used.

Further along the street contrasts can again be seen. No. 86 to no. 90 is a white, or off-white building of limestone, unusual in Glasgow. This is Portland limestone from Dorset which is well known in the south of England, e.g. in London, but was not often used in Scotland. It is of upper Jurassic age, is often oolitic and commonly contains fossils. When clean it is startlingly white but often becomes stained black. Next to it is more larvikite and a green brecciated serpentinous marble.

Continue on to the next block beyond Hope Street where, on the north side, are buildings of the red Locharbriggs sandstone and beyond is the Scottish Amicable Assurance Company Office (no. 150). This is clad with the dark Bleubraun granite from Sweden. The blocks show a distinct banding when viewed from a distance. The interior, in marked contrast with the sombre exterior, is finished in highly polished cream Botticino 'Marble'. This handsome rock shows a splendid development of stylolites. Originally all Botticino marble came from near Brescia, but now similar limestones are also quarried in Sicily and sold under the same name. There are sometimes small exhibitions open to the public, in the foyer.

A detour can be made here by turning north up Wellington Street past a sunken garden of cream travertine, to Ashley House at the corner with West George Street. This has columns faced with another version of Portland stone which comes from beds above the more commonly used Portland Whitbed; this is the highly fossiliferous Portland Roach. The shells have often been dissolved away leaving a rock full of cavities. There are many moulds of highly turreted gastropods e.g. *Aptyxiella* and bivalves like *Laevitrigonia*. Beneath the windows is the more typical Whitbed limestone. Retrace your steps down Wellington Street. On the SE corner of St Vincent Street (no. 145) is a 'traditional' red sandstone/red granite building where the sandstone shows good large scale cross bedding. Walk down Wellington Street noting the various uses of sandstone and limestone and then turn left (east) along Bothwell Street. At the corner with Hope Street, Imperial Mahogany granite from Dakota, U.S.A. has been used as cladding in the Abbey National Building Society office. From here Central Station can be seen, a sandstone edifice built mainly of Giffnock Sandstone in 1884. Opposite the station, on the corner of Gordon Street the Bradford and Bingley Building Society has made impressive use of two contrasting rocks. Much of the front is the Baltic Brown granite from Finland with its characteristic 'Rapakivi' texture of large round pink feldspar phenocrysts. In sharp contrast part of the front is of creamy pink limestone breccia, the fragments being of oolitic limestone. The rock is from Italy and is known as Rosaro Marble.

From here the walk can be continued in any direction. Attempt your own identifications.

References

LAWSON, J.A. 1981. *Building Stones of Glasgow*. Geological Society of Glasgow.
LAWSON, J.A. 1984. *Sandstone Quarries in Glasgow*. Proc. Geol. Soc. Glasgow.

Excursion 2 FOSSIL GROVE
Michael C. Keen

Themes: *In situ* remains of Carboniferous lycopod trees, their surrounding sediment, and intrusive late Carboniferous quartz dolerite sills, in Victoria Park, Glasgow.

Features: Sand-filled internal moulds of the root systems and basal portions of lycopods; drifted logs; shale and sandstones, the latter showing bedding plane surfaces sometimes with ripple marks; small scale cross bedding; intrusive quartz dolerite sheets exhibiting rapid lateral changes in thickness.

Maps: O.S.   1:50 000 Sheet 64 Glasgow & surrounding area
           B.G.S. 1:63 360 Sheet 30 Glasgow

Terrain: Paths in Victoria Park.

Time: 30 minutes -1 hour.

Access: Enter Victoria Park from the main gate in Victoria Park Road (where parking is easy) and follow the path past the tennis courts; signs to the Fossil House lead (past the minature golf course) to the western end of the park where the Fossil House is situated. Improvements are gradually being made in the viewing facilities and in the explanatory exhibits. It is hoped to have an attendant in charge from whom the helpful illustrated guide-book (MacGregor and Walton 1972) may be purchased. Being situated in a public park, the opening times are more restricted in winter. It is wisest to check times with the Glasgow Tourist Information Office (041-204. 4400) or with Glasgow City Council direct (041-221. 9600).

Hammering is forbidden and hammers should not be carried.

The Fossil House, gardens, and fish pond are situated in what was once a whinstone quarry which ceased to be worked over one hundred years ago. Whinstone is a dolerite, and was used as an aggregate for road construction. When the area of the quarry was incorporated into Victoria Park, a path being cut across the lower part of the floor in 1887 revealed the fossil trees, which were then carefully

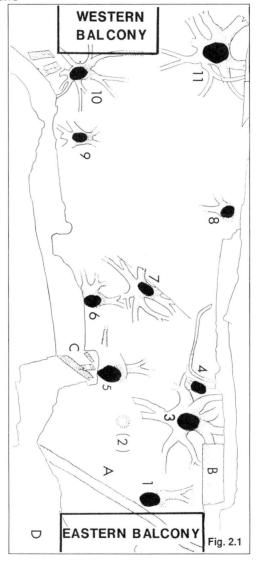

Fig. 2.1

excavated, and the present building constructed to protect them. Although occurrences of similar Carboniferous trees are not uncommon, this is the only site in the world where they have been preserved *in situ*. Fossil Grove is therefore truly unique and justifies its designation by the Nature Conservancy Council as a Site of Special Scientific Interest. The trees occur in the lower part of the Limestone Coal Group. The following geological itinerary is divided into two parts: the first a visit to the trees inside the building, the second a look at the surrounding rocks exposed in the grounds of Fossil Grove.

The public normally enters at the eastern end of the Fossil House, but the map (Fig.2.1) allows the itinerary to be followed from either end. The first objects noticed by the visitor are undoubtedly the tree stumps themselves (Fig. 2.2). There are 11 in all, although only 9 can be clearly seen today. The trees probably represent a mature stand with no saplings as they are roughly equally spaced and of a similar size. It is unlikely that they represent the whole of the plant community living at the time, but only the most durable part was preserved when buried by inundation: little or no foliage such as leaves occurs in association with the trunks. The preserved heights range from 15 cm to 68 cm. The trunks are elliptical in cross section, the longest diameter orientated in a N.E.-S.W. direction, with average dimensions of 91 cm in the long direction and 61 cm in the shorter. It is interesting to note that the stumps with the greatest preserved height also show the greatest deviation from a circular cross section.

Each stump has four main roots, each of which divides into two equal branches; some do this twice, giving 16 end branches. The roots do not penetrate very deeply downwards, which is very typical of modern swamp dwelling trees. Evenly spaced indentations are present on the roots, which in life were the sites of smaller rootlets capable of absorbing water. The stumps are preserved as internal moulds: when the trees died the soft inner material decomposed, leaving the tough outer bark to enclose a hollow cylinder; this cylinder was then infilled with sand which ultimately formed a mould of the inside of the tree. When the stumps were first discovered they still had a coating of carbonaceous material derived from the decomposition of the bark, but this has since decomposed.

Figure 2.1. Ground plan of Fossil Grove. See text for explanation (After MacGregor and Walton 1972).

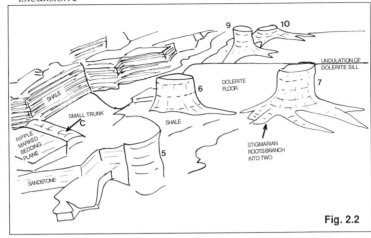

Figure 2.2. Sketch of the features seen from the eastern balcony. Numbers and letters refer to Fig.2.1.

Immediately in front of the eastern viewing balcony is a fallen tree trunk about 7m long which is clearly flattened, due to compression caused by burial in a thick sequence of sediments (A on Fig.2.1). It has a much smaller diameter than the stumps. Other pieces of trunk can be seen within the grove; a thicker piece(B) is present on the northern side of the house (right hand side when viewing from the eastern balcony), partially overlying Trunk no.3 (B on fig. 2.1), and a prominent piece is present on a projecting rock on the south side of the house (C). Closer inspection reveals a network of diamond-shaped meshes on the surfaces of some of these branches, which are scars left by leaves when they fell off the branch. This pattern has led to the name of "scale tree" for this type of Carboniferous tree. The bedding planes adjacent to C have ripple marks which are slightly asymmetric, and indicate water flow to the SW: another ripple marked surface (D) is present adjacent to the left of the viewing gallery.

Turning our attention to the rocks of the grove, four different types can be seen from the viewing gallery. The sediment in which the roots occur is a finely laminated sandy mudstone usually described as a shale, and this forms much of the floor of the house. This would have originally been a mud and subsequently a soil horizon in which

66

the trees grew; small rootlets are common, especially in the vicinity of stump 11. A dolerite sill is also present at this level and forms much of the floor in the central areas of the house away from the immediate vicinity of the trunks: the sill can be seen to have an undulating surface. It is a tongue of a much larger intrusive sheet which may be examined in the grounds outside the Fossil House. These thin tongues of dolerite intruded into the shales have been altered to a rusty yellow coloured rock by the liberation of carbon dioxide from the shales caused by the heat of the intrusion, although this has not affected the thick dolerite of the main mass of the sill. The trunks are preserved within a sandstone with occasional ripple marked bedding planes; none of the trunks reaches the top of this unit.

Overlying the sandstone are shaley sediments, including finely laminated siltstones with sand partings. Bedding planes with a dip to the NE are well displayed within the sandstone and the overlying shale. Further wedges of dolerite sill thickening to to the west occur along the walls of the house, and are best seen from the western balcony. One in the lower shale along the north wall is 80cm. thick in the west, but tapers out before the eastern viewing gallery is reached; this cuts two of the trunks, including trunk 9 which was repaired with a concrete spacer after damage during the Second World War.

The trees are obviously preserved in position of growth, which is believed to have been a lowland swamp environment. The roots of these trees are named *Stigmaria* (Figs 2.2 and 2.3), and are typical of a group of Carboniferous plants referred to as lycopods. Many different lycopods had roots and trunks similar to those found at Fossil Grove, so it is not certain to which they should be assigned, although they are commonly placed in the genus *Lepidodendron* (Fig. 2.3). These trees grew to a height of 30m., and had a straight trunk with a crown of branches; the younger parts of the branches and trunk were covered with small leaves which left diamond shaped scars when they fell off. The smaller branches bore cones up to a foot in length, which contained reproductive spores. These great forest-forming trees of the Carboniferous are now extinct, their only living relatives being the small club mosses found on wet hillsides or stream banks at the present day.

The trunks at Fossil Grove are preserved as sand moulds, so no original internal plant material is present. However, lycopod trees have been found with their original tissue preserved at other localities

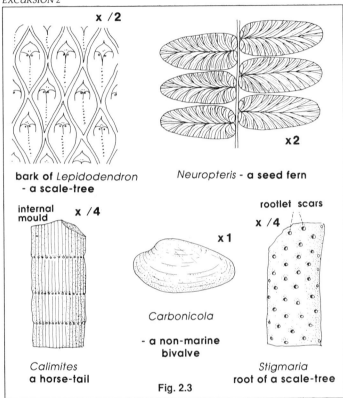

x /2

bark of *Lepidodendron*
- a scale-tree

Neuropteris - **a seed fern**

x2

internal
mould **x /4**

rootlet scars

x /4

x 1

Carbonicola

- a non-marine
bivalve

Calimites
a horse-tail

Stigmaria
root of a scale-tree

Fig. 2.3

Figure 2.3. Carboniferous non-marine fossils.

in Scotland (eg. Saltcoats: Excursion 17), so it is possible to describe the type of structure that would have been present in the trees of Fossil Grove. The trunk and branches had a thick strong bark, but only a relatively small amount of wood in the centre which in turn had a soft pith core; between the bark and the wood the cortex was mostly composed of a soft tissue. This structure meant that upon death selective decay occurred, with the soft inner bark, most of the cortex, and the central pith rapidly disintegrating, but the main part of the bark, parts of the cortex, and the inner wood being more resistant. It is this partial decay, with the trunks retaining their shape after death, that allowed the introduction of sand into the rotting interior of the trunks and hence their preservation as internal moulds.

So what were the events leading to the formation of the fossils? The trees were growing in the alluvial mud of a hot humid lowland swamp; an influx of sediment, represented by the siltstones covering the basal portions of the stumps, associated with flooding of the area, killed the trees. It is not clear whether the submergence of the lower parts of the trees in fairly permanent water, or the increased sediment supply was the more important factor in their death. After death the softer tissues of the trees decayed, and the trunks snapped at varying heights above the ground, perhaps due to slight variations in the rate of decay. The standing portions were already partially hollowed before the influx of the sands which subsequently filled them. The sandstone bed containing the trunks is 90cm thick. It is mostly thick-bedded with only occasional ripple marked surfaces, but becomes thinner bedded with more ripple marks in its upper layers. This suggests the the lower parts were deposited in much faster moving waters than the upper parts. This could have been the result of a nearby river channel breaking its levee banks, the water pouring out as a crevasse splay, and flooding the neighbouring areas of the lower lying swamps of the river's flood plain. The velocity of the water would have eventually slowed down, but by then the hollowed trunks had been partially infilled with sand. The ellipsoidal shape of the trunks has usually been attributed to deformation during folding of the rocks at a much later date. However in the scenario presented above, the deformation would have been the result of "streamlining" or distortion of the hollowed trunks. This would have been caused by sand deposition in a high energy flow regime of sediment laden flood waters coming from the north east (Gastaldo 1986).

The rock gardens outside the fossil house are in quartz-dolerite, the "whinstone" for which the original quarries were worked. It has already been seen that the thin dolerite tongues thicken westwards, and consistent with this the main sill in the gardens to the NW is seen to be at least six metres thick. The base of the sill can be seen at the end of the fishpond nearest the fossil house, where it rests on cross-bedded sandstone. Opposite the fishpond the edge of the sill intrudes the sediment and lifts up the overlying strata. These sandstone beds are well exposed on smooth surfaced bedding planes where the path from the fossil house descends towards the fishpond. It is possible to measure the true dip of the beds at this point where the bedding planes are well exposed; inside the Fossil House the sections cut through the rocks and exposed along the walls of the house show excellent apparent dips (true dip is the amount and direction of maximum inclination of the bedding plane measured from the horizontal, apparent dip is the amount of inclination in any other direction). The fishpond therefore lies at one end of the sill. The dolerite of the sill can be examined (but **no hammering!**) in a narrow passage cut through it opposite the fossil house; it coarsens towards its interior. The dolerite was intruded long after the depostion of the sediments and belongs to an intrusive episode that occurred at the end of the Carboniferous period.

References

MACGREGOR, M. and WALTON, J., 1972. *The story of the fossil grove*. Glasgow D.C. Parks Dept., 32pp.

GASTALDO, R.A., 1986. An explanation for lycopod configuration, 'Fossil Grove' Victoria Park, Glasgow. *Scott. J. Geol.* **22**, 77-83.

Excursion 3   MILNGAVIE and MUGDOCK
Judith Lawson

Themes:	Clyde Plateau Lavas, Craigmaddie Sandstone, dolerite sills and dykes, topography.
Features:	Sandstones and conglomerates, porphyritic basalts, dolerite sills and dyke, jointing, fault valley, scarp and dip, roche moutonnée.

Maps:

O.S.	1:50 000	Sheet 64	Glasgow
O.S.	1:25 000	Sheet NS 47/57	Milngavie
B.G.S.	1:63 360	Sheet 30	Glasgow

Terrain:	Easy walking, mainly on paths or roads.
Distance and Time	Total distance if walked as a round trip is 8 km (5 miles). If a car is used then walking is about 2 km (1.25 miles). Suitable for a half-day or a long summer evening.
Access:	Locality 1 is on Water Board property; phone Area Engineer, Loch Katrine Area (041) 336.5333 for permission which is willingly given. Localities 5-9 are on a Scottish Wildlife Trust reserve which has public access at all times. Mugdock Wood is an SSSI of biological interest but again there is no access problem.

Locality 1. Milngavie Reservoir: Craigmaddie Sandstone. (Fig.3.1).

Take the Mugdock road from the centre of Milngavie and park near the western entrance to Milngavie reservoir (NS 555 763). Cross the bridge over the reservoir and turn right along the cart track immediately beyond the water-side path. As the track turns left and a house comes into view turn obliquely left along a narrow path which passes behind the house and turn left again, uphill, behind the houses into a seemingly dense thicket of rhododendrons. The path quickly becomes an easy track which leads up to the quarry at the top of the hill (NS 558 761). On the way several small quarries can be seen to the right of the track. These, and the main quarry at the top, were worked for the sandstone which can be seen in the walls and buildings around the reservoirs. Dolerite was also quarried. The lower face of the quarry shows about 6m of uniform, medium-grained, rather soft siliceous sandstone which has a particularly shiny appearance in hand specimen.

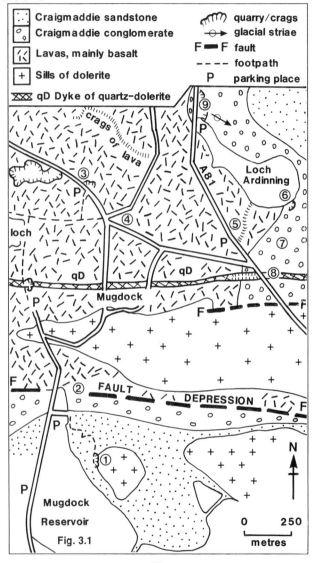

Legend:

- ⣿ Craigmaddie sandstone
- ⌀ₒ Craigmaddie conglomerate
- ⟨K⟩ Lavas, mainly basalt
- ⊞ Sills of dolerite
- ⧉ qD Dyke of quartz-dolerite
- 𝕄 quarry/crags
- ⊙→ glacial striae
- F▬F fault
- ---- footpath
- P parking place

crags of lava

P

Loch Ardinning

③ ⑨ ⑥ ⑤ ④ ⑦ ⑧ ② ①

A81

loch

qD Mugdock qD

P

Mugdock

F F FAULT DEPRESSION F

P

P

N

Mugdock Reservoir

Fig. 3.1

0 250 metres

Black plant fragments can occasionally be found. Bedding planes are not particularly obvious but there are two sets of joints approximately perpendicular to each other which can be seen in the quarry face. This is the Craigmaddie Sandstone. At the far end of the quarry it is possible to get on to the ledge formed by the top of the sandstone and inspect the dolerite sill which forms the upper 4m of the quarry face. Unfortunately the contact cannot be seen but can be located to within about 0.5m. The dolerite is highly weathered in hand specimen and is characteristic of the Milngavie sills confined to a small area between Mugdock and Milngavie. These are always, even in boreholes, highly altered. In thin section they can be seen to be olivine-free dolerites. The sill shows quite well developed columnar jointing. The different patterns of jointing in the sandstone and the dolerite are quite distinct.

Locality 2. Fault Valley. The pronounced valley which runs E-W for several kilometres immediately north of the reservoir is very straight and has been eroded along a fault. Here, the Craigmaddie Sandstone to the south is faulted against the Clyde Plateau Lavas to the north and the downthrow is to the south.

Return to the entrance and drive up the hill to the East Car park of Mugdock Country Park (NS 557 774). If walking, go up the road as far as the hairpin bend, noting the sill exposed at the corner, and continue straight on into the park. Following the signs to the car park, note an old quarry in a wide vertical dyke (NS 554 770) in a private garden to the right of the path and a line of lava crags to the east of Mugdock Loch.

Locality 3. Porphyritic basalt. This rock is exposed immediately opposite the entrance to the car park. This is one of the flows of the Clyde Plateau lavas and shows large (1cm) phenocrysts of plagioclase feldspar. It is thus a basalt of **Markle** type. The jointing is irregular and the exposure shows some spheroidal weathering towards the top. Numerous lines of lava outcrops, forming prominent crags can be seen in the area. It is noticeable that rock is very near the surface here. There are very few glacial deposits here and it was in general an area of glacial erosion.

Locality 4. View. Walk SE along the road until a good view to the north can be seen near the crossroads (NS 559 774). Figure 3.2

Figure 3.1. Simplified geological map of the Milngavie and Mugdock area.

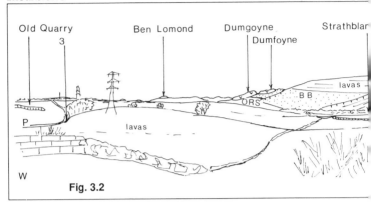

Fig. 3.2

Figure 3.2. View to the north from Locality 4. P = car park, ORS = Old Red

illustrates this view.

Locality 5. Top of lavas. Return to the car park and drive east taking the second left turning at the cross roads, or walk along this road to its junction with the main road A81. Park here and enter the field to the east of the road and look at the rock outcropping in the trees near the gate (NS 566 772). This is again a basaltic lava flow. None of these flows is as highly altered as the dolerite of the sills. Walk through the trees towards Loch Ardinning following the line of lava crags as they dip gently to the east. Continue east along the loch shore to an exposure in the next group of trees.

Locality 6. Conglomerate. The rock face at this exposure is in an unstable condition: it is safer to examine by eye rather than by hammer. Coarse, cross-bedded conglomerates with some sandstone beds, clearly very different from the lavas, are exposed.

Locality 7. Conglomerate. Walk SW along the edge of the wood where similar rock crops out as far as the corner at which point they can be easily inspected. The sediments at both these localities are the basal conglomerates of the Craigmaddie Sandstones which overlie the lavas. The pebbles are almost entirely of well rounded quartz. Notably, although they overlie the lavas, no obvious volcanic detritus from this source is visible. Both the bedding and the type of sediment

74

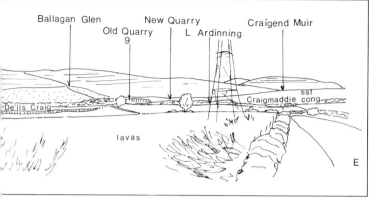

Sandstone, BB = Ballagan Beds, SST = sandstone.

suggest that these sediments were deposited by a braided stream flowing south from the Highlands. The conglomerates are common near the base of the Craigmaddie Sandstone but thin out both vertically and to the south. The higher beds are more uniformly sandy as was seen at Locality 1.

The relationship between the top lava and the basal conglomerate can be appreciated here although the contact is not visible. A series of westward facing scarp-faces mark the layers while the more gentle dip-slopes face east. This relationship can be particularly well seen looking south from Locality 9, at the north end of the loch, (Fig. 3.1). Although the contact between the lavas and the sediments is not visible it must run somewhere across the field. Standing in this field and looking north to the Campsie Fells it is easy to appreciate the magnitude of the Campsie Fault as you stand on the highest lava and look across to the lowest *i.e.* there must be a downthrow of some 1000m to the south.

Locality 8. Dyke and roche moutonnée. Now walk south across the field to a farm track. This follows the line of a quartz dolerite dyke about 5m wide. The dyke forms a feature above the general level of the field and can be followed for several kilometres; it was quarried on the other side of the road and also near Mugdock (see earlier reference to the walk through the park). The surface of the dyke is very smooth. It is a **roche moutonnée** and this is a glacially polished surface although no glacial striations can be seen here. The age of both the dyke and sills must be later than the Clyde Plateau Lavas as they cut the sediments above the lavas. They are probably of late Carboniferous age.

Locality 9. Craigmaddie Quarry.   Conglomerates and sandstones of the Craigmaddie Sandstone are well exposed here and show good sedimentary structures. Walk to the top of the quarry where a good general view of the scarp and dip slopes and the general topography can be seen. On the upper surface here are striations pointing to the SE and it is easy to imagine the ice grinding its way over the surface. On a clear day there is an excellent view of the Campsie Fells of Clyde Plateau Lavas, relatively uplifted north of the Campsie Fault, with Dumfoyne and Dumgoyne to the left and the Highlands beyond.

References

CLOUGH, C.T. *et al* 1925. The Geology of the Glasgow District. *Mem. Geol. Surv. U.K.*

Excursion 4   BALDERNOCK and BLAIRSKAITH

Judith Lawson and James D. Lawson

Theme: Sediments and fossils of the Lower Limestone Group (Carboniferous) and the environments of the time.

Features: Dolerite sills, waterfalls, coal seams, various limestones, stoop and room mining, desiccation cracks, flake breccias, ironstone nodules, black mudstones, nearshore shallow-water features, fossils and their ecology, Blackhall Limestone, Neilson Shell Bed.

Maps: O.S.   1: 50 000 Sheet 64   Glasgow
             O.S.   1: 25 000 Sheet NS 47/57   Milngavie
             B.G.S. 1: 63 360 Sheet 30   Glasgow

Terrain: Hummocky grass with muddy paths and potentially slippery rock at Baldernock; very muddy at Blairskaith after rain.

Distance: A few hundred metres at Baldernock and up to half a kilometre in the quarry at Blairskaith - providing transport is available.

Time: An hour is enough at Baldernock but at least two hours is needed at Blairskaith.

Access: At Baldernock cars can be parked on the adjacent road and access is open. There is also no restriction on access to Blairskaith Quarry at the moment, but there is a barrier across the road which leads past the quarry. If a large number of cars are being used the present residents at the house are very co-operative about unlocking the gate. One or two cars can be safely parked at the roadside near the farm and there is room for one coach (preferably not too large), which should approach via Bardowie to avoid tight bends.

Public transport is not convenient for this excursion and would add considerably to the walking distance, but there are occasional buses to Bardowie and Balmore to the south of these localities.

Locality 1. Linn of Baldernock (NS 591 758). In the stream section at the Linn of Baldernock is a good section through the lowest part of the Lower Limestone Group. Dolerite sills belonging to the Milngavie group have intruded into the sediments and generally form the series of waterfalls, or linns. The benches are formed by the baked sediments, (Fig. 4.1), which include coals and a thin limestone. Underneath the lowest sill which forms the largest waterfall is a limestone about 1 - 1.5m thick. Limestone was a valued commodity in Central Scotland (which is generally poor in limestones) and was often mined. The old stoops, or pillars, which supported the roof as the limestones were excavated in the rooms, or stalls, can still be seen. The mine extends some distance underneath the sill. It is wet and muddy and, as with all old mine workings, **should not be entered or explored.** This limestone is known as the Baldernock Limestone and occurs just below the Hurlet Limestone and Coal sequence of which it really forms part. The limestone is not obviously fossiliferous but is made up of **ostracode** shells from which it was formerly called the Entomostracan Limestone, after the old name for ostracodes. A small seam of coal can be seen about half way up the sill above the mine. The floor of the mine is formed of a hard sandstone, a "kingle" and below that are a limestone, another sandstone and shales of the top of the Calciferous Sandstone Measures.

Figure 4.1. Sketch of geology in stream section at the Linn of Baldernock.

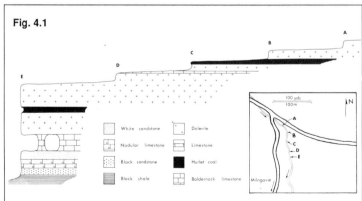

78

Fig. 4.2

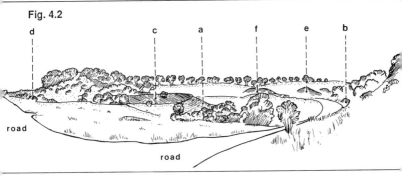

Figure 4.2. Sketch of Blairskaith Quarry.

Locality 2. Blairskaith Quarry (parking place south of quarry at NS 595 752).

This abandoned brick pit exposes the Blackhall Limestone and black mudstones of the Lower Limestone Group. The strata are of approximately the same age as the limestones and shales of Trearne Quarry (Excursion 20) and are also exposed at Corrie Burn (Excursion 6). They display a striking contrast in facies and conditions of deposition to the rocks at Trearne.

A sketch of the quarry is provided in Fig. 4.2. There is a small cliff (**a**) in the Blackhall Limestone but it is not very stable or easy to work. The casual visitor is advised to study the rock types in the fallen blocks both here and elsewhere in the quarry (e.g. **b**). The lower part of the formation includes dolomitic limestone and a pseudo-oolitic limestone which is probably an algal pellet rock, suggesting non-marine or restricted marine conditions. Blocks of a striking flake-breccia ("clay galls" of the Survey Memoir) can be found in the debris, representing partly lithified pale mud which has suffered penecontemporaneous erosion in shallow water so that the flakes have been incorporated in a later mud deposit. Some large blocks can still be found (*e.g.* at **b**) displaying moulds (*i.e.* ridges which infilled the grooves) of desiccation cracks ("mud-cracks") indicating emergence and drying out of the sediment. The shalier layers often contain fish remains, particularly scales (Fig. 4.3). Other layers contain tiny, smooth, oval ostracodes; their population structure (high density and low diversity) suggests a non-marine environment, probably brackish water. **Coprolites** also

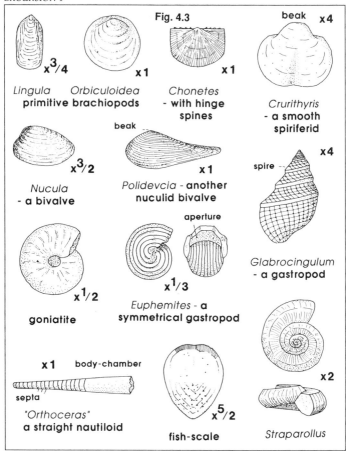

Fig. 4.3

Lingula   Orbiculoidea   Chonetes
primitive brachiopods   **- with hinge
spines**

beak

Crurithyris
**- a smooth
spiriferid**

beak

Nucula
- a bivalve

Polidevcia - **another
nuculid bivalve**

spire

aperture

Glabrocingulum
- a gastropod

goniatite

Euphemites - **a
symmetrical gastropod**

body-chamber

septa

**"Orthoceras"
a straight nautiloid**

fish-scale

Straparollus

Figure 4.3. Some fossils from Blairskaith Quarry.

occur commonly: these are fossilised faecal pellets - in this case,
probably of large predators (*e.g.* sharks) since the coprolites contain
shiny "ganoid" scales from smaller fish.

Spreads of similar feeding remains have been interpreted as shark
vomit, which is common in modern seas - although diarrhoea would

presumably give the same result! The top of the limestone, however, is a fully marine limestone composed mainly of small crinoid columnals. It is best examined on the extensive top bedding surface at **c** (and also at **e**). Other fossils are also small *e.g.* solitary corals of zaphrentid type and the brachiopods *Crurithyris, Chonetes* and productids(Fig.4.3): this size-reduction may be related to a limited food-supply in less than ideal marine conditions.

The black mudstones ("blaes") below the Blackhall Limestone are fine-grained organic-rich sediments with very few fossils and are considered to be dominantly non-marine deposits, perhaps from a large sluggish river system.

Ironstone nodules of various sizes are common; these are mostly of iron carbonate composition. Some of them show **septarian** structures *i.e.* internal shrinkage cracks infilled with walls (*i.e.* septa) of mineral precipitate, usually calcite. The nodules often show evidence of having been exhumed, eroded and resedimented indicating early formation and subsequent modification in nearshore conditions.

The black mudstones above the limestone are lithologically similar and also contain courses of ironstone nodules; some are tiny enough to be mistaken for goniatites and others are septarian nodules. However these upper mudstones contain a large and interesting marine fauna occurring in bands at various levels, mainly in the lower parts. They can be conveniently studied at a small exposure at **d** near the road but if enough time is available there are large exposures at **f**, **e** and **b**. This fossiliferous division is called the Neilson Shell Bed and has been fully described by Wilson (1966) and traced by him over most of the Midland Valley at this level. Most of the shells are complete and not compressed but they are mostly small and the same dark colour as the containing sediment, making them difficult to find until one gets the eye accustomed. Once a good layer is found it is wise to collect large blocks for processing at home.

Bivalves are common, particularly nuculids (*e.g. Nucula, Polidevcia* in Fig. 4.3) which today are superficial burrowers in silt or mud, feeding on organic detritus. Large thin-shelled pectinids and the concentrically furrowed *Posidonia* may have been able to swim, at least for short distances, above the mud. Gastropods are also common including high-spired forms (*e.g. Glabrocingulum*, Fig. 4.3), a very low-spired euomphalid (*Straparollus*, Fig. 4.3) and symmetrical bellerophontid genera (*e.g. Euphemites* Fig. 4.3). These gastropods probably crawled over the sea bottom, browsing on algal debris. A third group of molluscs, the cephalopods, is well represented by straight orthoconic nautiloids often of large size (*Orthoceras*, Fig. 4.3) and the occasional but stratigraphically important occurrence of goniatites (Fig. 4.3). A coiled nautiloid, *Catastroboceras*, also occurs and should not be confused with the smooth goniatites. These cephalopods would have been predatory carnivores and would have spent some time swimming above the bottom in search of food.

Brachiopods are less common. The tolerant *Lingula* (Fig. 4.3) presumably lived as a filter feeder in a burrow as at the present day. The other fairly common inarticulate, *Orbiculoidea*, however, had a strong pedicle and must have attached to something - most probably algal fronds. The occasional small productids and chonetids (Fig. 4.3) possessed spines for anchorage and to avoid sinking into the mud. The tiny, smooth spiriferid *Crurithyris* (Fig. 4.3) would have been very light and probably lived umbo-down in the mud like a productid.

Layers composed of spherical foraminifera are not uncommon. Fish scales and other remains have been found at all levels: *Watsonichthys* was recently recovered from the nodular mud-stones above the Neilson Shell Bed.

The combined evidence from the sediments and fossils in the Neilson Shell Bed suggests a shallow, quiet sea bottom rich in organic mud but with sufficient oxygen to support a fairly varied fauna of mainly small organisms including shallow burrowers, browsers, epifaunal filter feeders and swimming predators.

Dr C.J. Burton considers that the preponderance of gastropods and bivalves, together with the limited diversity of the fauna in general, suggests that 1) conditions were less than fully marine (marine marginal and river influenced) and 2) the faunas were in part **opportunistic**. They resemble modern delta-edge faunas occupying rich mud layers after the river activity has switched elsewhere.

References

CLOUGH, C.T. *et al*. 1925. The geology of the Glasgow District. *Mem. Geol. Surv.* U.K.

WILSON, R.B. 1966. A study of the Neilson Shell Bed, a Scottish Lower Carboniferous marine shale. *Bull. Geol. Surv. G.B.* **24**, 105-128.

Excursion 5   CAMPSIE GLEN
James G. MacDonald

Themes:	To examine part of the Lower Carboniferous succession, including the Clyde Plateau Lavas and the sedimentary sequences immediately above and below them, and the effect of the Campsie Fault. Minor intrusions and other evidence for faulting will be observed as well as the effects of Glacial and post-Glacial erosion and deposition.
Features:	The Campsie Fault Scarp, Cementstone Group, Campsie Lavas, dykes, the Lennoxtown essexite intrusions, Campsie Main (Hurlet) Limestone, fossils.
Maps:	O.S. 1: 50 000 Sheet 64 Glasgow B.G.S. 1: 63 360 Sheet 30 Glasgow
Terrain:	Muddy paths in Campsie Glen, some steep walking in vicinity of Campsie scarp, rough hill walking.
Distance and Time:	The normal itinerary is 9 km (5.5 miles) long : add 5 km (3 miles) if the ascent of Lairs Hill is included; a day is required to cover it fully on foot.
Short Itinerary:	The excursion can be shortened by missing out Localities 7 and 8 or, if returning via Campsie Glen, Localities 9 to 11.
Access:	Campsie Glen can be reached by private transport or by a frequent service from Buchanan Street Bus Station (Telephone (041) 332 7133 for departure times). Permission for access is not required but no dogs please as there are sheep on the hill. Care should be taken not to disturb livestock, particularly in the lambing season. The return bus to Glasgow can be boarded at Lennoxtown Cross.

Introduction

The first detailed account of the Campsie District (Young 1868) appeared in volume one of the Transactions of the Geological Society of Glasgow. The reprinting of this in new editions in 1868 and 1893 testifies to the early popularity of the area with members of the Society. The Campsie district is still recognised as an area for teaching the fundamentals of geology in the field.

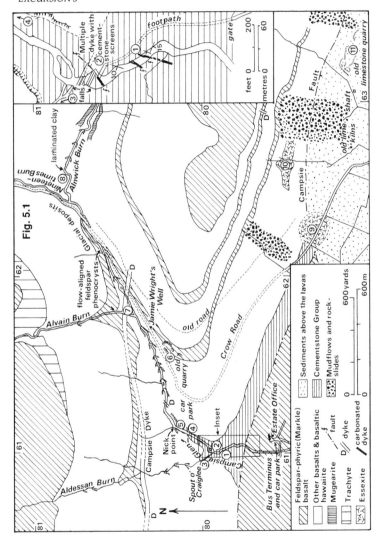

Fig. 5.1

Legend:

- Feldspar-phyric (Markle) basalt
- Other basalts & basaltic hawaiite
- Mugearite
- Trachyte
- Essexite
- Sediments above the lavas
- Cementstone Group
- Mudflows and rock-slides
- *f* fault
- D// dyke
- carbonated dyke

Scale: 0 — 600 yards; 0 — 600m

Inset scale: feet 0 — 200; metres 0 — 60

Labels on map: Multiple dyke with cement-stone screens, footpath, gate, falls, laminated clay, Nineteen Times Burn, Alnwick Burn, flow-aligned feldspar phenocrysts, Glacial deposits, Alvain Burn, Jamie Wright's Well, old road, Crow Road, old quarry, Campsie Dyke, car park, Nick point, Spout o' Craiglee, Aldessan Burn, Campsie Glen, Bus Terminus and car park, Estate Office, old lime kilns, old limestone quarry, Fault, Campsie, N

A major part of the local succession is occupied by the Clyde Plateau Lavas but parts of the Carboniferous sedimentary sequences above and below the lavas can also be studied. The scenery is dominated by the dramatic southward-facing scarp of the Campsie Fault. This fault, which has a downthrow to the south of possibly as much as 900 m, results in a dropping of the lava succession so that its top is encountered south of the fault (Fig. 5.1); as a result a large part of the Lower Carboniferous succession can be observed within a small area. Although not seen at the localities given here, the top of the lava sequence, to the south of the fault, occurs a little to the west of Campsie Glen in Fin Glen, as does the Campsie Fault itself.

The striking scenery of the area owes much to the effects of the Glacial Period and its aftermath. Results of the erosive power of ice and water are evident and there are extensive glacial and periglacial deposits. The broad valley between Strathblane and Lennoxtown is at present occupied, for the most part, by insignificant streams and there is a watershed about 5 km west of Lennoxtown. Its present form resulted from erosion by a major glacier, originating in the Loch Lomond area, which flowed eastwards past Strathblane and Lennoxtown, its path traced by boulders plucked from outcrops of the Lennoxtown essexite (see Locality 9). On the retreat of the ice, steep unstable scarps were left at Strathblane and to the east of Campsie Glen. In places these have collapsed to form major landslips (Fig. 5.1).

During the process of deglaciation enhanced run-off of melt waters led to the formation of gorges in Campsie Glen and neighbouring Fin Glen. The recent collapse of part of the Campsie Glen gorge (Locality 4) testifies to the continuing action of erosion of the unstable land forms which emerged at the end of glaciation. Other evidence of glacial processes is evident in the widespread deposits of boulder clay which blanket many of the higher slopes above Campsie Glen and are exposed in the banks of tributary burns.

From the car park and bus terminus at the Clachan of Campsie (NS 610 796) proceed to Locality 1 by the public footpath which starts to the east of the estate office. Although not visible the Campsie Fault crosses beneath the path some metres south of the gate which leads on to the hillside and into Campsie Glen. In the glen itself there are outcrops of the Cementstone Group and the overlying lavas (Fig. 5.1).

Figure 5.1 Geological map of the Campsie Glen district.

Papers relevant to the volcanic history include Whyte and MacDonald 1974 and MacDonald and Whyte 1981.

Locality 1. Ballagan Beds cut by carbonated dykes (Fig.5.1.). The first outcrops in the stream are of gently dipping strata of the Cementstone Group (Ballagan Beds), consisting of grey, green and dullish-red-brown mudstones, sometimes sandy, alternating with beds of nodular argillaceous dolomite (cementstones). At this locality the sediments have been intruded by a narrow N-S trending dyke which forms a waterfall and a cliff a little bit back from the west bank of the burn. The dyke was probably basaltic but has been very strongly carbonated and veined with calcite so that it is pale in colour, even on fresh surfaces. The line of the dyke is displaced by a fault which crosses it obliquely in the stream bed. Tilting of the sediments indicates a downthrow to the NW. The shales in the contact area have been indurated, sheared and brecciated, suggesting that faulting and intrusion were contemporaneous. About 15 m upstream similar structures occur in the bed of the burn, again indicating a small downthrow to the northwest along the line of a multiple carbonated dyke.

Locality 2. Multiple dyke complex (Fig.5.1). At this locality the burn is crossed by a multiple doleritic dyke complex which forms a prominent waterfall. The individual units of this intrusion are, in places, separated from each other by narrow screens of sediment which have been altered by contact metamorphism to such an extent that it is often difficult to tell which is dolerite and which is cementstone. The eastern end of the multiple dyke complex is displaced by a NE-SW trending dextral fault which is concealed below a jumble of boulders. This fault obliquely crosses the plunge pool of the waterfall where it is associated with another carbonated dyke, similar to those seen at Locality 1, clearly visible when the water level in the burn is low.

Across the flat area above the fall, other units of the dyke complex occur as far as the confluence with the Aldessan Burn which runs over a small waterfall of alternating cementstone and shales to join the main burn at this point. Between here and Locality 3 the uppermost part of the succession of the Ballagan Beds can be examined in Aldessan Burn and on the steep slope of its northern bank. Over 18 metres of sediments occur here, the lower half consisting of shales which alternate with both nodular and massive horizons of cementstone. The upper half of the succession consists mainly of shale but is interrupted by a thin sandstone bed about 4.6 m from the top of the sequence. At the top are red mudstones covered by a 46 cm (1.5 feet) layer of ash immediately below the lowermost lava flow.

Locality 3. Spout o'Craiglee. Here Aldessan Burn runs over a high cliff formed by the first three flows of the Campsie Lavas. Although thinner than the others, the second flow shows best the contrast between the more solid lower part and the upper vesicular part where gas bubbles were trapped as the lava cooled. The layer of red **bole** which lies on top of flow 1 shows that its slaggy top was subjected to a period of tropical weathering prior to the eruption of flow 2. Boles of varying thickness occur between many of the flows indicating that there were often time gaps of several years between some eruptions. The basal ash, below flow 1, can be examined to the left and right of the waterfall, where it contains occasional fragments of rock resembling Old Red Sandstone.

Returning to the main burn the path climbs up to the entrance to the gorge, the sides of which are formed by outcrops of the lowermost lava flows. Red bole is again exposed at the point where the path levels out. Note the size of the large boulders which have fallen from the sides of the gorge after it was excavated by the stream. It is probable that the most active period of downcutting took place during the process of deglaciation, when vast amounts of meltwater would have produced a more rapid rate of erosion than occurs at the present day.

Locality 4. Faults cutting the lavas. At this point a recent major rock fall confirms that erosive processes continue. The cliff has given way at the intersection of two fault planes. One of these, a normal fault, crosses the gorge and displaces the lava succession downwards to the SW by about the thickness of flow 2. The other plane of movement, now clearly exposed on the south-east side of the gorge has near-horizontal slickensides which indicate that it must have been a strike slip (tear) fault when it last moved. Near the intersection of the two faults, high up on the cliff, a dyke has been exposed with a trend close to that of the strike slip fault.

A little further on a set of rock-cut steps and some minor scrambling leads to the head of the gorge at Locality 5. **The conditions, however, are potentially dangerous here** for all but the sure-footed, particularly in wet weather when the rock can be very slippery. An easier and safer route involves retracing one's steps to the foot of the glen and climbing up to Locality 5 along paths through the trees above the east side of the gorge.

Locality 5. Nick Point. At the head of the gorge there is a pronounced nick-point above which the glen has a V-shaped cross-section. Note here the pot holes eroded in the top of flow 3. A short distance upstream flow 4 outcrops on the southeast bank. The central part of this flow, which forms the lower part of the small cliff, has pronounced platey jointing parallel to the flow orientation of feldspar microphenocrysts. This texture is characteristic of basaltic hawaiites. The lower part of the lava sequence at Campsie Glen consists of 17 flows of microphyric basalt and basaltic **hawaiite** referred to in BGS publications as Jedburgh basalt, a useful field term, although strictly speaking some of the flows are less basic than basalt (MacDonald and Whyte 1981).

From Locality 5 climb up the slope to the large car park at the corner of the Crow Road (NS 613 801). From here a path leads upwards to the east, crossing successively higher lava flows, until it reaches the cairn on Lairs Hill (504 m). On a clear day the energetic will find it worth while to make the ascent for the view from the summit but even from the car park one can see the easterly dip of the Kilpatrick Hills in the west and, far to the east, the Pentland Hills on the other side of the Midland Valley Syncline.

Locality 6. Markle basalt Quarry. To reach Locality 6 cross the road from the car park and start uphill along the path to the summit. About two hundred metres uphill from the Crow Road turn to the left just before a small concrete outhouse which was the explosives store of a long abandoned quarry in flow 18 (Markle basalt). The lava here is highly vesicular in places and rather weathered but is notable for the size of its feldspar phenocrysts, some of which exceed 25 mm (1 inch) in length. Comparatively fresh specimens can be obtained from loose material in the talus on the slope between the quarry and the Crow Road. Note the narrow dyke which cuts the basalt at the NE end of the quarry.

To reach Locality 7 descend to the Crow Road and follow it to the NE (keeping a watchful eye for traffic) past Jamie Wright's Well. The granite setting of the well has inscribed on it a verse by the Kirkintilloch Poet, James M.Slimmon, who died tragically in 1898 on the brink of a promising career. He did however see the first copy of his book, "The Dead Planet and Other Poems", on his death bed.

Locality 7. Campsie Dyke. Just north of the confluence of the main burn with the Alvain Burn both streams are crossed by the Campsie Dyke, one of the set of E-W trending quartz-dolerites which were intruded in late Carboniferous times. This dyke can be traced from Blanefield in the west as far east as Denny and it probably continues to the the Firth of Forth at Grangemouth. At Campsie Glen it is about 20m in thickness and shows well the contrast between the rounded spheroidal weathering of the central part (with its widely spaced cooling joints), and the much finer grained chilled margin which stands up as a cliff on the south side of the intrusion where its crosses Alvain Burn. To the north of the dyke in Alvain Burn the first two waterfalls run over the same Markle basalt flows as the one which occurs at Locality 5. On horizontal surfaces at the edge of the waterfall one can see that the elongate plagioclase feldspar phenocrysts display a pronounced preferred orientation suggesting a line of flow movement on a NNE-SSW trend (Whyte and MacDonald 1974). Similar phenocryst orientations occurs where this flow crosses the main burn about 300 m to the NE.

Locality 8. Varved Clays. Cars can be parked at the confluence of the Nineteentimes Burn and Alnwick Burn (NS 625 808). Just west of the first outcrops in the Alnwick Burn the steep northern slope of the bank contains outcrops of laminated glacial clays. The individual layers are graded indicating that they were laid down by successive influxes of sediment into a lake which probably occupied the ground on either side of Nineteentimes Burn. In places the layers have been disturbed by slumping. Much of the ground to the west is occupied by hummocky glacial deposits, including moraine which probably dammed the main burn to form the temporary lake in which the clays were deposited. Further up Alnwick Burn a variety of flows including mugearite occur.

Localities 9 and 10 may be reached either by returning along the Crow Road or by following, on foot, the old drove road which is situated farther up the hillside. Near locality 9 the drove road cuts across a major landslip which is thought to have been caused by an earthquake some hundreds of years ago.

Locality 9. Lennoxtown essexite (NS 623 794). This is the lower outcrop of the Lennoxtown **essexite** . Here the rock is a porphyritic microgabbro or dolerite with well shaped black augite **phenocrysts** which stand out well from the paler groundmass on weathered surfaces. In thin section the rock contains about 40% plagioclase feldspar, 30% augite and 10% olivine with lesser amounts of opaque ores, apatite, analcime, biotite and occasional nepheline. Note the well developed vertical joints. The magnetic anomaly associated with this intrusion suggests that it has a plug-like form. The exact position of the Campsie Fault here is uncertain but the combination of topographical and geophysical evidence suggests that it may run along the north side of the essexite plug, or indeed that the essexite may be intruded at the junction of the Campsie Fault with another, lesser, fault which splays off to the SW. A limited amount of car parking is available here by the side of the road.

The essexite is highly distinctive in appearance and so has proved to be a valuable tracer for ice movements. Fragments of this rock occur as far as 20 km (12.5 miles) to the east, within 2 km of Larbert (Shakesby 1978); traces of augite which may have originated in the essexite occur in sediments and soils even farther to the east. This confirms that the main movement of ice from the Loch Lomond area was to the east and there must have been a major glacier moving along the strath from Blanefield. Further evidence of the direction of ice movement is provided by Dunglass plug, opposite Ballagan Glen, 5 km (3 miles) to the west. Its pronounced **crag and tail** feature is visible from this locality.

Locality 10. Upper essexite intrusion. Further up the hillside to the NE, on the other side of the drove road, is the upper essexite intrusion. The lower contact occurs in a water course where the clay-rich weathered top of one of the basalt lava flows has been thermally metamorphosed by the essexite. The intrusion appears to have the form of a sheet which is dipping steeply northwards into the hillside. At its west end it ends rather abruptly against a line of basalt outcrops which show signs of thermal metamorphism and hence an intrusive contact; to the east outcrops peter out short of another major landslip. Although the essexite of the upper outcrops lacks the prominent augite phenocrysts of Locality 8, it is in every other way similar to the lower essexite.

Locality 11. Hurlet Limestone (NS 634 790). Further to the east, to the south of the Campsie Fault and above the golf course, there are sporadic outcrops of the sediments which lie on top of the Clyde Plateau Lavas. These include the Campsie Main (Hurlet) Limestone which was quarried during the 19th century and earlier. There are extensive grassed-over spoil heaps but part of the quarry face is still exposed. At the eastern end of the old quarry the flaggy upper part of the limestone has yielded numerous fragments of shelly fossils including productid brachiopods, bivalves and crinoids. Several shafts were sunk in the area to extract coal from a thin seam (the Hurlet Coal) which underlies the limestone. The coal was used as fuel in lime kilns, the remains of which occur at the corner of the Crow Road as it turns for the descent into Lennoxtown. It is reputed locally that lime from the Lennoxtown district was used in the construction of Glasgow Cathedral.

If on foot return to the main road and follow it into Lennoxtown. The bus to Glasgow can be boarded at Lennoxtown Cross and refreshments can be obtained in a nearby cafe.

References

MACDONALD, J.G. and WHYTE, F. 1981. Petrochemical evidence for the genesis of a Lower Carboniferous transitional basaltic suite in the Midland Valley of Scotland. *Trans. Roy. Soc. Edinb.* **72**, 75-88.

SHAKESBY, R.A. 1978. Dispersal of glacial erratics from Lennoxtown, Stirlingshire. *Scott. J. Geol.* **14**, 81-86.

WHYTE, F. and MACDONALD, J.G. 1974. Lower Carboniferous vulcanicity in the northern part of the Clyde Plateau. *Scott. J. Geol..* **10**, 187-98.

YOUNG, J. 1868. The geology of the Campsie district. *Trans. geol. Soc. Glasgow.* __ **1**, 9-72.

Excursion 6 CORRIE BURN
George E. Bowes

Themes:	Sedimentary and volcanic rocks of Lower Carboniferous age and evidence for the Campsie Fault.
Features:	The Clyde Plateau Lavas, Calciferous Sandstone Measures, Lower Limestone Group and Limestone Coal Group; sedimentary rocks include sandstone, ironstone, shale and limestone, some of which are richly fossiliferous; igneous rocks include waterlaid volcanic detritus, lavas and ashes, with some minor mineralisation (baryte veining) in the lavas. There is evidence for the Campsie Fault and the Cairnbog Fault.
Maps:	O.S. 1:50 000 Sheet 64 Glasgow
	B.G.S. 1:63 360 Sheet 30 Glasgow
Terrain:	The ground is rough in places, with some steep banks; the streams are normally easily crossed on foot.
Distance: and Time:	It is not necessary to cover the whole area in one visit. The minimum useful walking distance, say from Burnhead Farm to Locality 5 and back is about 3km (2 miles) and this can be accomplished in two or three hours. The whole excursion entails about 6km (4 miles) walking, and can be done easily in one day.
Access:	From the A803, at (NS 689 769), about 3km (2 miles) west of Kilsyth, follow a narrow unclassified road NNE for about 1.5km (1mile), until the road turns right at Burnhead Farm. Cars may be parked a short distance east of Burnhead Farm (NS 684 782) where the verge is wide enough to get a car clear of the carriageway. Enter the field north of the road, and follow the track northwards; leave the track to reach Locality 1. The Corrie Burn is a geological **SSSI** and it is advisable to ask permission at the farm: it is also courtesy to do so.

Locality 1. (Fig.6.1): **Limestone Coal Group.** About 100m west of Cairnbog Farm masonry of the entrance to an old mine is visible in the undergrowth a few metres up the west bank of the Queenzie Burn, indicating the proximity of coal-bearing rocks. Old maps show that

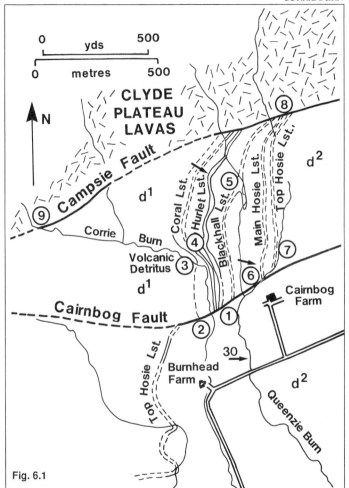

Figure 6.1. Geological map of the area near Corrie Burn.

the Kilsyth Coking Coal outcropped hereabouts. Some 90m upstream, about 30m below the confluence of the two branches of the Queenzie Burn, the Clayband Ironstone outcrops in the stream bed. The material is dark and shaly, but markedly heavier in the hand than the dark ferruginous shales forming the stream bank above it. The coal and the ironstone both belong to the Limestone Coal Group.

Locality 2. Cairnbog Fault. Beside the Corrie Burn some 250m north of Burnhead Farm, occur the outcrops of massively bedded coarse somewhat ferruginous sandstone of the Limestone Coal Group dipping at 25° to the east. Some 50m NW of these sandstones is an exposure of volcanic detritus of the Calciferous Sandstone Measures (see Locality 3 for description). The close proximity of these beds showing similar dip and strike, yet separated stratigraphically by some 100m, indicates that a fault must run between the two outcrops. This Cairnbog Fault is not exposed at the surface, but some indication of its course may be gleaned from the position of the southernmost exposure of the Hurlet Limestone, which is visible to the NE in the bank above the Corrie Burn, and from the occurrence of the Clayband Ironstone and evidence of mining at Locality 1 some 200m away to the east, in the Queenzie Burn. The Volcanic Detritus and the Hurlet Limestone lie north of the fault, while the massive sandstones and the Clayband Ironstone lie south of the fault.

Locality 3. Volcanic Detritus is exposed where the Corrie Burn turns southwards, some 400m north of Burnhead Farm. It comprises green and red-coloured lava and volcanic ash. Many of the fragments are rounded, and it is believed that this material has been transported by running water and deposited as a sediment. Towards its upper part, the volcanic detritus is interbedded with sandstones.

Overlying beds are now largely obscured, although some more resistant layers are exposed. Fragments of the richly fossiliferous Coral Limestone can be found in the burn.

Locality 4. The **Corrie Burn (Hurlet) Limestone** is well exposed in a series of quarries along the strike of the bed, and yields brachiopods including productids, strophomenids, athyrids and spiriferids, corals such as *Caninia* and *Lithostrotion*, bryozoans, crinoid fragments and bivalves (Figs 20,5, 20.6).

Locality 5. The **Blackhall Limestone** is seen in the bed of the burn. It is dolomitic and oolitic in the lower portion, and crinoidal in the upper part. A little further downstream the decalcified granular limestone or Shields Bed is exposed.

The dark shales (**blaes**) with abundant ironstone nodules which overlie the Blackhall Limestone form the cliff face immediately east of the burn. The ironstone nodules are curiously asymmetrical, one of the flattened sides commonly having a small local concavity or dimple. Many of the nodules show an internal structure of shrinkage cracks which have been filled with mineral matter - a **septarian** structure.

The cliff is capped by a thin band of sandstone, fallen blocks of which may be found showing structures on the lower surfaces (**sole marks**) due to deposition upon a scoured or fluted surface, and some blocks also show evidence of mud-cracks.

Upstream, where the burn first reaches the Blackhall Limestone, fossil plant roots (*Stigmaria*:: Fig. 2.3) may be seen in the limestone. Further upstream, in sandstones a short distance stratigraphically below the Blackhall Limestone, several layers show well-preserved ripple marks.

Locality 6. The **Main Hosie Limestone** outcrops in the eastern tributary of the Queenzie Burn. Eastwards, the burn follows the Cairnbog Fault so that sandstones overlying the Kilsyth Coking Coal occur in the south bank and sporadic outcrops of Top Hosie Limestone are exposed in the stream, having been dragged down against the fault plane.

Locality 7. The **Second Hosie Limestone** and **Top Hosie Limestone** are well exposed further upstream. The Second Hosie is somewhat arenaceous and more fossiliferous than the dark grey argillaceous Top Hosie. The intervening shales are also richly fossiliferous, yielding *Sanguinolites* and *Posidonia*. Further upstream there are outcrops of the shales overlying the Top Hosie Limestone.

Localities 8 & 9. Campsie Fault. There is a distinct change in slope associated with the Campsie Fault which brings Lower Limestone strata into juxtaposition with Calciferous Sandstone Measures lavas. The feature can easily be traced westwards from the head of the eastern tributary of the Queenzie Burn (Locality 8 at NS 687 793) to Corrie Burn (Locality 9) where vertical wedges of Corrie Burn (Hurlet) Limestone and basalt are caught up in the fault zone.

A short distance north of the fault small veins of **barytes** are present in the lava, and north and west of the fault a series of lava flows and ashes of varying composition are exposed (see Fig. 6.1).

References

BENNIE, J. 1868. On the Surface Geology of Glasgow. *Trans.geol. Soc. Glasg.* **2**, 100-115.

MACNAIR, P. and CONACHER, H.R.J. 1914. The Stratigraphy of the Limestones lying immediately above the Calciferous Lavas in the Glasgow District. *Trans. geol. Soc. Glasg.* **15**, 37-50.

The Geology of the Glasgow District. 1925. *Mem. Geol. Surv.*

ROBERTSON, T. and HALDANE, D. 1937. The Economic Geology of the Central Coalfield , Area 1. *Mem. Geol. Surv.*

Excursion 7 DUMBARTON ROCK
F.Whyte and D.S.Weedon

Theme :   An intrusive basalt plugging the root of a Lower Carboniferous volcano.

Features: Contact relationships, columnar jointing, amygdales, microphenocrysts, bedded tuffs, glacial striae and small-scale roches moutonnées.

Maps: O.S.   1 : 50 000 Sheet 63   Firth of Clyde
              B G.S. 1 : 63 360 Sheet 30   Glasgow
                      1 : 50 000 Sheet 30W   Greenock

Terrain: Rocky shoreline conditions exist and suitable footwear should be used : no climbing is entailed ; best visited at half to low tide.

    From Glasgow proceed to Dumbarton, 11 km (7 miles) and follow signs to Dumbarton Rock, which is approached via Castle Road. Parking is easy in the vicinity of the base of the Rock. Access to the shore is along the path from this point, between the rock outcrop and the sawmill (**SSSI**).

Distance: The total distance from the starting point to the shore section and return is not more than 0.5 km (0.4 mile).

Time: One to two hours on the exposure.

Introduction

In early Carboniferous times widespread volcanism occurred within the Midland Valley, predominantly extrusive in nature. This is seen in the Central (Glasgow) Region as the lavas of the Campsie and Kilpatrick Hills to the north, and those of the Renfrewshire heights to the south. Seemingly these were fed from localized vents along pronounced fissures. By its characteristics Dumbarton Rock stands out as a type example of such a feeder vent. Within its circumference it shows inwardly-dipping agglomerates, typical of a sub-aerial volcanic cone, together with large blocks of slumped overlying Cementstone alongside a central plug of intrusive basalt.

The intrusive basalt has columnar cooling joints, most of which are inclined radially outwards from the centre of the Rock at a steep angle suggesting that the plug narrows downwards, thus enhancing the

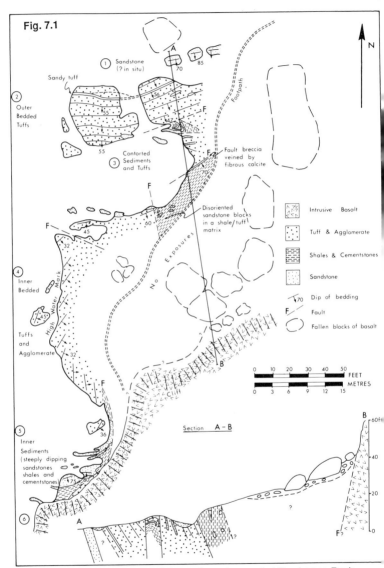

Figure 7.1. Geological map of the north-western part of Dumbarton Rock.

impression of an infilled crater.

In the immediate vicinity of the parking area the steep-sided cliffs provide an excellent area in which to study the general nature of the intrusive basalt. It should be noted that although the surface shows an orange/yellow rind of weathering this is very thin and unlike the normal deeper-weathering of basic igneous rocks of the Midland Valley. A fresh surface reveals a fine-grained black igneous rock, micro-porphyritic in part. The micro-phenocrysts are dominantly of plagioclase feldspar, but those of olivine and augite may be present. Using MacGregor's classification (1928) the intrusive basalt appears transitional between **Jedburgh** and **Dalmeny** types.

Locality 1. Exposures of sandstone. These *may* be erratic blocks but their conformity of strike with those of the nearby outer bedded tuffs indicates strongly that they are in place. It is suggested however, (Whyte 1966, p.110), that their steeper dips, 70°-85°, in contrast with the lesser dips of the outer bedded tuffs, 30°-50°, implies faulted contacts between them.

Localities 2 and 4. Outer and inner bedded tuffs. These are mainly composed of fragments of volcanic rocks (with subordinate fragments

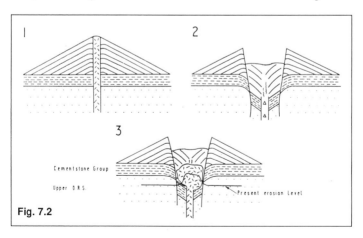

Fig. 7.2

Figure 7.2. Diagrammatic representation of three stages in the development of the Dumbarton Rock vent: 1) active volcano; 2) withdrawal of magma accompanied by fracturing and subsidence; 3) emplacement of plug basalt.

of sandstone, **cementstone** and shale) in a matrix of fine tuff, calcite and chlorite. A prominent bed of sandy tuff occurs within the outer bedded tuffs.

Locality 3. Contorted sediments and tuffs. Within this fault-bounded zone the rocks are brecciated, veined with fibrous calcite and show small folds related to the faults. Disorientated sandstone blocks in a shale and tuff matrix probably formed by explosive disintegration of shale and sandstone strata accompanied by tuff intrusion.

Locality 5. Inner sediments, comprising steeply dipping sandstones, shales and cementstones belong to the sequence of rocks immediately underlying the original volcano, and attained their present position, (as did the outer and inner tuffs), by a subsidence of the central part of the volcano, prior to the emplacement of the plug basalt.

Locality 6. Basalt plug . The contact between basalt and sediments dips steeply inwards at about 80 degrees. Near the contact, the normally blue-black colour of the basalt changes to dark green due to the development of chlorite in the groundmass and in **amygdales**; the plagioclase is albitic in composition.

Apart from this contact zone, throughout the remainder of the plug the blue-black basalt is consistently fine-grained, composed of **microphenocrysts** of olivine and plagioclase (labradorite) in a groundmass of plagioclase, augite and iron ore. According to MacGregor's classification (1928) this basalt is transitional between **Jedburgh** and **Dalmeny** types.

Other features of interest

In the high-level gully which crosses the central part of the Rock there are good examples of glacial striae, first described as long ago as 1855. In addition, the western face of the gully exhibits very small-scale **roches moutonnées**: looking one way along the face the basalt appears quite rough, whereas looking the other way the same surface appears smooth.

The summit of Dumbarton Rock is a good vantage point for viewing the following: the course of the River Clyde from the restricted channel near Bowling down the widening estuary: the valley of the River Leven and the Cowal hills to the west: Ben Lomond to the north, and Dumbuck volcanic vent and the lavas of the Kilpatrick Hills to the east.

References

BELL, D. 1885. *Among the rocks around Glasgow* . Glasgow.

HAMILTON, J. 1956. The mineralogy of basalts from the western Kilpatrick Hills and its bearing on the petrogenesis of Scottish Carboniferous olivine basalts. *Trans. Edinb. geol. Soc.* **16,** 280-298.

MACGREGOR, A.G. 1928. The classification of Scottish Carboniferous olivine-basalts and mugearites. *Trans. Geol. Soc. Glasg.* **18,** 324-360.

PRATT, A. 1882. Scottish trap rocks and their structure under the microscope. *Trans. geol. Soc. Glasg.* **6,** 58-62.

TYRRELL, G.W. 1913. The petrology of the Kilpatrick Hills, Dunbartonshire, with notes on the Scottish Carboniferous basalts. *Trans. geol. Soc. Glasg.* **14,** 219-257.

WHYTE, F. 1963. Volcanic vents of the Kilpatrick and Campsie Hills. *Univ. of Glasgow Ph.D. thesis* (unpubl.)

WHYTE, F.1966. Dumbarton Rock. *Scott.J.Geol.* **2,** 107-121.

WHYTE, F.1968. Lower Carboniferous volcanic vents in the west of Scotland. *Bull volcan.* **32-1,** 253-268.

Excursion 8 ARDMORE POINT AND AUCHENSAIL
B.J.Bluck

Themes: The stratigraphy and sedimentation of the Lower and Upper Old Red Sandstone rocks; the angular unconformity which separates them.

Features: Lower Devonian plants and trace fossils; various alluvial facies; structure, including possible faulting in unconsolidated sediments.

Maps: O.S.   1:50 000 Sheet 63   Firth of Clyde
B.G.S. 1:50 000 Sheet 30 W Greenock

Terrain: Muddy coastal path and foreshore: quarry exposures.

Distance   The circuit of Ardmore Point is about 3 km (1.8 miles):
and Time: allow two hours at least.

Access: Avoid high tides, most localities accessible at mid-tidal range. Parties visiting Locality 1 should obtain permission from Mr.Semple Findlay, Carniedrouth Farm, Barrs Road, Cardross G82 5EY.
Ardmore Point is an **SSSI** but no permit is required at this time.

Locality 1. Auchensail Quarry (NS 342798): **Devonian plants.**
Approaching this locality from Glasgow, follow the A 814 to the NW end of Cardross village (just before Geilston Burn crosses the A814) and take a minor road to the north which leads to Auchensail Farm and Darlieth House. It is important to take the left fork at Auchensail and travel north to cross Geilston Burn. The quarry is behind Auchensail Cottage.

Auchensail Quarry exposes gently dipping Lower Old Red Sandstone rocks cut by an E-W Carboniferous dyke. These Lower Old Red Sandstone rocks are in the axial zone of the Strathmore syncline where they form the youngest beds in the regional Old Red Sandstone sequence. On the basis of the plant identification they belong to the uppermost unit of the Lower Old Red Sandstone (Emsian).

There are two important lithologies in the quarry: grey-green lithic sandstones alternating with red irregular beds of siltstones and shales (Scott *et al* 1976). The sandstones are in upward fining sediment units about 2m thick, beginning with intraformational conglomerates of red mudstone clasts, followed by cross stratified sandstones and terminating with beds rich in aligned spiny carbonaceous plants. The commonest plant is *Sawdonia ornata*, but it is in a fairly poor state of preservation. Patient collecting, however, should yield identifiable specimens of the two main spiny bush-like plants (Fig.8.1). *Sawdonia ornata* has fertile tips with lateral sporangia and sterile branch tips with circinnate vernation: also branching styles with stem spines. The less common *Drepanophycus (Arthrostigma) spinaeformis* has less sterile branches and branch tips with typical spine-leaves. These plants were well adapted to the arid, semi-arid climatic conditions of the Devonian where they grew to a height of 0.5-0.7 m (Rayner 1983). Good collecting can be made from sandstone blocks on the quarry floor and particularly in the eastern end of the quarry.

Each of the upward-fining cycles is produced by the lateral migration of a river, so that the thickness of a cycle is approximately

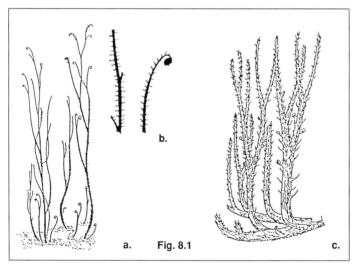

Figure 8.1. Plants from the Lower Old Red Sandstone of Auchensail Quarry.
a. *Sawdonia ornata* (reconstruction, x 0.1), **b.** *Sawdonia ornata* (stems, x 0.05),
c. *Drepanophycus spinæformis* (reconstruction, x 0.15).
[Redrawn after Rolfe, 1976]

equivalent to the depth of the river. On this basis the sandstones were laid down by rivers which were no more than 2-3m deep.

Red siltstone interstratified with these sandstones have yielded *Beaconites*, burrows produced by an organism of uncertain type. One view is that they are the resting burrows of amphibians or reptiles which may have lived within the muds of temporary pools in ephemeral streams. The red siltstones either infill channels or spread laterally as sheets and often have very well developed mudcracks which are vertically infilled with sandstone. Some mudcracked beds have roughly circular depressions 3-5mm in diameter: these are rain imprints. The siltstones with the sheet-like form are produced by deposition on the floodplains of the rivers which deposited the sandstones. Their periodic drying out caused the formation of mudcracks and subsequent floods washed sands over the flood plain to fill the cracks with sandstone.

An E-W, Carboniferous quartz dolerite dyke, c. 0. 8m thick runs the length of the quarry and is exposed in the far (eastern) wall. It has a good chilled margin and the sandstones adjacent to the dyke are slightly metamorphosed .

Ardmore Peninsula (NS 325 878) (Fig. 8.2) is reached by returning to the A 814 and following it NW to Lyleston Cottage: turn left onto a small road to cross the railway line and park cars at Ardmore Peninsula. The main outcrops are to the west of this car park and are reached by a track which follows the coastline (Fig. 8.2).

Ardmore Point exposes two sequences of rocks which are divided by an unconformity. The first, encountered at Locality 2, is Lower Old Red sandstone in age, on the basis that when the sequence at Ardmore is traced towards the NNE, it is seen to conformably underlie the sandstones of Auchensail Quarry which are known to be at the top of the Lower Old Red Sandstone. The second sequence (Locality 6), which unconformably overlies the first, has generally been regarded as Upper Old Red Sandstone because elsewhere the Upper is seen to rest unconformably on the Lower and also the Upper is generally bright red in colour in contrast to the dark red of the Lower. Current thinking in the B.G.S believes these lighter red rocks to be Lower Old Red Sandstone in age and the unconformity a local event within the Lower Old Red Sandstone sequence.

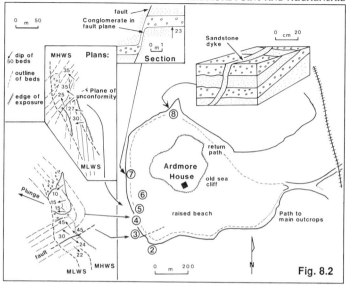

Figure 8.2. Map, with illustrative sections and plans, of Ardmore Point.

Locality 2. (NS 3145 7824): **Conglomerates and sandstones.** The main part of the foreshore is made up of alternating conglomerates and sandstones, dipping to the SE. Most of the conglomerates have a sheet-like form, but some are infilling channels: each contains well rounded pebbles and cobbles mainly of quartzite, vein quartz and andesite, plus other lithologies. The size of the clasts, up to 300 mm in diameter, suggests that they were deposited near their source. The high degree of rounding, particularly of the tough quartzite clasts, implies long distances of transportation, which is not consistent with their being close to source. This paradox is resolved if the clasts are assumed to have been derived from a nearby source which included a pre-existing conglomerate in which the clasts were already partly or largely in a rounded condition.

The composition of the clasts may be used to determine the **provenance** of the sediment. The provenance comprised metamorphic, igneous and, if the rounded quartzite is from a pre-existing conglomerate, sedimentary rocks.

Sandstones interstratified amongst the conglomerate have abundant small scale cross-stratification 10-20 cm thick. This is produced by the migration of small sand-bars and megaripples the height of which are, in a complex way, related to the flow depth: deeper flows produce thicker bars and larger megaripples which in turn may yield thicker cross strata. Lineations seen on the bedding surfaces are normally produced in shallow, fast flowing streams, and these structures together with the thin cross strata suggest deposition by flows which were probably less than a metre deep.

The conglomerates and sandstones, being red in colour were laid down in conditions where there was an abundant supply of oxygen to convert iron-bearing minerals to haematite, the red iron oxide grain-coating which gives these rocks their colour. This, together with the presence of mudcracks elsewhere within the sequence implies deposition in a terrestrial environment, and these deposits are considered to be alluvium laid down by ephemeral streams in an arid or semi-arid climate.

The directions in which these sediments were dispersed vary considerably within the region of Ardmore as well as in the Old Red Sandstone along strike towards the Balmaha. Because of this variability in the directions of sediment transport a cautious view is taken of the direction in which the source lay: sometimes it was in the south, SE, SW and north. The clear implication is, however, that the present Highlands were not so domiminant in Old Red Sandstone times that they controlled the dispersal of sediment. Indeed they may have lain a little further to the north or were so flat that they were not the main source of the sediment (Bluck 1984). Some of these points are made in Excursion 9 (Balmaha).

Locality 3. Faulted anticline. This structure is easily recognised by a sudden change in the dip of the beds. The low foreshore to the SE comprises a SE dipping sequence of coarse conglomerates and dark red sandstones terminated at this point by a series of fractures with fault-breccias which locally mark the path of a fault running SW towards the Clyde. On the NW of the fault the beds dip to the NW so the structure of this ground is a faulted anticline.

Locality 4. Plunging syncline. Follow the path northwards, noting that the beds which form the faulted anticline change dip to form a plunging syncline on the foreshore. This syncline has a steep limb to the south with a shallow limb to the north, and in walking from one limb to the other it is possible to stop at the axis and look down the plunge of the fold which extends out into the Clyde.

Locality 5. Slickensides and raised beach. The plunging syncline is terminated NW by a fault the plane of which forms the low cliff at the NW side of this Bay. This cliff face shows almost horizontal slickensides suggesting that there was a horizonal movement along it for at least part of its history. A small burn reaches the shore near the cliff and raised beach gravels are exposed along its banks. This raised beach sediment, or the erosion surface upon which it was laid is now covered with peat and forms the low ground up to the old sea cliffs which surround Ardmore House. This beach and the cliff behind it was abandoned c. 7000 years B.P. (Before Present).

Locality 6. Unconformity between the Lower and Upper Old Red Sandstone. This unconformity is not well displayed, and to see it requires a careful examination of the ground. The purple-dark red rocks of the Lower Old Red Sandstone strike almost N-S, and as they are traced in a northerly direction they are truncated by the, brighter red, Upper Old Red Sandstones which dip to the NW. The irregular contact between the two rock groups can be traced across the foreshore, and is particularly well seen at the low cliff on the upper part of the shore. In places along and sometimes above the unconformable surface there are faults above which the Upper Old Red Sandstone has been slightly rotated, and the unconformable surface has, in places been used as a plane of detachment—a fault along the surface of the unconformity.

There is not only a contrast in the colours of the two red sandstone units but the compositions of the clasts in the conglomerates are also different. The Lower Old Red Sandstone contains quartzite, vein quartz and volcanic rock fragments; but the Upper is particularly rich in vein quartz and greenschist.

This unconformable relationship is clearly not the sharp break seen in many other unconformities. One possible reason for this is that the Lower Old Red Sandstone was not fully indurated at the time the Upper was laid on top of it. If, as seems likely these Lower Old Red Sandstone rocks occur towards the top of the Lower Old Red Sandstone sequence, then they may not have been buried to a great depth before the Upper was laid over them. Pebbles and the dark-red sand from the

Lower have been incorporated into the basal beds of the Upper and this, as well as the nature of the exposure, makes it difficult to clearly see the contact between them.

The sequence of events which must have taken place in order for this unconformable relationship to be established are as follows: after deposition of the Lower Old Red Sandstone the beds were tilted and those which were at the top of the pile, such as at Ardmore, may not have been fully consolidated. Either as they were tilted or after tilting they were eroded, probably by river action. New beds, the Upper Old Red Sandstone, were then laid on top this surface of erosion. These new beds, along with the underlying Lower Old Red Sandstone strata were then folded. It follows that before this second folding event the Lower Old Red Sandstone of Locality 2 had a very diffent dip than it now has: some of the beds there were dipping in the opposite direction.

Recently the B.G.S. have indicated that the beds which are referred to as Upper in this account are indeed Lower, and this unconformity is a local one within the Lower Old Red Sandstone sequence.

Locality 7. Upper Old Red Sandstone and soft sediment faulting.
Rocks of the Upper Old Red Sandstone comprise an alternation of light red, cross-stratified sandstones and whitish conglomerates. The sandstones are cross-stratified, with larger scale cross strata than at Locality 2, and the conglomerates are finer grained than in the Lower Old Red Sandstone and have abundant vein quartz. The conglomerate beds are often channelled into the underlying sandstones with the relief on the channels being up to 1 metre.

These rocks, like the Lower Old Red Sandstone, were probably laid down by shallow braided streams which spread sediment in sheets over the alluvial plain surface. Cross-stratification indicates a southerly palaeoflow for these rivers, so a source from the north is indicated. The location and nature of that source is difficult to establish, but the abundant vein quartz and the associated greenschist and phyllite clasts suggest a source in low grade metamorphic rocks where there were abundant quartz veins. When metamorphic rocks of this kind weather in a source region, the phyllites and schists are usually broken down by chemical or physical action quite quickly, but the quartz veins are very resistant and remain intact. This results in a high concentration of the vein quartz and a loss of the host rock so that the gravels produced are greatly enriched in what may be the minor lithology of the source. The Dalradian Highlands to the north could well be the source of this Upper Old Red Sandstone sequence.

Particularly fine examples of faulting can be seen at this locality, most of which appears to be normal. A series of fractures oriented N-S displace the conglomerates and sandstones by c. 0.5 m. A more detailed examination of these fractures reveals that screens of conglomerate have been dragged down into the interleaved sandstone; the sandstone has been folded and deformed adjacent to the fracture and some of the elongate clasts have been re-orientated during the faulting so that they lie flat in the plane of the fracture. Some faults have sandstone sheets which have been injected up them. These observations suggest rather than prove that the sediment was poorly consolidated at the time of fracturing. Faults cutting Recent or unconsolidated Tertiary sediments are certainly accompanied by similar features.

Locality 8. Sandstone dykes. This locality is near the far northern end of the Ardmore Peninsula. The outcrop on the headland comprises alternations of sandstone and fine conglomerate. Some of the thin sandstones (c. 20 cm thick) cut across the bedding for short distances. These features are sandstone dykes which are formed when waterlogged sands liquefy and intrude upwards.

Follow the path adjacent to the fence and return to the road on the track indicated (Fig. 8.2).

References

BLUCK, B.J. 1984. Pre-Carboniferous history of the Midland Valley of Scotland. *Trans.Roy. Soc. Edinb. Earth Science.* **75**, 274-295.

RAYNER, R.J. 1983. New observations on *Sawdonia ornata* from Scotland *Trans. Roy.Soc. Edinb. Earth Science.* **74**, 79-94.

SCOTT, A.C., EDWARDS, D and ROLFE W.D.I. 1976. Fossiliferous Lower Old Red Sandstone near Cardross,Dunbartonshire. *Proc.Geol.Soc.Glasgow.* **117**, 4-5.

Excursion 9 BALMAHA
B.J.Bluck

Themes: The principal reasons for visiting the Balmaha area are:

1. To examine the evidence for the presence of a terrane boundary within this general area.

2. To examine the evidence for the types of movements which have occurred along the Highland Boundary Fault and associated fractures, bearing in mind that movements along terrane boundaries are complex and diverse.

   There need not be a single phase of movement but a sequence of separate movements each of which may be different in nature and sense.

3. To examine the Highland Border Complex which here has great diversity in lithologies.

4. To examine both the Lower and Upper Old Red Sandstone rocks with a view to determining the nature of their accumulation and their provenance.

Features: Conglomerates, alluvial fans, cross-stratification, unconformity, overlap, inverted cross-strata, cherts, serpentinite conglomerate, faults.

Maps: O.S. 1: 50 000 Sheet 56   Loch Lomond & Inveraray.
O.S. 1: 25 000 Sheet NS 49/59 Buchlyvie & Balmaha.
B.G.S. 1: 63 360 Sheet 38   Loch Lomond.
B.G.S. 1: 50 000 Sheet 38W   Ben Lomond.

Terrain: Lochside with muddy paths for first part of excursion; hillside for the later part.

Distance and Time; 4 km: walking time 5 hours.

Access: A809 to Drymen and the B837 from Drymen to Balmaha, On the A809 at Queen's View (NS 511 807) there is a splendid panoramic view of the Balmaha region in the context of the Highland Boundary Fault and the Old Red Sandstone of the Strathmore syncline.

   The low, fertile ground in the immediate foreground belongs to the Old Red Sandstone; the high ground in the distance is mainly the metamorphic basement of the Dalradian block. The northern limb of the Strathmore

Syncline forms the rugged ground, with prominent ridges, between these two regions; and between this limb of the syncline and the Dalradian block lies the Highland Boundary Fault. At Balmaha it is possible to see a section through the north limb of the Strathmore Syncline to the Dalradian rocks. At the time of writing there is a service bus from Glasgow to Balmaha: further particulars should be sought from the Bus Station, Buchanan Street. The Island of Inchcailloch is well worth a visit for its geological and other natural history features. It is an SSSI (no permission needed at time of writing - except for parties), and a booklet is available from the Nature Conservancy Council for Scotland, Balloch Castle Country Park: transportation can be arranged through MacFarlane, The Boat Yard, Balmaha (Tel Balmaha (036087) 214).

Introduction

The Balmaha area has long been of considerable interest as being one of the most accessible places for viewing the Highland Boundary Fault - a fracture which has commanded a great deal of attention over the years. But over the past decade this fracture and its associated rocks have received renewed geological attention with the discovery that large-scale movements associated with terrane boundaries were to be found in the Caledonides (see Terrane Accretion in Western Scotland), and that they may be concentrated partly on the Highland Boundary Fault.

In this region it is possible to demonstrate the ways in which terrane boundaries may be analysed and the ways in which we are able to recognise terranes as being far travelled blocks, each of which has a history distinguishable from those now lying adjacent to it. Before discussing the localities to be visited at Balmaha, an introduction to the general problems of terrane analysis as demonstrated by these outcrops is now undertaken.

Terranes often travel such great distances that it is not possible to indentify the rocks on one side of a fault and look for their displaced equivalents on the other: i.e. the distances travelled by terranes often exceed the lateral extent of rock units. The other problem is that terranes often move along the strike of the beds, so that correlation across the faults is often not possible.

The problem posed in terrane identification at Balmaha is one of recognising differences in geological history between a basement and a sedimentary basin: the basement is the Dalradian and the sedimentary basin is the Highland Border Complex.

The Dalradian block comprises a thick sequence of sandstones,

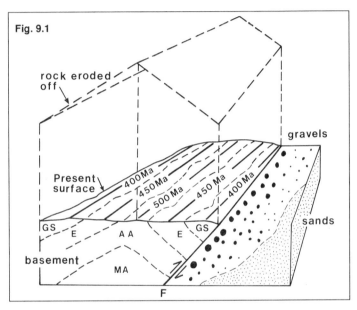

Fig. 9.1

Figure 9.1 Showing the relationship between the uplift of a basement and the accumulation of the sediments, sand and gravels, which have been eroded off it. The basement in this example has been thrust over the sediment pile which has accumulated in a basin which is to the right in the diagram. Gravels accumulate near to the source and sands further away. The volume of material removed from the basement is represented by the envelope in dotted lines; the present land surface exposes the metamorphic zones, with the lowest (GS=green-schist) going via E=epidote-amphibolite facies; AA=lower amphibolite facies, to MA=middle amphibolite facies (the highest). The times at which the rocks cooled are given in Ma= millions of years, and the thick lines join all points which cooled at the age given. In the example illustrated the centre of the basement pile was uplifted first (it has the oldest ages of 500Ma) and from this region there was the greatest removal of overlying rock.

limestones, lavas and shales laid down in the Late Proterozoic. After a period of folding which occurred before 590 Ma there followed a prolonged interval when the sequence was thickened and became hot and suffered fairly intensive metamorphism. At the present erosion level there is a changing mineralogy of these Dalradian metamorphic rocks as they are traced through the Highlands: generally low metamorphic grades occur in the south; and higher grades to the north. These changing grades are a response to the changing heat and pressure which occurred during their burial, so that in a very general way the rocks in the north were more deeply buried than those to the south. In the same general sense these metamorphic grades or zones lie roughly parallel with the Highland Boundary Fault. Superimposed on this general trend, there are some anomalies, the largest of which is that the rocks in the SW of the Dalradian belt underwent a cooler but higher pressure type metamorphism than the rocks to the NE.

After burial and metamorphism the whole sequence was subject to considerable uplift. Estimates of the burial-depths of rocks now at the surface range from 15 km in the south, along the Highland Boundary Fault to > 30 km in the central regions, so that these thicknesses of rock had to be removed to expose those rocks we can at present study at the surface.

When were these overlying rocks removed? A clue to this comes from the radiometric dating of some of the metamorphic minerals. As the rocks are uplifted they cool, and certain of the minerals they contain record in their isotopic systems the time of cooling. By taking sections through the Dalradian basement one is then able to 'map-out' the cooling behaviour of the surface i.e. which metamorphic zone cooled first, second etc.

In the fictitious example given in Figure 9.1 there is a section through a metamorphic belt showing the grades ranging from low (GS, green-schist) to high (MA, middle amphibolite). The solid lines are the contours for the uplift; i.e all the rocks which fall on these lines were uplifted through the same temperature at that specified time (e.g. uplifted through 500 C at 400 Ma, 500 Ma etc). On the diagram the highest grade rocks with the greatest thickness of rock overlying them were uplifted first at 500 Ma; and the lowest grade much later, at 400 Ma. The envelope above that surface represents the relative amount of rock which has to be removed. And, if at the same time we take account of the fact that the high grade rocks were uplifted first, then the surface, in a very general way, approximates to the attitude of the land surface during uplift.

When basement blocks rise in this manner, they often yield a great deal of sedimentary detritus. The whole rock volume illustrated in the envelope in Figure 9.1 is removed in this way or, in some cases by tectonic sliding i.e. detachments which resemble huge lithospheric landslides. The detritus yielded by erosion normally accumulates around the flanks of the mountain chain as piles of coarse alluvium, which gets finer-grained away from the source as illustrated in Figure 9.1. This situation characterizes many of the great mountain chains we now see such as the Himalayas, the Andes and the Alps.

If we find a sequence of rock which formed at the same time as an adjacent basement was known to have been rising and yielding sediment we would expect the sedimentary sequence to be dominated by coarse clastic debris. We know therefore that a paradox exists when this relationship fails (Fig. 9.2) and deep-water shales with volcanic rocks typical of extensional tectonics lie next to the basement.

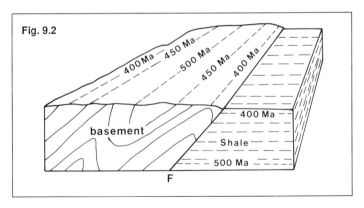

Figure. 9.2. Illustrates a similar structural situation in which the basement (as in Fig. 9.1) was uplifted at the same time as sediments were accumulating in a basin which is now juxtaposed against it. The sediment in the basin is shale which is not the sediment expected from the erosion of an adjacent mountain (compare Fig. 9.1). This situation implies that these two blocks (shale basin and basement) had a history which is not compatible with their having been formed adjacent to each other.

In this situation we would suspect that the basement and basin did not lie adjacent to each other during the periods of their individual activity, but that both or one of them to be a terrane which has moved into its present position from some distance.

The Dalradian block was uplifted in Ordovician times from 515Ma-430Ma and a huge volume of sediment was lost from it. Rocks of the Highland Border Complex, which were laid down at roughly this time, comprise fine grained sediments such as cherts and shales which accumulated in deep waters at some distance from a land source; sediments found in positions of stability and low rates of sedimentation, such as limestones and quartz-arenites, and volcanic rocks which typify regions of extension. These rock types are all totally unlike those accumulating in front of a rising mountainous source block such as the Dalradian would have been in Ordovician times. They are presently juxtaposed at Balmaha and leave us with two problems: firstly, we have to dispose of the sediment pile which the Dalradian uplift created, and secondly, we have to put in its place a basin with a totally different history. The Highland Border Complex is clearly a terrane with respect to the Dalradian block.

Once a terrane boundary has been established one must then attempt to recognise the history of terrane assembling, i.e how and when did the blocks we now see lying adjacent to each other get into that position. There is good reason to believe that a substantial portion of the assembly record was poorly recorded, has been lost or is covered over by rocks emplaced by younger events. However there is also good reason to suspect that part of the later history of amalgamation is recorded in the sediments of the Old Red Sandstone and it is to these rocks we now turn to pick up the rest of the story.

The Lower Old Red Sandstone rocks comprise a steeply dipping assemblage of conglomerates and sandstones which rest unconformably on the Highland Border Complex. The unconformity can best be seen on the Island of Inchcailloch, but can also be seen on the mainland. The Highland Border rocks beneath the unconformity have yielded very few clasts to the overlying Old Red Sandstone, so it is fairly clear that the Highland Border Complex formed the floor to the basin rather than its source.

When the whole Lower Old Red Sandstone assemblage is traced out laterally from near Aberfoyle in the NE to Inchmurrin in Loch Lomond in the SW it is seen as a sequence of overlapping lenses of

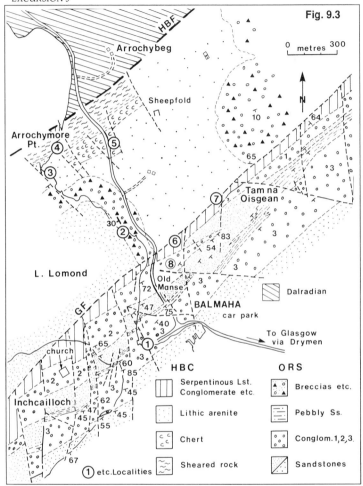

Figure. 9.3. Geological map of part of the Balmaha region with Localities. HBC = Highland Border Complex; ORS = Old Red Sandstone; GF = Gualann Fault; HBF = Highland Boundary Fault. Serpentinous Lst, Conglomerate etc. refers to rocks which include detrital as well as tectonic fragments of serpentinite. The conglomerates are marked 1,2,3 in the local order; they bear no relationship to the regional order.

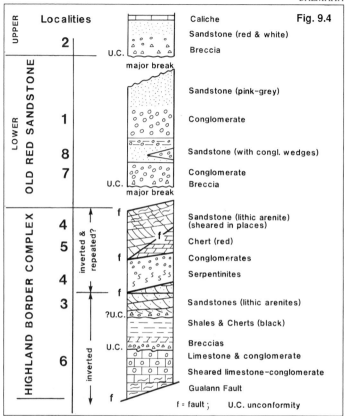

Figure. 9.4. A compound section of the post Dalradian rocks at Balmaha, together with the localities where they are to be seen. In this section the Highland Border Complex is seen to be repeated: there is a southern sequence (mainly overlain by Upper Old Red Sandstone) and a northern sequence which is seen at Arrochymore Point.

conglomerate with interspersed sandstone (Fig.9.3). The conglomerates overlap each other in a southwesterly direction, so that it appears that we are dealing with a basin which is progressively being filled in that same direction (Fig.9.6). One explanation for this, bearing in mind also the coarseness of these deposits, is that they accreted in an extensional basin generated within a strike-slip fault belt.

There are three distinctive stratigraphical units exposed south of the Dalradian block at Balmaha: The Highland Border Complex; the Lower Old Red Sandstone and the Upper Old Red Sandstone (Fig. 9.4). Each records a distinctive phase in the history of terrane accretion.

Locality 1. Balmaha Pier (NS 4155 9008) (Fig.9.3) : **Lower Old Red Sandstone.** Lower Old Red Sandstone conglomerates occur in the low ground to the immediate south of the pier and in the cliffs to the NW. The bay at Balmaha probably lies at the junction between the coarse conglomerates and the finer sandstones and siltstones which form most of the low ground around the southern end of Loch Lomond. The conglomerates contain fairly large clasts (up to 400 mm) mainly of quartzite, volcanic rocks mostly of intermediate type, together with a few orthoclase and biotite bearing granites. This conglomerate, no.3 in the local sequence (Fig.9.3), forms the uppermost conglomerate at Balmaha. It outcrops on the Island of Inchcailloch to the SW, and is responsible for the prominent hills, including Conic Hill, to the NE. When traced across the loch, it is seen to rest finally on the Highland Border Complex, thus overlapping about 200m of section. The significance of this relationship will be discussed later at Locality 7.

The conglomerates have a dispersal from the SE and NE, and taken as a whole, contain very well rounded clasts of tough quartzite and sometimes slightly less well rounded softer volcanic rocks. Some of the quartzite clasts have been broken and then re-rounded, indicating a provenance in a pre-existing, compositionally mature conglomerate comprising metamorphic clasts. The volcanic clasts may be first cycle. On the basis of the palaeocurrents in the conglomerates, this source block is thought to have existed within the Midland Valley and probably in the region which is now the Dalradian of the Southern Highlands.

At this stage it is not at all clear whether the Dalradian block along with the Highland Border Complex provided the floor to this Old Red Sandstone basin, or whether the entire Old Red Sandstone basin has been floored by the Highland Border Complex and the Dalradian block has been subsequently emplaced. From evidence in Western Ireland (Bluck and Leake 1986) it is clear that in a general sense the

Dalradian and Highland Border Complex lay near to each other by Silurian times.

The conglomerates are thought to have been deposited in bars built by braided streams. Generally speaking the thickness of the bar structures in these conglomerates increases with coarser grain size. From the study of the conglomerate **lithosome** shape and the distribution of clast sizes within it, it is concluded that these conglomerates formed in alluvial fans.

Follow the path north along the shore of the loch, passing a thick sandstone unit which underlies the conglomerate at the Pier, and head for the northern margin of the sandy bay.

Locality 2. Upper Old Red Sandstone. The conglomerates and breccias exposed beneath these low-lying cliffs are assigned to the Upper Old Red Sandstone, partly on the basis of their upward transition into quartz-arenites and caliches, which normally characterize the top of the Upper Old Red Sandstone where it grades into known Carboniferous. The Upper Old Red Sandstone rocks are also typically a brighter red colour than the Lower, and in this region rest unconformably on the Highland Boundary Rocks (as can be seen south of Locality 3, Fig.9.3) and possibly on the Dalradian.

Clasts of 'grits', slates and other rocks of greenschist metamorphic facies and vein quartz comprise most of the rock-types in these breccias. This clast assemblage strongly resembles rocks now seen in the local Dalradian block to the immediate north and serve to remind us of the appearance of a typical conglomerate of Dalradian **provenance**. They are in sharp contrast to the conglomerates of the Lower Old Red Sandstone to the south. Sedimentary structures abound in these conglomerates, and fine examples of sand-shadows behind proud clasts, imbrication and cross stratification in various scales are found. All these features indicate dispersal from the north, NW and NE, the direction in which the Dalradian is now seen to lie; the deposition was probably by braided streams.

From this outcrop it is clear that wherever the Dalradian block was with respect to the basin in which the Lower Old Red Sandstone accumulated, it was certainly close to the Highland Border Complex and the Midland Valley at the time these sediments were laid down. It therefore seems probable that the Highland Border Complex, the Midland Valley and the Dalradian had docked (united) by this time.

Follow the path (West Highland Way) northwards to Arrochymore

119

Point.

Locality 3. Highland Border Sandstones are exposed near the tip of Arrochymore Point (Fig.9.5), and are well exposed in a low, vegetation-covered cliff section on the right of the path as it turns to the NE. These beds have been referred to as the Loch Lomond Clastics (Henderson and Robertson 1982), and are probably equivalent to the Aberfoyle Arenites of Bluck *et al.* (1984). They are red-pink sandstones with many lithic fragments of **ophiolitic,** acidic volcanic rocks and detrital mica. The coarser members of this division contain rhyolitic clasts which are quite angular and are probably first cycle. The sequence shows abundant cross-stratification, which in the vicinity of this Point are all inverted but it has yet to be demonstrated whether this is a regional or local inversion associated with isoclinal folding.

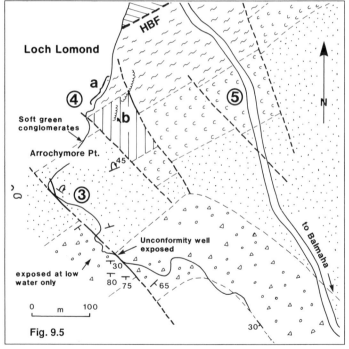

Figure. 9.5. Detail of the geology of Arrochymore Point, with localities.

These sandstones are probably of Caradocian age, for although no faunas have been obtained here, **chitinozoa** from what are probably equivalent rocks near Aberfoyle are of that age.

Locality 4 Serpentinite and sheared rock. There are two main exposures to visit here (Fig.9.5): the highly sheared rocks at the lochside (**4a**) and the serpentinite, which is comparatively unaltered, (**4b**). The sandstones of Locality 3, when traced NE along the shore, show a surprising degree of contortion, and are in places almost broken down to mylonites (**a** on Fig.9.5). Within these sheared rocks are pods of relatively undeformed red breccias of uncertain age, and in places just below the beach-gravels of the loch are soft green conglomerates with abundant ophiolitic clasts (see Fig.9.5). The outcrops have abundant shears which have a range of dips, striking in a NE-SW direction, parallel with the Highland Boundary Fault. Rocks of this type are in contact with the Dalradian farther to the NE, but along the shore the nearest exposures of Dalradian are north of the bay.

The small outcrop of serpentinite 4b (Fig.9.5) forms part of a somewhat larger mass which is terminated on either side by faults. Neither its age nor its associations are known but it differs from the southern serpentinite in being unaltered. The soft green conglomerate exposed on the lochside may be the equivalent of the southern serpentinite which, as discussed at Locality 6, is mainly or even totally a conglomerate with serpentinite and other clasts.

Follow the path NE for *c.* 200 m along the lochside to a car park, and then head south along the road (B837) back towards Balmaha. Locality 5 is an overgrown road cut on the western side of this road.

Locality 5. Red cherts belonging to the Highland Border Complex are exposed on the roadside and in the wooded area to the NE. Although quite massive here, elsewhere the cherts are interstratified with red shales. They have not yielded any fossils to date, and differ from other cherts in the Highland Border Complex which are grey-black, well stratified and associated with black shales. The age of these red cherts is unknown, but from evidence elsewhere in the Complex cherts are widespread during the Llanvirn and early Caradoc.

Walk along the road towards Balmaha, and in a shallow valley where the stream crosses the road (there is a field used as a car park here), a stile on the north side of the stream and opposite the car park allows access to a muddy footpath which winds through the trees and up the hill. The first ridge (i.e. furthest north) is distinctive because of its brown coloured soil.

Locality 6. Serpentinite conglomerate and breccias of the southern 'serpentinite'. The rocks comprising this hill are mainly breccia, conglomerate and a sheared mixture of carbonate and serpentinous rock which may be a sheared conglomerate with serpentinite pebbles in a carbonate matrix. In places the breccias and conglomerates are very distinctive and are formed of very well rounded clasts of serpentinite, basic rocks and sometimes sub-rounded quartz grains almost all of which are monocrystalline. On the continuation of this ridge to the shore at the lochside, distinctive marbles and conglomerates, normally underwater, have yielded a range of lithologies including dolerite, gabbro, spilite and well rounded clasts of quartz-arenite, and metaquartzite. Some of these metaquartzite clasts are > 300 mm in length and have ages of 1863Ma, which dates the uplift in the metamorphic block from which they were derived. This metamorphic block is substantially older than the Dalradian block, so the clasts were derived from a metamorphic terrane of unknown affinities and of uncertain location (Dempster and Bluck 1989).

These rocks on the shore have also yielded chitinozoa which suggest an Arenig age, and it is from rocks with this type of lithology that Curry *et al.* (1982) and Ingham *et al.* (1985) recovered a definite Lower Arenig fauna at Aberfoyle. It is almost certain therefore that these rocks are Arenig in age. Because they contain ophiolitic debris, there must have been in this region an ophiolite which is older than the limestone. From data elsewhere (Dempster and Bluck 1991) this ophiolite may be *c.*540Ma or older.

Along the south-eastern face of this exposure are very small outcrops of red sandstone which map out into the overlying Old Red Sandstone (see Fig. 9.3). At a few places on the hillside these sandstones are seen to rest unconformably on the Arenig rocks of the Highland Border Complex. This contact was formerly thought to be a fault and with the Old Red Sandstone conglomerates faulted against the Highland Border Complex its base was not seen, so the total thickness of conglomerate was unknown. However since the contact is now seen as an unconformity, the complete thickness of Old Red Sandstone is exposed - and that thickness is far less than previously supposed.

The serpentinite ridge is terminated along its northern margin by a fault which drops the Upper Old Red Sandstone down to the north. This fault is not the Highland Boundary Fault, as had previously been supposed: it is the Gualann Fault, named after a prominent hill on the NE termination of the conglomerate ridge. The Upper Old Red Sandstone steeply dips at the contact with this fault, as can be seen at the base of the ridge (see Fig.9.3)

Locality 7. Basal conglomerates and the overlapping fans. A line of old quarries, parallel with the ridge, exposes the conglomerates of the Lower Old Red Sandstone and rocks of the Ordovician Highland Border Complex. Conglomerates of the Lower Old Red Sandstone lie unconformably on the Highland Border Complex in most places but in others, as here, there is a small fault at the contact. The ORS conglomerates comprise well rounded or very well rounded quartzite clasts together with some volcanic clasts and very few clasts from the Highland Border Complex. In composition they closely resemble the conglomerate at the pier (Locality 1; conglomerate 3 in Fig.9.3) and probably share the same source, which lay in an approximately northeasterly direction.

The conglomerate exposed in these quarries is the oldest Lower Old Red Sandstone conglomerate in this area; it is overlain by the sandstones of Locality 6, which in turn are overlain by a conglomerate (2 of Fig.9.3) exposed on the shore and seen to rest on the Highland Border Complex on the island of Inchcailloch. The third conglomerate which forms the impressive ridge to the SE (3 of Fig.9.3), rests on sandstones in the valley: both sandstone and conglomerate have a source from the NE, east and SE. The third conglomerate is seen to rest on the Highland Border Complex on the island of Creinch further to the SW across the loch, so that they all overlap each other in that direction.

To the NW lies the low ground of the Highland Border Complex and the Upper Old Red Sandstone and a little beyond that the higher, rougher ground of the Dalradian, outcrops of which are seen on the low hills to the NNE. Between these outcrops and the lower ground of the Highland Border Complex lies the Highland Boundary Fault. The distant high peak to the east of the loch is Ben Lomond.

From this vantage point the following features can best be appreciated:

1. The low ground immediately below the ridge comprises black shales and cherts which at low water in the loch are seen to overlie the Arenig rocks which make up the ridge upon which you are standing. These rocks are replaced to the NW in the sequence by the sandstones seen at Locality 9.3 near Arrochymore Point. In a general sense this sequence of Highland Border rocks is steeply dipping and youngs towards the NW. The Old Red Sandstone rocks are also steeply dipping, but to the SE, so that at the time of the deposition of the Old Red Sandstone the Highland Border Complex was inverted (Figs. 9.5B; 9.7B).

2. As the Ordovician rocks of the Highland Border Complex were being deposited, the Highlands to the north were being uplifted. Profiles across the Dalradian metamorphic belt show that they were being uplifted from c.515Ma- 440Ma (Dempster 1985), and this is roughly the time span of deposition of the Highland Border Complex. Calculations suggest that well over 20 km of rock was removed from parts of the Dalradian highlands at this time, so rivers emerging from these early Dalradian mountains would be the principal agent dispersing this sediment. If the Highland Border Complex had formed where we now find it, right next to the Dalradian Block, then the basin in which rocks of the Complex accumulated would have been dominated by this sediment. Recent mountain chains and the basins which occur in front of them comprise mainly coarse detritus—gravels and sands, which are in direct contrast to the mudstones, shales and cherts of much of the Highland Border Complex.

It is therefore clear that the Dalradian block was nowhere near the Highland Border Complex in Ordovician times (Bluck 1985), and from the discussion at Locality 1, they were probably not in their present juxtaposition even in Lower Old Red Sandstone times.

3. The Upper Old Red Sandstone rocks form a thin cover over the Highland Border Complex in the immediate low ground and are disposed in a series of folds with axes running NW. The outcrops are terminated against the ridge of Arenig rocks by the Gualann Fault (Figs 9.3, 9.7). This Upper Old Red Sandstone sequence, in comparison with the Upper Old Red Sandstone to the south, is almost complete in the sense that it begins with a conglomerate (Locality 2) and is terminated by caliche beds which occur almost always just beneath the Carboniferous.

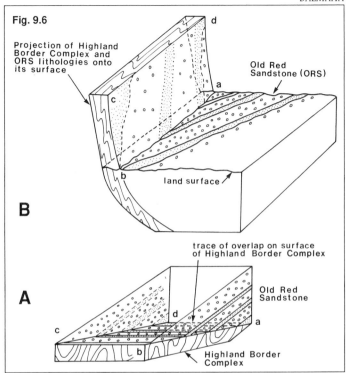

Figure. 9.6. **A** showing the simple overlap of sediment towards the SW as mapped out in Figure 9.3, but with the beds brought back to horizontal as at the time of deposition. The sediments rest on an eroded surface of Highland Border Complex, a,b,c,d. **B,** showing the overlap of the beds now rotated as seen in the map (Fig. 9.3) where they outcrop on the land surface. The basement to the basin and the basin itself is projected vertically and along the plane of unconformity. The present map is then seen to be a section through a basin which extends upward and downward.

The disposition of the Upper Old Red Sandstone implies that the Upper Old Red Sandstone sequence thins from >1 km where it is exposed on the south limb of the Strathmore syncline to <100m as one goes to the NW, and it thins against the Dalradian Block, which was therefore in place at this time. Moreover, if the base of the Upper Old

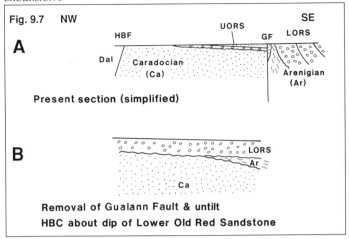

Figure. 9.7. Simplified sections through the rocks at Balmaha, **A** shows the present configuration of the rocks, **B,** the configuration at the time of deposition of the Lower Old Red Sandstone.

Red Sandstone is projected to the NW, then in order to be in this position the Gualann Fault would need to have a vertical throw of at least 500 m. It also follows that the Strathmore syncline formed before the deposition of the Upper Old Red Sandstone since these rocks are clearly not part of that structure.

Locality 8. Edge of second conglomerate NE of Old Manse which at this point is surrounded by sandstone (Fig.9.3). This conglomerate, which makes up a distinctive small conical hill has the same composition and textures as the lowest seen at Locality 7. From this point, looking over The Old Manse it is possible to see the Island of Inchcailloch, and to the SE, the valleys cut into the faulted conglomerates. From SW to NE lies the ridge of conglomerate 3 which reaches its thickest development at Conic Hill to the NE.

From this position, from the examination of Figure 9.3 and from the evidence further mapping along the outcrop a number of points emerge about the disposition of these conglomerate beds and their significance:

1. The conglomerate bodies are lensoid and this can be partly seen on Figure 9.3, SE of Locality 6. It is also clear that conglomerate 3 thins towards the SW, and (not seen of Figure 9.3) it also thins to the NE.

2. There is evidently a sequence of conglomerate bodies which overlap each other to the SW (Fig.9.6); they all had a roughly similar source in the NE, east and SE, and they form an impressive sequence which can be traced for at least 3 km to the NE.

3. There is no evidence for a local Dalradian provenance. The source area included first cycle volcanic and plutonic rock and polycyclic quartzite; it did not include a metamorphic basement. The source extended from the SE to the NE and probably lay across the region now occupied by the Highland Boundary Fault.

4. **Fanglomerate** stacks of this kind can be modelled as forming in a basin, the SE, NW and NE margins of which were bounded by faults. One has to imagine the basin as a vertical extension of the present outcrop, so that its NW margin may have been 1 or 2 km in the vertical sense (Fig.9.6). This basin was probably formed in response to a sinistral strike slip movement.

5. The sedimentation of these rocks is effectively controlled by faults other than the Highland Boundary Fault—a considerable departure from former views (including my own !!). The basin margin of the ORS sediments was probably a fault and that fault would have been in a position some distance to the north of the present Highland Boundary Fault, and therefore positioned beneath the Dalradian block. Clasts at the top of the sequence are more angular than those at the base. This suggests that the source has been firstly stripped of its overlying conglomerates and that the feeder streams began eroding the original basement which, in this instance, comprised metaquartzite.

Conclusions

The principal conclusions to be drawn from this excursion are as follows:

The Dalradian and Highland Border blocks were not juxtaposed during the Ordovician; the Midland Valley, Lower Old Red Sandstone basin received sediment which was **not** derived from the local Dalradian; by Upper Old Red Sandstone times the two blocks (Midland Valley and Highland Border Complex) were joined and therefore the Highland Boundary Fault is not the terrane boundary. It is a comparatively young fault which brought terranes together probably by thrusting during the Middle Devonian (at which time the Strathmore basin formed). The terrane boundary was probably hidden by this thrust and it now lies beneath the Dalradian block.

On a fine day it is well worth going up to the summit of Conic Hill; there is a splendid view in all directions and it is an ideal place (in good weather) to sit and muse on a majestic terrane boundary. To the SW, across Loch Lomond on a fine day it is possible to see the the tall chimney stack of Inverkip power station, beyond which lies the northern peaks of Arran. To the SE it is possible to see through the gap of the Blane Valley, Tinto Hill (the Late Silurian felsite) and the highest point in the Midland Valley. Tinto lies just north of the Southern Upland Fault, so from this point the whole width of the Midland Valley is seen. The low ground running parallel with the strike of the conglomerates, and occupied partly by the southern end of Loch Lomond is made up of sandstones and siltstones which occur in the axis of the Strathmore syncline. The impressive line of hills immediately beyond the low ground of the Strathmore syncline comprise Upper Old Red Sandstone in the foothills and Carboniferous basalts in the higher ground. The distinctive conical hills are almost all Carboniferous volcanic plugs.

References

BLUCK, B.J. 1985. The Scottish paratectonic Caledonides. *Scott. J. Geol.* **21,** 437-464.

—————. and LEAKE, B.E. 1986. Late Ordovician to Early Silurian amalgamation of the Dalradian and adjacent Ordovician rocks in the British Isles. *Geology* **14,** 917-919.

—————., INGHAM, J.K. CURRY,G.B. and WILLIAMS,A., 1984. Stratigraphy and tectonic setting of the Highland Border Complex. *Trans. R. Soc. Edinb. Earth Sci.* **75,** 125-133.

CURRY, G.B., INGHAM,J.K.,BLUCK,B.J. and WILLIAMS,A. 1982. The significance of a reliable Ordovician age for some Highland Border rocks in Central Scotland. *J.Geol.Soc.* **139,** 451-4.

DEMPSTER,T.J. 1985, Uplift patterns and orogenic evolution in the Scottish Dalradian. *J. Geol. Soc.* **142,** 111-128.

—————. and BLUCK, B.J. 1989. The age and origin of boulders in the Highland Border Complex: constraints on terrane movements. *J.Geol. Soc.* **146,** 377-380.

—————————————, 1991. The age and tectonic significance of the Bute amphibolite, Highland Border Complex, Scotland. *Geol. Mag.* **128,** 77-80 .

HENDERSON, W.G. and ROBERTSON,A.H.F. 1982, The Highland Border rocks and their relation to marginal basin development in the Scottish Caledonides. J. *Geol. Soc.* **139,** 433-450.

INGHAM,J.K. CURRY, G.B. and WILLIAMS, A. 1985. Early Ordovician Dounans Limestone fauna, Highland Border Complex, Scotland. *Trans. R. Soc. Edinb. Earth Sci.* **76,** 481-513.

B.J.Bluck and James D. Lawson

Themes:	The relationships between the Dalradian block and the Midland Valley; some details of the structure and stratigraphy of the Highland Border Complex; recumbent folding in Upper Dalradian rocks.
Features:	Serpentinite, serpentinite breccias, fossiliferous limestones, unconformity, conglomerates; Aberfoyle Grits and Slates, grading, bedding-cleavage relationships, recumbent fold.
Maps:	O.S. 1:50 000 Sheet 57 Stirling
	O.S. 1:25 000 Sheet NN 40/50 The Trossachs
Distance	B.G.S. 1:63 360 Sheet 38 Loch Lomond
and Time:	10 km in total, including 3 km walking : 8 hours.
Access:	Unrestricted, but stay on the forestry paths as much as possible and leave vehicles at the car parks provided. Do not drive vehicles through the forests.
Short itinerary:	Localities 3 a,b,c,d, 4, 5, 6 and 8.

In the vicinity of Aberfoyle there are fine sections through the Dalradian where details of its structure may be simply seen and sections through the Highland Border Complex where fossiliferous carbonates, critical in determining its age and association, are well exposed.

The age and affinities of the Highland Border Complex have been debated for a long time. Some workers (e.g. Henderson and Robertson 1982) maintain that these beds were folded together with the Dalradian and are therefore either part of the Dalradian sequence, or lay on top of the Dalradian at the time of folding. Others (e.g. Longman *et al* 1979) took the view that the Highland Border Complex was younger than the rocks of the Dalradian and represented an entirely different rock assemblage formed in a totally different tectonic setting.

Two important discoveries resolved this difference:

1. The age of the Dalradian sedimentary rocks and their folding. There are a number of granites which cut the folded Dalradian rocks, and are therefore younger than both the Dalradian rock sequence and

the episodes of folding which occurred prior to their intrusion. One of these granites (Ben Vuirich) has cut through Dalradian rocks which at the time of intrusion had already undergone two initial phases of folding. This granite yielded an age of 590Ma (Late Precambrian; Rogers *et al* 1989), indicating that the sedimentation of the Dalradian and the two phases of folding which affected it are older than this date.

2. The age of the Highland Border Complex. This and the association of the Highland Border Complex were both solved with the rediscovery of a fauna in Lime Craig Quarry (Locality 3). A lens of limestone exposed in this quarry yielded a fauna of trilobites, brachiopods and other fossils to Curry *et al* (1982) and Ingham *et al* (1986) which demonstrated their lower Ordovician age. With the sedimentation and two phases of folding already completed in the Dalradian Block by Late Precambrian times this part of the Highland Border Complex could not have been associated with the Dalradian block as had been previously suggested.

In the Upper Dalradian grits and slates adjacent to the Highland Border Series, sedimentary structures led Shackleton (1957) to conclude that the Aberfoyle Slates occupy the core of a major fold of which grits form the limbs. Shackleton (1957) has also shown that the axial planar slaty cleavage of the Aberfoyle "Anticline" has a downward-**facing** relationship to bedding (*ie.* the axial plane of folds on all scales encounters successively *younger* rocks when traced *downwards)*. Consequently, he concluded that the Aberfoyle "Anticline" is a **synform** - the downbent nose of a major gravity **nappe**, the Tay Nappe, which has its roots far to the north across the Cowal Anticline.

From the west end of Aberfoyle take the small road south over the Forth, and head SSW to a car park at Balleich (c.1km from Aberfoyle). Follow the forestry road west from the car park to the locality where this road crosses Bofrishlie Burn

Locality 1. Bofrishlie Burn (NS 5003 9901): **Black shales and cherts** Fig. 10.1). In both the stream section and along the forest road are good exposures of folded and sheared black shales and **cherts**. These rocks have yielded brachiopods, bivalves and radiolaria to Jehu and Campbell (1917) and **chitinozoa** to Downie et al (1971). On the basis of chitinozoa these beds are probably Llanvirn-Llandeilo in age, and beds with these characteristics have been recorded in Stonehaven, where they are also assigned to that age-span.

Fig. 10.1

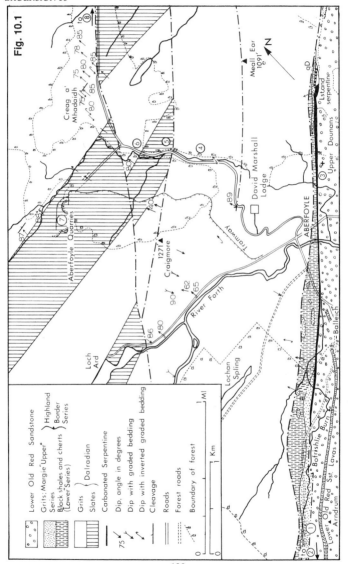

On the the NW and SE side of the Burn there are exposures of grey sandstone with interbedded siltstones and black shales. These beds make up most of the ridge lying parallel with the road on the NW side. The contact between these sandstones and the black shales is faulted, although Jehu and Campbell (1917) record an unconformable relationship between them. Some grey sandstones have black mudstone and shale clasts in them which may support the view that they rest unconformably on the shale-chert sequence.

Locality 2. (NX 4954 9861): **Unconformity between Highland Border Complex and Old Red Sandstone** (Fig. 10.1). From Locality 1, continue SW along the forestry track. Take the left fork at the first road junction and the right fork at the second junction. Walk 90 m on the road over a small hill to the low lying outcrops 20m from the road. The unconformable contact between the Old Red Sandstone and the underlying Highland Border Complex is seen in these bare rock exposures (Fig.10.1). The basal Old Red Sandstone is a breccia with clasts of shale and sandstone and forms the base to a sequence of coarse, quartzite bearing conglomerates, sandstones and a thin andesitic lava which partly forms the high ridge to the south.

Locality 3. Lime Craig Quarry (NN 533 018): **Fossiliferous lime-stones and section through the Highland Boundary Fault** (Fig. 10.2). This locality is on Forestry Commission land, and is best approached from the David Marshall Lodge where there is parking, refreshments and (at the time of writing) a simple introduction to the rocks at Lime Craig Quarry. From the David Marshall Lodge the trail to the quarry is clearly marked and is about 1 km long.

(a). Before reaching the quarry, there are exposures in steeply dipping sandstones and shales on the north side of the track. These sandstones belong to the Achray Sandstones and the interbedded shales have yielded pale yellow (unheated) chitinozoa of middle Ordovician age (Burton and Curry 1984). The same shale has also yielded black chitinozoa of lower Ordovician age which have probably been derived from an older formation which experienced elevated temperatures after deposition.

Lime Craig Quarry lies c100 m south of the Highland Boundary Fault (Figs.10.1 and 10.2) and east of the high quarry spoil. It exposes Lower Old Red Sandstone conglomerates, Ordovician limestones,

Figure 10.1. Geological map of the Aberfoyle district with locality numbers.

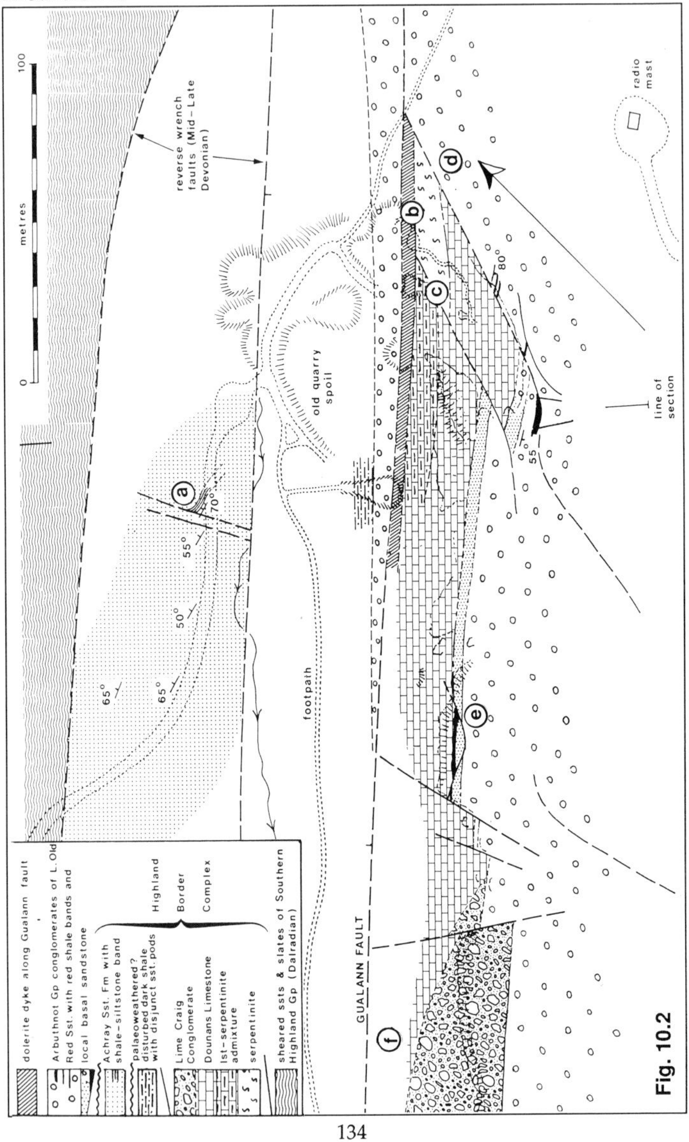
metres
0
100
reverse wrench faults (Mid–Late Devonian)
old quarry spoil
footpath
radio mast
line of section
GUALANN FAULT
a
b
c
d
e
f
65°
65°
50°
55°
70°
80°
55
dolerite dyke along Gualann fault
Arbuthnot Gp conglomerates of L. Old Red Sst. with red shale bands and local basal sandstone
Achray Sst. Fm with shale–siltstone band
palaeoweathered? disturbed dark shale with disjunct sst. pods
Lime Craig Conglomerate
Dounans Limestone
lst–serpentinite admixture
serpentinite
Highland Border Complex
sheared ssts & slates of Southern Highland Gp (Dalradian)

Fig. 10.2

serpentinite-limestone mixtures, serpentinite and the trace of the Gualann Fault along which there is now a Carboniferous dyke (*cf.* Balmaha excursion). Mechanical excavation here has exposed the rocks and clarified their relationships (Fig.10.3).

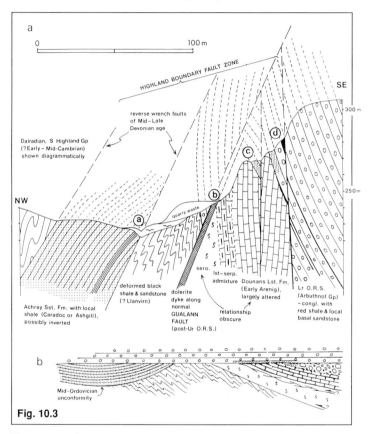

Figure 10.2. Geological map of Limecraig Quarry and environs, with locality numbers (From Bluck *et al* 1984).

Figure 10.3. (a) Geological cross section (as indicated on Figure 10.2); (b), the attitude of the Highland Border Complex at the time of Lower Old Red Sandstone deposition. (from Bluck *et al* 1984).

(b). A vertical dark rock surface exposes the dolerite dyke, to the north of which is the serpentinite and to the south a thin sliver of Old Red Sandstone conglomerate. Conglomerates are also visible in the very high east face of the quarry, so the thin outcrop at (b) is a downfaulted part of this thicker conglomerate sequence to the NE. The fault responsible for this displacement is the Gualann Fault which can be traced as far as the west side of Loch Lomond.

On the east side of the dyke lies an outcrop of soft dark serpentinite. This rock differs in colour and texture from the brown weathering carbonate-serpentinite which is associated with the limestone: this latter rock is probably a sheared breccia and conglomerate made up of serpentinite clasts.

(c). The high ground to the SW of the quarry is partly formed of brown weathering, pale grey limestone from which an abundant fauna has been collected (Curry *et al* 1982; Ingham *et al* 1986). The limestone contains sand-gravel sized clasts of serpentinite, gabbro, dolerite, spilite and other clasts of basic igneous rock. It was probably deposited in shallow water and was partly sourced in a pre-existing mass of oceanic crust (Bluck *et al* 1984). The discovery in the Isle of Bute of a metamorphic sequence which resembles one produced beneath obducted ocean crust provided further evidence for the existence of an ophiolite along the Highland Border. Furthermore, the age of 540 Ma for the cooling of this metamorphic assemblage indicated that the ophiolite was older than the limestone found at this locality and could therefore be the source of the ophiolitic detritus found within it.

Although a large fauna has been obtained from this limestone, the fossils are small and difficult to see without the aid of a hand lens. The faunas include the trilobites: *Distazeris, Punka, Ischyrotoma, Illaenus;* brachiopods: *Archaeorthis, Orthidium, Orthambonites* and gastropods, bryozoans and crinoids. These and many others are figured in Ingham *et al* (1986) and indicate a Lower Arenig age.

(d). Steeply dipping Lower Old Red Sandstone conglomerate with clasts up to cobble and small boulder size interstratified with thin red sandstones. The cobbles are mainly quartzite and andesite and both are very well rounded. The brittle quartzite clasts are often fractured and the significance of these fractures has been recognised by Ramsay (1964) as indicating shear, as well as reverse movement along the Highland Boundary and related faults.

(e). This locality, and to a lesser extent (f) are difficult to find, particularly in the summer when there is much vegetation. (e) is also fairly inaccessible so only the agile and enthusiastic should attempt this part of the excursion. Follow the cliff made by the limestone along the path for c. 100 metres, then scramble and climb to the limestone-Old Red Sandstone boundary. Here the Old Red Sandstone is seen to rest on the limestones of the Highland Border Complex. The contact is an unconformable one but with some minor movement along the plane of the unconformity. The formerly held view that this is the Highland Boundary Fault is now discarded.

(f). Conglomerates with abundant quartzite and psammitic clasts up to small boulder size. This is a conglomerate which is considered by Bluck *et al* 1984 to be part of the Highland Border Complex and probably younger than the Lower Arenig Dounans Limestone. Some of the psammitic clasts have yielded ages of 1800 Ma (Dempster and Bluck 1988) suggesting a source in a metamorphic terrane far older than the Moine and Dalradian.

Locality 4. Quarry (NN 5205 0225): Graded grits (Fig. 10.1). Return to David Marshall Lodge and take the A 821 northwards to traverse the Dukes Pass. Along this road there are numerous exposures of the Aberfoyle Grits and Slates belonging to the Southern Highland Group of the Upper Dalradian. It is possible to determine the way up of the strata and recognise the presence of a major recumbent fold with a downturned nose.

Along the winding part of the road there are many **roches moutonnées** in the grits, some with glacial striations, but parking here is difficult. As the road straightens out before the quarry, the stream on the right displays good water worn surfaces of a **graded** grit with **load casts** indicating that the beds are inverted, as they dip north-eastwards but young to the SW. However , the best exposure is not easy to find and there is not room for a group of people. It is normally preferable to carry on a short distance and park the car or bus at a lay-by on the right, close to a small quarry.

Cross the small (unless in flood) stream to enter the quarry, the floor of which is usually very wet. It should be possible to appreciate from the lay-by that the grits are dipping steeply to the left (i.e. roughly northwards). These so-called "grits" are really **greywacke** type sandstones deposited by **turbidity currents** in deep sea fans. At the entrance to the quarry two graded units can be recognised (often

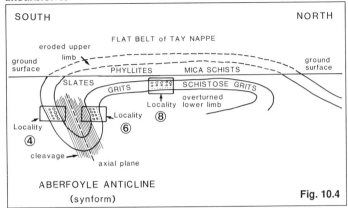

Figure 10.4. Diagrammatic section from south to north along the excursion route to show how the folding can be interpreted from the exposures visited.

with difficulty) at and below eye level. The basal layers are coarse and pebbly, containing subangular fragments of quartz, feldspar and rock e.g. shale. The bottom of the graded unit is often irregular and rests sharply on finer sediment. The grading is not very convincing in these exposures but the top layers are distinctly finer and may show lamination. On the north (far) side of the quarry there is an interbedded purple slate and an impressive grit with large feldspars: some visitors are more convinced by the graded bedding here. The conclusion that should be reached is that the grits in the quarry are younging approximately southwards although the dip is roughly to the north. In other words the grits are inverted (Fig.10.4).

Locality 5. Forestry track (NN 5210 0228): **Bedding-cleavage relationships in slates.** About 30 m north of Locality 4 is a forestry road with a cutting through the Aberfoyle Slates. The grits of the quarry dip steeply below these slates but as the strata are inverted, the slates must be older that the grits. Careful examination along this section will reveal folded bedding, often picked out by colour changes (maroon and green) in the slates, cut by a constant cleavage. It is possible for a qualified geologist to determine from the relative dips of bedding and cleavage that the major structure is closing downwards (Fig. 10.4).

Locality 6. Hill Cottage crags (NN 5158 0290): **Graded grit on slates.** Drive about one km northwards over more slates and grits which are involved in faulting (Fig. 10.1). Park on the left-hand (west) side opposite some prominent crags and before reaching the cottage where the road branches off westwards into the slate quarries. The roadside crag shows grits dipping at about 80 degrees to the north and resting on slates which are at road level. The base of the grit is very coarse and obviously grades upwards: the under-surface displays large elongate lumps which are considered to be **sole markings** known as load-casts and are characteristic of the base of turbidite sediments. This evidence indicates that the grits here are younging to the NNE in the same direction as the dip and are therefore not inverted. The cleavage dips more steeply than the bedding. Between Localities 3 and 5, therefore, we have crossed the axis of a fold: the slates in the middle are older than the grits and the fold can be shown (from bedding-cleavage relationships) to close downwards. Although the structure is **synformal** the presence of older rocks in the centre indicates that it is an inverted anticline (Fig.10.4).

The crags behind this exposure and those near the little waterfall opposite also show graded bedding which confirms the northward younging. Just to the south there are roadside exposures of purple and green slates in which bedding can be recognised as well as cleavage.

Locality 7. Aberfoyle Slate quarries. Seven main bands of slate can be distinguished with occasional thin bands of grit and limestone. The rocks in the quarry are intersected by at least six north-easterly trending faults in a distance of approximately 370m. They are presumably **sinistral** tear (strike-slip) faults trending sub-parallel to the larger fracture indicated on the map (Fig.10.1). Faint laminae and cross-laminae representing original bedding occur in several places, intersected by the slaty cleavage planes. These indicate that cleavage is oblique to bedding at least in the hinges of the minor folds and that the cleavage in the slates faces downwards.

Locality 8. Creag Noran (Loch Achray) (NN 5041 0658): **Flat-lying grits.** Continue northwards along the road for about 4 km, skirting the southern shore of Loch Achray. Immediately after a sharp right turn at the Loch Achray Hotel there is a cliff on the left with limited parking space opposite. *En route* one passes exposures of grits and slates although these finer sediments are now altered to the shinier **phyllites**, with larger white mica crystals due to the higher degree of metamorphism.

The roadside cliff exposes mainly flat-lying grits but they have obviously suffered a greater degree of deformation than the grits on the Duke's Pass with a wavy cleavage developed. The distinct graded bedding indicates that these almost horizontal beds are upside down. The finer sediments have been altered beyond phyllite grade to **chlorite** schist. We are here on the inverted lower limb of the flat part of the large recumbent fold shown in Figure 10.4.This is the Flat Belt of the Tay **Nappe** which affects most of the southern Highlands.

References

BLUCK,B.J. INGHAM. J.K. CURRY,G.B. AND WILLIAMS,A. 1984.Stratigraphy and tectonic setting of the Highland Border Complex. *Trans. R. Soc. Edinburgh, Earth Sci.* **75,** 124-133.

BURTON, C.J. and CURRY,G.B. 1984 Chitinozoa and miscellanea from the Highland Border Complex, *Trans. R. Soc. Edinburgh, Earth Sci.* **73,** 119-121.

CURRY, G.B., INGHAM,J.K., BLUCK,B.J. and WILLIAMS, A. 1982. The significance of a reliable Ordovician age for some Highland Border rocks in Central Scotland. *J. Geol. Soc. London.* **139,** 451-4.

DEMPSTER, T.J. and BLUCK, B.J. 1988. The age and origin of boulders in the Highland Border Complex: constraints on terrane movement. *J. Geol. Soc. London.* **146,** 377-9.

———————————————————1990. The age and tectonic significance of the Bute amphibolite, Highland Border Complex, Scotland. *Geol. Mag.* **128,** 77-80.

DOWNIE,C., LISTER,T.R. HARRIS, A.L. and FETTES,D.J. 1971. A palynological investigation of the Dalradian of Scotland. *Rep. Inst. Geol. Sci. Lond.* **71/9.**

HENDERSON,W.G. and ROBERTSON,A.H.F. 1982. The Highland Border rocks and their relation to marginal basin development in the Scottish Caledonides. *J. Geol. Soc. London.* **139,** 433-50.

INGHAM,J.K. CURRY,G.B.,and WILLIAMS, A. 1986. Early Ordovician Dounans Limestone fauna, Highland Border Complex, Scotland. *Trans. R. Soc. Edinburgh, Earth Sci.* **76** (for 1985) , 481-513.

JEHU T.J.and CAMPBELL, R. 1917. The Highland Border rocks of the Aberfoyle district *Trans. R. Soc. Edinburgh, Earth Sci.* **52,** 175-212.

ROGERS, G., DEMPSTER T.J. BLUCK,B.J., and TANNER, P.W.G. 1989.A high precision U-Pb age for the Ben Vuirich granite: implications for the evolution of the Scottish Dalradian. *J. Geol. Soc. London.* **146,** 789-798.

RAMSAY, D.M. 1964 Deformation of pebbles in Lower Old Red Sandstone conglomerates adjacent to the Highland Boundary Fault. *Geol. Mag.* **101,** 228-248.

SHACKLETON, R.M. 1957. Downward facing structures of the Highland border. *J. Geol. Soc. London* **113,** 361-392.

Excursion 11 **LOCH LOMONDSIDE**

D.R. Bowes

Themes: Polyphase deformation and polymetamorphism in the Caledonides; Barrovian-type metamorphism; Grampian and Athollian episodes.

Features: Dalradian Supergroup, folds, lineations, metamorphic mineral growth, schistosities, schists (chlorite, biotite, garnet, albite porphyroblast).

Maps: O.S.   1 : 50 000   Sheet 56   Loch Lomond & Invararay
           1 : 63 360   Sheet 53   Loch Lomond
      B.G.S.   1 : 50 000   Sheet 038 W   Ben Lomond

Terrain: Roadside exposures.

Distance and Time: About 21 miles (34 km) one way. With many localities facing east, morning light is advantageous. Because of the clearly displayed relationships of the structural elements at Rudha Mor and Rudha Dubh, a northerly traverse is recommended. The major features can be examined in 4 - 5 hours. If only 1 1/2 - 2 hours are available, the Rudha Dubh Localities,(5 to 8), provide the greatest range of features and relationships. For those en route with only a very brief time to spare, Localities 9, 10 and 11 give a brief glimpse of many of the features.

Access: A82 on the western side of Loch Lomond. At most times the road is very busy, with many heavy trucks and buses as well as much tourist traffic, **so care is essential.** South of Tarbet the road is a clearway with roadside parking prohibited. North of the loch, through Glen Falloch to Crianlarich, much of the road is a succession of broad, sweeping curves with vehicle speeds generally high and roadside parking can cause potentially dangerous bottlenecks. Many of the recommended localities are on parts of the old road or adjacent to lay-bys and car parks. While new road cuttings may look excellent for study, many have numerous vertical drill markings and lack three-dimensional exposure such as that available on the old road. Here also, absence of passing traffic permits examination of representative outcrops without the potential danger of members of the party inadvertently straying on to an exceptionally busy road. It should be noted that because of much road improvement, published maps do not consistently show road location precisely.

There are toilets open throughout the year at car parks in Luss and Crianlarich. Those at the car park opposite the Loch Sloy hydro-electric power station are open during the tourist season only. Although occasional long-distance buses stop at Tarbet, this excursion is not easily accomplished using public transport.

Road log: Distances from Inverbeg (NS 345 978) travelling north and in brackets from Crianlarich (NN 384 253) travelling south.

0.0 miles, 0.0 km (21.2, 34.1): Inverbeg.

1.0 miles, 1.6 km (20.2, 32.5): lay-by on western side of road - entrance from south only.

1.1 miles, 1.8 km (20.1, 32.3): old road leading to Rudha Mor Localities 1 to 4 (Fig. 11.3) abuts against embankment of new road - **no vehicular access**.

1.3 miles, 2.1 km (19.9, 32.0): large cutting begins - dangerous bend ahead.

1.6 miles, 2.6 km (19.6, 31.6): large cutting ends.

1.7 miles, 2.7 km (19.5, 31.4): lay-by on eastern side of road - entrance from north only (cars and minibuses can enter or exit with a U-turn, but **not coaches**); nearest stopping place for Rudha Mor Localities 1 to 4 (Fig. 11.3).

2.4 miles, 3.9 km (18.8, 30.2): lay-by on western side of road - entrance from north not prohibited.

2.5 miles, 4.0 km (18.7, 30.1): on eastern side of road, small access road for Rubha Dubh Localities 5 to 8 - **not suitable for coaches** which should park in lay-bys to south or north. 3.1 miles, 5.0 km (18.1, 29.1): **small** paved area on western side of road suitable for one **car or minibus** only (Locality 9).

3.2 miles, 5.1 km (18.0, 29.0): lay-by on eastern side of road - entrance from south not prohibited; for Rubha Dubh Localities 5 to 8 walk 200 m south on road verge to where there is direct access (without fences) down a bank to the old road 300 m north of Figure 11.4.

3.9 - 4.0 miles, 6.3 - 6.4 km (17.2 - 17.3, 27.7 - 27.8): large lay-by on western side of road; AA telephone at southern end; Localities 10, 11, 4.9 miles, 7.9 km (16.3, 26.2): Tarbet; turn right at A82 - A83 junction.

8.9 miles, 14.3 km (12.4, 20.0): viewpoint, picnic area, large car park on eastern side of road (NN 322 098) with Loch Sloy hydro-electric power station on western side (Locality 12).

14.8 miles, 23.8 km (6.4, 10.3): Inverarnan (setting off point for Garabal Hill intrusion).

16.8 miles, 27.0 km (4.4, 7.1): entrance to picnic area on eastern side of road - **cars only** (2 m headroom) (Locality 13).

18.3 miles, 29.4 km (2.9, 4.7): road bridge over railway.

18.4 - 18.9 miles, 29.6 - 30.4 km (2.3 - 2.8, 3.7 - 4.5): road cuttings on western side; off road parking on eastern side possible for **cars** on remnant of old road at 18.5 miles, 29.8 km (2.7, 4.3) (Locality 14).

21.2 miles, 34.1 km (0.0, 0.0): Crianlarich; toilets on northern side of railway bridge and 50 m from A82 (Glen Coe, Ballachulish, Fort William) (A85 Oban) - A85 (Perth) (A84 Stirling) junction.

Geological context

The rocks seen on this excursion are mainly quartz - mica schists and mica schists of the Leny - Ben Ledi Grits Formation of the Southern Highland Group of the late Proterozooic Dalradian Supergroup. They are on the inverted lower limb of the Tay Nappe within a structural domain known as the "flat belt" because of the generally flat-lying disposition of the lithological units (S_0), the dominant (composite) schistosity (S_c) and many blind veins of quartz that are generally concordant with the schistosity (Fig. 11.1b). Structures formed in five deformational phases (D_{1-5}) are seen: these reflect the tectonic evolution of the region over more than 150 million years from about the Precambrian - Cambrian boundary until Silurian times. However the most prominent structures are (1) a composite fabric (S_c) incorporating the Dalradian sedimentary layers and two

143

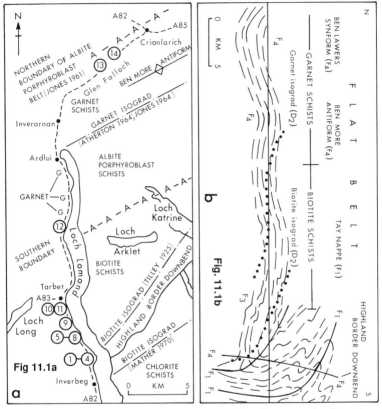

Figure 11.1. Locations (a), metamorphic isograds and cross-section (to east of Loch Lomond - b) illustrating the main geological features.

essentially concordant penetrative schistosities (S_1 and S_2 formed during D_1 and D_2) that represent phases of the Grampian episode (pre-590 million years) (Fig. 11.3a, b) and (2) upright, open folds (F_4) (Fig. 11.3d) having subhorizontal axes with a NE - SW ("Caledonian") trend associated with a period of major uplift in late Ordovician times (c. 450 million years).

From south to north there is a change in metamorphic grade from chlorite through biotite to garnet (Fig. 11.1). However many of the

Episode	———— Grampian ————			Athollian ___?		
Age (Ma)	Before 590 Ma			c.490	c.450	
Phase	Syn-D$_1$	Post-D$_1$	Syn-D$_2$	Syn-D$_3$	Syn-D$_4$	Post-D$_4$
Quartz	——	——	——	——		——
Muscovite	——	——	——	——		——
Chlorite	——	——	——	——		——
Albite	——			——		——
Garnet		— —	——	——		
Biotite				——		——
Epidote				——		
Tourmaline	——			——		

Figure 11.2. Summary of phases of metamorphic mineral growth in relation to major episodes.

minerals have grown at more than one stage (Fig. 11.2) so that what has been considered to be a relatively simple pattern of metamorphic **isograds** is complex because of (1) the superimposition of two major episodes of prograde mineral growth up to garnet grade, (2) the overprinting of albite **porphyroblasts** (post-D$_4$) over Barrovian-type isograds, metamorphic zones and mineral assemblages and (3) the extensive effects of retrograde metamorphism during which much chlorite was formed at the expense of biotite and garnet. The peak of the earlier episode of prograde metamorphism was during D$_2$ (in the Grampian episode that generally corresponded in time to the Cadomian (or Middle Pan-African) orogeny of NW Europe). The regional distribution of isograds in the district (and in SW Scotland generally) is largely the result of this episode, but there is no unanimity about their precise locations (Fig. 11.1a). The peak of the later episode that also reached garnet grade was during D$_3$: this is related to a corresponding (D$_3$) metamorphic peak during early Ordovician times associated with the development of Barrovian zones in their type area in NE Scotland (in the Athollian episode). There is a general correspondence of events in the Irish Caledonides in Connemara where D$_2$ dynamothermal metamorphism is overprinted during early Ordovician times by metamorphism associated with D$_3$ tectonic and igneous activity.

The albite porphyroblast and related mineral growth was post-D$_4$. Its regional expression southwestwards through Kintyre to Antrim, controlled by major F_4 structures (including the Cowal antiform), and its characteristics of a post-tectonic thermal overprint could be related to large masses of basic magma at depth whose higher level expressions are the early Silurian explosion-breccia - appinite - diorite masses that are common in the Loch Lomond district (e.g. Arrochar, Garabal Hill). The control of F_5 and S_5 on the emplacement of some of these masses means that the upper time limit on the D_{1-5} features is c. 425 million years.

While the Loch Lomond district is within the Caledonides, the term "Caledonian" has no precise meaning in relation to the evolution of rocks whose structural imprint spans from the Precambrian - Cambrian boundary to early Silurian times: the NE - SW "Caledonian trend" is shown both by D_1 and D_4 structures that are separated by c. 150 million years. Hence while a sequential development from D_1 to D_5 can be demonstrated from refolding and cross-cutting relationships in the Loch Lomond district, and in adjacent regions, not only must these deformational phases be considered in cognate groups based on an integration of structural and geochronological data (D_1, D_2 - Grampian; D_3 - Athollian; D_4 - regional uplift, possibly late in the Athollian episode; D_5 - continued uplift to development of transcurrent faults of the Loch Tay set), but also as a partial record of geological evolution: evidence for the existence of other phases that had only limited structural or metamorphic expressions may have been masked by superimposed, more strongly expressed features, or may be identifiable only by isotopic data. In addition the metamorphic zones - isograds developed before 590 Ma (in the Grampian episode) as the result of Barrovian-type metamorphism need to be separated from the metamorphic zones - isograds formed 100 million years later (in the Athollian episode at the time of development of the type Barrovian metamorphic zones). This applies not only in the Loch Lomond district but in reconstructions of "Barrovian zones" throughout the Scottish Caledonides to ensure that metamorphic isograds whose formation was separated by c. 100 million years are not joined to give patterns without geological significance.

At the level now exposed D_1 and D_2 resulted in the structural and metamorphic modification of cover rocks (Dalradian Supergroup) during the Grampian orogeny. However at the time of D_3 deformation the rocks of the Loch Lomond and adjacent regions must have been crystalline basement to an as yet unrecognized early Palaeozoic cover assemblage that was involved in crustal thickening during early Ordovician tectonism. Which stage(s) of deformation in cover rocks during the Athollian episode relates to D_3 deformation in the basement schists is not known. However at the initiation of that phase the total effect of D_1, D_2, and any as yet unrecognized later deformational phases of the Grampian episode (or any tectonism between the Grampian and Athollian episodes), left both schistosity and lithological layering essentially flat-lying. This was a favourable attitude to facilitate the essentially horizontal tectonism, deduced from D_3 structural features, that resulted in SSE (to S)-directed movements during the Athollian episode.

Structural elements

The most prominent structural element (S_c) consists of $S_1 + S_2$ (+ S_0). Variations in its attitude result largely from folding during D_4: F_4 deforming S_c on the long limbs of F_3 can be seen at almost every exposure (cf. Fig. 11.1b). To a lesser extent, and generally in localized zones, hinges of F_3 folds are seen to deform S_c. The expression of D_5 structures is very limited. Field photographs and photomicrographs of D_1, D_2, D_3 and D_4 structures are given in Bowes (1979). They and the structures in Figures 11.3 and 11.4 correspond to features present throughout the many hundreds of square kilometres of the flat belt. However the number of F_3 fold hinges at Rudha Mor (Localities 1 - 4) and Rudha Dubh (Localities 5 - 8) is far in excess of that normally seen.

(i) *Structural elements of the first deformational phase :* Evidence for a large D_1 recumbent fold (Tay Nappe) is given by a regional inversion of the stratigraphical sequence. **Mesoscopic** F_1 folds are not seen but there was growth of quartz, muscovite and chlorite in S_1 and the development of blind quartz veins as the result of metamorphic segregation. The progressive development and modification of D_1 structures are particularly well expressed near Rosneath (Excursion 13) and axial traces of large F_1 structures, with near-vertical axial planes because of superimposed D_4 deformation, pass through Luss (to the south) and north of Aberfoyle (Excursion 10) (Fig. 11.1b).

(ii) *Structural elements of the second deformational phase:* Locally, and particularly in the more psammitic units, there are much dissected intrafolial folds that deform S_1 and S_0 (Figs 11.3a, b; 11.4a). Some are tight but most are isoclinal. Commonly fold noses are much thicker

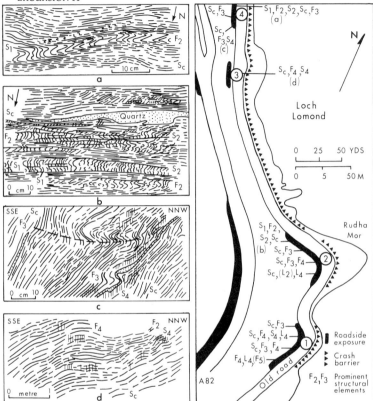

Figure 11.3. Map of Rudha Mor and examples of structural features.

than fold limbs and many occur as isolated fold hinges. There is a prominent axial planar schistosity (S_2) but on fold limbs, that greatly predominate over fold hinges, the schistosity is composite (S_c - S_1 + S_2) with evidence of **transposition**. Within, or at a very low angle to S_c, are abundant quartz masses with lensoid sections having the appearance of boudinaged quartz veins. Development as the result of syntectonic metamorphic segregation during D_1 with subsequent tectonic modification during D_2 is consistent with at least most of the textural observations. The dominant metamorphic zonation (chlorite

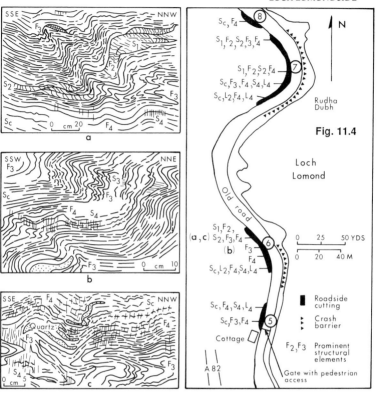

Figure 11.4. Map of Rudha Dubh and examples of structural features.

in the south, biotite, garnet in the north) formed as a response to D_1 and D_2 crustal thickening with the peak during D_2 and the isograds generally flat-lying (Fig. 11.1).

A lineation expressed as a fine colour banding formed by the alignment of micas and other mineral aggregates is present within S_c. The micas that are muscovite and chlorite in the lower grades and biotite (in places with muscovite) in the higher grades are generally < 1 mm across and a few mm long. The expression of the lineation is very patchy being best shown in **pelitic** units. It is deformed by F_3

folds and on their generally flatly-disposed long limbs it trends NW - SE to NNW - SSE with variations in attitude related to the effects of open F_4 folds. This lineation appears to be equivalent to the "stretching lineation" that is so widely expressed in the SW Highlands. Whether it is solely related to D_2 has not been determined but it is expressed in S_c, pre-dates D_3 and is referred to here as L_2. Whether D_2 is itself polyphase is not known, but it is one explanation of variations in attitude of F_2 fold hinges.

(iii) *Structural elements of the third deformational phase* : Folds (F_3) deforming S_2 and F_2 (Figs 11.3c; 4a, b) are commonly asymmetrical with generally gently to moderately inclined axial planes and axes that plunge west or east at low angles. They are not large structures with maximum observed wave length of < 2 m. The folds consistently face SSE or south and in places there is evidence for axial planar thrusts on which the movement was also consistently towards the SSE (or south). Curvature of axial planes and thrusts due to superimposed F4 folds is evident, but in some of the more psammitic assemblages the curvature is like that shown by **ramps** in **thrust duplexes**. However, utilization of the generally flat-lying S_c for much of the D_3 movement would account for both some of the retrogressive development of chlorite and the patchy expression of (remnants of) L_2. D_3 folding was dominantly **flexural** in psammitic units but **flexural-flow** in interbanded pelitic - psammitic assemblages with localized development of S_3 (Fig. 11.4b).

(iv) *Structural elements of the fourth deformational phase* : Folds (F_4) that deform the axial planes of F_3 folds and the earlier formed F_2 and S_c are the most common **mesoscopic** structures throughout the region (Figs 11.3d; 11.4b, c). They correspond to the Cowal antiform, its continuation in the Highland Border downbend, the Ben More anti-form and the Ben Lawers synform (Fig. 11.1) whose subhorizontal NE - SW ("Caledonian")-trending axes can be traced for many tens of kilometres. The folds are generally open and upright with a prom-inent axial planar cleavage (S_4) in pelitic units (Figs 11.3c, d; 11.4a, b, c) associated with microfolds and a crenulation lineation (L_4) that is prominent on most micaceous surfaces of S_c. However both the profiles of F_4 folds and the attitude of axial planes vary with box-folds occurring where asymmetrical folds with SE- and NW-dipping axial planes are juxtaposed. In places, F_3 and F_4 folds affect the same layer of S_c without the F_4 fold affecting the F_3 fold hinge: the resultant structures have the appearance of box-folds. Where F_4 folds are superposed on F_3 folds interference structures occur and these play a major structural control on the emplacement of explosion-breccia - appinite - diorite complexes in the district.

(v) *Structural elements of the fifth deformational phase*: These are very weakly developed but are much more prominent further west. Very open, upright flexures (F_5) deform F_4 hinge zones and L_4; axes trend N - S to NNE - SSW. Strong N - S joints also occur and these also exert a structural control on the development of some of the explosion-breccia - appinite - diorite complexes.

Localities 1 - 4. Rudha Mor (NN 346 000) **and nearby** (Fig. 11.3). Park in one of the lay-bys indicated in the road log. S1 deformed by F_2 with development of S_2 (and S_c) is shown in psammitic rocks in NNE-facing near-vertical faces at the northern end of Locality 2 and in subhorizontal faces at the northern end of Locality 4. S_c is the dominant planar fabric in all four exposures and its deformation by F_3 is well shown in the northern - central parts of Locality 2, the northern part of Locality 1 and the northern - central parts of Locality 4. F_4 deforming S_c dominates in Locality 3 and in much of the central and southern parts of Localities 1 and 2. In the more pelitic layers, such as at the most southerly part of Locality 1, L_4 crenulation is prominent and curvature around very open N - S-trending F_5 is seen. F_2 - S_2 deformed by F_3 is shown in the northern parts of Locality 2. F_3 deformed by F_4 with the development of S_4 and L_3 crenulation at a low angle to L_4 crenulation can be seen in a number of places in Localities 1 and 2 and at the southern end of Locality 4.

Localities 5 - 8. Rudha Dubh (NN 345 017) **and nearby** (Fig. 11.4). Park in one of the lay-bys indicated in the road log, or for cars and minibuses only, park on the access road 50 m from the A82 or south of the second white house ("Cottage" on Fig. 11.4) from the turn off.

In the central - northern part of Locality 6 and the central and northern parts of Locality 7, S_1 is deformed by F_2 folds, most of which are much dissected with S_2 developed. L_2 is best shown on the SE-facing micaceous schistosity surfaces in the southern part of Locality 7: it is at millimetre scale and its general NW - SE trend is nearly perpendicular to F_4 fold hinges and L_4 crenulation. L_2 is also shown in the southern part of Locality 6, again at a high angle to the very prominent L_4. F_3 folds little affected by later deformation are shown in the central part of Locality 6. F_4 folds, S_4 crenulation cleavage and L_4 crenulation are very prominent in the southern part of Locality 6 where L_3 and L_4 show only a small angular difference. There are also L_4 crenulations corresponding to the F_4 folds having SE- and NW-dipping axial planes. F_4 folds are also strongly expressed at the northern end of Locality 5 and at Locality 8. F_3 and F_4 folds commonly occur in juxtaposition, with F_3 axial planes strongly folded and complex patterns displayed, particularly where thin units with marked competence contrasts are adjacent, as in the northern part of Locality 6. In the southern - central parts of Locality 7 some faces are dominated by F_3 deforming S_c and others by F_4 deforming S_c.

Locality 8. S_c and blind quartz veins are deformed by open, upright F_4 folds with the development of S_4 and L_4. Adjacent to the parking place F_3 folds with subhorizontal axial planes are seen and their axial planes are curved around F_4.

Localities 10, 11. Two large vertical faces with little three dimensional exposure are composed mainly of massive psammitic units that define open F_4 folds. In the more northerly Locality 11 some inter-banded pelitic units show L_2 on S_c, tighter F_4 folds than in psammitic units, as well as S_4 and L_4. There are a few poorly expressed F_2 folds near the northern end of this exposure. In the more southerly Locality (10) there are F_3 folds with flat-lying axial planes near the southern end (near the AA box) as well as upright F_4 folds..

Locality 12. Near-vertical faces at the southeastern corner of the car park show F_4 folds deforming S_c in semipelitic and psammitic quartz - biotite schists. There are also small F_3 folds, S_1 and S_2 intersecting at a very low angle and, in schistosity surfaces near the landing stage, NW - SE-oriented biotite flakes (at mm size) define L_2. The F_4 folds are much tighter than generally seen, are commonly asymmetrical with the shorter steep limb inclined towards the northwest and have axial planes that dip towards the southeast. On subhorizontal surfaces curvature of F_4 hinges indicates D_5 folding.

Locality 13. Exposures in the vicinity of the picnic area, including a small side stream to the south, show albite porphyroblasts that have overgrown steeply-disposed NE -SW-striking S_4 in garnet - mica schists (in places with much chlorite due to retrogression). Upright F_4 folds and L_4 crenulation deforming S_c are the most prominent structures, but in places they deform F_3 folds with subhorizontal (to gently inclined) axial planes, that in turn deform the schistosity in which garnet (almandine) porphyroblasts have grown.

Locality 14. In most of the road cuttings S_c, and near-concordant blind quartz veins, are seen to be deformed by F_4 folds in psammitic, semipelitic and pelitic micaceous schists in which D_2 garnet (almandine) and post-D_4 albite (many with cores of $Ab_{100-99.5}$) occur as porphyroblasts in suitable lithologies. Chlorite is common in S_c as the result of retrogression. F_4 fold profiles vary and on the steep limbs of some F_4 folds the prominent NE - SW-trending subhorizontal crenulation is associated with F_4 axial planes and S_4 that are subhorizontal rather than steeply inclined as is generally the case. Where S_c is not steeply inclined, F_3 asymmetrical folds have E-W-trending axes and curved (by F_4) subhorizontal to gently inclined axial planes. Their distribution is patchy while the occurrence of F_2 is rare.

References
ATHERTON, M.J. 1964. The garnet isograd in pelitic rocks and its relation to metamorphic facies. *Am. Mineral.* **49**, 1331-1349.

BOWES, D.R. 1979. Structural patterns in polyphase deformed schists as illustrated by Dalradian rocks, Scotland. *Krystalinikum* **14**, 145-154.

HARTE, B., BOOTH, J.E., DEMPSTER, T.J., FETTES, D.J., MENDUM, J.R. and WATTS, D. 1984. Aspects of the post-depositional evolution of Dalradian and Highland Border Complex rocks in the Southern Highlands of Scotland. *Trans. R. Soc. Edinburgh Earth Sci.* **75**, 151-163.

JONES, K.A. 1961, Origin of albite porphyroblasts in rocks of the Ben More - Am Binnein area, Western Perthshire, Scotland. *Geol. Mag.* **98**, 41-55.

————————1964. Metamorphism of the Ben More - Am Binnein area, Western Perthshire, Scotland. *Q. J. Geol. Soc. London* **120**, 51-76.

MATHER, J.D. 1970. The biotite isograd and the lower greenschist facies in the Dalradian rocks of Scotland. *J. Petrol.* **11**, 253-275.

MENDUM, J.R. and FETTES, D.J. 1985. The Tay Nappe and associated folding in the Ben Ledi - Loch Lomond area. *Scott. J. Geol.* **21**, 41-56.

ROGERS, G., DEMPSTER, T.J.., BLUCK, B.J. and TANNER, P.W.G. 1989. A high precision U - Pb age for the Ben Vuirich granite: implications for the evolution of the Scottish Dalradian Supergroup. *J. Geol. Soc. London* **146**, 789-798.

————————and DUNNING, G.R. 1991. Geochronology of appinitic and related granitic magmatism in the W Highlands of Scotland: constraints on the timing of transcurrent fault movement. *J. Geol. Soc. London* **148**, 17 - 27.

TILLEY, C.E. 1925. A preliminary survey of metamorphic zones in the southern Highlands of Scotland. *Q. J. Geol. Soc. London* **81**, 100-112.

Excursion 12 SITHEAN SLUAIGH
C. D. Gribble

Theme :   The thermal aureole seen around the basic igneous plug at
Sithean Sluaigh represents an excellent and very rare
example of progressive metamorphism of pelitic country
rocks to extreme temperatures (called pyrometamorphism). Primarily of specialist interest.

Features :   High temperature mineral assemblages in pelitic rocks;
gabbroic plug with marginal dolerite.

Maps :   O.S.   1: 50 000 Sheet 56 Inveraray and Loch Lomond
B.G.S. 1: 63 360 Sheet 37 Inveraray
1: 50 000 Sheet 37 E Lochgoilhead

Terrain: The going is steep and rough, with the gabbro plug
presenting an area of exposed rock right at the summit of
Sithean Sluaigh.

Distance :   Sithean Sluaigh is about100 km (60 miles) by road from
Glasgow. To get there, take the A82 Loch Lomond road to
Tarbet, and then the A83 past the Rest and Be Thankful
(where there is a magnificent southerly view). Near Loch
Fyne, take the A815 south along the eastern shore of the
loch to the village of Strachur where the A886 is encountered. From the crossroads, continue along the A886 for
7.25 km (4.5 miles) until reaching the end of a forestry
plantation on the north side of the road (about 2 km beyond the junction with the B8000). The walking distance
from here is about 5 km (3 miles).

Time :   This trip takes a full day from Glasgow including the time
spent driving there and back.

Access: Parking spaces can be found at the side of the road, just
beyond the forestry plantation mentioned above.

Sithean Sluaigh is the more northerly of two summits,
the southerly one (about1 km away) being Cruach nan
Capull. Sithean Sluaigh is 435m in height and the ascent
should be made along the edge of the forestry plantation
from about grid reference (NS 060 965). Climb to the NE
for about one kilometre and then swing round to the north

and head towards the summit of Sithean Sluaigh, some 1.5 km distant. As the climb is steep take it slowly, and, once above the level of the plantation, pause frequently to admire the views of Loch Fyne.

The Gaelic word *Sithean* (pronounced shee - hen) means "a fairy hill": *Sluaigh* (sloo - ah) means "of the multitude" or "people".

Introduction

The geology of the area was first described by Gunn *et al.* (1897) as being underlain by Dalradian country rocks; in particular by **phyllites** (of the Garnetiferous Mica Schist Group described by Hill 1905) which vary in composition from **psammitic** rocks to **pelitic** rocks, and which contain quartz, albitic feldspar, muscovite and **chlorite**, and with occasional garnet, biotite and other accessory minerals also present.

The gabbro plug at the summit of Sithean Sluaigh is oval in plan with its long axis trending NW to SE; it is about 180m by 90m in size (Fig. 12.1). The plug is very well exposed, and the geological variations can be seen with ease. However, the aureole rocks are not well exposed and the best plan is to try to locate the positions of the samples shown on Figure 12.1 which were given to the Hunterian Museum, since *in situ* exposures of rock occur at these points. The numbered locations below are shown on the map (Fig. 12.1). Note that these rocks are often fine grained and their mineralogy is difficult to identify with certainty in the field, even with a hand lens.

Locality 1. The centre of the intrusion is gabbro containing basic plagioclase feldspar, augite, olivine and iron ores, with **zeolites** occasionally present.

Locality 2. The plug has a fine grained margin of dolerite exhibiting good **ophitic texture** which can be seen by the naked eye. This dolerite is exposed in places as a low, broken ledge of rock surrounding the main mass of gabbro.

Locality 3. A finer grained dolerite occurs on the north edge of the plug (Fig. 12.1), forming an outer 'skin' to the marginal dolerite. All the dolerites have a mineralogy similar to that of the main gabbro.

Locality 4. A coarse grained rock (called a **pegmatite** by Smith 1965) occurs between the gabbro and the marginal dolerite on the west side of the intrusion. It is not marked on Figure 12.1 as it is discontinuous,

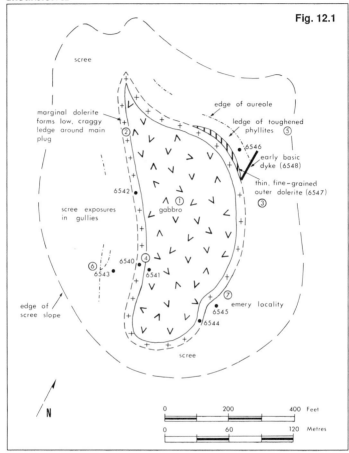

Figure 12.1. Geological map of Sithean Sluaigh (adapted from Smith 1965). Numbers (e.g. 6543) refer to specimens in the Hunterian Museum.

but this coarse material is easily identified.

Since an extensive scree is present, the exact limit of the thermal **aureole** is difficult to ascertain, but is estimated to be about 9m wide. At this distance the country rocks are baked and hardened.

156

Locality 5.   At the northern edge of the intrusion a narrow ledge of toughened phyllites occurs (Fig. 12.1). This ledge may originally have been continuous around the plug but is now seen only in a few isolated exposures which are not precisely identified on the Figure.

Locality 6.   On the SW side of the plug, a gully in the scree exposes country rocks (R6543) about 5m from the contact, and the rocks here contain **cordierite** and dark green **spinel**. The mineralogical changes which occur in these rocks depend to a large extent on the type of rock involved, with pelitic rocks showing the greatest changes.   Further breakdown of the original minerals in the country rocks can be observed as the contact is approached. At about 1.5m from the contact, the dark **hornfelses** contain spinel, cordierite and orthopyroxene, with occasional **sanidine** present. The grain size here is small and the rock is dark grey or black in colour, and also has a high specific gravity.   Nearer the contact the grain size increases and spinel, sanidine and orthopyroxene occur as constituents.

Locality 7.   On the SE side of the plug (Fig. 12.1), spinel, green **corundum** (emery), and **mullite** may occur (Smith 1965), and a specimen from this locality (R6545), a few centimetres from the contact, is entirely composed of dark green spinel set in a matrix of plagioclase.

Note that many of the minerals described above are dark coloured and fine grained, and are difficult to distinguish in the hand specimen. However they are rare minerals and many of them (spinel, orthopyroxene, etc.) are particularly beautiful when viewed in thin section, under the microscope.

Geological History

The basic igneous plug of Sithean Sluaigh was emplaced into a volcanic vent during Tertiary times; temperatures of about 900 °C were produced in the aureole. When temperatures as high as this occur, affecting pelitic rocks, the rocks start to melt with the production of a low temperature liquid (rather like a granitic liquid). When this liquid forms, any unmelted fractions remain as high temperature residua rich in alumina, magnesia and iron, and low in silica and alkalis. The major minerals formed from such material will include spinel, corundum and cordierite.

Many of the contact rocks seen at Sithean Sluaigh represent these high temperature unmelted residua which remained after the Dalradian country rocks were subjected to the high temperatures in the aureole. The low temperature (or granitic) liquid, which must have been formed when the rocks were first melted, is not seen; and this low temperature liquid was possibly added to the gabbroic magma, which is unlikely since it has a normal gabbro composition, or, more probably, was removed elsewhere. This type of hypothesis has been used to explain other rock associations of a similar nature (Evans 1964; Gribble 1968). Smith (1969) gives a very good account of the mineralogy and geochemistry of the plug and its thermal aureole.

References

EVANS, B. W. 1964. Fractionation of elements in the Cashel-Lough Wheelaun intrusion, Connemara, Eire. *Geochim. Cosmochim. Acta* **28**, 127 - 156.

GRIBBLE, C. D. 1968. The cordierite-bearing rocks of the Haddo House and Arnage districts, Aberdeenshire. *Contrib. Mineral. Petrol.* **17**, 315 - 330.

GUNN, W., CLOUGH, C. T. and J. B. HILL. 1897. The geology of Cowal. *Mem. geol. Surv. U. K.*

HILL, J. B. 1905. The geology of Mid-Argyll. *Mem. geol. Surv. U. K.*

SMITH, D. G. W. 1965. The chemistry and mineralogy of some emery-like rocks from Sithean Sluaigh, Argyllshire. *Am. Mineralog.* **50**, 1982 - 2022.

_____ 1969. Pyrometamorphism of phyllites by a dolerite plug. *J. Petrology* **10**, 20 - 55.

Excursion 13   ROSNEATH PENINSULA and LOCH LONG
P.W.G. Tanner

Themes: To examine the small-scale, mainly tectonic, structures in the Dalradian rocks immediately north of the Highland Boundary Fault and show how they can be used to deduce the geometry and relative ages of two of the largest fold structures in the UK: the Tay Nappe (D1/D2) and the Downbend antiform (D4).

Features: Dalradian greywackes, slates and phyllites; way-up structures; identification and geometry of a great variety of minor folds, lineations, and cleavages (especially those resulting from pressure-solution processes); progressive development and overprinting of one set of minor structures upon another; minor intrusions; glacial features.

Maps: O.S.   1:50 000 Sheets 56 Loch Lomond and 63 Firth of Clyde.
B.G.S   1:50 000 Sheets 30W Greenock and 38W Ben Lomond
1:63 360 Sheets 29 Rothesay and 30 Glasgow

Terrain: Coastal sections, mainly exposed to the prevailing SW wind: often slippery underfoot.

Distance and Time   The driving distance from Locality 1 to Locality 8 is about 22 km(13 miles), all on good roads. Examination of the Portincaple sections involves 1·5 km of easy walking. Allow 6 hours for this excursion, preferably starting at Locality 1 some 2 - 3 hours after high tide.

Short itinerary   If the tide is unsuitable, or if it is intended to link this excursion with a visit to the A82 Loch Lomond road sections (see Excursion 11), brief visits to localities 1, 4 and 6 are recommended.

Access: The section at Locality 1 is best examined at low tide and certainly within the period between 3 hours after high tide (HT) and 3 hours before the succeeding HT. All of the remaining sections are accessible (and more comfortable to work on) in the period between 2 hours after HT and 2 hours before the next one.

Beware slippery rocks: those at Localities 1, 4 and 6 are particularly treacherous when it is raining.

You are advised **not** to stop on the Ministry of Defence (MOD) road north from Coulport (Fig. 13.1) nor on the road over Peaton Hill a few kilometres to the SE as these areas are under constant MOD surveillance.

NOTE: there are public toilets in Kilcreggan, just to the west of the pier, with sufficient parking space for coaches.

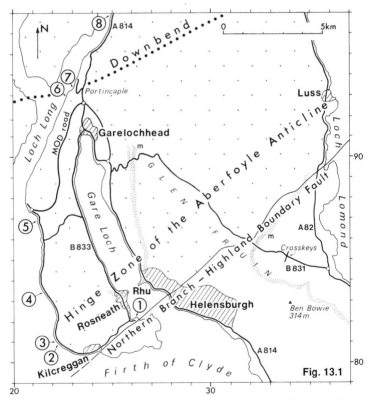

Figure. 13.1   Regional setting of the Localities 1-8 described in this guide. Dalradian rocks are shown by a dotted ornament. m, Loch Lomond Readvance terminal moraine.

Introduction

The excursion consists of a south-to-north traverse across the Dalradian rocks of the Southern Highland Group (Fig. 13.1). Starting at the Highland Boundary Fault, the traverse crosses the regional 'Steep Belt', which contains the hinge zone of the Tay **Nappe**, and then continues across the Downbend Antiform and into the 'Flat Belt' (Fig. 13.2). The Tay Nappe, which in this area is represented by the downward-facing Aberfoyle Anticline (Shackleton 1958), developed during the first deformation (D1) to affect the Dalradian rocks, prior to 590 Ma ago (Rogers *et al.*. 1989). It is folded around a much younger structure, the Downbend Antiform, which is of D4 age and probably formed at around 460-440 Ma ago (Harte *et al.* 1984)

The Tay Nappe is generally considered to have been a flat-lying structure prior to D4 and have been bent into its present attitude in the 'Steep Belt' by the Downbend Antiform. Thus a traverse northwards from the Highland Boundary Fault along the present ground surfaces takes us from the rocks which were originally at a high structural level on the upper limb of the Tay Nappe, to rocks at a lower structural level on the inverted limb of the nappe around Portincaple. Prior to D4, the latter were some 7-9 km deeper in the crust (Fig.13.2) than rocks now seen at the Highland border.

Along this traverse, we can therefore examine a progression from rocks which have only been deformed once (D1) and which show a single set of folds with an axial-planar cleavage (Locality 1, Fig. 13.3) to rocks at a deeper level in the nappe which have been affected by a later folding (D2) (Locality 2, Fig. 13.3 ; Fig.13. 5), and which develop

Table 13.1 Stratigraphy of the Dalradian rocks of the Rosneath - Loch Long area

Southern Highland Group	
south of the Aberfoyle Anticline	north of the Aberfoyle Anticline
Bullrock Greywacke Dunoon Phyllite	Beinn Bheula Schists ? Dunoon Phyllite

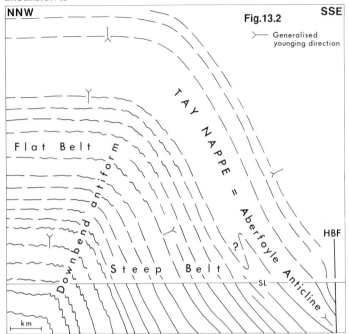

Figure. 13.2 Schematic cross-section parallel to the Gare Loch (Fig.13.1) showing the main structural elements in the area. HBF, Highland Boundary Fault.

a penetrative D2 fabric which overprints (Localities 3 & 4, Fig. 13.3 ; Fig. 13.6b), and in some cases obliterates, the D1 cleavage. Farther north along the section, between Localities 5 & 6 (Fig. 13.3) a further deformation (D3) affects the rocks and the D2 **microlithons** (seen as parallel-sided stripes on the rock surface bounded by D2 cleavage surfaces and containing the microfolded D1 fabric, see Fig. 7) are deformed by D3 minor folds. These folds are characterized by having a Z-shaped profile when viewed down the plunge of the fold hinge towards the east (i.e. they verge consistently southwards), and are not known to be associated with any major folds in the area. Finally, in the vicinity of the D4 Downbend (Localities 6-8, Fig.13.3), minor D4 folds become common: their vergence is related to their position within the

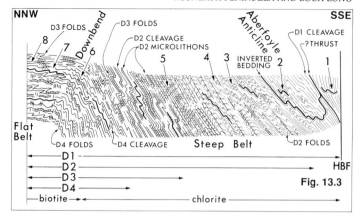

Figure. 13.3 Vertical section showing in cartoon form the style, orientation and sequence of deformations along the section shown in Fig. 13.2. Numbers 1-8 refer to the Localities described in this guide.

structure and they give rise to complex fold interference patterns.

The oncoming of the D2, D3 and D4 deformations occurs in sequence from south to north (Fig.13.3), as is well shown for the adjoining area to the east by Mendum and Fettes (1985) and in the series of synoptic structural maps on BGS Sheet 38W (Loch Lomond). Bedding in the finer-grained rocks is progressively destroyed northwards along the Rosneath-Loch Long section, largely by pressure-solution processes, but is still recognizable at the deepest levels in areas of low-strain and where the rocks are especially competent and thick-bedded. Metamorphic grade is low throughout the section, but grain size increases northwards, the rocks become increasingly recrystallized, and biotite is developed in rocks north of the Downbend. Quartz-carbonate± chlorite veins form at all stages of the deformation sequence from syn-D1 to post-D4, the early veins being subsequently deformed in rocks found in the more northerly part of the section. Quartz veining increases in abundance from south to north.

Roberts (1977) has published an excursion guide to the Dalradian rocks of Rosneath and south-east Cowal which provides a summary of the stratigraphy and structure and gives brief descriptions of localities in the Rosneath-Loch Long area which are largely alternative to those described here. D1 (this account) = B_1 (Roberts); D2 = B_{2a}; D3 + D4 = B_{2b}. Accounts of the stratigraphy and structure of Dalradian rocks in other parts of the Highland Border zone are given by Shackleton (1958), Harris *et al.* (1976), Bradbury *et al.* (1979), Harte *et al.* (1984), and Mendum & Fettes (1985).

The aim here is to provide a well-illustrated guide to a few carefully chosen localities which together demonstrate the sequence of development of minor structures and fabrics in the Dalradian rocks. It is hoped that by describing in detail relatively small rock exposures this will assist geologists who have either little experience of structural geology or are unfamiliar with the area or the structural features found there, to identify the structures shown in cartoon form in Figure 13.3. The excursion also illustrates the nature of the field evidence which can be used to analyse the sequence and geometry of structures in polyphase-deformed rocks. It is therefore essential that these exposures be preserved in their present state as there is little to be gained from hammering these low-grade rocks .

Please do not take hammers on this excursion

Itinerary

Travelling from Glasgow, coaches should proceed direct to Rosneath via Garelochhead using the A814 and B833. Note that Rhu Point, the prominent spit which extends into the Gare Loch 3 km (1.9 miles) NW of Helensburgh (Fig.13.1) marks the position of an important terminal moraine which is of the same age as that mentioned below. Mini-bus and car drivers can follow a more scenic route along Glen Fruin: they should follow the A82 to Loch Lomond, take the B831 at the Arden roundabout to Crosskeys, and thence the single track road along the glen (Fig.13.1). 1·8 km (11 miles) NW of Crosskeys there is a large parking area (NS 323 857) opposite the end of the track to Inverlauren, which provides an excellent view of the Loch Lomond Readvance end-moraine. This moraine was deposited c. 10,000 years ago and consists of a sand and gravel ridge with parallel meltwater channel (see Rose 1980 for further details). Ben Bowie with its cap of Lower Carboniferous lavas can be seen to the SE. The same end-moraine is crossed again at the head of the glen before the road descends in a series of hairpin bends (1:6 or 17% gradient) to join the A814.

Locality 1.   Camsail Bay, Rosneath (NS 262 822) : Downward facing D1 folds in a structural situation analogous to that of the hinge zone of the Aberfoyle Anticline (Tay Nappe). (Figs 13.1 & 13.4b)

The first locality is 1.2 km (³/₄ mile) SE of Rosneath church. Travelling south from Rosneath on the B833, take a left-hand turn in 1 km (0.6 miles), keep left at fork in minor road and after 200 m park in the lay-by at the bend in the road. From the lay-by, walk back up the road for 40m for easy access to the beach, then skirt around the seaweed-covered exposures of steeply dipping **greywackes** and slates on the SE side of the small bay (Camsail Bay), and clamber up on to the promontory. Note in passing the smooth glaciated surfaces on some of these exposures. The surfaces dip moderately NW and show sharply incised glacial scratches and grooves trending NW-SE; the manner in which the rock has been plucked away along the SE edge of some surfaces indicates ice flow towards the SE. The rockhead was once covered by boulder clay and this is sometimes exposed in the steep bank by the refuse tip.

The rock exposure on the small promontory illustrates well the importance of choosing the most appropriate direction for viewing, and hence interpreting, structures in the field. Looked at from above, it presents a rather featureless glaciated rock surface crossed in places by cm-spaced, irregular, anastomosing stripes which are the end-on view of a near vertical **spaced cleavage**. However, if you make your way down the steep front face of the exposure and, tide permitting, stand on the shingle and look back southwest towards the rock face, you can see the structures sketched in Fig. 13.4a. The low cliff represents a profile section through a series of gently plunging, upright folds.

The rocks belong to the Bullrock Greywacke (Fig. 13.4b; Table 13.1) and consist of thick beds (>1 m) of feldspathic greywacke with thin intervening layers of siltstone and slate. Many of the rocks are coarse-grained sandstones with clasts a mm or two in diameter: such rocks are informally referred to in the Dalradian literature as 'grits' or 'gritty sandstones' although they were probably deposited as **turbidites**. Some contain pebbles (to 0·5cm) and show inverted **graded bedding** (Fig.4a). Some of the quartz grains are of the pale blue opalescent type characteristic of Dalradian rocks in Scotland and occur together with less common clasts of pink feldspar and some pinkish-orange quartz grains, typically found in   sandstones of the Southern Highland

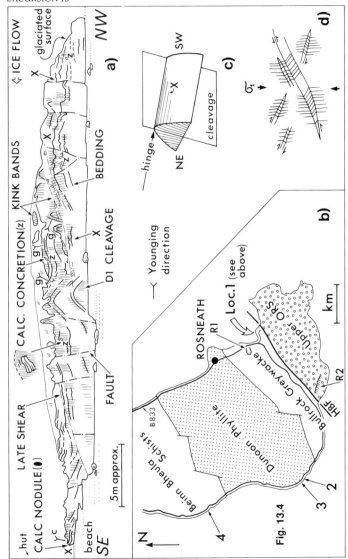

a) NW ← ICE FLOW
glaciated surface
X
Z
X
KINK BANDS
X
Z
BEDDING
CALC. CONCRETION(z)
g
Z
g
g
g
D1 CLEAVAGE
X
N
FAULT
LATE SHEAR
CALC NODULE (●)
hut
X c
beach SE
CALC NODULE (●)
5m approx.

c) SW
X
cleavage
hinge
NE

d) σ₁

b)
N
B 833
Beinn Bheula Schists
Dunoon Phyllite
ROSNEATH
R1
Loc.1 (see above)
Bullrock Greywacke
HBF
R2
Upper ORS
km
2
3
4
Fig. 13.4
~ Younging direction

Group. Excellent inverted **cross-bedding** is found in laminated siltstones at the far SE end of the exposure at the top of the beach (Fig. 13.4a).

Bedding planes in these rocks are marked by narrow zones of gnarled-looking rock with irregular pits and sets of grooves where a more calcareous horizon a few cm thick has become carious by differential weathering. The thick greywacke units contain occasional isolated rounded or elongate areas which weather differently from the enclosing rock and in which bedding laminations are commonly preserved as a series of fine ridges or ribs. These calcareous concretions formed during diagenesis and because of their quartz-poor composition did not readily develop a spaced cleavage. The concretion at location **a** (Fig. 13.4) has developed oblique to bedding. Near-vertical joint planes trending NW-SE cut across the bedding: master joints with this trend form the large surfaces on which the fold structures are displayed, and control the shape of the small headland.

A series of open to close, upright, downward **facing** D1 folds are seen in the section (Fig. 13.4a); most of them plunge gently SW towards 210-225° but locally they have slightly curved hinges and plunge NE. A spaced cleavage, consisting of cm-scale alternating quartz-rich and mica+chlorite-rich **microlithons**, which has formed as a result of **pressure-solution** processes, occurs in most of the greywackes. The cleavage is **axial planar** to the folds (Fig. 13.4c), although slightly fanned in places, and dips vary between 77° to the NW, and vertical. In places there are traces of an embryonic second cleavage which is oblique to the spaced cleavage and dips at 70-80° SE. Clasts are locally flattened in the plane of the cleavage. **Slaty cleavage** occurs in mudrocks now seen as grey laminated slates; an isolated calcareous concretion or nodule at the SE end of the section (Fig.13.4a) is flattened parallel to the cleavage trace and, assuming that it had an initially near-spherical form, its present shape gives an approximate

---

Figure. 13.4   a) True-scale drawing of geological features seen at Locality 1 on the headland in Camsail Bay, viewed from the NE. Younging directions are shown by a short arrow: c, cross-bedding; g, graded bedding. x, locality where bedding-cleavage intersection lineation can be seen. b) Locality and outline stratigraphical map of the area around Rosneath. R1 & 2 are localities from Roberts (1977). c) three-dimensional sketch of an idealised fold. d) Geometry of kink bands at Locality 1. s_1, maximum principal compressive stress. HBF, Highland Boundary Fault.

measure of the strain in the XZ plane. A **bedding-cleavage intersection lineation**, which is parallel to the hinges of the D1 folds (see Figure 13.4c for a schematic representation of these structures), is locally seen on cleavage surfaces in mudrocks as a colour banding. Localities marked 'X' on Fig. 13.4a show good examples of this feature; that at the SE end of the exposure is of particular interest as the inter-relationships between bedding, cleavage, inverted cross-bedding and the intersection lineation can be seen clearly. The spaced cleavage is deformed by small **kink bands** in a few places (Fig. 13.4a): their overall geometry is summarised in Figure 13.4d. They apparently result from sub-vertical compression (?gravitational loading) late in the Caledonian history of the area.

Several faults marked by small gullies can be seen to displace the bedding: they strike 207-225° and dip steeply to either the NW or SE. Minor quartz-carbonate ± chlorite veins (carbonate: yellowish colour, often weathered out; chlorite: grey-green to dull green, powdery appearance) trending oblique to bedding are seen; some are parallel to the spaced cleavage but none are deformed or lineated. The significance of the last observation will be seen later on.

The rocks making up the rock platform on the SE side of the small bay past the hut (off the left hand side of Figure 13.4a) are greywackes with a strongly developed D1 spaced cleavage. If you walk out on the nearest exposure to the beach just past the edge of the seaweed and turn to face the shore, two flat-lying blocks of greywacke up to 1m long are seen within the regularly-cleaved rock. Both preserve gently dipping bedding surfaces and resemble the calcareous concretions described above. They are slightly folded by D1 folds and show evidence of cleavage oblique to that in the adjoining rock. The manner in which they terminate along strike is also problematical, but one of them is cut and displaced by small fractures associated with kink bands and they may be fault-bounded. Farther SE along this section is a small quarry formerly used to provide building stone. The outcrop of the Dalradian rocks then ceases and the wide muddy bay to the SE of it marks the position of the northern branch of the Highland Boundary Fault (Fig.13.4b).

Across the bay (Fig. 13.4b) is a short section exposing Upper Old Red Sandstone conglomerates and sandstones which strike N-S and dip at 40-50° to the west. The conglomerates contain pebbles and cobbles up to 40 cm across, mainly of vein quartz, basalt, andesite, granite, **porphyry** and greenschist. Some of the clasts of metamorphic rock have a spaced cleavage and resemble the local Dalradian rocks. The Upper ORS rocks of the Rosneath Peninsula were described by Bluck (1980), who concluded that they were deposited in an alluvial fan environment. At the SE end of the exposure a 30 cm-thick sandstone-conglomerate unit is offset by three faults which trend between 230-260° and dip to the north, and a large fault with a cemented fault breccia, which trends at 113°.

Retrace your route across the bay and exit from the coast along a small path which passes between the Navigation Beacon and the large fenced compound. This leads to a road; turn right, then left at the next junction to regain the lay-by after 200m. Please note that the track leading to the hut is **private** and must **not** be used. Although it is nearby, locality 1 of Roberts (1977) (Fig. 13.4b, R1) is not recommended: it is a disused, partially flooded quarry with dangerous rock faces emblazoned with graffiti.

Locality 2.   Barons Point, Kilcreggan (NS 223 808): **Medium-sized D2 fold with axial-planar spaced cleavage** (Figs 1 & 4b).

From the lay-by return to the B833 and turn left for Kilcreggan. The road traces the margin of the Dalradian outcrop, with the Highland Boundary Fault occupying the broad hollow to the south of it.

If you are interested in the Upper Old Red Sandstone, Roberts (1977) locality 2 is worth a visit. Take a sharp left hand turn at the bottom of the hill into Kilcreggan, keep left along the single track road, and where it divides drive between the stone gateposts to park inside the King George V Recreation Ground. [Note: This area has been offered for development, so access to the section may change in future.] The Upper ORS conglomerates and sandstones are exposed in an old sea cliff: the beds dip 20-30° NW and are cut by steep SE-dipping extensional (normal) faults. The section demonstrates the variation in size and composition of the clasts in the ORS conglomerate (see Bluck 1980 for further details and regional setting).

After leaving Kilcreggan, pass the Tut-Tut (two painted glacial erratics on the foreshore) after 1km (0.6 mile) , and 1 km farther on park in a large car park on the right hand side of the road by Cove Burgh Hall and Craigrownie Parish Church. From the car park walk 140m north beside the A833 and when opposite the house named Kirklea take the small path to the beach. Bear left for 15m along the

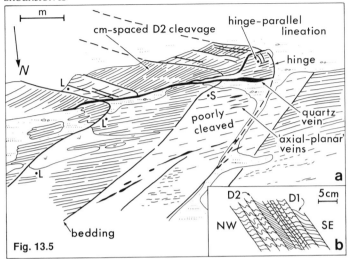

Figure. 13.5 a) Down-plunge true-scaled drawing of a D2 fold at Locality 2. L, location of bedding-cleavage intersection lineation; S, possible stretching lineation. b) Close-up view of the D2 cleavage showing the deformed D1 cleavage.

beach and examine the coarse-grained greywacke exposed in the small cliff face. The rock is made up of closely spaced, rather discontinuous layers - are these of sedimentary or tectonic origin? If tectonic, are they of D1 or later age? The answer to this puzzle can be found a few metres farther south along the beach by climbing a little way up on to the sloping rock face and looking down towards the south. The clear relationship between these closely-spaced surfaces, and bedding planes marked by the margins of thick greywacke units, can be seen (Fig. 13.5).

The bedding planes define an **antiform**, with a measured inter-limb angle of 50°, which has a well-developed, slightly fanned axial-planar spaced cleavage. The cleavage dips at 34-36° towards the SE and SSE. The hinge of the fold, which plunges at 40° due south, is well exposed and at several places around the structure the bedding-cleavage intersection lineation is seen (L on Fig. 13.5), both as a bedding intersection on the cleavage and as cleavage stripes on the

170

bedding. These lineations vary slightly in plunge, but all fall within 13° of the orientation of the exposed hinge line. A possible **stretching lineation** is found on the cleavage surface at location S (Fig.13.5) and sets of late kink bands are found on each limb of the fold.

Thin quartz veins, some of which are lineated, are either approximately parallel to the spaced cleavage or are more steeply dipping and oblique to it. A quartz-carbonate vein up to 9cm thick cuts the fold and bifurcates to the west. It contains abundant euhedral pyrite and has a 'bleached' alteration zone up to 1.5 cm wide on either side of it.

Evidence that the spaced cleavage is of D2 age has been found in thin-section but can also be seen in the field at nearby exposures. Return to the path onto the beach and closely examine the spaced cleavage by looking ENE along strike at clean, vertical rock faces. Traces of the D1 spaced cleavage can be seen within the D2 microlithons and this is particularly clear in the last exposure SE of the path as you leave the beach (Fig.13.5b). This feature will be examined in more detail at Locality 5.

The rocks at Locality 2 have been previously included with the outcrop of the Dunoon Phyllite (Roberts 1977, fig 2) but are greywackes which possibly have more lithological affinity with the younger Bullrock Greywacke (Table 13.1), although lacking the detrital pink feldspars which characterize the latter. Rock types typical of the Dunoon Phyllite are seen at the next locality.

Locality 3. Barons Point, Kilcreggan (NS 222 809) : **Disharmonic, curvilinear late folds (?D4) and crenulation cleavage in the Dunoon Phyllite.** (Figs 13.1 & 13.4b).

The locality is out of geological sequence in that features such as the D2 stretching lineation are better studied at Locality 4, where they are unaffected by later folding. However, this is impractical.

From Kirklea (Locality 2) walk 110m north along the pavement to the start of a wall made from alternating panels of stonework and iron railings, cross the road, take the path on the right into the small recreation area. Here, turn left down a path on to the beach after 35m. The area of interest lies between the iron pipe and the low cliff to the south of it.

The rocks are black phyllites (originally mudstones and siltstones) with quartz veins, and buff brown lenses and bands of limestone to

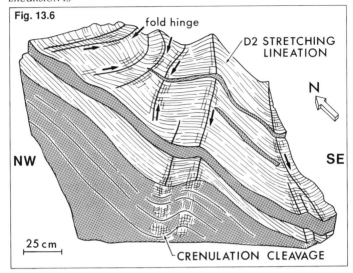

Figure. 13.6 Sketch showing the salient features of the disharmonic, curvilinear late folds (?D4) at Locality 3. Arrows indicate the approximate direction of plunge of the fold hinges.

40cm thick, all belonging to the Dunoon Phyllite. The fold structures in these rocks are best viewed from the rock platform looking east towards the shore (Fig.13.6). They consist of a series of asymmetrical warps with wavelengths of a few cm to 0·5m which verge northwards and fold a prominent lineation. The folds are **disharmonic** and when viewed from above are seen to have quite strongly curved hinges which cannot be traced for a long distance; these features are best seen in the rocks around a grass-topped knoll just south of where the path reaches the HT mark, and on a large exposure near the low-tide mark.

The asymmetrical folds in the phyllites deform a penetrative, slaty-looking cleavage which from thin-section examination is concluded to be of D2 age. Later structured fabrics such as these are typically more strongly developed in the finer-grained rocks than they are in the more competent grits and greywackes. Some quartz-carbonate veins are folded and **boudinaged**, probably during the same event which gave rise to the cleavage, and these contain a **quartz fibre lineation** which is parallel to the down-dip stretching lineation seen on the cleavage surfaces. These lineations are also folded by the late asymmetrical folds which show the same style, **vergence** and geometry as D4 minor folds seen farther north in the vicinity of the Downbend Antiform. The folds result from localized D4 strain in an incompetent, fissile unit SE of the general zone in which the D4 deformation typically affects all lithologies (Fig. 13.3).

A new **crenulation cleavage** is developed parallel to the axial surfaces of the late folds. Both discrete (marked by small fractures) and zonal (marked by microcrenulations) types of cleavage are present, and a crenulation lineation is seen parallel to the fold hinges.

Return to the car park either by retracing your route along the B833, or if the tide is sufficiently low, by an easy walk along the coast to the Memorial cross opposite the car park.

Locality 4. Knockderry Castle (NS 215 834): **D2 minor folds with northerly vergence associated with a new D2 fabric and a stretching lineation.**

From the car park travel north on the B833 through Cove for 3 km (1.9 miles) to Knockderry Castle. **Beware of meeting coaches** at the very sharp right-hand bend just before the Castle. Park in the lay-by (large enough to take a coach) which is on the left-hand side of the road just after the road straightens out following the double bend.

The whole section adjacent to the lay-by shows features of interest but it is best to start in the short stretch at the north end of the section before examining the remainder. The rocks here are greywackes and phyllites belonging to the Beinn Bheula Schists.

Walk northwards along the road for 65m and take the small path left to the shingle beach. Northwards from here there are numerous examples of minor folds with a Z-profile (northward vergence); they plunge at about 35° to the SSE (204°) and have axial planes which dip at 45-50° to the SE. Careful examination of the hinge zones of these minor folds shows that they fold both the lithological layering and an early spaced cleavage (D1). A new, generally widely-spaced, pressure solution cleavage is developed parallel to the axial surfaces of the folds and where the two cleavages are locally of equal development (especially in the more siliceous rocks) the layers are divided up into columns with a rhombic cross-section. These features are illustrated in a composite sketch in Figure 13.7a.

After about 40m there is a small overhanging face with an iron pipe

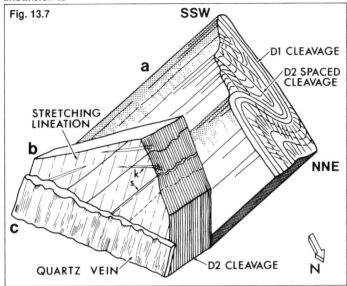

Figure. 13.7 Composite diagram showing the geometrical relationships between:- a) D2 folds; b) D2 penetrative cleavage in phyllite, and c) lineated quartz veins, at Locality 4. k, kink bands; s, bedding trace on D2 cleavage.

to the north of it. On the low rock platform between the pipe and the wall at the end of the section is an exposure of grey-brown phyllite. Bedding in the phyllite is marked by rusty-coloured bands which make a high angle with the cleavage and give rise to a very clear bedding-cleavage intersection lineation. Although the cleavage looks like a first generation penetrative slaty cleavage in the field, under the microscope it is seen to be a very closely spaced D2 crenulation cleavage with much new growth of white mica parallel to the D2 cleavage surfaces. The same features are seen at the southern end of the section where the main fabric in a thick band of phyllite is a micro-scale (D2) crenulation cleavage axial planar to folds revealed by colour banding in the rock. In the phyllite at the north end of the section, a fine D2 stretching lineation plunging at 48° to 137° is seen on the cleavage planes and, in good light, a very fine near-horizontal **crenulation lineation** can be seen on some of these surfaces, in addition to variably-orientated kink bands. These features of the phyllite are summarised in Figure 13.7b.

It is an instructive exercise to measure the orientation of the axial surfaces and hinges of folds in the greywackes, and the orientation of the cleavage surfaces and bedding-cleavage intersection lineations in the phyllites and compare them. It should be clear that, if sufficient measurements are made, the axial surfaces of the folds and of the cleavages are statistically parallel, as are the hinges of the folds and the bedding-cleavage intersection lineations. The geometry and vergence of these D2 structures is particularly well shown in a good three-dimensional exposure of a Z-fold at a point on the rock platform exactly in line with the wall at the end of the section. As we move northwards into the Flat Belt such D2 folds become difficult to identify as the pressure-solution cleavage becomes dominant and strongly overprints and obscures the bedding.

Deformed quartz veins are found in both rock types and many of them carry a fairly coarse quartz fibre lineation which represents the direction of extension during D2 and is parallel to the stretching lineation seen in the phyllite (Fig. 13.7c). Later quartz veins oblique to the D2 cleavage are also seen, and two thick siliceous greywacke beds (up to 0.6m thick) near the iron pipe have behaved as particularly competent units and show several sets of extensional quartz veins.

Other features to note on the return journey along the rock platform to the lay-by are: - a) intersection lineations between the D1 and D2 cleavages on the sides of upstanding D2 microlithons, b) a few brown-weathering limestone bands, and c) centimetre-scale graded sandstone units which if thin-sectioned give clear evidence that the beds are inverted and that the D2 folds face down to the south.

Locality 5. Letter Layo, Coulport (NS 212 869) : Modification of bedding and D1 cleavage during formation of D2 microlithons
(Fig. 13.1)

From Locality 4 continue north for 3.5 km (2.2 miles), past the turning to Garelochhead, and park at the northern end of the second long lay-by, opposite the track to Letter Layo. This locality is valuable in showing different stages in development of the D2 microlithons which, in the more deformed rocks farther north, provide a datum for identifying the D3 and D4 structures. Superb examples of these structures were once exposed on the coast just past the Royal Naval

Armaments Depot at Coulport but these have now been destroyed as a result of the Trident expansion programme.

The best examples of D2 microlithon development are seen at the extreme north end of the section. This is reached either by walking north along the road (**beware traffic on bend**) and turning on to the beach after 100m, or walking along the coast and around the small headland. The 75m of wave-washed exposures north of the iron pipe are best, and at the far north end clear relationships between bedding (marked by brown uncleaved or poorly cleaved greywackes), the D1 cleavage (clockwise to bedding at various angles), and the D2 cleavage and microlithons (anti-clockwise to both bedding and D1 cleavage) are seen. These relationships are shown schematically in Figure 13.8. Grading shows the beds to be inverted at the north end of the section and both the D1 and D2 folds are downward facing (Fig. 13.8). There are numerous deformed quartz-carbonate-chlorite veins in these rocks.

In places the mean orientation of the deformed D1 fabric is at right angles to the trace of the D2 cleavage: a relationship commonly seen in the former exposures at Coulport. The D2 hinges and the intersection lineation between the D1 cleavage stripes and the D2 microlithons plunges at 38-52° to 176-206°, similar to their orientation at Locality 4. The green phyllite bands have a penetrative D2 micro-scale crenulation cleavage, similar to that of the brown phyllite at Locality 4, which is

Figure. 13.8   Composite diagram showing the relationships between inverted bedding (b), D1 cleavage and D2 microlithons (m) at Locality 5.

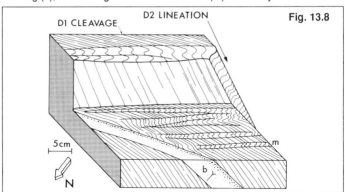

axial planar to folds defined by lithological banding plus D1 cleavage. D2 microlithons appear pale in some rocks due to their probable enhanced quartz content.

Similar relationships to those described above are found in the rest of the section and are best viewed by looking down-dip at the rocks on the return journey to the lay-by. Near the iron pipe, glacial scratches and grooves on WNW - dipping ice-smoothed surfaces trend 333° and plucking structures indicate ice flow to the SSE.

Locality 6.   Portincaple, south section (NS 228 932) : **Steep south limb of the Downbend   Antiform adjacent to the hinge zone; development of D3 and D4 minor folds and fabrics** (Figs 13.1 & 13.9).

From Letter Layo drive a short distance north to the Coulport roundabout, take the MOD road to the Whistlefield roundabout (Fig. 13.1) where you take the first exit (A814, Arrochar) and 200m after passing under a railway bridge, make a sharp left turn to Portincaple (signposted). Limited roadside parking is available in the village for cars and mini-buses (see Fig. 13.9); coaches should drop the party at the road junction and return to pick them up at an appointed time. Allow at least 2 hours for the stop at Portincaple (Localities 6 & 7).

The rocks at Localities 6 and 7 are greywackes with thin phyllite

Figure. 13.9   Sketch map showing the location at Portincaple of sections **AB** (Locality 6), **CD** (Locality 7) on Fig. 13.10 and of dykes D^{a-d} mentioned in the text.

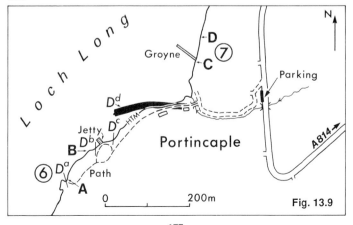

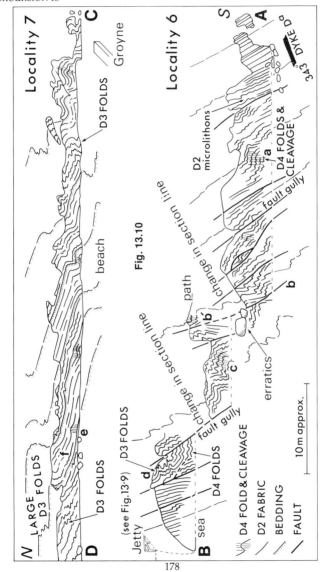

Fig. 13.10

horizons belonging to the Beinn Bheula Schists. No clear and entirely unambiguous way-up structures have been noted in these rocks, which is not surprising since they have been affected by two episodes of penetrative deformation and pressure-solution (D1 & D2), and two further episodes of folding (D3 & D4). Three roughly N-S trending dykes labelled here D^{a-c} occur at Portincaple. All are pale brown in thin section, consisting largely of an interlocking mosaic of cloudy feldspar laths (to 0.3mm long) and some quartz, and are highly altered with much calcite and chlorite. They can probably be correlated with the felsic dykes of the Lower Devonian age shown in the adjoining area of BGS Sheet 38W (Loch Lomond). The thick dyke D^d (Fig. 13.9) is less altered and is a continuation of the Permo-Carboniferous quartz-dolerite (Q^d) that has been traced ENE to just south of Inverbeg Hotel on sheet 38W.

Please do not hammer the Dalradian rocks at Portincaple.

The route to the beach is shown on Figure 13.9: near the end of the main track turn left across the bridge over the stream, take the path through an iron gate, past the boatyard. Follow the path through a second iron gate, keeping to the left hand path (muddy) which leads down to a small bay with a large grass-covered knob of rock on the north side. Asymmetrical gently plunging D4 folds can be seen on the south side of the knoll, and are best viewed downplunge to the ENE (065°). The folds are reminiscent of those seen at Locality 3 (Fig.13.6) but here occur in more siliceous greywackes. Section **AB** (Fig. 13.10) starts at the gully on the north side of this exposure. Deep water lies close to the edge of the rock platform at all states of the tide and the rocks are slippery - **take care!**

Section **AB** (Fig. 13.10) lies on the south limb of the Downbend, a regional monoform whose axial trace passes approximately between Localities 6 and 7. The axis is poorly defined because the structure has a complex rounded hinge zone. The section is dominated by a steep southerly dipping composite **foliation** which comprises bedding modified by the D1 and D2 cleavages and is now largely seen as a strongly developed D2 fabric. As shown in cartoon form in Figure 13.3 (between Localities 5 & 7) this foliation is locally affected by minor D3 folds which have a southerly vergence (Z-shaped down-plunge

---

Figure. 13.10 True-scaled N-S sections at Portincaple along lines **AB,CD** (Localities 6 & 7) on Fig. 13.9. Locations **a-f** referred to in the text.

profile). A new D3 spaced or crenulation cleavage is developed in places, although this is seen best farther north in more pelitic units. Superimposed on all of the earlier folds and fabrics are abundant, gently plunging, D4 minor folds which verge north towards the antiform (Fig. 13.3, Locality 6) and are locally accompanied by yet another crenulation or spaced cleavage. As deformation increases northwards across the area, where bedding can be seen it generally parallels the D2 fabric.

The section is dissected by ten faults, several of which occupy gullies and give rise to pronounced steps in the rock platform (Fig. 13.10). They dip at 44-84° S and strike consistently at 070-075° broadly parallel to the mean trend of the main foliation. In detail, however, beds are cut out at the fault planes, especially in the footwall.

Dyke D^a is poorly exposed: it trends 343° and occupies the gully at the beginning of the section **AB** (Fig. 13.10). In the first 10m of the section a planar D2 fabric (identification checked in thin section) dipping at about 60° S dominates the exposure, and by careful searching, D2 microlithons can be found (Fig. 13.10). Thus the structural situation is approximately equivalent to that at Letter Layo (Locality 5) except that here the D2 fabric is more intensely and uniformly developed and it is also affected by later folds and warps. The D1 'stripes' in more siliceous beds are with few exceptions preserved as relics within D2 microlithons. Farther along the section most of the folds are of D4 age and have a northerly vergence (with one steep and one gently dipping limb) and steep NNW-dipping axial surfaces. A typical, rather widely-spaced, D4 crenulation cleavage is developed locally in the more argillaceous rocks, as at location **a** (Fig.13.10), and D2 microlithons are folded.

To maintain the same profile view of the D3 and D4 structures, a new line of section has to be taken when the two glacial erratics are reached. Fault **b** (Fig. 13.10) is traced eastwards across the rock platform to its inferred position in a grassy knoll at **b'**. At location **c** (Fig. 13.10), on a low cliff face formed parallel to a N-S fault, small symmetrical D4 folds occur on the gently dipping middle limb of a much larger D4 fold. A steeply dipping D4 cleavage is developed locally and regularly-spaced D2 microlithons are folded around the structures. On the rock platform in front of these structures, **curvilinear** (?D4) folds seen in three dimensions deform a clear D2 stretching lineation which trends NW-SE and is parallel to a quartz fibre lineation seen in nearby deformed quartz veins (cf. Locality 4, Fig. 13.7b).

The line of section changes again at the next fault, which occupies a pronounced gully and in its footwall at location **d** (Fig. 13.10) are a set of well-exposed curvilinear E- and W-plunging D3 folds which fold the D2 fabric. They have axial surfaces dipping at <20° N which are parallel to a D3 crenulation cleavage and are in marked contrast to the generally more steeply dipping D4 structures. At a lower level in the footwall section, and also affecting the D3 folds, is a train of symmetrical, open, doubly-plunging, upright D4 minor folds which deform the D2 stretching lineation and show hinge-parallel crenulation lineation trending ENE-WSW.

Having reached the end of the section at **B** walk along the rock platform to the jetty. Dyke D^{b,} which strikes N-S and is 1.5m thick, crops out just south of the jetty. From here to section **CD** (Locality 7) the rock exposure is neither as good nor as continuous as in the other two areas but there are several small cliff faces which display relationships between the various sets of structures similar to those described above.

In the rock face on the north side of the track to the jetty is an example of D2 microlithons being reworked to form D3 microlithons. Dyke D^c forms a wall-like exposure 40m farther north: it has an almost N-S strike, dips 50-56° W, and is partially brecciated and highly carbonated. A prominent rock face some 50m north of the dyke shows a 0·8m-thick band of pebbly greywacke with prominent clasts (to 8mm) of blue quartz and cloudy feldspar; there is a thin skin of fault breccia adhering to the face . This massive uncleaved rock contrasts with the thin greywacke sandstones, quartz veins and phyllites noted above, which contain D4 folds with a discrete crenulation cleavage superimposed on D3 folds. It shows that even in rocks as deformed as these are, competent units still appear to remain relatively undeformed and unaffected by pressure-solution processes. Another clean rock face is seen 15m farther on and 5m south of the southern margin of a quartz dolerite dyke, D$^{d.}$ It occurs at the end of a small cliff near a group of large boulders and is the best example in this section of D2 microlithons and early quartz veins folded by D3 folds and overprinted by a steep to vertical D4 crenulation cleavage in the phyllites. The dyke has a chilled margin, is of probable Permo-Carboniferous age, and trends approximately east-west; it is ~18m thick and both contacts with the Dalradian rocks can be examined.

Locality 7. Portincaple, north section (NS 231 934): **Hinge zone and north limb of the Downbend Antiform; large D3 folds.** (Figs 13.1 & 13.9) .

From dyke Dd cross the beach and head NE for the landward end of the large groyne which marks the start of the section **CD** (Figs 13.9 & 13.10). This section lies slightly to the north of the main hinge zone of the Downbend Antiform (Fig. 13.3). Features of interest are the thick-bedded, coarse grained greywacke units (grits) making up much of the sequence, part of the Beinn Bheula Schists, and the presence of several key bedding surfaces which can be traced right

Figure. 13.11   Sketch of the fabrics seen on a flat rock face at location **f**, Fig. 13.10 at Portincaple. See text for explanation. The convergence of the top right and bottom left sides of the drawing is partly the result of perspective.

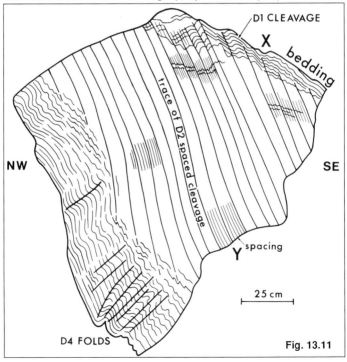

across the exposures and are marked by a dotted ornament on Figure 13.10. The greywackes contain clasts up to 0·5cm across and have a finely spaced (1-3mm) pressure-solution cleavage which is discontinuous in appearance, resembling that seen earlier at Locality 2, and here folded by D3 and D4 folds. Large-southward verging D3 folds and minor D3 folds are overprinted by upright, symmetrical D4 warps and small folds which have an axial-planar crenulation cleavage (Fig 13.3, Locality 7; and section **CD**, Fig.13.10).

At location **e** (Fig.13.10) D2 microlithons containing the D1 fabric are affected by gently plunging (11° to 062°) D4 warps with a near vertical crenulation cleavage striking at 060°. Nearby, at location **f** (Fig. 13.10), is a rock face over a metre across which, when dry and seen in good light, shows the initially puzzling, set of structures shown in Fig. 13.11. A partial explanation for this complex pattern is that the lamination seen approximately parallel to bedding at X (and apparently anticlockwise to bedding on the lower face) is the D1 spaced cleavage; the steeply dipping fabric reworking it is the D2 spaced cleavage (Y); and the folds which deform the early spaced cleavage along the bottom edge of the surface are minor D4 folds. The unit is a single bed of non-graded coarse-grained greywacke containing blue opalescent quartz pebbles to 5cm across.

Locality 8.   Glenmallon, Loch Long (NS 249 965) : **Structures illustrating the geometry of the 'Flat Belt'** (Fig.13.1).

From Locality 7 return to the main road (A814) and travel some 4km (2.5 miles) to the dock at Glenmallon. After passing the entrance to the MOD private road to Glen Douglas on the right hand side, continue for a further 370m and park in the large lay-by on the left. Prior permission has to be obtained from the MOD (at the nearby control post, if manned) to park in the MOD car park on the Glen Douglas road.

The locations noted below are all in the greywackes and associated rocks of the Beinn Bheula Schists. These locations when taken together give on the one hand a good impression of the beguiling structural simplicity of the "Flat Belt" and on the other hand give indications of the true complex structural state of the rocks i.e. that these rocks have undergone the same D1-D4 structural events as rocks on the steep, south limb of the Downbend (see Locality 8, Fig. 13.3) but with greater intensity. The structural age of spaced fabrics in the 'Flat

Belt' is not easy to determine as DI stripes are sometimes preserved and may be reworked by D2, D3 and even D4 microlithons. Typically, D2 cleavage dominates the exposures and related megascopic D2 folds if present are difficult to discern. Rock exposures are accessible from two platforms constructed on Loch Long side and in a small cutting at the entrance to the turning to Glen Douglas.

From the lay-by, walk back south 160m to the path and steps down to the first platform. The exposures here show a nearly horizontal D2 fabric corrugated by D4 minor folds, which plunge towards 055° and are accompanied by a strong crenulation lineation. A faint stretching lineation (?D2) trending 133-143° is seen on some surfaces and flat-lying D2 microlithons can be seen in the exposure by the foot of the lamp post. Return to the road, past the path to the second platform (no access to rocks) and continue south for a further 40m to platform 3. Access is via a steep 4m steel ladder and there is a good view of exceptionally planar (for these rocks), flat-lying beds to the south of the platform. D2 microlithons deformed by D4 folds are seen along the seaward edge of the exposure north of the platform. Having returned to the road then walk a farther 150m south, cross the A814 to examine the rock face on the south side of the road to Glen Douglas. The part of the face closest to the main road shows evidence of all of the deformation phases. The overall near-horizontal foliation is folded by upright D4 folds, which locally have a chevron style, and there are many thick, irregular, sub-horizontal quartz veins. Note that these veins are not deformed and lineated, and are later in age than the syn- or pre-D2 veins noted farther south. D3 minor folds verging south are common (good examples occur 4m north of the 'parking area' sign near the north end of section) and deform a spaced cleavage that can be seen to be of D2 age; they also fold D2 isoclinal folds which themselves fold the D1 spaced cleavage. The early stages of both D3 and D4 microlithon development are seen in these rocks as 1-2-cm wide bands of folded or kinked D2 fabric.

There are three possibilities for the return journey to Glasgow:

a. Retrace the route via the A814 through Helensburgh; **b.** Continue north along the A814 past the old Murlaggan landslip to Arrochar, then turn east to Tarbet and examine some of the localities along the A82 Loch Lomond section (Excursion 11); or **c.** if travelling in a car or mini-bus continue north for 5km (3 miles) on the A814 and take the single track road (some hairpin bends and steep gradients) through Glen Douglas to join the A82 at Inverbeg. Note the landslip on Tullich Hill immediately to the north on entering Glen Douglas from this direction.

Acknowledgements

I am grateful to John Mendum for reviewing, and suggesting valuable improvements to this article : to Bill Henderson for his comments on the geology of the Coulport-Kilcreggan area; and to Alec Herriot for advice on the igneous dykes.

References

BLUCK, B.J. 1980. Evolution of a strike-slip fault-controlled basin, Upper Old Red Sandstone, Scotland. *Spec. Publ. int. Ass. Sediment.* **4**, 63-78.

BRADBURY, H.J., HARRIS, A.L. and SMITH, R.A. 1979. Geometry and emplacement of nappes in the Central Scottish Highlands. *In* Harris, A.L., Holland, C.H. & Leake, B.J. (eds), The Caledonides of the British Isles-Reviewed. *Spec. Publ. Geol. Soc. London* **8**, 213-20.

HARRIS, A.L., BRADBURY, H.J. and MCGONIGAL, M.H. 1976 The evolution and transport of the Tay Nappe. *Scott. J. Geol.* **12**. 103-13.

HARTE, B., BOOTH, J.E., DEMPSTER, T.J., FETTES, D.J., MENDUM, J.R. and WATTS, D. 1984. Aspects of the post-depositional evolution of Dalradian and Highland Border Complex rocks in the Southern Highlands of Scotland. *Trans* R. Soc. Edinb. : Earth Sci. **75**, 151-163.

MENDUM, J.R. and FETTES, D.J. 1985. The Tay nappe and associated folding in the Ben Ledi-Loch Lomond area. *Scott. J. Geol.* **21**, 41-56.

ROBERTS, J.L. 1977. The Dalradian rocks of Rosneath and south-east Cowal. *Scott. J. Geol.* **13**, 101-11.

ROGERS, G., DEMPSTER, T.J., BLUCK, B.J. and TANNER, P.W.G. 1989. A high precision U-Pb age for the Ben Vuirich granite: implications for the evolution of the Scottish Dalradian Supergroup. *J. Geol. Soc. London* **146**, 789-98.

ROSE, J. 1980. 'Rhu' and 'The western side of Loch Lomond' *In* : Jardine, W.G. (ed.) *Quarternary Research Association Field Guide: Glasgow region.* 31-39.

SHACKLETON, R.M. 1958. Downward-facing structures of the Highland Border. *Q.J. Geol. Soc. London* **113**, 361-92.

Excursion 14 GREENOCK to LARGS
E.M. Patterson

Themes: Upper Old Red Sandstone and basal Carboniferous sediments: dyke swarms of three ages.

Features: Cornstones, cementstones, dykes of Lower Carboniferous, Permo-Carboniferous and Tertiary age, vent agglomerate, sill.

Maps: O.S.   1: 50 000 Sheet 63   Firth of Clyde
              B.G.S. 1: 63 360 Sheet 29   Rothesay
                      1: 50 000 Sheet 30W   Greenock

Terrain: For walkers the coast road is essentially level but carries heavy traffic. The footpath is discontinuous, and is on the side distant from the shore exposures. There are occasional lay-bys for car users. Shore exposures are readily accessible but slippery.

        The inland route is almost entirely single track road: there are sufficient lay-bys for car users. The surface is good. Rough walking on moorland grass flanks the higher parts of the route. There is no public transport. The road climbs to 269m (nearly 900 feet), and for 8km (5miles) there is no human habitation or shelter.

Distance and Time: About 48km (30miles) of driving for the round trip with short walks to the exposures. A full day excursion which can be reduced by selecting exposures of personal interest.

Access: If no car is available there is rail access to Largs (from the south) and to Wemyss Bay (from the north) both taking an hour from Glasgow. Between Largs and Wemyss Bay there is a bus service. No previous permission needed for access to exposures.

Figure 14.1. Geological map of the area from Greenock to Largs.

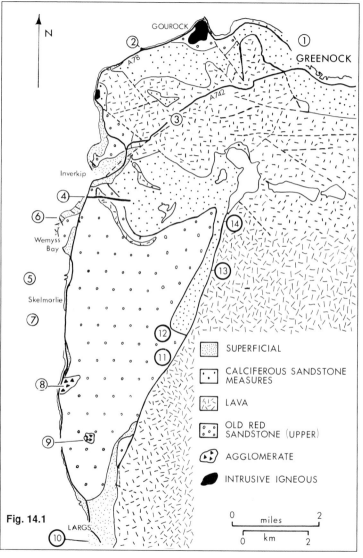

Fig. 14.1

SUPERFICIAL

CALCIFEROUS SANDSTONE
MEASURES

LAVA

OLD RED
SANDSTONE (UPPER)

AGGLOMERATE

INTRUSIVE IGNEOUS

Introduction

This excursion follows a circular route (Fig. 14.1) by the coast road and by a moorland road, and may be taken either clockwise or anti-clockwise. The coastal route affords particularly good opportunities for the study of three different dyke swarms. These are of Lower Carboniferous, Permo-Carboniferous and Tertiary age, and cut sedimentary rocks of Upper Old Red Sandstone and Lower Carboniferous age.

Itinerary

Locality 1. Craigs Top, Greenock. A good vantage point from which to see the raised beaches, a large quarry in the Craigmuschet sill, and a general view of the Clyde Estuary. The Craigmuschet sill is formed of quartz-**keratophyre**, and contains **phenocrysts** of oligoclase and soda-orthoclase, together with finer quartz and felspar. In the quarry, the rock is **drusy,** with well developed crystals of quartz, **barytes, fluorite** and **tourmaline**.

Locality 2. Pier (NS 768 219). Along the coast between Gourock and Cloch Point there is a repeated alternation of two facies: shales and cementstones alternating with calcareous sandstones, red **marls** and **cornstones**. There is thus produced an interbanding of types of sediments generally regarded as typical of the Calciferous Sandstone (Ballagan Beds) and Upper Old Red Sandstone respectively.

At M'Inroy's Point, midway between Gourock and Cloch Lighthouse, two Tertiary olivine **tholeiite** dykes outcrop above low water. One is **xenolithic: tridymite** has developed in sandstone fragments, and **cordierite-buchite** from shale (Herriot 1971).

The Highland Boundary Fault lies offshore, and metamorphic rocks of the Dalradian series form the Cowal hills on the opposite shore.

Locality 3. Spango Valley, the inland route between Greenock and the coast at Inverkip, is taken by the railway; and follows a deep valley eroded along a splay-offshoot of the Highland Boundary Fault. In spite of the marked erosion feature, there is apparently no great displacement of the rocks on each side.

From the village of Inverkip to Largs, the shore gives almost continuous exposures in the Upper Old Red Sandstone. In the 13km (8 miles) of coast between the two places, at least 100 dykes are exposed.

During 1971, 0.8km (0.5 mile) south of Inverkip, excavation work for a new power station opened extensive new exposures of red-brown sandstones, cut by Tertiary dykes. On the widened road section between the village and the power station site, a rock face offers fresh material in sandstone, cornstone, and in dykes and a sill-feeder of **trachyte**.

Localities 4-5. Lower Carboniferous dykes. These are the intrusive representatives of the Clyde Plateau Lavas. While the bulk of the extrusive activity was basaltic in nature, the Misty Law-Knockside hills area (NS 295 620), ENE of Largs, was the focus of early **rhyolite** and trachyte eruptions, with associated vent-**agglomerates** and ash beds. The maximum density of occurrence of the swarm is aligned on the Misty Law centre. Though no systematic petrographic study has been made of them, they are mostly felsic or semi-felsic in type, and probably correspond to the **bostonites** of the Great Cumbrae. There are few basalts; the dykes typically trend ENE and average about 1.2m (4ft) in width. Fifty dykes of this swarm occur between Inverkip and Largs, but the maximum density of occurrence is between Knock Castle and Largs, where there are 30 in 1.6km (1 mile) of shore. Their aggregate thickness of 34m (115ft) corresponds to a crustal stretch of 2 per cent.

The Permo-Carboniferous dykes of the Midland Valley and the Highlands are quartz-dolerites, and are typically solitary and thick. Two examples are encountered in this section. The first is 12m (40ft) in width and occurs 400m (440yds) south of Inverkip (Locality 4). The other is 25m (80ft) across, and appears through the boulder beach just south of the railway station at Wemyss Bay (Locality 5). Both have the E-W direction which typifies this swarm.

Locality 6 (NS 188 701). **Tertiary dykes** of the Mull swarm, numerous in the Lorne and Cowal districts of the mainland of Argyll, extend across the Firth of Clyde and are seen on this shore section. They trend principally NW or NNW, but occasional E-W and N-S variants are present. On the promontory near Castle Wemyss (Locality 6), 13 dykes outcrop along 1.6km (1 mile) of shore, and as many in the railway cutting alongside the main road. A triple intrusion, 11m (35ft) in width, occurs 400m (440yds) north of Castle Wemyss.

Locality 7. Tertiary dykes are also plentiful at Skelmorlie, where 19 may be counted in 1,213m (4,000ft) of shore. A striking example, 4.5m

(15ft) in width, and crowded with fresh **porphyritic** felspars is well exposed just south of the southernmost house between the main road and the sea.

Locality 8. Auchengarth (NS 191 645): **Cementstones and agglomerate.** Midway between Skelmorlie and Largs, the ubiquitous red sandstones are replaced over a distance of 0.8km (0.5 mile) by Cementstone strata and by black basaltic agglomerate. The Cementstones consist of red, grey and green shales, white and lilac cementstone bands and pebbly white sandstone. They are faulted against Old Red Sandstone to the north but disappear under a boulder beach to the south. They dip at 60°-70° to the west, and have been brought down by a series of faults whose course is parallel to the coast.

The basaltic agglomerate appears to be later than the fault, and rises steeply through the Cementstone strata over a N-S distance of about 121m (400ft). Sparse inland exposures suggest that the vent has a roughly oval plan, 1,200m x 400m (1,320yds x 440yds) in extent, and elongated towards the NE. It is cut by a small trachyte mass on its southern margin, and by three dykes of the Tertiary swarm.

Locality 9. The Knock (NS 202 628) : **Vent agglomerate.** 0.8km (0.5 mile) east of Knock Castle and 3.2km (2 miles) north of Largs, the rising ground culminates in The Knock 217m (715ft) high which is formed of basaltic agglomerate infilling a roughly circular vent, 400m (440yds) across: **Dalmeny** and **Dunsapie** type basalts have been recognised in the component blocks. A vent intrusion of Dunsapie type basalt cuts the agglomerate.

As the north end of the town of Largs is approached, the outcrops of red-brown sandstones and the numerous and rather similarly coloured dykes, disappear below boulder-strewn beach, and rock is then only seen in the cliff backing the lowest raised beach.

Locality 10. The Pencil (NS 207 577). About a kilometre south of Largs stands the Pencil monument, commemorating the defeat of the Norsemen by the Scots at the Battle of Largs in 1263. Turn off the A78 at the access road to Largs Yacht Haven (NS 210 576) opposite the Golf Course. The road crosses the railway and there is a car park immediately on the left. From here a well-defined path leads around the small bay to The Pencil. Here, particularly at low tide, can be seen excellent exposures of Old Red Sandstone with sedimentary structures, dykes and 'sills' with baked and chilled margins, and minor faults.

From Largs there is the choice of returning to Greenock along the coast road or completing a roughly circular tour by taking the inland route. This commences from the town of Largs, about one mile from the northern end of the town. Turn off the A78 at the 'Brisbane Glen' signpost, turn left after a quarter-mile, and enter the Brisbane Glen. The scenic contrast between the western and eastern slopes of the Glen are well seen. To the west, smooth, grass-covered ground is underlain by Old Red Sandstone, rising to the volcanic vent of The Knock. To the east, downfaulted volcanic rocks of the Clyde Plateau Lavas produce rock-scarps and terraces which rise inland towards the rounded summits of Hill of Stake 522m (1711ft) and Misty Law, 507m (1662ft).

Alluvium and raised beach gravels and sand extend into the lower reaches of Brisbane Glen. At higher levels the Noddsdale Burn has cut through red till. Approaching Whittlieburn Farm what may be a river terrace remnant lies to the east of the burn, but detailed mapping of the area has yet to be undertaken.

Locality 11. Castle Hill (NS 222 638) forms a striking conical feature just north of Tourgill Bridge. The area of its summit is insufficient to have held a fortification and it is considered to be a large exhumed basaltic erratic derived from the lava country to the north.

Locality 12. Permo-Carboniferous dyke (NS 228 647). A quarry on the east side of the road is in one of the solitary E-W quartz dolerite dykes. It is of Permo-Carboniferous age, crosses the valley, and is cut at the Noddsdale Water by a NW Tertiary dolerite. The two dykes form the sill of a picturesque waterfall, just below a stone bridge that takes a road to the abandoned steading of East Grassyards.

Outerwards Reservoir lies athwart the Noddsdale Water and since the road here lacks passing places, **care in driving** is necessary for a quarter mile. An extensive lay-by is reached at the north end of the reservoir. Sections in red till are seen across the valley in two small burns.

From here there are good views of several tributary burns, notably the South Black Burn and North Black Burn, which descend the steep east side of the Brisbane Glen. Their courses are deeply incised in basic lavas and are provisionally regarded as sub-glacial chutes, which originated when the glen was still occupied by downwasting ice. The gentler slopes on the shaded western side of the glen lack any such features.

Locality 13. As the road climbs to a summit at 273 metres, the watershed between the Noddsdale Water and the North Rotten Burn is passed, and a descent is made to Rottenburn Bridge. For a kilometre to the north, the burn follows the course of a N-S fault that brings basalt and mugearite lavas against Lower Carboniferous sandstones. A spectacular slot-gorge that possibly originated as a glacial meltwater channel is at (NS 2505 6985), close to an isolated ruin known as The Back of the World. About half a kilometre to the north of it, a cliff of cementstones of Ballagan Beds type forms the western bank of the burn. Since a belt of thick woodland intervenes between the road and the burn, the stream sections are best reached by walking northwards from Rottenburn Bridge, where a car can be parked.

Locality 14. Loch Thom is reached 1.5 km from Rottenburn Bridge. It is an artificial stretch of water, named after the design engineer Robert Thom, who planned both it and its associated aqueducts or 'cuts' to feed the water mills of Greenock. The disused outfall aqueduct passes below the road beside Shielhill Farm. It has been replaced by a tunnel from the north end of the Loch.

At the south end of Loch Thom turn left, skirting the margin of the water, to reach Cornalees Nature Reserve centre, where turn left and descend the valley of Shielhill Glen. This is a major glacial meltwater channel, now occupied by the Kip Water. The A78 coast road is regained at Inverkip village.

References

HERRIOT, A. 1971. A xenolithic dyke at M'Inroy's Point, Gourock, Renfrewshire. *Scott. J. Geol.* **7,** 153-161.

JOHNSTONE, G.S. 1965. The volcanic rocks of the Misty Law -- Knock-side Hills district, Renfrewshire. *Bull. geol. Surv. Gt. Br.* **22,** 53-64.

PATTERSON, E.M. 1952. Notes on the tectonics of the Greenock-Largs Uplands and the Cumbraes. *Trans. geol. Soc. Glasg.* **21,** 430-435.

RICHEY, J.E. 1939. The dykes of Scotland. *Trans. Edinb. geol. Soc.* **13,** 393-435.

Excursion 15 GREAT CUMBRAE
D. S. Weedon
(after W.G.E. Caldwell)

Themes:	Old Red Sandstone and Calciferous Sandstone Measures sediments and dykes of three ages, Calciferous Sandstone, Carboniferous-Permian and Tertiary.
Features:	Minor sedimentary structures, marls and concretionary cornstones, faults, upstanding dykes (notably cumbraite), bostonites, flow-banding.
Maps:	O.S. 1:50 000 Sheet 63 Firth of Clyde B.G.S. 1:63 360 Sheet 29 Rothesay
Terrain:	All exposures are accessible from the flat coastal road.
Distance and Time:	Total distance around the island approximately 16-18 km (10-11 miles); examination of main exposures (using car) half-day but better as a leisurely full day's outing.
Access:	By vehicle/passenger ferry from Largs to Holm Bay (in 1991, approximately £10 for car). If travelling on foot, buses from the ferry terminal run to Millport where, if desired, bicycles are available for hire.

Introduction

The island and its neighbour, Little Cumbrae, lie in the Firth of Clyde midway between the mainland and South Bute. Little Cumbrae, composed largely of Carboniferous basalts, is privately owned and not easily accessible; it is not here described (for details of its geology, see Tyrrell, 1918). Great Cumbrae, however, is easily accessible from Largs, either on foot or by car. Its shores offer excellent exposures of sediments of the Upper Old Red Sandstone and the overlying Calciferous Sandstone Measures sediments, cut by suites of dykes of early Carboniferous, Permo-Carboniferous and Tertiary ages. Structurally the island is divided by the N-S trending Great Cumbrae Fault (Fig.15.1). Sedimentary rocks to the east of the fault are entirely of Upper Old Red Sandstone, whereas to the west they range from Upper Old Red Sandstone in the north into overlying Calciferous Sandstone Measures sediments in the south.

The Upper Old Red Sandstone, more than 600m (2000 ft) thick,

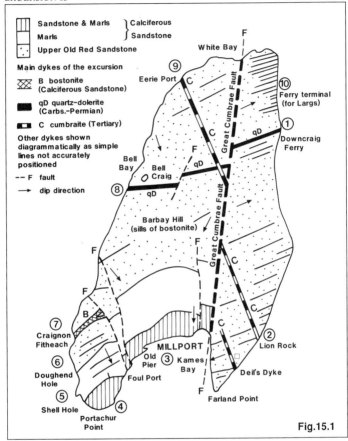

Figure 15.1. Simplified geological map of Great Cumbrae.

comprises mainly red sandstones and conglomerates in contrast with the Calciferous Sandstone Measures, about 300 m (1000 ft) thick, which are dominated by finer-grained red marls and grey sandstones. The latter are exposed by a southward-plunging syncline, present to the west of the Great Cumbrae Fault; the complementary southward-plunging anticline lies to the east of the fault. Examination of the relationships of recognisable dykes across the Great Cumbrae Fault shows that it has undergone at least two major movements: a sinistral tear movement of 1.6 km (1 mile) which is later than the Carboniferous/Permian dykes but earlier than the Tertiary dykes, and a dextral tear movement of 1.07 Km (0.67 ml) in post Tertiary dykes period (Patterson 1952). Great Cumbrae island is perhaps most notable geologically for the great number and variety of dykes that are easily accessible and magnificently exposed around its shores. Broad groupings into three categories can be made on directional trends, cross-cutting relationships and their individual distinctive petrological features. The accompanying map (Fig.15.1) indicates sufficient examples to show the major dyke trends; (1) Calciferous Sandstone Measures suite, trend approximately NE-SW: (2) Carboniferous-Permian suite, trend approximately E-W: (3) Tertiary suite, trend approximately NW-SE. Suite (1) is made up predominantly of dykes together with plugs and bosses representing old volcanic vents: these are generally of **Jedburgh**, **Dunsapie** and **Markle** basalts. The suite (1) dyke swarm is largely of **bostonites** and **felsites**, the main difference between them being the finer-grained texture of the latter. They often show well-developed fluxion structures, in the case of the bostonites by aligned phenocrysts. Both are characterised by a predominance of alkali feldspars (albite and orthoclase) and a paucity of ferro-magnesian minerals.

On Great Cumbrae albite is predominant in the dykes, the rocks being termed albite-bostonites. The felsites also show flow-banding, often due to streaked-out vesicles contained within a dense, crypto-crystalline matrix. (The dykes of Craignon Fitheach, Locality 7, are typical of these rocks). Suite (2) is exemplified by the E-W trending quartz-dolerite dyke which can be traced across the island from Bell Craig to Downcraig Ferry and is identical petrologically with other E-W dykes present in the Clyde area. It consists essentially of well-shaped plagioclase (labradorite) laths sub-ophitically enclosed by augite crystals, together with skeletal ilmenite and appreciable amounts of interstitial quartz. Suite (3) has dykes of both olivine-dolerite and tholeiite types, but the most striking are those named after the island, **cumbraite**. One forms the spectacular Lion Rock in the SE of the island, from whence it can be traced in a NW direction to Eerie Point at the NW end. It was here described by Tyrrell (1917, pp. 306-15) as the type rock. See Locality 9 for a full description.

Locality 1. The conspicuous promontory at **Downcraig Ferry** (NS 580 182) formed from a thick 23m (75ft) quartz-dolerite dyke of the Carboniferous- Permian Suite is well exposed on the shore. As mentioned above, this is the dyke which can be traced across the island to Bell Craig. In the intertidal zone some 230m (250 yds) north of this locality, a small complex of felsite dykes (Suite 1) is cut by an olivine-dolerite Tertiary dyke. The felsite dykes show excellent flow banding.

Locality 2. The **Lion Rock** (NS 549 179) and the **Deil's Dyke** (NS 544 174) are spectacular upstanding parallel dykes composed of cumbraite, a rock type described by Tyrrell (1917). It is a porphyritic rock, with large yellowish-white phenocrysts of plagioclase feldspar in a black, vitreous groundmass. The type rock was described from Eerie Port (Locality 9). Both dykes form sheer natural walls, with horizontal cooling joints well displayed. The Lion Rock (4.8m, 16ft thick) is exposed on the shore near the roadside, where it cuts a bostonite dyke of Suite 1. The Deil's Dyke is 3-3.6m (10-12ft) wide on the shore, where it encloses a lens of bleached conglomeratic sandstone. Between the Deil's Dyke and Millport, the road swings northward and runs parallel with the Great Cumbrae Fault, crossing a series of Old Red Sandstone sediments. These are dominated by flaggy red sandstones and quartz conglomerates. Many macro-porphyritic dykes of Suite 1, average width 2-3 m (6-10ft), are exposed along this shore line. The Great Cumbrae Fault lies to the seaward side of these exposures.

Locality 3. At **Kames Bay** are exposed many isolated outcrops of rocks of Upper Calciferous Sandstone age. Although there are slight variants, the general dip is southerly. The rocks are sugary textured, white to greyish-white sandstones, with pink and purple horizons which are more silty. The latter become more prevalent in the higher horizons, exposed on the two offshore islands. A few olivine-dolerite dykes of the Tertiary suite (3) cut these rocks. At Millport Old Pier (NS 547 161) a sill of macro-porphyritic dolerite is well exposed at the roadside. Between Millport and Portachur Point two small faults emerge at Foul Port (NS 546 156) and bring Lower Calciferous Sandstone red marls to the west against grey sandstones of the Upper Measures to the east.

Locality 4. The rocks forming the region of **Portachur Point** (NS 538 152) comprise the upper unit of the Calciferous Sandstone Measures and are here well exposed. They form a continuous sequence of rocks of the same age as those described in isolated outcrops at the last locality, namely pale-grey to white thick sandstone beds, often strongly cross-bedded. These alternate with red, purple and green marls and fine-grained sandstones: the latter generally prove less resistant to weathering and hence produce lower erosional features. The marls are associated with concretionary **cornstones**; detrital cornstones are fairly common in thin lenses beneath more massive sandstone layers.

Locality 5. At **Shell Hole** (NS 540 150) the junction between Upper and Lower Calciferous Sandstone Measures has been placed: this is somewhat arbitrary and difficult to pinpoint. However, between here and Doughend Hole (Locality 6) the rocks are dominated by red-brown marls with associated calcareous and non-calcareous laminated sandstones and limestones (2.5-15 cm thick), many showing ripple-marks and desiccation cracks. Towards Locality 5 occur "three thin clast-bearing limestones. The middle one (60cm, 2ft) thick is the most prominent and has a strongly ripple-marked surface. It is mid-grey in colour and shows undulating internal layering that suggests algal origin" (Quote Caldwell 1973).

Locality 6. At **Doughend Hole** (546 149) a series of Old Red Sandstone sediments, mainly sandstones and silty sandstones, are in juxtaposition with the red-brown marls which form the basal unit of the Calciferous Sandstone Measures on Great Cumbrae. The junction is inferred to be faulted but little movement appears to have occurred, judging from field evidence. A vertical macro-porphyritic dyke 3.6m (12ft) thick of Suite 1 is present to the NE of this locality. Between here and Locality 7 the highest beds of the Upper Old Red Sandstone are continuously exposed on the intertidal foreshore. These include coarse-grained sandstones with cross-bedding, finer grained sandstones and spectacular lenses of conglomerate with pure-white quartz pebbles. The sedimentary sequence from Doughend Hole to Craignon Fitheach (Locality 7) is cut by many non-porphyritic dolerite dykes of the Calciferous Sandstone Measures suite.

Locality 7. Old sea cliffs form **Craignon Fitheach**, a marked feature striking NE-SW and extending across the road to the sea. Parking of cars is relatively easy at this locality, but it is a rather popular picnic stop! The cliffs and seaward extension are formed from two thick dykes of porphyritic bostonite, with an intervening thinner dyke of porphyritic dolerite, in all some 39m (130ft) thick. On the shore the bostonite is seen in contact with quartz-conglomerate and pebbly sandstone. Tyrrell (1918, fig.3) described the bostonite as chilled against baked conglomerate, which is in turn in contact with blue porphyritic dolerite. Lenses of pebbly sandstone, 15cm thick, in places separate the dolerite from the more southern bostonite. All these dykes are cut by yet another, a thin dyke of olivine-dolerite of the Tertiary suite (3). From here to Locality 8 the shore section shows little variation, as the dip is generally SE at low angles. The Upper Old Red Sandstone sediments which are exposed are of red and purple sandstones, some more massive beds, and some flaggy with sparse conglomerates.

Locality 8. To the south of **Bell Bay** (NS 576 162) is a circular, flat-topped sheer-sided crag situated at the end of the old sea-cliff. This is formed from a basaltic volcanic plug, which contains large phenocrysts of augite and occasional xenoliths of country rock: agglomerate is plastered against the side of the plug. Somewhat to the south of the plug, a thick (30m, 100ft) dyke is exposed on the shore. This is a quartz-dolerite dyke of the Carboniferous-Permian suite (2) and although displaced by two faults, can be traced across the northern part of the island and equated with the dyke of similar characteristics present at Locality 1.

Locality 9. At **Eerie Port**, alongside the building indicated on the OS map (NS 588 168), is exposed the 9m (30ft) wide dyke selected by Tyrrell (1917, p. 307) as the type locality for the rock he named cumbraite. It is conspicuous on the shore by the road-side, where it is seen to dip at 70 degrees to the WSW. It is directly comparable with the rock of the Lion Rock and the Deil's Dyke, being dense, hard and flinty, black or dark grey in colour and with a vitreous lustre from its hemi-hyaline groundmass; large well-shaped phenocrysts of plagioclase feldspar are prominent. The groundmass of the central part of the dyke has a more vitreous lustre than the rest, a feature common in dykes of this nature. Microscope examination shows that the euhedral plagioclase crystals are calcium-rich, average composition mid-bytownite, usually with a narrow outer zone of labradorite, a composition comparable with that of the laths in the groundmass. The remainder of the groundmass is made of enstatite, augite and abundant dark glass. The freshness or degree of alteration of the glassy groundmass accounts for variations in colour of the overall weathered appearance of these rocks.

Locality 10. From **White Bay** (NS 592 178) where the Great Cumbrae Fault emerges at the northern end of the island, to the Ferry Terminal, the Suite 1 dyke swarm is particularly dense, with more than sixty dykes cutting the Upper Old Red sandstones of the shore section. Most are of the macroporphyritic feldspar type, but two microporphyritic varieties form prominent exceptions, 4.5m (15ft) and 7m (23ft) in thickness. Also recorded from this shore section have been a 12m (40ft) dyke of porphyritic bostonite, a 10m (34ft) quartz keratophyre and two NW-trending dykes of the Tertiary suite.

The car queue for the return ferry to Largs forms to the **south** of the jetty, on the seaward side of the road.

References

GUNN, W. and others. 1903. The geology of North Arran, South Bute, and the Cumbraes, with parts of Ayrshire and Kintyre. *Mem. Geol. Surv. U.K.*

PATTERSON, E.M. 1952. Notes on the tectonics of the Greenock-Largs uplands and the Cumbraes. *Trans. geol. Soc. Glasg.*, **21**, 430-435.

TYRRELL, G.W. 1917. Some Tertiary dykes of the Clyde area. *Geol. Mag.*, **6**, 305-315, 350-356.

_____ 1918. The igneous geology of the Cumbrae Islands. *Trans. geol. Soc. Glasg.*, **16**, 244-274.

Excursion 16 UPPER OLD RED SANDSTONE
OF THE FIRTH OF CLYDE
B.J.Bluck

Theme: Recognition of different alluvial deposits in the Upper Old Red Sandstone.

Features: Characteristics of channel-bar sediments and features distinguishing them from floodplain-floodbasin sediments; the upward coarsening unit, and its significance in recognition of the deposits of river bars; the diverse types of alluvium and the use of related channel bar and floodplain sediment to determine the nature of the alluvial sequence; the significance of the range of alluvial types in terms of environmental and tectonic controls; recognition of the scale of rivers and its significance in palaeogeography; megasequence stratigraphy and its meaning in terms of basin type and evolution; the structure and significance of carbonate palaeosols (caliche) and the stratigraphical evolution of the Upper Old Red Sandstone in the Firth of Clyde.

Maps: O.S. 1: 250 000 Sheet RM 3 Western & Central Scotland
              1: 50 000 Sheets 63   Firth of Clyde
       B.G.S. 1: 50 000 Sheet 29   Rothesay
              1: 50 000 Sheet 22W Irvine
              1: 50 000 Sheet 30W Greenock

Terrain: Coastal pathways and low coastal cliffs. Some walking on rough and sometimes slippery coastal sections.

Distance and Time: c.30 km from Localities 1-10; 6-8 hrs. Most localities are near the roadside but Localities 5-8 will require a walk of 2km. Short itinerary, localities 3,5,6,7,10 ; time 4 hrs. Car travel is assumed in these times, but at the time of writing there is a bus service which passes close-by all localities.

Access: No restriction

Introduction

a. Stratigraphical setting of the sequences

The Upper Old Red Sandstone deposits of the Firth of Clyde range in thickness from c. 4 km in the region of Helensburgh, to <100m in the southern Midland Valley. Their age is not known precisely , but they are older than the Carboniferous lavas which rest on them and younger than the oldest rocks (upper Lower Devonian) of the Strathmore syncline, upon which they rest.

The rocks comprise a series of mega-sequences which fine upwards, beginning with coarse conglomerates and ending with a blanket deposit of quartz-rich sandstones and **cornstone (caliche)**, the latter being themselves overlain by the Clyde Plateau Lavas (Fig. 16.1). There are three upward fining mega-sequences within the Clyde district: between Helensburgh and Rosneath (not seen on this excursion), at Wemyss Bay (Locality 3) and at Portencross (Locality 7). Only at Portencross can the Upper Old Red Sandstone be seen to rest on certain Lower Old Red Sandstone; there is an unconformity at the base of the sequence at Wemyss Bay, but the rocks beneath the unconformity are almost certainly Upper Old Red Sandstone belonging to the top of an earlier cycle of upward fining sediment, possibly the one which begins between Helensburgh and Rosneath.

The general tectonic regime within which the sediment has accumulated has been discussed by Bluck (1978, 1980), who favoured deposition in an extensional basin which opened along a series of normal faults. Each fault created in the basin a megasequence beginning with conglomerate and ending with sandstones and caliche. In addition, as the basin extended to the SW, younger faults were created and younger megasequences produced at the foot of them (Fig.16.1 A,B). The conglomerates produced at each fault scarp during the early stages of fault growth have their own distinctive clast assemblages related to the particular source. This migrating fault margin to the basin is thought to have been produced during a sinistral movement of the Highland Boundary Fault or a fault related to it (see below). It is thought likely that the Fault entered a locking segment in the region of the Firth of Clyde (the Fault trace bends to the SW). If the ground to the south of the Fault is then stretched to the NE, but is locked in the Clyde region, the result is extension of the south (Midland Valley) side. The southern side responds to this extension by developing a

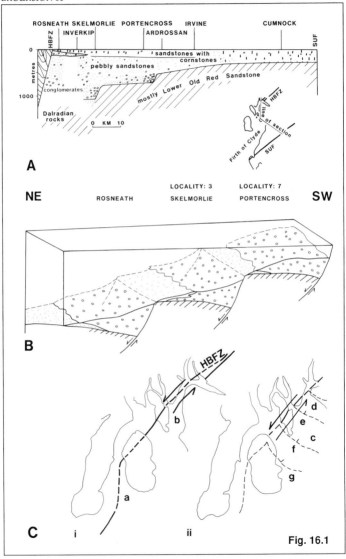

Fig. 16.1

series of normal faults lying roughly perpendicular to the Highland Boundary Fault, with each being the margin to successive basins which extended towards the SW (Fig.16.1C). This explanation, however, still requires more factual evidence before it can be accepted with any confidence, and as the Highland Boundary Fault may itself be a Late Devonian or Carboniferous structure, the main fault responsible may be an earlier but related fracture which has been obscured by this later movement.

b. The structure of alluvial deposits

The structure of a wide range of alluvial deposits can be seen in this region of the Firth of Clyde, and this introduction merely sets out to discuss some of the most common types so that their significance can be better appreciated at outcrop. Details of the interpretation of the alluvial sequences will be discussed at the appropriate localities, but there are some general points which need to be stressed about the general way in which ancient alluvium should be critically examined and assessment made of the significance of its presence at any one locality.

The processes which transport and deposit sediment in terrestrial environments generally vary in characteristics with their distance from source. Areas of sediment accumulation close to source are dominantly under the influence of the steep slopes and the often abundant supply of coarse sediment. Where there is high relief, the area of drainage is fairly small, the supply of sediment abundant and the rainfall occurs in heavy bursts, so that alluvial fans are likely to form. Depending on the ratio of sediment to water, these may be sites

---

Figure.16.1. Explanation of the structural and stratigraphical context of the Upper Old Red Sandstone basin. A, Cross section, B, Interpretation of the upward fining megacycles in terms of contemporary faulting, C, Explanation of the regional control on the basin formation. A sinistral movement on a fault (the Highland Boundary Fault or some fault which may be associated with it) which has a bend in the region of Arran, caused extension in the areas **a-b** in **Ci**. There is extension here because it is difficult to move material on the south side of the fault around the bend at (**a**). Because of this extension there is a sequence of normal faults developed which form the basins at (**d,e,f,g**) **(Cii)** where (**d**) is the basin at Rosneath, (**e**) at Wemyss Bay and (**f**) at Portencross. (**g**) is a remaining source block on Arran. HBFZ, Highland Boundary Fault Zone; SUF, Southern Uplands Fault

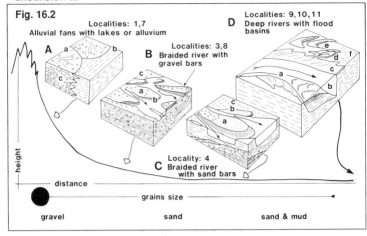

Figure.16.2. The effects of changing slope, distance from source, grain-size and the water depth on the structure of alluvium. These changes are seen not only in the structure of the bars but also in the structure of the overbank (floodplain) areas. A, alluvial fans (**a**), lakes or alluvium (**b**) and internal structure (**c**). **B,** gravel bars with coarse heads (**a**) and fine tails (**b**) and with coarse floodplain sediments (**c**). **C,** deeper channels than **B**, with well defined bars (**a**) and splays of sand (**b**) into the floodplain areas (**c**). **D,** deep channels (**b**) with sandy bars (**a**) and crevasse splays (**c**); deltas (**d**), dunes (**e**) and temporary lakes (**f**).

of mass flow deposition, where a chaotic jumble of sediment is laid down, or sheet-flood deposition, where shallow sheets of sediment-laden water spread out over the fan surface to deposit thin, laterally persistent, gravel beds. Both mass flow and sheet flood deposits can be seen at Localities 1 and 7.

When the area of drainage expands, a more regulated flow is attained in a longer and more stable channel system. In areas of high sediment discharge, and/or high channel slope, there is a non-sinuous wide zone of channels (braided river) flanked by an often poorly defined floodplain which is subject to flooding and sediment accretion only during high flow stages. Deposits from these river systems comprise many well defined gravel bars which dominate the channels and which grow generally in a downstream direction. The flood plains bordering these channels are frequently liable to flooding and are normally devoid of fine sediment, which has either been eroded away or was not deposited from the fast-flowing flood waters. Braided sediment bars of this kind are illustrated at Locality 8.

Farther away from the source where there are often slopes of lower gradient, drainage is often confined to one main, fairly deep channel which can be either straight or sinuous, flanked by a well defined floodplain which, if very extensive, may form a floodbasin. The channels are characterised by many sediment bars which either form the central zone or are attached to one of the banks. With increasing depth of the river the bars become very thick units of sediment which reach down to the deepest parts of the channel and up as far as the top of the bank. Thick sediment bars in confined channels can be seen at Localities 4,9,10.

Another result of the deeper, confined flow of the river is that the floodplain is quite distinct from the channel, and is typified by flat sheets of sediment which overspill from the channel during flood events. On river systems we see around Glasgow today the floodplains are grassed over, but in Devonian times plants were not well developed and the climate was fairly arid, so floodplains were bare. Where the floodplains are well drained and not subject to a great deal of flooding, as when the rivers are near low upland areas, a particular palaeosol may develop on them which is typically found in arid and semi-arid regions today. This 'soil' is called caliche or cornstone, and is made up of carbonate. It is particularly well seen at Locality 2. Where there are wide floodplains with a good supply of flood sediment and a dry windy climate, then dunes may form. The floodplains and floodbasins associated with the deep rivers at Seamill (Locality 11) have dune deposits in the floodplain sequences. It is a characteristic of most river systems which have a source separated from the basin, that the grain size of the sediment bed-load decreases downstream. This grain-size difference, coupled with the factors discussed above, result in the alluvial facies acquiring a wide range in structure; there is not only the diversity associated with the differences between floodplain and channel-bar sediment, but also the differences in both these regimes when traced from source. These differences in the structure of alluvium are very clearly demonstrated in the sediment of the Clyde coast.

Channel-bar deposits, despite their heterogeneity in structure, are all united by one characteristic: they comprise units of sediment which coarsen upwards from a recognisable base. This coarsening

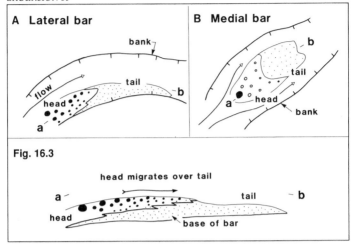

Figure.16.3. Explanation of upward coarsening units with head (coarse) differentiated from the tail (fine) and with the head migrating over the tail to form the upward coarsening structure.

upward is brought about by the presence of an areal grain-size segregation within the channel (Fig.16.3). There is very little known about why this segregation has taken place, or indeed its significance in the mechanics of bed-load transport. Nevertheless this type of segregation is found abundantly in recent sediment throughout the world. When the coarse-grained part of the bar (the head) moves or extends downstream it often builds over the fine downstream part (the tail). The resulting structure is a unit of sediment which coarsens upward (Fig.16.3): this coarsening upward sequence may take place in sandstones (coarse sandstone overlying fine sandstones (Localities 4,9,11); or conglomerate (coarse conglomerate overlying fine conglomerate or sandstone (Localities 3,8). The two sequences are at greatly different scales and have radically different appearances, but they share this common and fundamental attribute. Upward coarsening units abound in the Firth of Clyde, and will be a special feature of this excursion.

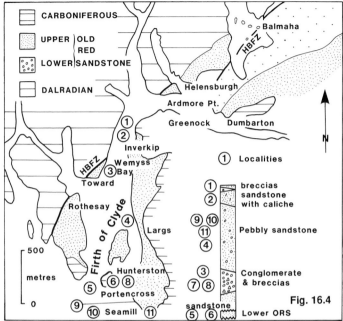

Figure.16.4 Map of localities along the Firth of Clyde, which are also positioned on a composite stratigraphical sequence.

Locality 1. North end of Lunderston Bay (NS 202 748): **Breccias with Dalradian clasts** (Fig.16.4).

Parking is quite easy here, as there is a large car park on the west side of the road. The hills to the NE above the garden centre are in thick caliche and white sandstone. They belong to the upper part of the Upper Old Red Sandstone sequence, and the breccias which occur on the shore here and in the raised beach along the road are stratigraphically below these caliche beds. The breccias are therefore also high in the sequence, and imbrication and cross stratification show a dispersal towards the SE, away from the Dalradian block to the NW. The breccias contain slates and and psammitic clasts which are very similar to the local Dalradian, and Bluck (1980) believed that they were from this source. The clasts show convincingly that the Dalradian block was in contact with the Midland Valley by Dalradian times and that it was in sufficient relief to shed debris to the south.

These breccias are laid down in sheets which can be traced for some distance over the outcrop. They are probably the result of sheet-flows, where sediment-laden water disperses over a surface which has little relief. The flat shaped clasts are well oriented and in some instances can be seen to be aligned in a swirling pattern suggesting that the flow was sometimes quite "viscous": in this case the breccia sheets may be thought of as mass-flows.

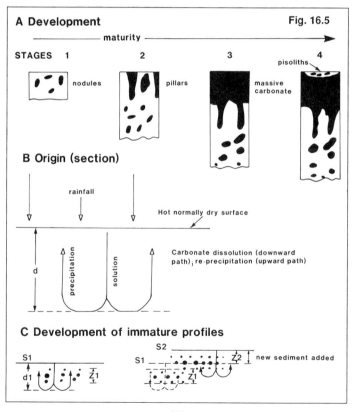

A Development — Fig. 16.5

maturity

STAGES 1 2 3 4

pisoliths

nodules — pillars — massive carbonate

B Origin (section)

rainfall

Hot normally dry surface

d — precipitation — solution — Carbonate dissolution (downward path); re-precipitation (upward path)

C Development of immature profiles

S1 — $d1$ — $Z1$

S2 — S1 — $Z2$ — new sediment added — $Z1$

Locality 2. Inverkip (NS 200 718): **Caliche** (Figs 16.4, 16.5, 16.6). This exposure occurs on the shore just below the car park (with toilet, but not open continuously) on the headland, and can be reached at high tide, although it may be examined to much greater advantage at low tide. The rocks comprise white quartz-rich sandstones, red mudstones and carbonate beds (caliche). The sandstones are cross stratified and have occasional clasts of a fine, dense carbonate which resembles the caliche layers to be discussed below. These sandstones are channel deposits of small-scale river systems which are either at some distance from source or are near to low-lying source blocks which were yielding very little coarse sediment. The interstratified mudstones and carbonates are the overbank floodplain deposits to the same or allied systems.

The caliche is preferentially found in the mudstones of the floodplains, although it can also be seen in some of the sandstone units. The most complete profile can be seen at the NE end of the exposure, where sparse, nodular carbonates are replaced upwards by elongate carbonate pillars and finally by massive, irregular carbonates (Fig.16.5 A). This is a section through an almost complete caliche profile. The nodular phase represents the immature, early stages of caliche development: the dense, massive unit represents the final most mature stage. Other sections at this outcrop have only immature profiles which are at the pillared or nodular stages.

Caliche occurs when water, usually from rainfall seeps down through the surficial layers of sediment only to return towards the surface because of the intense evaporation at the surface. It therefore

---

Figure.16.5. Explanation of the development of caliche. **A** traces the stages in its development through time in section. Stage 1, at the initial stage only nodules form but as time proceeds the nodules coalesce into pillars if the muds are mudcracked or into larger nodules if not. Stage 3 occurs when the pillars and nodules grow into a massive bed; and stage 4 occurs when the massive bed no longer lets water through and pools appear on the surface in which pisoliths form. **B,** provides an explanation for the growth of caliche; **d** refers to the depth to which percolation of the rainwater normally goes. **C**, the development of thick beds of stage 1 or 2 etc occurs when there is a continous addition of sediment to the surface, so that the depth of water percolation **d1**, and the zone of nodule formation **Z1** rises as the sediment is added. The surface does not mature because the process is not operating in the same zone (**Z1**) for a sufficient length of time.

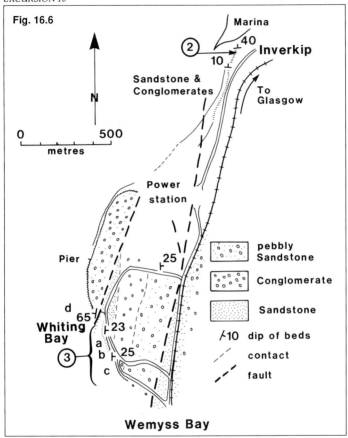

Figure. 16.6. Map of the region: Inverkip-Wemyss Bay.

characterizes arid or semi-arid regions of the world where the rainfall is low and the ground surface is hot. Carbonates are dissolved as the waters pass down and are then precipitated as they migrate up towards the surface (Fig.16. 5 B). At first only nodules develop, then the nodules grow to coalesce in the zones where the water is more concentrated. Where there are spaces along which water may move easily, as along mudcracks, carbonate is concentrated to form pillars. The next stage is reached where the nodules have amalgamated into a massive unit of carbonate which will no longer allow the water to percolate through. At this stage the rainwater concentrates on the surface as pools in which **pisoliths** may form.

Caliche grows very slowly, normally far more slowly than the rate of sedimentation. It only develops on fairly stable surfaces, such as river floodplains, rather than channels which have mobile sediment which is not stationary long enough for caliche to develop. The depth to which the rainfall percolates below the surface is fairly constant, and the depth below the surface reached by the return flow is fairly constant too, so that there is a distinctive zone in which the nodules grow below the surface (Fig.16.5 C,Z). If the surface is building up by sedimentation, then the depth to which the rainfall descends below the surface rises all the time, as does the depth of nodule growth. By this means, the profile is hindered in its development of maturity, and remains an immature profile. There are a number of such profiles at this outcrop.

This section occurs towards the top of the Upper Old Red Sandstone, where there are many such profiles, some of which are > 5 m thick. On the basis of other evidence there was slow subsidence in the entire Upper Old Red Sandstone basin across the Midland Valley towards the end of its development and floodplain surfaces were exposed for a long period before being buried. For this reason caliche surfaces are well developed in floodplain sediments at this time and can be traced for kilometres where the oucrops are favourable; the presence of thick caliches is an indication that the sequence is at the top of the Upper Old Red Sandstone.

Locality 3. Wemyss Bay (NS189 699): **Unconformity, megacycle and faulting** (Fig.16.6). Parking at this locality is difficult as the road leading to the outcrops is private but no permission is needed to go down the road on foot. However, there are parking facilities just outside the grounds (See Fig. 16.6). The rocks at Wemyss Bay illustrate a number of important issues which are essential to the understanding of the Upper Old Red Sandstone history:

1. Unconformities within the Upper Old Red Sandstone.
2. The initiation of an upward fining megacycle and the sequence of facies associated with it.
3. Faulting.

There are 4 sub-localities which are used to illustrate these points.

a. A cross stratified conglomerate rests discordantly on bright red sandstone. The red sandstone has been extensively used for building, and to the north of this outcrop a small harbour has been quarried into it. The sandstones are best seen in the low cliffs to the north of this quarry, at the foot of the wall which runs along the road. Here they comprise alternations of flat stratified, rippled and mudcracked sediment and cross stratified sandstones. The environment of origin of this sandstone unit is uncertain; it is probably aeolian, with the flat stratified irregular beds being interdune deposits (see Locality 9).

b. The conglomerates have large-scale cross strata which dip towards the NNW. They are associated with more gently dipping strata some of which dip at low angles to the SSE. These are backset beds, and in combination show that these sediments were deposited from gravel-dominated sediment bars the height of which was equal to the thickness of the foresets and backsets (Figs 16.3, 16.10, 16.11). The bar height is the minimum depth of the stream, and in this instance streams of about 2-3 m depth are likely to have laid down this alluvium. They flowed to the NNW. On the basis of data collected here and on the outcrops to the south of the pier at Wemyss Bay, the rivers are thought have been braided and fairly near to source.

The conglomerates contain a wide variety of clasts which include white vein quartz, quartzite, schist, amphibolite, acid-intermediate volcanic rocks, and very few granites. Many of these clasts are well rounded and those of the more durable lithologies such as vein quartz and quartzite are probably in their second or more cycles.

c. These beds are discordantly overlain by cross stratified pebbly sandstones which contain the same assemblage of pebbles as the lower conglomerate. This overlying conglomerate has upward coarsening sediment units (see Fig.16.3 for explanation) which were deposited by river systems flowing towards the NNW.

The beds are repeated by two faults, one of which can be seen at (**d**) in Figure 16.3.

Interpretation: This is the lower part of an upwards fining mega-sequence which has been cut by a number of roughly N-S fractures. The sequence ends with caliche and sandstones which can be seen in the region of Leap Moor.

Locality 4. Shore at Knock Castle (NS1913 6303): **Cyclical sediments of channel-bars and floodplains** (Figs 16.7: 16.8). These exposures can be visited at any state of the tide, but are best viewed at low tide. From just north of Largs to this locality they comprise numerous alternations of coarse cross stratified sandstones and conglomerates (coarse member), with flat stratified sandstones in alternation with thin mudstone bands (fine member). Together they form units 2-10 m thick.

The exposure under consideration is 330 m north of the lodge at the entrance to Knock Castle and is situated below a car park on top of the low-lying cliff and can be easily identified by its presence beneath a wall. Here a coarse member, resting erosively on a fine member, begins with units of upward coarsening sediment which are 0.5-1.0 m thick. In its upper part, the coarse member comprises a unit which is a level of organization above that of the basal, in that it comprises four different lithologies (Fig. 16.7 A):

   b1.   A wedge of ductile folded and refolded sandstone which thins
         to the east;
   b2.   A unit of cross stratified sandstone in the middle of the
         outcrop, which also wedges out to the east;
   b3.   A sheet of coarse pebbly sandstone which underlies the wall
         and caps the outcrop to form an upward coarsening unit;
   b4   A coarse grained unit of uncertain affinities.

All three units, b1-3, are in part transitional or interfingering.
An explanation for this outcrop (Fig. 16.7 B) involves the following lines of reasoning:

   1.   The cross strata dip towards the NW indicating that the flow
        was in that direction.
   2.   With the divisions b1-3 being transitional or interfingering,
        then the coarse sediments of b3 are partly equivalent to the
        finer sediments of b2 and b1, and all divisions were therefore
        laid down at the same time. The palaeoflow is towards the NW
        and the whole outcrop becomes finer in that direction, i.e.
        downflow, so that there was on the river bed a pile of sediment
        which became finer downstream. This type of size-segregation
        within alluvial channels is typically found in sediment bars
        (see Introduction).
   3.   The sequence coarsens upwards indicating that the sheet of

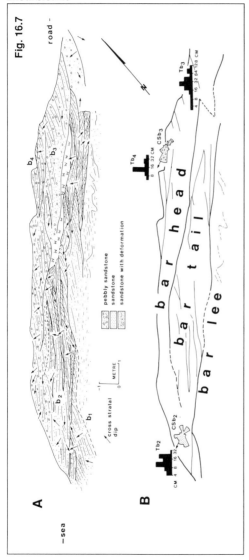

Figure. 16.7. A, Section through sediment bar, Locality 4. **b1** etc. refers to lithofacies described in the text **B,** interpretation in terms of an alluvial bar where the head refers to the upstream (coarse) segment and the tail, the downstream fine. The farthest downstream facies is the bar lee where the finest sediment accretes. **T**=thickness of cross strata; **CS**=cross stratal dip orientation, both given for the lithofacies (**b2** etc). The wall is to the right of the section.

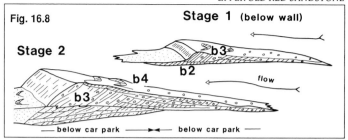

Figure.16.8. Interpretation of the development of the bar complex at Locality 4; **b2** etc. refer to the lithofacies discussed in the text and in Figure 16. 7.

coarse sediment of the upstream margin (to the SE) has migrated over the fine to give an upward coarsening unit (compare Fig.16.3); and the direction of coarse sediment migration was in the direction of stream flow.

4. Such mechanisms of sediment migration and the sequences they produce are typically found when bars of sediment migrate downstream. Sequences like this can be seen, for example, now forming in the Endrick Water.

5. The whole sediment sequence thickens downstream and this may be due either to the bar migrating into deeper water, or the whole sediment bar building up on the stream bed.

It is clear that if this explanation applies then the minimum depth of the river is given by the height of the bar, which in this instance is *c.* 3 m

Locality 5. Farland Head (NS 178 484): **Faults** (Fig.16.9). There is a free car park at the first farm entering Portencross. The exposures lie on the coast in front of the car park and extend to the south. Walk south beyond Sandy's Creek to the begining of the sandy beach of Ardneil Bay (Fig. 16.9) **(a)**. This beach is underlain by fairly gently dipping (up to 35°), bright red sandstones of the Upper Old Red Sandstone which patchily emerge from beneath the beach sands. To the west of the sandy bay, these fairly gently dipping sandstones are in fault contact with steeply dipping, and sometimes overturned, bright red, flat-stratified sandstones rocks of uncertain age, but which are provisionally regarded as belonging to the Upper Old Red Sandstone.

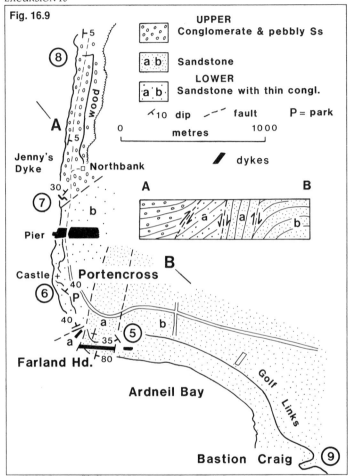

Figure.16.9. Map of Farland Head with localities and a simplified cross-section A-B.

To the west are fault bounded, sheared grey siltstones and lithic arenites at Sandy's Creek. These beds are c. 50 m thick, and on spore evidence are considered to be Lower Devonian or possibly Late

Silurian in age (Downie and Lister 1969).

The Upper Old Red Sandstone rocks of Ardneil Bay do not appear within the Upper Old Red Sandstone sequence to the north where the basal Upper Old Red Sandstone rests on the Lower (Locality 7). The beds in Ardneil Bay belong to a group of sandstone which extends at least to Ardrossan and was built by a large, contemporary river system (Localities 9,10,11). If these sandstones once overlaid the sequence north of Portencross (as seems probable) the throw of the fractures at Arneil Bay and Sandy's Creek would therefore be substantial, since they fault out not only the Lower Old Red Sandstone sequence but also the whole of the upward fining megasequence at Portencross. The nature of the faulting is not clear, but elswhere in the sequence there is evidence for much high angled reverse faulting (see Fig.16. 9, section A-B).

Locality 6. Car park: Lower Old Red Sandstone (Fig. 16.9). These rocks form the foreshore and the raised beach platform from the car park to the castle. They are a brown-red colour and are thought to belong to the Lower Old Red Sandstone. They comprise alternations of flat stratified and cross stratified sandstones and conglomerates. There is a wide variety of sedimentary structures to be seen in these deposits: sedimentary lineations, mudcracks (seen in section as pillars of sand in shale but as polygonal surfaces in plan), and a wide variety of cross stratification. Some of the cross strata are in tabular sheets with mudstone drapes over the foresets and mudstones at the base (bottom sets) and rippled strata at the top (top sets). These deposits resemble the flat-topped bars of sandy sediment described from recent braided stream deposits, representing a facies not depicted in Figure 16.2.

The interstratified conglomerates which can be readily seen on the northern margin of the outcrop near the castle, comprise clasts of mainly volcanic rock which include andesite and andesitic tuff as well as basic volcanic rocks. Clasts of a green sandstone present here are particularly abundant further up in the sequence.

The palaeoflow for these sediments is from the south in which direction we can infer from the composition of the sandstones and conglomerates there was a source made up of dominantly volcanic rock.

Locality 7. Northbank: Unconformity between Lower and Upper Old Red Sandstone and an upward fining megacycle (Fig.16.9). Follow the path northwards through the gap in an E-W Carboniferous dyke. The faulted unconformity between Lower and Upper Old Red Sandstone is exposed on the rocky foreshore. The Lower beds are mainly dark red sandstones which range in dip direction from north to NW. They are overlain by a quite distinctive conglomerate which contains clasts of quartzite, sandstone, vein quartz and minor amounts of green sandstone, chert and lavas. At the base of the sequence these conglomerates are coarse and massive; they were probably laid down by some mass-flow mechanism. Cross stratal dip and clast imbrication show that they were laid down by a flow running from south to north, and the source block was almost certainly a pre-existing conglomerate with abundant clasts of quartzite. The quartzite clasts are generally very well rounded, but some have been broken before entering this sequence. Some of these broken clasts have rounded edges suggesting transportation after being broken.

This basal unit fines upward and is replaced by mudstones with mudcracks, minor caliche beds and thin conglomerates and sandstones. These strata form a distinctive hollow on the shore and are succeeded to the north unconformably by a sequence of cross stratified conglomerates and sandstones. These conglomerates are particularly rich in green sandstone clasts.

Locality 8. Hunterston: Gravel bar of a braided river (Figs 16:9,10,11). This locality is reached by following the track along the top of the shoreline beyond Jenny's Dyke to the boundary fence of the Hunterston power station. The section under discussion occurs in a distinctive hollow south of this fence and in the present-day cliffs exposing sandstone. The map (Fig.16.10) is of the top of the low cliff section south of this hollow and includes most of the low cliffs along the shore. These beds are gently dipping to the east in contrast to the beds near the unconformity and are roughly equivalent in stratigraphical position to the conglomerates and pebbly sandstones of the section south of Jenny's Dyke.

There are three lithofacies to be seen at this outcrop (Fig.16.9): (**d**), a flat stratified alternation of sandstone and conglomerate; (**c**), a sheet of cross stratified conglomerate and pebbly sandstone and (**b**), a wedge of cross stratified sandstone. Lithofacies (**a**) is below this outcrop and is exposed in the cliff on its western side.

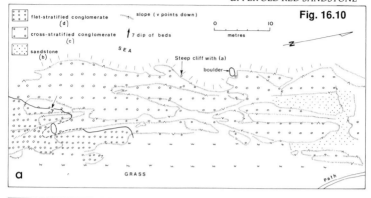

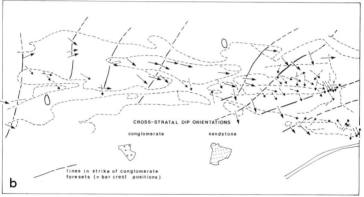

Figure.16.10. Map of gravel bar (**a**) at Locality 8 together with cross stratal dip orientations (**b**).

The sandstone is overlain by the cross stratified conglomerate and itself wedges out to the south where the overlying bed replaces it. Further to the south the cross stratified sheet of conglomerate is replaced gradually by the overlying flat to gently dipping alternation of sandstone and conglomerate (see Fig.16.10). The cross strata and clast imbrication indicate a flow to the north, and the dips of the cross strata are in a fairly constant direction in the case of the conglomerate, but variable in the case of the sandstone.

219

Fig. 16.11

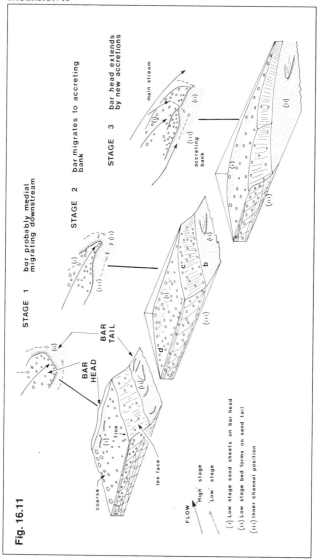

Figure.16.11. Explanation of the development of the gravel bar at Locality 8; **a**, **b** etc refer to the location of lithofacies discussed in text and shown in Figure 16.10.

Bluck (1986) has interpreted these rocks in the following way (Fig.16.11):

The cross stratified conglomerate (**c**) represents the successive lee faces of a bar which migrated to the north. On the upstream margin of this bar were the back sets and top sets of the flat stratified unit (**d**), and on the downstream margin were the fine grained sands of the bar tail (**b**). The lee face over the bar climbed over the tail to produce an upward coarsening sequence as seen at Locality 3. The lithofacies (**a**) represents the channel deposits below the bar.

Locality 9. Bastion Craig: Channel sand body (Fig.16.12). This locality at Bastion Craig may be reached by foot from Farland Head or by car by driving past the golf club and down to the shore. **On no account should buses go down this road.** They may park elsewhere e.g. just south of Seamill where parking is suggested for Locality 11. This part of the coastline is made up of low ground underlain by fine, soft sediments, of large-scaled cross-stratified sandstones and alternations of red mudstone and sandstone and upstanding outcrops of red cross-stratified pebbly sandstone.

Bastion Craig is a sand body the top part of which comprises, at its western margin, pebbly sandstone and conglomerate (**C5**), and at its eastern margin mainly sandstone (**C3**) overlain by pebbly sandstone (**C4**). With the dispersion of sediment being from SW to NE the coarse sediments belong to the head and the fine to the tail, but as with other bars, the coarse head has migrated over the fine tail to give an upward coarsening sequence and the gradation between the lithofacies **C4-C5** is seen at (**b**); and between **C4** and **C3** at (**a**). At (**a**) it is possible to trace this gradation by reference to bands of conglomerate, where between two conglomerate units **C4** grades downstream into **C3**. The whole structure is best viewed from a vantage point near the golf course where this latter gradation in facies is particularly well seen (Fig. 16.9,16.12). **C1** and **C2** do not appear on the map; they refer to facies which, although seen here are best seen at Locality 11, where the lithofacies notation (**C1** etc.) is the same as for this bar.

The mid-part of the bar comprises trough cross strata, sometimes organised into small upward coarsening units, and the tail of the bar comprises planar cross strata which wedge out towards the west (Fig.16.12). This sandstone is enclosed in beds which comprise alternations of sandstone and mudstone and which outcrop to the south and west.

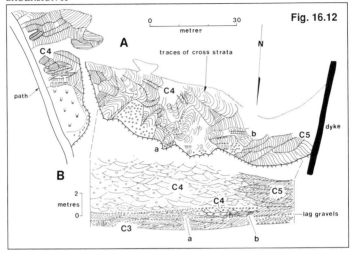

Figure.16.12. Map of Bastion Craig **(A)** together with section **(B)**. Letters in bold capitals refer to lithofacies; letters in lower case to localities. **C3** refers to tabular cross strata at the base of the section; **C4,** to trough cross stratified sands which are the main part of the outcrop; **C5** to the thick, coarse-grained tabular cross strata which can be seen only at low tide. At **(a)** there is a transition between the tabular cross stratified sands of **C3** and the trough cross strata of **C4**; at **(b)** the **C5** the tabular cross stratified pebbly sandstones of **C5** grade into the trough cross strata of C4. P = the point from where it is best to see the transitions.

Locality 10. Bell Stane (NS 190 476): **Floodbasin deposits, dunes overbank deltas** (Fig.16.13). The foreshore to the north and west of Locality 9 is interpreted as floodbasin deposits and these can be examined on the foreshore. The floodbasin comprises a number of lithological elements each of which can be related to the processes known to take place in present-day floodbasins:

F1. Thinly stratified (1-10 cm) alternations of siltstone and rippled sandstones. These are interpreted as thin overbank sand sheets dispersed out of the channel either during a slight flooding or the distal ends of thicker sand sheets such as described under **F2**, or simply lacustrine sediment accumulated during periods of flooding.

F2, Cs cross stratified, pebbly sandstone sheets which occur amongst

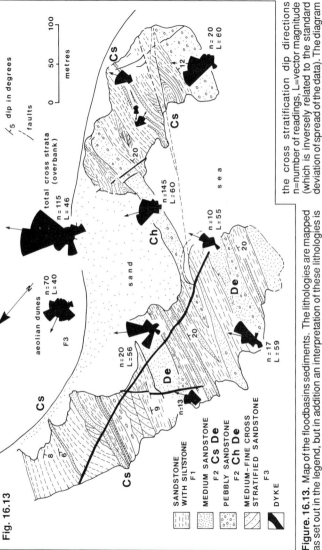

Figure. 16.13. Map of the floodbasins sediments. The lithologies are mapped as set out in the legend, but in addition an interpretation of these lithologies is given by the following codes: **Cs**=crevasse splays; **De**=deltas; **ch**=channels. In this notation deltas (which are the result of crevasse sands building onto the floodplains) are a combination of two gradational or interfingering lithologies- mediumgrain-size sandstone and pebbly sandstone. Rose diagrams refer to the cross stratification dip directions n=number of readings, L=vector magnitude (which is inversely related to the standard deviation of spread of the data). The diagram *total cross strata (overbank)* refers to dip directions of the cross strata in the sandstone sheets which have originated as sandstone crevasse splays i.e. **De** and **Cs**.

SANDSTONE
WITH SILTSTONE
F1

MEDIUM SANDSTONE
F2 **Cs De**

PEBBLY SANDSTONE
F2 **Ch De**

MEDIUM-FINE CROSS
STRATIFIED SANDSTONE
F3

DYKE

total cross strata (overbank)
n=115
L=46

aeolian dunes
n=70
L=40
F3

n=20
L=56

n=13

n=17
L=59

n=10
L=55

n=145
L=60

n=20
L=60

dip in degrees

faults

Fig. 16.13

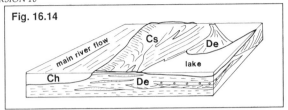

Figure. 16.14. A model of floodbasin deposition for the Bell Stane region. **Cs** etc refers to text and Figure 16.13.

1 and represent crevasse splays. These occur quite near to the bank of the river and were produced during times of flooding in the main channel and breaching of the river bank followed by the spread of sand sheets onto the adjacent floodbasin area. They can be seen at several positions as marked on the map of the foreshore.

F2, De large-scale sand sheets which are upward coarsening and contain abundant wedge-shaped cross strata. These could be confused with channel deposits (**ch**) but are thought to be deltas of sand produced when there was a strong overbank breach during flood so that the floodwaters and their entrained sediment filled the lakes and other bodies of standing water which was in the low ground in the floodbasin (Fig.16.14). They may be the distal terminations of **F2 Cs** above.

F3, very large scale, often trough-like, cross strata in soft friable and pebble-free sand. These lithologies are thought to be the lower parts of aeolian dunes which transported sediment on the floodbasin when it had dried out. This suggests that the floodbasin and river system existed in a fairly dry climate. Beneath these large-scale cross strata are often very irregular red sandstone and claystone beds with indistinct ripples. These are interdune sandstones and mudstone which occur between the dunes and are therefore more likely to be buried and preserved than any other of the dune lithologies.

Locality 11. Seamill: Large-scale sand body (Figs 16.15 : 16.16). Park cars on the main road just south of Seamill, and approach this locality by following the pathway, south of the river and alongside a large, red sandstone house which backs onto the shore. This locality is in a major sandbody which may be 8-10m thick. The far distant, west (seawards) side of the sheet (**C5**, Fig.16.15) can only be examined at low tide and comprises planar cross stratification in coarse pebbly sandstone. As

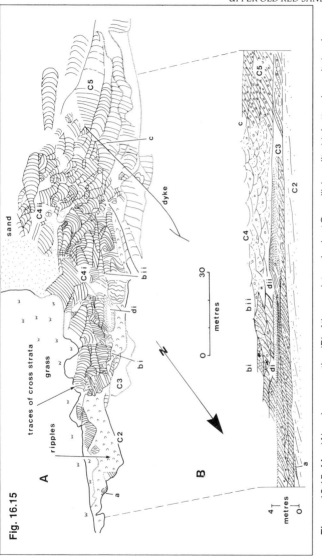

Figure.16.15. Map (A) and cross section (B) of the sandstone body at Seamill, Locality 11. Letters in capitals refer to lithofacies, letters in lower case to localities. **C2**, refers to the soft, friable large-scaled cross strata; **C3**, to the tabular cross stratified sand sheets; **C4**, the trough cross stratified deposits and **C5** the tabular, pebbly sandstones. At **a**, **C2** interfingers with **C3**; at **bi** and **bii C4** interfingers and grades into **C3**; and at **c**, **C5** grades with **C4**.

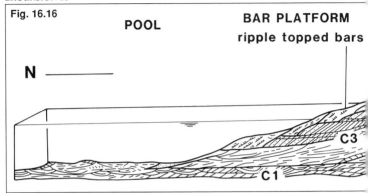

Figure. 16.16. Explanation of the Seamill sandstone body, Locality 11. **C2** etc as for Fig. 16.15 and text.

the section is traced to the east (landwards) these cross strata are replaced by trough cross strata (**C4i,C4ii,** Fig.16.15) and the zone of transition can be seen at (**c**). These trough cross strata are seen to overlie planar cross strata which form the upper part of the cliff section at the most landward margin (**C3**) of the sand body. Below the planar cross strata, soft, cross stratified sandstones (**C2**) are seen to interfinger with the overlying planar cross stratified beds (Fig.16.15, **a**), and form the more deeply eroded part of the cliff section, and the low ground to the north of this outcrop.

There is a prominent pebbly sandstone unit on the foreshore north of the main outcrop and south of the stream. This sandstone is easily recognised by the presence of concrete all along its outcrop (there is a pipe-line buried here). In the notation for these lithofacies this is **C1** and may belong to the same bar-channel system as the main outcrop being discussed.

A detailed examination of the outcrop shows a number of important features: at (**bi**) the trough cross strata of **C4i** interfinger with the planar cross strata of **C3**. At (**di**) a mass-flow of sandstone has probably been produced during the de-watering of a sandstone at (**dii**).

The cross strata dip in the same direction as the lithofacies change and from these observations a number of significant points can be made (Fig.16.15): the large scale foresets on the seaward side of the

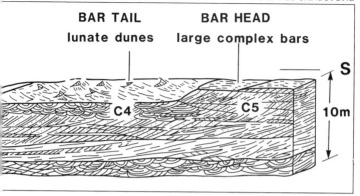

outcrop (**C5**) are replaced, when traced landward, by the trough cross strata of the main part of the outcrop (**C4**). These trough cross stratified sandstones overlie the planar cross strata of **C3** with which they also partly interfinger. **C3** dominates the outcrop on the eastern (landward) side of the map (Fig. 16.15). Together the whole section forms a large upward coarsening unit some 8-10m thick, which has C5 at its upstream end C4 in the central areas and C3 in the downstream regions; and all these facies overlie the sediments of C2 to which they are related by interfingering. The position of C1 in this scheme is uncertain but may be the basal channel deposits as illustrated in Figure 16.16. The whole sequence is interpreted in terms of a large river bar with head and tail regions (Fig. 16.16) and which migrated downstream to build up the upward coarsening unit.

The whole development of this bar complex is similar to that described at Localities 4 and 8, but because now the scale of both the bar and the river is much greater so the lithofacies are thicker, more complex and the transitions take place over a greater distance.

Trough cross stata in the main part of the outcrop are beautifully exposed in 3-D: they are themselves arranged in upward coarsening units which can be as much as 1m thick. The top of this sequence is gradational upwards into overbank deposits exposed on the rock platform to the south and which comprise very large aeolian dunes and interdune sediment as described at Locality 10.

These sediments were laid down by a river which was at least 6m deep, and was fairly distal, being in its floodplain-floodbasin reach (see Fig.16.2). It flowed to the east through the Midland Valley and out towards the North Sea. Deep rivers are normally also wide and carry a considerable quantity of water and sediment; and there is now a good deal of evidence to suggest that the Old Red Sandstone rocks were deposited under the influence of large-scale river systems. Large scale rivers normally have large catchment areas to supply the great sediment and water loads and usually drain to the sea; an inland lake would soon be filled by these rivers (see Introduction).

The palaeogeography of the whole North Atlantic region for Devonian times involved a large sea to the south, in England, and very high mountainous areas to the north in Greenland and Scandinavia. It is probable that the large river which built these Upper Old Red Sandstone bars at Seamill drained these northern mountains, was diverted through the Midland Valley and then drained southwards through the North Sea to the Devonian coast in the south.

Summary of excursion and significance of observations

1. In terms of the distribution of alluvial facies as shown in Figure 16.2, alluvial sediments have been examined from the proximal regions (mass-flow deposits, probably on alluvial fans; Localities 1 and 7: proximal braided alluvium; Localities 3, 7 and 8: mid-distance alluvium; Locality 5: and distal alluvium: Localities 9, 10, and 11. These localities show a proximal-distal increase in bar thickness from c. 2m in the proximal; 3-4m in the medial and 8-10m in the distal. This almost certainly reflects an expected change in river depth from proximal regions. At the same time as there is a change in the scale and complexity of the bars there is also a change in the nature of the overbank sediment: from little or no overbank sediment in the proximal sediments of Hunterston (Locality 7) and Wemyss Bay (Locality 3) to a greater thickness of overbank sediments in the bars north of Largs (Locality 4), to well developed floodbasins in the Seamill area (Localities 10,11,12). It is emphasised however that this sequence of alluvium does not belong to the same river system: the very large river system which occurs at Seamill (Locality 12) had its drainage well outside the present Midland Valley, whereas the river systems which deposited the conglomerates north of Inverkip (Locality 1) and Portencross (Locality 6) were clearly local.

2. The clasts in the conglomerates at Portencross differ greatly from those at Wemyss Bay. It is therefore inferred that the nature of the source which gave rise to these sediments also differed. However both were deposited by river systems draining areas from the south: they share the same dispersal direction but they clearly do not belong to the same dispersal system, so a source block is inferred to have existed *between* Wemyss Bay and Portencross. It is on this and other evidence that Bluck (1980) postulated that the conglomerates were deposited in separate basins. With each conglomerate belonging to an upward fining sequence, each was thought to form at the foot of a fault scarp (see Fig. 16.1). One explanation for a series of fault bounded basins is that they formed as a result of a shear movement along the Highland Boundary Fault or its equivalent.

3. There is ample evidence for post-Upper Old Red Sandstone N-S faulting, and this late-stage fracturing has controlled the orientation of the coastline and may have been responsible for the development of the Clyde Basin.

References

BLUCK, B.J. 1967. Deposition of some Upper Old Red Sandstone conglomerates in the Clyde area: a study in the significance of bedding. *Scott. J. Geol.* **3,** 139-167.

—————. 1978. Sedimentation in a late orogenic basin: the Old Red Sandstone of the Midland Valley of Scotland. *In: Crustal evolution of NW Britain and adjacent regions* (eds D.R.Bowes and B.E.Leake), *Geol J. Spec. Issue* **10,** 249-278.

—————. 1980. Evolution of a strike-slip, fault-controlled basin, Upper Old Red Sandstone, Scotland. *In: Sedimentation in oblique-slip mobile zones* (eds Ballance, P.F. and Reading, H.G.). *Internat. Assoc. Sedimentol. Spec. Publ.* **4,** 63-78.

—————. 1980. Structure, generation and preservation of upward fining, braided stream cycles in the Upper Old Red Sandstone of Scotland. *Trans. R. Soc. Edinb. Earth Sci.* **71,** 29-46.

—————. 1986. Upward coarsening sedimentation units and facies lineages, Old Red Sandstone, Scotland. *Trans. R. Soc. Edinb. Earth Sci.* **77,** 251-264.

DOWNIE,C and LISTER,T.R. 1969 The Sandy's Creek beds (Devonian) of Farland Head, Ayrshire. *Scott. J. Geol.* **5,** 193-206.

PATERSON, E.M. 1952. Notes on the tectonics of the Greenock-Largs Uplands and the Cumbraes. *Trans. geol.Soc. Glasg.* **21,** 430-435.

Excursion 17 **SALTCOATS**
D.S.Weedon

Theme: Sediments of Coal Measures (Carboniferous) age and the intrusive igneous rocks associated with them.

Features: Baked mussel bands; fossil trees in their growth position; differentiation in a picrite/teschenite sill.

Maps: O.S.   1:50 000   Sheet 70   Ayr, Kilmarnock and surrounding area.

B.G.S. 1:50 000   Sheet 22W   Irvine

Terrain: Coastal section comprising low-lying rocks, generally fairly close to the Saltcoats promenade.

Distance: Saltcoats lies about 16 km (10 miles) SE of Largs
and   on the coast road (A78).
Time   Easily accomplished in half a day.

Access: Any part of the shore section is easily reached via one of the sets of steps down from the promenade. Cars can be parked in many places along the B714, but preferably in one of the official car parks along the sea front.**(SSSI)**

Locality 1. (NS 249 411) **Coal Measure sediments and sill.** Opposite Seaview Road. Here Coal Measure sediments are well exposed, together with the top of the underlying teschenite sill, whose resistance to erosion has formed the headland which terminates at the pier (Fig 17.1). Heat from the underlying igneous intrusion has produced noticeable thermal metamorphism in the sediments immediately above, which are baked and hardened. The sill outcrops at the base of the promenade wall and immediately above occur two mussel bands, which contain the basal fauna of the similis-pulchra Zone, with *Anthraconaia salteri, Anthracosphaerium turgidum* and species of *Anthracosia*. With the baking and hardening, the non-marine bivalves in the lower of the two bands are well preserved but have become welded together: hence individual specimens are difficult to obtain. The overlying Wee Coal is visible at low water.

Locality 2. Fault. Between here and Locality 1, the succession has been displaced seawards by a NW-SE trending normal fault. This latter feature is well worth examination, as the respective rock units can be

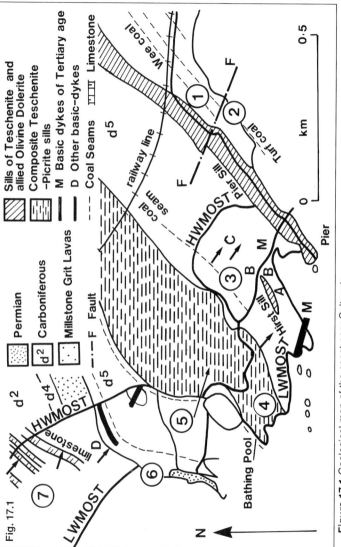

Figure 17.1 Geological map of the coast near Saltcoats.

231

easily traced to the line of the fault from each side and their displacement measured. These are excellent exposures for study by those new to geology. Only the top of the sill is seen to the east of the pier, as the greater part of the sill has been built over: however, in a cutting of the former Caledonian railway, some 1 km inland, the sill consists of three layers, an upper and lower teschenite layer and a median **picritic** layer (cf Saltcoats Main Sill, Locality 4).

Locality 3. Fossil trees. Coal Measure strata are well exposed in the extensive inter-tidal platform known locally as the Hirst. A thin coal (probably the Lower Wee Coal) is exposed together with overlying sandstones. These are cut by a sinuous, generally NW-SE trending, basic dyke which forms a distinctive feature across the bay at low water. On the seaward side of the dyke two small teschenite sills are exposed. It is immediately above the larger sill (shown on the map) that fossil trees are located (Yuill 1963). The trees occur in three groups within the sandstones lying immediately above the larger sill (approximate positions indicated on (Fig 17.1) at localities A, B, and C. In all, some 30 tree stumps were identified by Yuill, each in its position of growth. It should be noted that they were located after a succession of gales had swept clear the area of sand and shingle: as this is in constant motion, some or all of the stumps may not be exposed at any one time. The trees have been eroded to the general overall surface level and therefore diligent searching is necessary to locate them. The original outer layers have been preserved (unlike the trees at Fossil Grove) and they are of the sigillarian type, showing a ribbed appearance.

Please do not use hammers at this locality

Locality 4. Saltcoats Main Sill. The foreshore south of the Bathing Pool is formed by the Saltcoats Main Sill, an intrusion of Permo-Carboniferous age about 18.5m (60ft) thick, conformable with the regional dip towards the SE. It comprises three main units, believed to have been intruded successively (Patterson 1946): flow-banded **teschenite,** biotite-teschenite and **picrite.** A flight of steps leads directly on to the upper margin of the sill, whose topmost unit, comprising flow-banded teschenite, is in sharp contact with the overlying sandstones, which are hardened and altered to spotted hornfels. Stoping of the overlying sediment has occurred as xenoliths of hornfels

are common within the marginal teschenite: they normally lie parallel with the flow-banding. The flow-banded teschenite is about 2.7m (8ft) in thickness. Its contact with the underlying biotite teschenite is somewhat irregular but generally conformable with the overall dip of the sill. The contact between these two rock types is relatively sharp.

The biotite teschenite is characterized by its weathering into smooth rounded masses of fresh black rock accompanied by segregation veins and patches rich in pink analcite. The latter have been related mineralogically to **lugarite** (Patterson 1946) albeit with a higher percentage of potassium than the type rock (Lugar Sill, Excursion 23). There is no apparent chilling of the veins against the host teschenite and they appear to be segregation veins formed at a late stage in the cooling history.

The underlying central picrite occupies the central portion of the sill. It is approximately 9m (30ft) in thickness, and is essentially hornblende-picrite. There is no visible chilling of either picrite or the overlying biotite teschenite, but offshoots of picrite appear to intrude the teschenite and 'rafts' of the latter are present in the uppermost part of the picrite. The lower contact of the picrite with the underlying biotite teschenite shows similar relationships, namely no visible chilling of either rock type.

The Lower biotite teschenite forms the base of the sill, a layer about 3.6m (12ft) in thickness. The lower contact is with the Kilwinning Main Coal, which has been metamorphosed by the intrusion into a columnar coke. The lowermost part of the sill (some 1.5m or 5ft) has been altered into '**white trap**'.

Locality 5. Dykes. Below the Main Sill and the underlying Kilwinning Main Coal the Carboniferous sedimentary rocks, dominantly sandstones, are cut by a number of sinuous dykes with an overall E - W trend: they are generally doleritic affinities.

Locality 6. Ayrshire Bauxitic Clay. Further west, close to the low-water mark, the Ayrshire Bauxitic Clay is poorly exposed (**bauxite,** see Glossary). Varying in thickness from 1.2 - 1.6m (4 - 5ft), its upper highly-oolitic portion passes down into a reddish clay which contains specks of **sphaerosiderite**. The clay is underlain by decomposed lavas.

Locality 7. Limestones. Exposure of the limestones present at this general locality is unpredictable, owing to the shifting beach sand cover. Three limestone bands may be exposed, the highest being distinctly siliceous (note the relative hardness) and underlain by an arenaceous **fireclay** rich in ferruginous concretions. These limestones have been correlated with rocks of the Upper Limestone Group exposed to the north of Saltcoats, but this age is problematical.

A further feature of geological interest in this general area is the picrite sill forming the headland of Castle Craigs at Ardrossan (NS 226 414). It is described by Falconer (1907) as a banded intrusion composed of a lower marginal layer of olivine-feldspar rock (picrite) overlain successively by hornblende-dolerite and a fine-grained banded dolerite. The sill is exposed both on the shore at Castle Craigs and also inland along Hill Street, where curved columnar jointing is pronounced.

It is not recommended that the **far end** of Castle Craigs be visited, unless specimen collecting is vital. The intertidal rocks are seaweed covered and slippery and little may be observed on the weathered surfaces. Also, they are accessible only at low tide and as there is an overhanging unclimbable breakwater along the headland, unless **care** is exercised one may easily become cut off by the tide; this would result in at least a very wet return journey.

In contrast, there are many exposures of the sill which are easy to find inland, in the vicinity of the ruined castle on the hill above the headland.

References

BLUCK, B.J. 1967. Deposition of some Upper Old Red Sandstone conglomerates in the Clyde area: a study in the significance of bedding. *Scott. J. Geol.* **3,** 139-167.

DOWNIE, C. and LISTER, T.R. 1969. The Sandy's Creek Beds (Devonian) of Farland Head, Ayrshire. *Scott. J. Geol.* **5,** 193-206.

FALCONER, J.D. 1907. The Geology of Ardrossan. *Trans. R. Soc. Edinb.* **45,** 601-610.

PATTERSON, E.M. 1946. The Teschenite-Picrite Sill of Saltcoats, Ayrshire. *Trans. geol. Soc. Glasg.* **21,** 1-28.

———— 1951. The Old Red Sandstone Rocks of the West Kilbride-Largs district, Ayrshire. *Trans. geol. Soc. Glasg.* **21,** 207-236.

RICHEY, J.E., ANDERSON, E.M. and MACGREGOR, A.G. 1930. The Geology of North Ayrshire. *Mem. Geol. Surv. U.K.*

YUILL, M. 1963. Fossil tree stumps at Saltcoats. *Trans. geol. Soc. Glasg.* **25,** 1-3.

Excursion 18 LOANHEAD QUARRY
C. D. Gribble

Themes :   Clyde Plateau Lavas; a Permo-Carboniferous dyke; minerals and their occurrence.

Features :   Lava flow characters, red boles, rock joints, vesicular and amygdaloidal texture, porphyritic texture.

Maps :   O.S.   1: 50 000 Sheet 63 Firth of Clyde
             B.G.S. 1: 63 360 Sheet 30 Glasgow

Terrain :   Quarry floor and rock faces.

Distance :   Loanhead Quarry (NS 365 555) is situated near the A737 road, about 2 km (over 1mile) north of the village of Beith, which is about 20 km (12.5 miles) from central Glasgow.

Time :   About 45 minutes travelling time, and about 3 hours in the quarry (about a half day).

Access :   The quarry is operated by Tarmac Roadstone (Scotland) Ltd., at 134 Nithsdale Drive, Glasgow (041) 423 6611: for permission telephone the Quarry Manager direct at Loanhead Quarry (041) 234 . 2534 or 3758 . There is ample car parking space at the quarry offices, but first obtain permission from the Manager.

> **This is a working quarry.**
> **Hard hats must be worn.**
> **Beware of heavy vehicles which**
> **are continually moving around.**

There is a regular bus service from Buchanan Bus Station in Glasgow, taking about 1 hour and 40 minutes to Beith; the driver may be willing to stop near the quarry.

Introduction

In Lower Carboniferous times (about 360 million years ago), the Glasgow area was subjected to intense and widespread volcanic activity. Basic lava flows and volcanic ash were poured out over an area of more than 2500 km^2 reaching a maximum thickness of 800m,

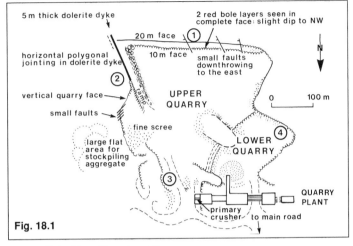

Figure 18.1. Plan of Loanhead Quarry.

and these are known as the Clyde Plateau Lavas. They now form the flat-topped Campsie Fells, Kilpatrick Hills and Renfrew Heights lying to the north, west and south of Glasgow respectively. Loanhead Quarry is excavated in the basalts which form the high ground to the SW of the city.

Three successive lava flows can be seen in the quarry, although the continuous removal of rock from the faces may make them difficult to identify from time to time.

Locality 1. (Fig 18.1). In the long south face in the Upper Quarry two layers of **red bole** are observed which separate the basalt flows. Judging from the position of the boles, the uppermost lava flow is more than 10m thick, the lower one at least 15m thick, and the middle lava flow about 8m thick. The high face is benched, i.e. it is split into an upper and lower face; the top two flows can be seen in the upper face, with the lower red bole running along the bench between the two faces. The lowermost flow occupies the complete lower face. These lava flows tend to undulate but, in general, dip at a shallow angle towards the north west. Examination of the basaltic rock shows that the lava is vesicular; that is it contains **vesicles**, which are gas holes in the rock formed by dissolved gases being released under reduced pressure

236

when the original molten lava was erupted on to the land surface. These vesicles are often empty, but sometimes may be filled with minerals formed by the deposition of various salts from solutions in which they had been dissolved. When this occurs, the lava is said to be amygdaloidal, and the mineral-filled cavities are called **amygdales**. Individual lava flows tend to have vesicles and amygdales near the top and bottom surfaces. When lava was first erupted gas bubbles formed and tried to escape from the molten rock. However the top of a lava flow would have congealed quickly, preventing the escape of these gas bubbles; and therefore a concentration of these would occur near the top. The movement of the lava flow over the land surface dragged the upper surface down at the front of the flow, so that concentrations of vesicles (or amygdales) occur at both the top *and* bottom of the flow.

Close inspection of the more non-vesicular blocks of lava occasionally reveals the presence of minerals which show good crystal faces, and are conspicuously bigger than the surrounding matrix. Such minerals are called **phenocrysts**, and the lava containing them is said to be **porphyritic**. This type of rock occurs when the molten lava has remained for some time in the magma chamber at depth, so that early formed minerals have had time to develop and grow to an appreciable size before the molten magma (containing both crystals *and* melt) is finally erupted on to the land surface. In the basalts at Loanhead the phenocrysts were originally olivine, but this has since been altered and replaced by an aggregate of **iddingsite** (a hydrated silicate of iron and magnesium) and iron oxide. A microscope examination of the basalt shows that it contains both fresh and altered olivine phenocrysts, in a matrix of feldspar laths and augite, together with some minute magnetite granules. The feldspar laths show a poor flow texture, being roughly aligned by the flow of the lava before it consolidated.

The lava flows in this quarry were originally erupted sub-aerially: i.e. poured on to a land surface. The presence of red boles shows that the top surface of each lava flow has been weathered in the presence of oxygen with the ferrous iron (Fe^{2+}) contained in the basalt being oxidised to ferric iron (Fe^{3+}), which reaction involves a colour change to red-brown (the colour of ferric iron); the thickness of the red bole gives an estimate of the length of time over which weathering took place. These weak, weathered surfaces or red boles have been preserved by the protection offered from the overlying lava flows.

Locality 2. An extremely fine example of a red bole can be observed on the small rock face to the east of the road leading away from the primary crusher towards the Upper Quarry (Fig. 18.1). The bole is up to half a metre thick and rests on top of a chloritised zone in which the principal mineral chlorite, a greenish, secondary mineral, was formed from the original ferromagnesian minerals in the basalt, either by late stage hydrothermal processes or by sub-horizontal shearing in the lava pile.

Joints occur throughout the quarry, appearing as vertical cracks running through the basalts. Crystallisation took place at point centres during the cooling of the basalt, and, as these cooling centres grew in size, thermal contraction of the igneous body also occurred which produced small gaps between adjacent cooling centres. A series of polygonal joints developed which grew in towards the centre of the igneous body; these joints developed at right angles to the margins of the cooling body. At Loanhead the joints are usually vertical since the lava flows are horizontal or sub-horizontal, although a few flat-lying joints may be seen on the extreme east face of the upper quarry near the very fine grained 'scree falls'. The basalt jointing should be compared with that of the dolerite dyke described below.

Locality 3. A dolerite dyke is seen in the south east face of the Upper Quarry near the corner, where it exhibits superb polygonal jointing over the entire face. The dolerite dyke is a thin igneous sheet (5m thick here) intruded vertically, and, since cooling takes place from the margins inwards, the joints affecting the dyke are horizontal. A dark green, soapy mineral known as **bowlingite** (a variety of saponite) frequently coats joint surfaces, often in association with a finely divided red **heulandite**. Native copper may also occur in the joint planes, but is more common as small flakes widely disseminated through the basalt.

Locality 4. In a few places in the upper quarry, especially on the west side of the lower face, a thin layer of volcanic ash or **tuff** may be seen. These ash bands are discontinuous and it is impossible to tell if they were deposited in water.

Mineralisation in the rocks at Loanhead Quarry

Most of the interesting minerals in the basalt lavas are not primary minerals, originally crystallising as an integral part of the rock, but secondary minerals formed in the vesicles and joints of the basalt after it had consolidated. The most common mineral is calcite, found as 'dog-tooth' crystals, cleavage rhombs and as massive aggregates. Pale green, botryoidal (grape-like) masses of **prehnite** are common, and also snow-white crystals of **analcime**. Copper may be found native on joint surfaces and also as the hydrated carbonate **malachite**, and the oxide **cuprite**. **Zeolites** are present though rather rare, especially red heulandite, and the white fibrous minerals **thomsonite** and **natrolite**. An important collection of the zeolite minerals of the Glasgow district can be seen in the Hunterian Museum of Glasgow University.

As regional vulcanicity waned, hot waters, perhaps bearing carbon dioxide, percolated through the consolidated lava pile. The existing primary minerals (olivine, feldspar, augite) were altered, and elements released during this episode contributed to the formation of low-temperature secondary minerals such as calcite and zeolites in the cavities and fissures of the basalts. Either copper was magmatic in origin, or it was formed by the percolating waters concentrating the minute quantities of copper originally found in the basalt.

Excursion 19 **BOYLESTON QUARRY**
D.S.Weedon

Themes ;   Examination of the nature and relationship of three Clyde Plateau lava flows: collection of minerals, mainly of hydrothermal origin present in amygdales and veins of basalt in spoil-heaps within the quarry: glacial topography viewed from a vantage point above the quarry.

Features: Columnar jointing: bole weathering: vesicles: erosional channel showing graded bedding; minerals particularly of the zeolite group.

Maps: O.S.   1 : 50 000   Sheet 64   Glasgow
          B.G.S.   1 : 63 360   Sheet 30   Glasgow

Terrain: The extensive quarry floor is generally flat, but some scrambling is necessary when searching for minerals on the spoil heaps.

The main quarry face is unstable and should not be approached too closely.

Also, the quarry floor to the SE is flooded and marshy and should be avoided.

Distance and Time   Boyleston Quarry, Barrhead is within easy driving distance of Glasgow, lying some 10 km. (6 miles) to the SW. A half-day should be adequate to visit the quarry, examine the lavas and to collect representative minerals.

Access: At present there is no prohibition of access into the quarry, but this might change in the future. The quarry (NS 492 598) lies to the west of the B774, NW of Barrhead. Travelling from Barrhead on the B774 pass under the railway bridge and take the fourth turning to the left, Quarry Road.
Cars should be parked at the bottom of the track leading up to the quarry. The track is rough, but ingress is easy on foot. **(SSSI)**

Introduction

Formed from a large excavation near the base of the Clyde Plateau Lavas the quarry has been disused for many years, but is still accessible by a rough track from a local road in Barrhead. At the present time it is not prohibited to the general public and indeed is quite popular with the local youth.

At the top of the path the view is of an extensive old quarry floor extending towards a three-sided vertical face,in which individual lava flows may be distinguished (Fig 19.1). The quarry face is some 20m high and should not be approached too closely. Indeed, apart from studying the individual lava flows and their characteristics from a distance, it is unnecessary to hammer the main faces, as lava and mineral collecting and examination of the contact relationship of the lower two lava flows is much more productive within the main quarry floor.

Locality 1. The contact of lowermost lavas (1 and 2) can be studied in the mound within the quarry floor, to the north of the quarry face towards its eastern side (Fig. 19.1). Only the topmost 1.5 m of the bottom lava is exposed, appearing as a highly vesicular reddened surface, indicative of **bole** weathering: both **vesicles** and **amygdales** are present, the latter containing mainly calcite and quartz. The contact with the base of the overlying lava (number 2) is readily descernible, as the latter is non-vesicular but rich in veins of calcite, analcime and prehnite and upwards quickly becomes dense and greenish-black in colour. The absence of vesicles and amygdales at the upper contact implies that here there was no overturn of the advancing front of the second lava flow as it overwhelmed the earlier.

Locality 2. The centre of Lava 2 . Viewed from a distance the eastern end of the quarry displays the massive nature of the centre of the second lava by its well-developed columnar jointing. The lava is dark-green in colour and the jointing is vertical. The jointing, which is typical of many of the thicker Clyde Plateau lavas, is formed by contraction during cooling at right angles to the upper and lower surfaces. As the lava flows are nearly horizontal, the joints are vertical. Native copper occurs somewhat rarely along the joint planes: it also occurs as disseminated flecks throughout the basalt groundmass , again not commonly. The lava is of the **Dalmeny** type but in hand-

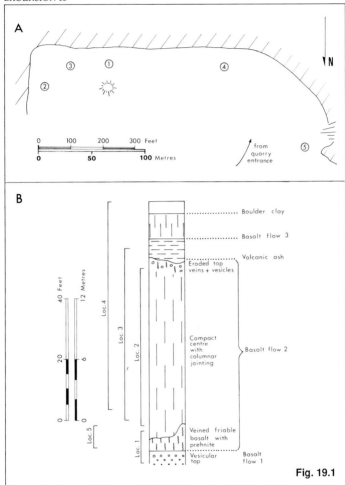

Figure 19.1. Plan view and section of Boyleston Quarry showing the approximate positions of Localities 1 - 5.

specimen micro-phenocrysts seem to be infrequent. However, when viewed in thin section it can be seen that pseudomorphs after olivine occur quite frequently : also in thin section can be seen a tendency towards a trachytic (flow) structure due to the alignment of the groundmass feldspars.

Locality 3. A vesicular top of Lava 2 can be seen at this part of the quarry, above the massive centre described at the previous locality. The vesiculation results from originally dissolved gases 'boiling off' and escaping upwards through the cooling liquid and becoming trapped at the top as the surface lava rapidly congealed. The resulting cavities and fissures have been subsequently filled with a variety of minerals, here mainly calcite. Also at this locality can be seen a red-brown bed, flaggy consolidated volcanic ash, lying directly above the vesicular top of the lava.

Locality 4. Bedded volcanic ash features prominently at this most interesting face in the quarry (Fig. 19.2.) ; it is perhaps unique within the exposures of the Clyde Plateau Lavas. In essence, it illustrates beautifully the periodicity of the local volcanism. The interface between the top of Lava 2 and the overlying Lava 3 is clearly visible (Fig.19.2) and two features are immediately apparent: the top of Lava 2 is not flat but undulating, and one down-warp is pronounced and filled with bedded material. These are erosional features and it is readily apparent that there has been a break in volcanicity in this area of sufficient duration to allow fairly extensive weathering of the underlying Lava

Figure 19.2. Sketch section, from photographs, of the erosional channel in the upper surface of Lava 2.

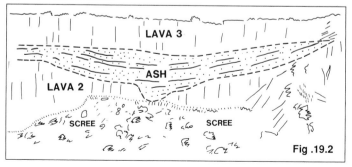

243

2 to take place. The undulations are erosional channels and the sediment laid down within them shows evidence of graded bedding, indicating river action. The sediments within the channel are entirely of volcanic material, as might well be expected within a wide-spread province of early Carboniferous volcanicity. It has been noted that volcanic bombs, present within the channel sediments, have disturbed the bedding by impact, implying that volcanicity was still proceeding in the vicinity while fluviatile deposition was taking place. It is also noteworthy that scree derived from the outwash channel vicinity has yielded well-formed crystals of augite and olivine.

Locality 5. An outcrop at the NW side of the quarry (Fig.19.1) is part of the Number 2 lava flow in which there is fairly extensive mineralization. The cavities and fissures present contain calcite, analcime and malachite: prehnite is also common towards the bottom of the exposure.

It should be emphasised that when hammering this or any other exposure within the quarry, the greatest care should be exercised and **protective goggles should be worn**. The fresh basalt is very fine-grained and tough and thus splinters when hammered. It is, of course, tempting to "open up" new exposures, but often the weathered rocks present in the spoil heaps will break more readily and diligent searching can reveal quite large cavities in which the minerals were deposited.

The probable origin of these minerals is the late-stage hydrothermal alteration of the lavas. The hot waters, charged with carbon dioxide, altered the high-temperature silicate minerals present in the lava and re-deposited lower temperature carbonates (particularly calcite) and hydrous silicates mainly of the zeolite group. Some of the minerals present, for example native copper, may have been of primary magmatic origin: other copper-bearing minerals such as malachite, a copper carbonate, are probably of secondary, hot water derivation.

There is a fine collection of zeolites and other minerals from various localities in the local Clyde Plateau Lavas displayed in the Hunterian Museum, within the main building of Glasgow University. It is open to everyone and a visit there would simplify identification of the minerals you have collected.

Before leaving , if the visibility is reasonable, it is well worth the effort to follow the old road to the top of the quarry, to look at the surrounding countryside. Here, one is standing on the eastern termination of the basalt outcrop; the junction of the Clyde Plateau Lavas and the overlying Upper Sedimentary Group extends generally westwards from this point. Looking NE towards Glasgow, one moves up through the Carboniferous succession to the Carboniferous Limestone Series. Apart from the contrast of the higher terrain formed by the basalts and the lower relief of the softer Carboniferous sediments, the most striking feature is in the more immediate foreground and is dominantly of glacial origin. A series of elongate mounds (drumlins), with their long axes parallel, indicate that moulding of glacial material has occurred with the passage of an ice sheet. This is a fine example of "basket of eggs" topography, the shallower slopes of each mound indicating the direction in which the ice was moving. Which direction was that?

Excursion 20 **TREARNE QUARRY**
C.J. Burton
with mineralogy by **J.G. Todd**

Themes: Fossil faunas and their ecologies in a complete transgression-regression sequence in the Lower Carboniferous.

Features: The ecology of a marine transgression and the relationships within fossil communities, and between fossil communities and rock types. Coal, seat-earth, mudstone, shale, limestone, dykes, fossils, minerals.

Maps: O.S.   1:50 000   Sheet 63   Firth of Clyde
          1:25 000   Sheet NS35 (1st edition)   Kilbirnie
                     Sheet NS25/35 (2nd edition) Largs
                     & Kilbirnie
        B.G.S. 1:63 360   Sheet 22   Kilmarnock

Terrain: Exclusively within the quarry. Trearne is a working quarry with a safe, flat floor. Keep clear of haulage roads and unstable working faces.

Distance: Trearne quarry is situated 24km (15 miles) SW of Glasgow. It lies 2.5km (1.5 miles) east of Beith.
          Approach Trearne from Glasgow via Barrhead (Fig. 20.1) and Lugton village on the A.736. At Lugton village turn onto the Beith road (B.777) at the Paraffin Lamp Inn. After about 4.0km (2.5 miles) take the by-road to Trearne quarry, an inconspicuous left turn just before a small brick house is reached on the right hand side of the main road.   The quarry entrance lies 0.4km (0.25 mile) along this road opposite a bungalow. There is abundant parking opposite the bungalow, or within the quarry itself.

Time: Within the quarry walking distance is minimal and the itinerary can be accomplished in around 3 hours, although keen fossil and mineral collectors will require far more time. **(SSSI)**

246

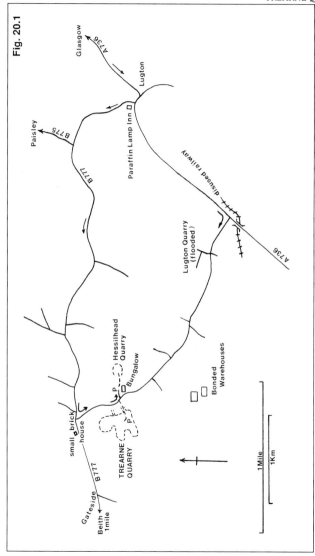

Figure 20.1. Location map for Trearne Quarry.

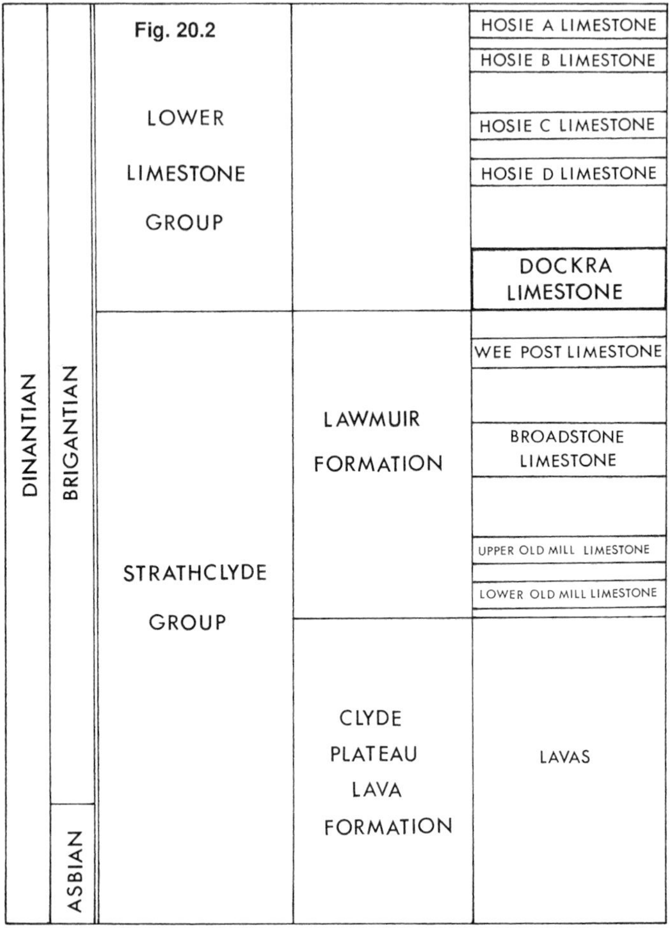

DINANTIAN	BRIGANTIAN	Fig. 20.2 LOWER LIMESTONE GROUP		HOSIE A LIMESTONE
				HOSIE B LIMESTONE
				HOSIE C LIMESTONE
				HOSIE D LIMESTONE
				DOCKRA LIMESTONE
		STRATHCLYDE GROUP	LAWMUIR FORMATION	WEE POST LIMESTONE
				BROADSTONE LIMESTONE
				UPPER OLD MILL LIMESTONE
				LOWER OLD MILL LIMESTONE
	ASBIAN		CLYDE PLATEAU LAVA FORMATION	LAVAS

Figure 20.2. The Carboniferous stratigraphy of North Ayrshire.

Access :   *Apply to:*   James Reid & Co. (1947)
Lugton Lime Works, Lugton,
Kilmarnock KA3 4EB
Tel: 8751 435

If it does not prove possible to telephone prior to arrival at the quarry, then contact the quarry foreman at the bungalow by the entrance for permission to enter the workings. **Hard hats should be worn.** Recently, the owners have become increasingly reluctant to allow access to large parties, except those local groups which visit the quarry annually.

Introduction

Trearne quarry lies within the upper Brigantian Stage of the Lower Carboniferous, (Fig.20.2) and the rocks within the quarry belong to the Lower Limestone Group of the Kilmarnock Basin. Below this Group lies the Strathclyde Group (Paterson & Hall 1986), the base of which is formed by the basaltic lavas of the Clyde Plateau Volcanic Formation. These lavas appear in the prominent hills to the west and north of the quarries. Above the lavas, going towards the centre of the basin, are beds of the succeeding Lawmuir Formation, rich in volcanic detritus at the base and having, higher up, shales, seat-earths and sandstones representing terrestrial deposition, and limestones representing occasional marine incursions. On entering the Lower Limestone Group, marine incursions become more widespread, evidence for these being seen in the many limestones and shales within the Group. The Dockra Limestone of Trearne is one of the oldest of these limestones, although current opinion is divided as to whether it should be correlated with the Hurlet Limestone (Whyte 1981) or the higher Blackhall Limestone (Wilson 1979). Traditionally (Richey *et al.* 1930), and with some justification, the Dockra Limestone is equated with the Hurlet Limestone of the Paisley area and as such forms the base of the Lower Limestone Group. In North Ayrshire the Lower Limestone Group is, on this basis, 38metres (124 feet) thick, compared to 90m (300 feet) near Hurlet and 180m (600 feet) in west Midlothian. The Dockra Limestone follows a marine transgression, and was deposited in the shallow, tropical waters of the North Ayrshire Shelf. The general geography of these waters was of a wide marine channel open to the SW and communicating with the Glasgow Basin to the north. The limits of this channel are supplied by the thinning out of the Dockra Limestone against the underlying lavas (Richey *et al.* 1930). At Trearne the limestone is about 7.5m (25 feet) thick, but 8km (5 miles) or so to the east it thins to zero against a contemporary land area which seems to have been a large island, and of low relief - judging by the lack of anything more than clay-sized detritus in the limestone. Similarly the limestone thins to the NW, indicating a western land area which was probably the margin of the Laurussian continent.

Itinerary

Trearne Quarry (NS 372 533) (Fig. 20. 3).

In this quarry two major patterns of variation may be seen within the Dockra Limestone and the beds immediately below it. These patterns are in the horizontal and the vertical aspects of the quarry respectively. In the horizontal it is clear that massive and irregularly bedded limestones are dominant in the southern bay of the quarry, but that towards the central bay these beds become thinner and less massive and thin dark shale horizons are intercalated between them. By the time the north-western and northern bays are reached limestones, in thin, regular beds, have become subordinate to dark shales, thus confirming an overall and rapid decrease of limestone content from south to north.

The vertical succession (Fig. 20.4) begins, quarrywide, with a pale seat earth, followed by a coal horizon, then marine marginal, and finally marine, black shales, signalling a marine transgression. Above, in the southern half of the quarry, lies a marine limestone succession, whereas, in the northern half of the quarry, above the black shales, lies an initial limestone followed by an alternation of dark shales and limestones. Both successions culminate in a final limestone, the top of which shows a Carboniferous weathering surface and, rarely, the imprint of stigmarian roots. Both trees and weathering signal a regression to terrestrial conditions. Within this major cycle are minor cycles of emergence and submergence marked by faunal changes and **hard grounds.**

These variation patterns, and the environmental changes behind them, acted as cues for the prolific local fauna, since the dark shales and the limestones each have their own well-defined fossil communities which supplant one another when the environment changes (Shiells and Penn 1971). The basal black shales also contain a fauna transitional between the fluvial and the marine environment. Within both limestones and dark shales minor environmental variations in both the horizontal and the vertical senses, as well as variations in sea bed topography and thus energy levels, have led to the establishment of

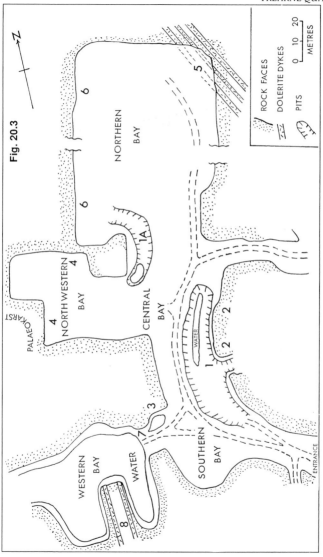

Figure 20.3. Trearne quarry and localities within it.

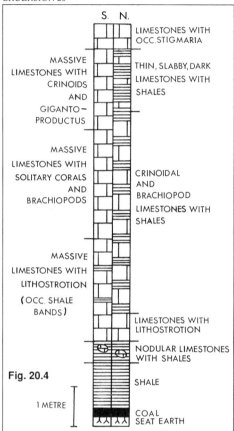

S. N.

LIMESTONES WITH
OCC. STIGMARIA

MASSIVE
LIMESTONES WITH
CRINOIDS
AND
GIGANTO-
PRODUCTUS

THIN, SLABBY, DARK
LIMESTONES WITH
SHALES

MASSIVE
LIMESTONES WITH
SOLITARY CORALS
AND
BRACHIOPODS

CRINOIDAL
AND
BRACHIOPOD
LIMESTONES WITH
SHALES

MASSIVE
LIMESTONES WITH
LITHOSTROTION
(OCC. SHALE
BANDS)

LIMESTONES WITH
LITHOSTROTION

NODULAR LIMESTONES
WITH SHALES

Fig. 20.4

SHALE

1 METRE

COAL
SEAT EARTH

Figure 20.4.
Stratigraphical column for Trearne Quarry.

strongly localized variants of the major communites, as well as a detailed chronicle of changes in time as reflected in the succession of the communities and their variants.

Mineralization is widespread within the Dockra Limestone (Todd 1989) and at Trearne can be found in three situations. Firstly, in fissures in the limestone, especially where doleritic dykes have caused minor faulting; secondly filling the interiors of fossil brachiopod shells, and thirdly as nodules and mineralized shells in the basal black shales. The minerals themselves can be grouped into five major classes - carbonates, sulphides, sulphates, silicates and halides, with the majority of crystal specimens being fine but small, and best studied under the microscope, or with the hand lens. It seems likely that the fossil brachiopod minerals (quartz, dolomite, barite, **strontianite** and fluorite) are the result of later mineralising solutions percolating through the rocks rather than forming during **diagenesis** of the original sediments. Inspection of a large number of specimens suggests the **paragenetic**

sequence calcite (first generation brown crystals) - quartz - calcite (second generation large white crystals) - dolomite - chalcopyrite/ **millerite** - fluorite - chalcopyrite - strontianite. The faulting of the limestone by doleritic dykes has caused fissuring with the emplacement of chalcopyrite, pyrite, barite and fluorite, the crystals of the latter being much larger than in the fossil cavities.

Trearne is a working quarry and it must be emphasised that the itinerary which follows deals with localities as they exist at the time of publication. Thus some localities will disappear, others will be better exposed and new areas will appear as quarrying goes on.

Locality 1. This lies within a lengthy, shallow pit in the floor of the quarry immediately to the right of the main entrance. The marine transgression is recorded in a section 2.9 metres thick, below the Dockra Limestone, in this pit. Along the eastern wall of the pit and in the deeper parts of the western wall the following succession can be seen (Fig. 20.4). Firstly a pale, grey-white clay approximately 1m thick. This clay is crumbly when dry and contains comminuted, blackish plant material, and has a layer of calcareous nodules at its base. It forms the **seat-earth** (soil) in which grew the plants which formed the succeeding coal. This coal, probably the Hurlet Coal, is of variable thickness, ranging from thin, carbonaceous partings in black shale to a seam 12 cm thick, interbedded with black shales and thin, fine-grained limestone beds. Within the coal and on the carbonaceous partings are plant fossils, including the bark of *Lepidodendron* and its root *Stigmaria* (Fig. 2.3). The coal is a bright, bituminous coal with occasional nodules of pyrite and numerous thin calcite veins. The presence of limestones and the variable thickness of the coal suggests a location very close to the sea, with patches of peat surrounded by, and interspersed with, the lime-mud precipitated from marine waters.

Immediately above the coal are 21.5cm of grey to black, very fine-grained mudstones with scattered plant remains, mainly the twigs and straplike leaf fragments of *Lepidodendron*, and occasional small fish. Succeeding this is a thicker bed (53.5cm) of splintery, black shale with irregular claystone nodules. This shale contains large numbers of two species of the brachiopod *Lingula*, (Fig.4.3) these being *Lingula squamiformis* and *Lingula mytiloides*. In this locality *L. squamiformis* is concentrated near the base of the bed and *L. mytiloides* is not seen. Elsewhere in the quarry *L. mytiloides* is common near the top of the bed. *Lingula squamiformis* can occasionally be found in life position.

Fig. 20.5

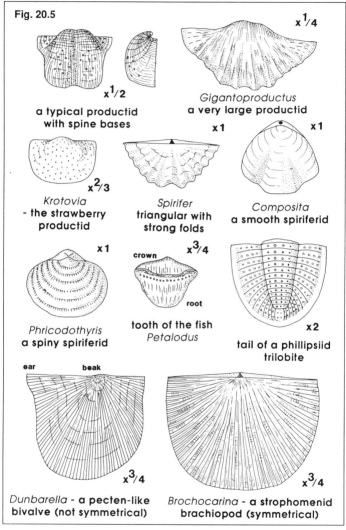

x¼

Gigantoproductus
a very large productid

x½

a typical productid
with spine bases

x⅔

Krotovia
- the strawberry
productid

x1

Spirifer
triangular with
strong folds

x1

Composita
a smooth spiriferid

x1

Phricodothyris
a spiny spiriferid

crown   x¾

root

tooth of the fish
Petalodus

x2

tail of a phillipsiid
trilobite

ear   beak

x¾

Dunbarella - a pecten-like
bivalve (not symmetrical)

x¾

Brochocarina - a strophomenid
brachiopod (symmetrical)

Figure 20.5. Fossils from Trearne Quarry.

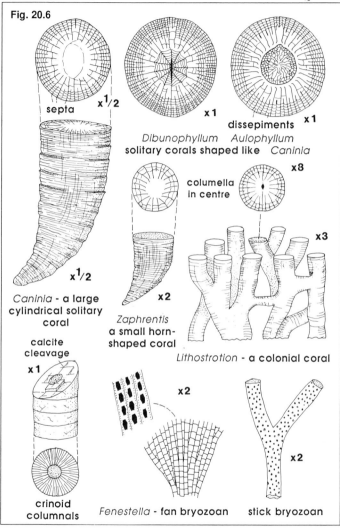

Fig. 20.6

septa x$\frac{1}{2}$

x1

dissepiments x1

Dibunophyllum *Aulophyllum*
solitary corals shaped like *Caninia*

columella
in centre x8

Caninia - a large
cylindrical solitary
coral x$\frac{1}{2}$

Zaphrentis
a small horn-
shaped coral x2

x3

Lithostrotion - a colonial coral

calcite
cleavage x1

crinoid
columnals

x2

Fenestella - fan bryozoan

stick bryozoan x2

Figure 20.6. More fossils from Trearne Quarry.

At this point the marine transgression has progressed to a position at which brackish water has spread over the site of the coal swamp. At the top of the *Lingula* bed is a black shale 1m thick, forming the last bed before the Dockra Limestone. Within this bed the sediments become fully marine, heralded at the base by the presence of the rhynchonellid brachiopod *Pleuropugnoides*. The fauna of the bed is very rich and of various life styles - infaunal (buried), vagrant benthos (free-moving seabed forms) and epifaunal (attached) - the whole representing a thriving community dominated by brachiopods and bivalves, together with gastropods, bryozoans and crinoids (Figs 20.5, 20.6). The dominant brachiopod is the small to medium-sized *Antiquatonia insculpta,* but others are also present in some numbers including *Eomarginifera præcursor, Martinothyris, Spirifer* (sometimes colonized by the inarticulate brachiopod *Crania), Composita, Dielasma* and *Orbiculoidea.* Among the bivalves are *Edmondia, Sanguinolites* and *Polidevcia* of the burrowers and free-movers, and the dominant, smooth or slightly ribbed *Pernopecten* of the attached forms. Gastropods include the flat-coiled *Straparollus* and, rarely, the minute *Glabrocingulum.* (Fig. 4.3). The stick-bryozoan, *Rhabdomeson*, is common as are the broken stems, arms and, occasionally, cups of crinoids. Rare goniatites also exist at this level. The preservation of brachiopods with intact spines, and the cups of crinoids suggest very low energy levels and quiet waters.

About 50cm above the base of the bed there is a horizon in which pyritization of the brachiopods has taken place and where pyrite nodules up to 8cm in diameter have formed. The individual crystals in these nodules are octahedral.

The beds seen in full section at Locality 1 may be seen as partial exposures in other parts of the quarry, especially at Locality 1A, where weathered shales from the heaps release many fossils.

Locality 2. This comprises the face immediately above Locality 1 and is variably accessible from that locality at its southern and northern ends. The section thus exposed includes the entire thickness of the Dockra Limestone (7.5m) with, at the base, a 1m thick horizon in which calcareous shales alternate with thin limestone horizons or bands of calcareous nodules. The shales, best exposed at the southern end of the locality, close to the quarry entrance, are considerably more calcareous than the black shales of Locality 1 below them, and have a distinctly different fauna. Bivalves are rare in these shales, the fauna being dominated by a rich, though restricted, community of crinoids, brachiopods and bryozoans which lived in quiet waters. Several crinoid genera are present and the scatter of semi-intact stems, arms and even cups suggest that minimal post-mortem movement has taken place. The genera range in size from forms up to 1m tall to forms of much less than half that height, suggesting a layered community rather like a forest. Commonly found are the large stems and intricately ornamented plates and arms of *Rhabdocrinus scotocarbonarius*, as well as the distinctive stems of *Ureocrinus* with their alternation or semi-alternation of large and small **ossicles**. The dominant brachiopod, found in large numbers is *Eomarginifera præcursor* a tiny and very common fossil here, the thin metallic-looking spines of which are common in the shales.

Growing among the crinoids was the stick-bryozoan *Rhabdomeson*, a sure indicator with its branching tree-like shape of a quiet low-energy environment. Other bryozoans encrust shell fragments and fallen crinoids on the sea bed. The small solitary coral *Zaphrentis* is also commonly present. The community, its layering and the maximum size of the larger crinoids all suggest that water depth was of the order of ten metres over the area.

The thin or nodular limestones accompanying the shales represent times at which input of **clastic** mud was restricted and limited carbonate deposition was possible - the nodules representing local patches of lime mud. These limestones are detrital and above them are thicker limestones which represent a period during which clastic muds were rarely present in the area. However, in this section, and elsewhere in the quarry some limestone beds have very thin, unfossiliferous shales between them. Such shales do not represent original deposition, but are **stylolitic** in origin, being the result of pressure-solution between beds of limestone, in which calcium carbonate is removed and a deposit of the clay originally in the limestone is left behind.

These massive limestones themselves reflect changing environments, and for the first 2m it can be shown that water depth had diminished and that the water itself had become clearer, although the area was still below wave-base in this area. The evidence lies within the many patches of the colonial coral *Lithostrotion* (Fig. 20.6) found in this area. These patches, still in life position, formed a series of branching bushes of coral up to a maximum of 1m high and perhaps 3m in diameter, scattered across a wide area and separated from one another by flat areas of sea-bed. In these spaces between the coral "bushes" flourished several genera of small, bushy bryozoans, including *Septopora*, a few small fenestellid bryozoans and crinoids. Distributed throughout the lower two-thirds of the limestones, as well as between the corals, are the productid brachiopods *Eomarginifera longispina, Pugilis scoticus, Krotovia spinulosa* and *Echinoconchus punctatus*, as well as the distinctive spiriferid *Brachythyris*. Many of these fossils are closed and contain a small amount of fine mud, infiltrated into the cavity, layered gravitationally and capped by minerals. These **geopetals** indicate the original attitude of the shell to the horizontal, and the fact that the vast majority of the geopetals do not now conform to bedding horizontal suggests that after deposition the shells were disturbed by **bioturbation**. On numerous lower bedding surfaces are the brown, now calcareous and sugary-looking tethering strands, up to 1m long, of the siliceous sponge *Hyalostelia smithi*. Dense grey mudclots within the limestones are associated with the remains of these sponges, and may be algal precipitates.   More certainly, horizontal and sub-horizontal grey banding reflect the former presence of algally bound lime-muds at the sea-bed.

At five or more distinct levels within the limestones, the first about 2m above the base, are horizons where it is clear that massive destruction of the corals and other members of the fauna has taken place. Some of these horizons are in the form of large, irregular lenses of debris, up to 7cm thick, draped in the lee of large groups of coral colonies. The debris consists of smashed *Lithostrotion* branches, broken solitary corals and brachiopod fragments and appears to be due to either storm damage or a period of shallowing above wave-base - the former being the more likely.

The upper 3.5m of the limestones reflects a change in environment from an occasionally disturbed but relatively quiet environment to one which was at first quieter and then more agitated. Quieter conditions are signalled by a decrease in the number and size of *Lithostrotion* colonies, although in the southern part of the locality these do persist up to the top of the limestones, and also by the incoming of numerous solitary corals of the genera *Dibunophyllum, Caninia* and occasionally the clisiophyllid *Aulophyllum*. (Fig. 20.6). These are sometimes found rolled together in "nests" by current action in brief episodes of higher energy.

As the top of the succession is approached evidence for more agitated conditions is found, firstly in a horizon rich in the extremely large productid *Gigantoproductus* (Fig. 20.5), but poor in all else but rolled and broken debris. The huge brachiopods, of mature size, are upside down and appear to have been moved by powerful currents. Secondly, above this level, and forming limestone pavements at the top of the face is a thick horizon of crinoidal **grainstone**, visible over much of the southern and central bays of the quarry. The crinoidal debris includes long, but randomly oriented lengths of stem, locked together with an extensive meshwork of the spines of *Eomarginifera*. On this pile of debris grew extensive colonies of the bryozoan *Fenestella*, a **fenestrate** form common in agitated water (Fig. 20.6). The anomalous length of the crinoid stems, unbroken in the agitated water, is explained by the fact that they were joined to each other by **cirri**, in large forests, fell joined together and were locked into place by the bryozoans and brachiopods. Occasional examples of the flattened, but sharp-edged, mollusc-crushing teeth of the shark-like fish *Petalodus* can be found here (Fig. 20.5).

In the northern part of this locality, close to the steep quarry road running east, mineralization is widespread in limestone fissures. In these fissures fluorite is found associated with "dog-tooth" calcite. The cubic, pale yellow fluorite crystals are up to 1cm across, and some have chalcopyrite inclusions. Occasionally, in the same area, veins of barite are exposed.

Locality 3. This is a face on the right of the entrance to the flooded area of the quarry, and is itself fringed by a marshy area. The base of this face is in *Lithostrotion* limestone, but a little higher up, perhaps 1m above the base, is a horizon displaying every sign of extremely agitated water over a rough and bumpy seabed. This horizon is marked by masses of rolled and smashed corals and brachiopods sedimented as a hummocky surface on which are growing colonies of the **sclerosponge** group, the chaetetids. These form pancake-shaped patches which, in cross-section, look like miniature colonial corals and which effectively preserve the contemporary sea-bed. Their low aspect is a sign of powerful agitation well above wave-base, as is the presence of single gigantoproductid shells piled into one another like stacked bowls. This horizon is about 1m thick and gradually fades out upwards into finer lime-muds with crinoidal debris. Its thickness suggests that rather than a storm-induced horizon, it marks a period of shallowing which, since it does not appear at Locality 2, also suggests that sea-bed topography was marked by sharp rises and depressions of a very local nature.

> **Please do not hammer this locality.**

Locality 4. Now go northwards along the line of faces into the northwestern bay of the quarry and approach the northern face of this bay. This actively quarried face, which should be approached carefully, reveals the first evidence of a series of facies changes which bring in muds to alternate with the limestone horizons. The advent of muds suggests, and the fossils bear out, quieter and perhaps deeper waters on what appears at first to be a regular alternation. However the limestones are grain-supported, i.e, the shelly materials within them touch and thus resist compression, and a closer look reveals that large areas of the limestone face show fossils which are uncrushed and smaller areas lateral to them where the fossils are crushed and flattened. This represents areas where diagenesis happened in two distinct phases, early and late; early diagenesis supporting the shells and resisting the later diagenetic flattening. Thus the límestones resist much of the crushing and may be as much as 70%-90% of their original thickness, whereas the mudstones have no such grain support, most of their fossils are crushed flat, and they represent perhaps 20% of their depositional thickness. The regular alternation is a diagenetic artefact and periods of mud accumulation are in the majority in this face. The fauna of these mudstones will be dealt with under Locality 6.

Within the limestones the dominant association is that of brachiopods and crinoids in relatively quiet water conditions. Brachiopod diversity is high,and among the smaller forms the productids are represented by the small and elongated *Avonia*, together with *Promarginifera, Eomarginifera, Pugilis* and *Krotovia*, with its multitude of spine bases resembling the surface of a strawberry (Fig. 20.5). The larger productids include *Buxtonia* and the rare, broadly flanged *Kochiproductus. Rugosochonetes* and *Martinothyris* are common and the small terebratuloid *Dielasma* appears. The most common bivalve present is the large, fan-shaped *Pinna*, living upright in the lime muds. The rare and enigmatic square, cone-shaped fossil *Paraconularia* is also present.

The many crinoids occur usually as long lengths of current-stacked stems, although occasionally they may be found as large pockets of debris. These pockets appear to have formed by the rupture of an algal mat and the consequent current erosion of the loose underlying lime mud, this being replaced by rolled and disjointed crinoidal debris. Limestones higher up the face are often stylolitically bedded, appearing to have flat bedding planes. However close examination shows that the sea bed was far more uneven than it thus appears, with early diagenesis forming hard grounds of limestone rock which appear to have eroded to form an irregular topography of ridges and hollows with cavities of up to 30 cm height. The formation of such hard grounds suggests that at times the lime muds were above sea level where hardening and erosion took place. On later submergence the cavities were colonized by calcareous sponges and other fixed animals. A marked tendency in this bay, and to the north, is the development of a separate limestone facies which reflects a different environment with its own specialized faunas. The facies is represented by darker, more muddy limestones which break to form thin, flat slabs which weather to a pale surface. These limestones can be seen at higher levels in all faces of the bay. In the northern face these beds contain solitary corals (*Dibunophyllum*), probably in growth position, and the large coiled gastropod *Straparollus*. However in the western bay the fauna is better developed, and here large slabs, quarried from the upper levels, and large flat slabs on the quarry top, bear prolific assemblages of fossils which are certainly in life position.

The main component of these assemblages is the large, flat brachiopod *Brochocarina*, the semicircular shells of which, attached one to another, form large oyster-like colonies. On these shells, which may have hinge-line widths of 12 cm or more, *Crania* sometimes colonises. Around these colonies lived productids, including *Kochiproductus, Spirifer, Composita*, large numbers of *Martinothyris* and a variety of branching and small fan bryozoans. The waters were generally very quiet, evidence for this being seen in the remains of the sea-urchin *Archaeocidaris*, some of which are collapsed and unscattered individuals, and in the occasional complete crinoids also present. Meandering across the surfaces of some of the slabs are the long, thin, fluted **coralla** of the coral *Heterophyllia*, an unusual prostrate form. In the more muddy horizons are relatively rare specimens of the trilobite *Phillipsia* (Fig. 20.5). The limestones of the northern parts of this bay contain many hollow brachiopods, these are lined with a first

261

generation of brown rhombohedral calcite, followed by a second generation of clear "dog-tooth" calcite, brown saddle-shaped groups of dolomite and micro-cubes of colourless fluorite. Some of the brachiopods are rich in strontianite which forms white, hemispherical aggregates to 2mm, or minute, spiky, pseudohexagonal crystals. On the flat surfaces above the faces there are signs of extensive **palaeokarst** development subsequent to the marine regression and, very rarely, slabs of a yellowish crinoidal limestone can be seen, on the surfaces of which are large stigmarian roots.

Locality 5. This lies at the far north-eastern end of the quarry's northern bay. Here three NW-SE trending dolerite dykes crop out, a wide one and two narrow ones, all with horizontal columnar jointing. Minor faulting can be seen in the limestones here, associated with veins of calcite, and the cavities within the productid brachiopods often contain fluorite, minor strontianite and occasional sulphides, including hair-like needles of millerite. The large dyke has a considerable influence on the surrounding sediments, decalcifying the limestones and baking the mudstones. Some brachiopods near the dyke contain sugary white microcrystalline gypsum and yellow-brown siderite. Cubic calcite pseudomorphs after halite, or possibly fluorite, project from some dolerite surfaces at the contact zone. Flat golden marcasite "pennies" are found in the coal seam below the main succession. At other places along the face the productids in the limestones contain flat, salmon-pink barytes crystals together with calcite and quartz.

An important feature here is the increasing dominance of mudstones over limestones, with the limestone beds becoming thinner, often as elongate lensoid units, and the mudstones becoming thicker and interpolating between the limestone units.

Locality 6. This locality covers the western face of the northern bay, within which the increasing dominance of the mudstone horizons, already noted in localities 4 and 5, can be seen as it develops northwards. The mudstones themselves contain a quiet water fauna with abundant small horn corals including *Zaphrentites* (Fig. 20.6), *Allotropiophyllum* and *Fasciculophyllum*. The larger *Caninia* is also present, as are the brachiopods *Spirifer*, *Composita* and *Antiquatonia* (Fig. 20.5). Molluscs include various bivalves and rare goniatites. *Lingula* occurs in some mudstone horizons, suggesting periods in which marine conditions may have been replaced by more brackish water conditions as the sea retreated temporarily.

The limestones are rich in many of those species of brachiopod noted at Locality 4, with the addition of *Gigantoproductus*. Solitary corals, such as *Aulophyllum* are present, but colonial corals are rare, only a few small colonies of *Lithostrotion* being visible in beds low down on the face.

Once again it is the slabby, pale-weathering, dark, muddy limestones which contain the most interesting fossils. Many such beds contain *Brochocarina* (Fig. 20.5) and solitary corals as before, but in a series of beds just below the lip of the quarry, is a large and unusual fauna of molluscs. This fauna contains abundant cephalopods and large bivalves, the latter often with their valves either still tightly closed, or fully open as "butterfly" fossils. Such groupings can only occur in the quietest conditions well below wave base, suggesting deeper than usual water, perhaps correlating with the penultimate quiet episode seen at Locality 2. The fauna consists further of a wide range of genera with unusually large adult forms and is atypical of the usual faunas of the quarry, but has much in common with those faunas to the south, especially those of Ireland. This may suggest a marine transgression opening up hitherto closed routes from the south west. The fauna is in the process of being described (by C.J.B.), but among a provisional list of forms are large examples of the straight cephalopod *Orthoceras* and the slightly curved *Campyloceras*, as well as the coiled nautiloids *Stroboceras* and *Vestinautilus*. Large beyrichoceratid goniatites may also be found. Among the bivalves are huge examples of *Pinna flabelliformis* and *Sedgwickia gigantea*, as well as large examples of *Limipecten*, *Myalina* and *Edmondia*.

The limestone in this area can contain bands of chert over 30cm thick. Perfect hexagonal quartz crystals line the hollow interiors of brachiopods, while some fossil shells are completely replaced by chalcedony. Occasionally the familiar banded variety agate can be found. Between here and the spur separating the locality from the northern bay (Locality 4) fine specimens of scalenohedral calcite covered in lustrous cubic pyrites turn up in limestone fissures.

Locality 7. This locality lies in the western part of the southern bay, near the edge of the flooded area. Here, in the upper parts of the low cliffs on the north side of the track can be seen the last stages of the history of the quarry. These consist of dense crinoidal grainstones in the top 2 metres or so of the succession. These grainstones occupy the same horizons as the quiet water areas of Locality 6 but, as relatively high energy crinoid forests, are likely to have developed on a submarine mound well above wave base. However the topmost beds here, and almost everywhere else in the quarry are similar crinoidal limestones, suggesting a general shallowing as part of the final retreat of the sea in this area.

Locality 8. This is within the flooded area, but can be approached by going to the quarry entrance, taking the short, steep wagon road up the southern face, and walking west along the quarry rim. On the promontory are two small dolerite dykes around which minor faulting has led to some mineralisation including iron pyrites and chalcopyrite.

References

PATERSON, I.B. and HALL, I.H.S. 1986. Lithostratigraphy of the late Devonian and early Carboniferous rocks in the Midland Valley of Scotland. *Rep. Br. Geol. Surv.* **18**, 1-14.

RICHEY, J.E., ANDERSON, E.M. and MACGREGOR, A.G. 1930. The geology of northern Ayrshire. *Mem. Geol. Survey, UK.*

SHIELLS, K.A.G. and PENN, I.E. 1971. Notes on the geology of Trearne Quarry (Upper Visean), Ayrshire and on the palaeoecology of its productid brachiopods. *Scott. J. Geol.* **7**, 29-49.

TODD, J.G. 1989. Minerals of Trearne Quarry, Beith, Ayrshire, Scotland. *UK Journal of Mines and Minerals* **6**, 18-20.

WHYTE, M.A. 1981. The upper Brigantian (Lower Carboniferous) of Central Strathclyde. *Scott. J. Geol.* **17**, 227-46.

WILSON, R.B. 1979. The base of the Lower Limestone Group (Visean) in North Ayrshire. *Scott. J. Geol.* **15**, 313-19.

W.D. Ian Rolfe

Theme: Transition from marine to terrestrial deposits in one of the Silurian inliers of the Midland Valley of Scotland.

Features: Turbidites, graded greywackes with sole markings and shelly fossiliferous bases, lower Wenlock resedimented faunal assemblage, Caledonian sills, Llandovery-Wenlock siltstones with fossil crustaceans in concretions, Tertiary dyke, alluvial fan conglomerates and playa sediments, lacustrine fish bed yielding some of the oldest, most complete fossil fish known, industrial archaeology of Muirkirk.

Maps: O.S.   1: 63 360   Sheets 67 Ayr and 68 Biggar,
                                           Moffat and Sanquhar
                 1: 50 000   Sheet 71   Lanark & Upper Nithsdale

                B.G.S. 1: 63 360   Sheets 23 Hamilton and 15 Sanquhar

Terrain: Exposures in burns and loch-sides: some easy walks, some rough hill walking with occasional scrambling: wellington boots recommended.

Short
Itinerary: Omit localities 13, 14.

Distance   The road distances between different parts of the excursion
and Time: are 15.3 kM (9.5 miles), and on foot 5.4 km. (4.5 miles). One day is recommended, but the excursion can be rushed through in 5 hours. The short route is 5.4 km (3.3 miles) on foot and can be covered in 4 hours.

Access: The Ree Burn section is now an SSSI and permission must be obtained from the owner, Mr.E.Renwick at Debog Farm (NS 775 280). This is on the A70 one mile east of Parish Holm.

Collecting is listed as a Potentially Damaging Operation (P.D.O.) by the Nature Conservancy Council at localities 9 and 12, which are also SSSIs.

It is therefore essential to obtain a permit from the N.C.C. before attempting to collect at these sites, lest the site-owner be responsible for permitting unauthorised collecting. Such permits should be applied for **at least** three weeks in advance of the intended visit giving an indication of the reason for collecting at these sites, e.g. to obtain teaching, museum or research material. A package of information detailing local access arrangements will then be given. Write to NCC, 2 Beresford Terrace, Ayr, KA7 2EG or to Dr D. Norman, Earth Science Division, NCC, Peterborough, PE1 1UA.

Cars may be left in the turn-off to Monksfoot (NS 786 284).

Introduction

This excursion examines the transition from marine Llandovery to Old Red Sandstone terrestrial deposits that typifies sequences in the Silurian inliers of the Midland Valley of Scotland. Prior to the plate tectonic interpretation, this transition was thought to represent the end of the marine phase of the Caledonian geosyncline in Scotland. Currently, opinion differs on how to interpret the significance of this sequence of rocks. The Glasgow School of thought (Bluck 1983, 1984 and Ingham) suggests the sequence represents a passage from deposits in an older, fore-arc basin to the silting up of an inter-arc basin by sediments eroded northward from the upthrusting Midland Valley basement. This upthrusting was an early manifestation of the collision of two continental plates: the Anglo-Welsh Avalonia with the southern margin of the Scottish Laurentia. As the oblique collision continued, emergent greywackes of the Scottish Uplands accretionary prism were obducted over the by-then-eroded upthrust basement. The eroded fragments of that prism form the Greywacke Conglomerate that is taken as the local base of the Lower Red Sandstone.

Up until comparatively recently, the Silurian inliers of the Midland Valley were variously dated, ranging between the extremes of Carboniferous and Ludlow/Downtonian of the Silurian. Recent refinement, largely initiated by the late Dr. Archie Lamont, has established that the lowest beds of the sequence are in fact much older - of uppermost Llandovery to lower Wenlock age. Evidence for secure dating of higher beds in the succession is lacking since the fossils that do occur, fish and arthropod species largely unique to these areas are clearly strongly **facies** controlled, and correlation with beds elsewhere is scanty. It is suspected that these higher beds are of

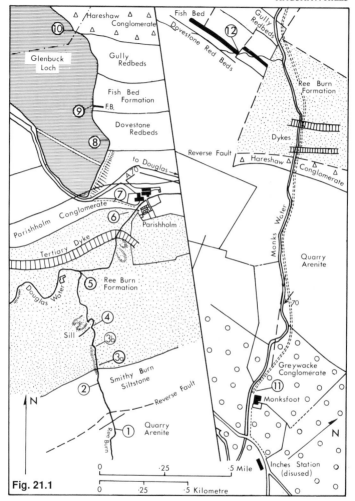

Fig. 21.1 Sketch maps of geological section seen in the Ree Burn - Glenbuck Loch traverse (left) and of position of Shiel Burn Fish Bed locality (right).

267

Wenlock/Ludlow age, partly by overall comparison with the similar fauna of Ludlow age in Norway, and partly because they are overlain by the Lower Old Red Sandstone which has yielded the Lower Devonian fish *Cephalaspis* in Ayrshire.

Itinerary

Walk through the farmyard to the south front of Parish Holm (Fig. 21.1) and follow the north bank of the Douglas Water 330m (360yds) upstream to the first side stream on the south bank, the Ree Burn. Proceed up the Ree Burn (noting *en route* at NS 761 279 the grassed-over walls of the large ree or sheepfold from which the burn takes its name), walking along the top of the west (left) bank for 460m (500yds), before descending to the valley floor to Locality 1.

Locality 1. Quarry Arenite. Red sandstones of the Quarry Arenite are here seen to be vertical, and further upstream they are overturned to dip northwest at 40°. These sandstones underlie the thick Greywacke Conglomerate that constitutes the local base of the Lower Old Red Sandstone, and which forms the high ground south of this locality. The sandstones are best studied at this locality, since they are not so well seen later on: they are mainly **subgreywackes**, and show good cross-stratification. According to McGiven (1958) these rocks were laid down by braided streams, the intercalated mudstones being due to deposition of overbank fines during floods. Subsequent subaerial exposure produced mudcracks and mudflakes, the latter now found in desiccation breccias (intraclast conglomerates).

The Quarry Arenite and Greywacke Conglomerate make up the southern limb of the Hagshaw Hills NE—SW ("caledonoid") trending anticline. This structure is mainly asymmetrical, having an axial plane dipping steeply northwest, the northern limb dipping up to 70° northwest, and the southern limb dipping from 50° southeast, through verticality to overturned beds dipping up to 40° northwest. Locally therefore the structure is isoclinal.

About 46m (50yds) north of Locality 1, dark grey siltstones, mudstones and shales of the Smithy Burn Siltstone, which forms the local base of the succession, are brought up by the major north-dipping reverse or thrust fault which runs along the axis of the anticline. A small exposure of the Hareshaw Conglomerate may be found on the south side of the reversed fault, which is here intruded by a small dyke. Henceforward, the remainder of the section to be examined ascends the succession on the northern limb of the anticline.

The succession is as follows:

(f) Greywacke Conglomerate
      (base of terrestrial Lower Old Red Sandstone).
(e) Quarry Arenite
(d) Hareshaw Conglomerate
(c) Glenbuck Group   iv Gully Redbeds
                             iii Fish Bed Formation
                             ii   Dovestone Redbeds
                             i   Douglas Water Arenite
(b) Parishholm Conglomerate
(a) Hagshaw Group   ii   Ree Burn Formation
                                   (marine Silurian)
                             i   Smithy Burn Siltstone

Locality 2. Smithy Burn Siltstone (NS 761 275). This formation contains few fossils. The following graptolites have been collected at this locality, however, which suggest the *crenulata* Zone of the topmost Llandovery: *Monoclimacis* [*Monograptus*] *?crenulata*, *M. ?griestonensis*, *M. ?vomerina*, *Monograptus ?spiralis*, *M. priodon*, *M. ?marri*. Unfortunately, the specimens upon which the list was based were lost before their significance was appreciated or their determination verified, so that any graptolites found in the Hagshaw Hills should be carefully preserved and deposited for public reference in a museum.

Locality 3a. Ree Burn Formation: sedimentary structures. Moving downstream, hard bands of **greywacke** and siltstone characterise the succession, and alternate with medium grey shales and mudstones. These 280m (900ft) of "grits and shales" constitute the Ree Burn Formation. Many of the greywackes show **graded bedding**. The bases of individual coarse greywackes are commonly full of large angular fragments of igneous and metamorphic rocks, whereas the tops of them are of shale with conspicuous black laminae. Such grading originates from large debris-charged clouds of sediment which are thrown into suspension. These high density tongue-like masses of water (turbidity currents) flow rapidly down the slope, transporting material from shallower water areas, eroding the plastic sediments over which they travel and depositing their suspended grains *en route*

- coarse grains and fossil shell fragments first and fine last as the weaker tail of the current passes by.

Collecting is easiest from the bases of greywackes which have been decalcified: these are obvious since they are dark brown and soft, the fossils consisting of casts and moulds. A partial list of the fossils is as follows (fuller list given by Rolfe 1962a, and some new forms described by Lamont 1965). Brachiopods - *Lingula, Atrypa reticularis, Glassia, "Catazyga" pentlandica, Protochonetes* aff. *edmundsi, Leptaena rhomboidalis, Howellella, Dicoelosia,* dalmanellids and rhynchonellids; bivalve molluscs - *Nuculites, Ctenodonta, Orthonota* cf. *scotica, Pteronitella, ?Grammysia;* snails - ?*Holopella, Bellerophon, ?Pycnomphalus, Hormotoma;* conoidal fossils - *Cornulites, Tentaculites, Hyolithes forbesii;* water flea - *Beyrichia* cf. *kloedeni;* trilobites - *Calymene* aff. *carlops, C.* aff. *nodulosa,* cheirurid, *Hemiarges rolfei, Encrinurus hagshawensis, E. knockgardnerensis, Eophacops* aff. *sufferta, Phacops* aff. *stokesi, P. straitonensis,* proetid.

This fossil assemblage is probably identical to that which occurs at Knockgardner near Girvan, and which has been identified by Cocks as the lower Wenlock *Howellella-Protochonetes* assemblage, an assemblage that characterises shallow water in Wales and the Welsh Borderland. **Acritarchs** from the highest units beneath the Knockgardner redbeds are also of early Wenlock age (Dorning 1982). Most of the fossils are fragmentary or disarticulated which, together with their shallow water nature, suggests that they have been resedimented by turbidity currents to their present position, in deeper water downslope.

Locality 3b. Sole markings (NS 762 277). South of the sharp bend in the stream, the under sides of the greywacke units should be inspected for their variety of **sole markings.** Some of these linear structures have bulbous ends which indicate the up-current direction. These are casts of flutes formed by the scouring vortex action of the current (**flute casts**). Others are casts of grooves cut by angular particles dragged along by the flow (**groove casts**). On the right bank of the burn (NS 762 277), 73m (80yds) downstream from the Smithy Burn Siltstone and 130m (140yds) upstream of the junction with the Douglas Water, an 18cm thick greywacke carries orthocone **prod and skip casts** - casts of impact marks left by the empty shells of orthoconic nautiloids borne along by the turbidity current. Greywackes in the vicinity also yield casts of orthocone fragments that presumably lay on the sea floor until whisked away by an incoming current.

All these sole markings indicate that the currents responsible for their formation must have originated to the south. This turbidite sequence and its southerly derivation have been taken as evidence that a ridge-like land area - Cockburnland - appeared in upper Llandovery times, running NE—SW along the southern margin of what was then the Midland Basin of deposition. Currently "Cockburnland" is interpreted as possibly emergent greywackes forming the Southern Uplands accretionary prism.

Locality 4. Continue downstream for 82m (90yds), where running up the left bank is a 1.5m (5ft) thick sill of **amygdaloidal plagiophyre**. This is only one of eight such Caledonian sills intruded into the Ree Burn Formation, some of them thin enough to confuse with greywacke units.

Locality 5. Pod-shrimp concretions. Approaching the junction of Ree Burn with the Douglas Water the greywackes disappear from the sequence, and the sediment is a striking laminated siltstone. Calcareous septarian concretions occur which may contain the fossil pod-shrimp *Ceratiocaris papilio* (Fig. 22.1) preserved "in the round". Both small and large moult stages of this 60cm (2ft) long crustacean occur, and the smallest microstructures of its cuticle are preserved. The large and heavy **mandibles** of this animal may be found isolated in some concretions, and local thin siltstones may contain concentrations of the toothed cutting edges of these mandibles. Such pod-shrimps characterise a group from which evolved many later groups of crustaceans (e.g. the shrimps and their allies). The concretions also contain plant fragments and orthoconic nautiloids, and one specimen of the fish *Logania* [*Thelodus*] has been found; the mineral wax hatchetite also occurs, but rarely.

Cross over the Douglas Water and follow the north bank downstream to the 20m (65ft) thick **tholeiitic** quartz dolerite dyke which forms the waterfall 150m (160yds) SW of Parish Holm. This Tertiary dyke was quarried for road metal in the north bank, and John Smith observed (in his 1897 notebook) the local baking of the siltstones to Lydian stone. Six subsidiary dykes (locally sills) may be traced above and below the main intrusion.

Locality 6. Whilst walking towards Parish Holm, notice the Hareshaw Conglomerate feature striking across the south face of Hareshaw Hill (NS 764 287), above Glenbuck Loch. About 18m (60yds) downstream from the Tertiary dyke, large bulbous sole markings can be seen on the thick sandstones forming a bluff on the left bank of the Douglas Water (at locality 6). These are **load cast structures.** The sandstones may represent a shallowing of the depositional basin.

Locality 7. Parish Holm: alluvial fan conglomerates. Turn left through the gate, westwards, before reaching the gate into Parishholm farmyard, and take the track that leads along the wall towards Glenbuck Loch. Parishholm Conglomerate (the Igneous Conglomerate of Peach and Horne) forms the bluff along the south side of this track (Locality 7). This is the first of three such conglomerates that will be encountered, and which have been studied by McGiven, whose results are summarised here. All three conglomerates contain the same six main groups of rock types, but in different proportions, reflecting changes with time in the composition of the source area. These groups are, 1 - fine grained igneous rocks (soda rich rocks - spilites, **keratophyres**, **quartz-feldspar porphyries**, together with andesites and **tuffs**) 2 - medium-coarse grained igneous rocks (**microperthitic adamellites** and alkali granites, granodiorites, quartz monzonites and diorites) 3 - sedimentary rocks (greywackes and rare limestones) 4 - metamorphosed sedimentary rocks (quartzites, schists and **phyllites**) 5 - **chert** and cherty mudstones 6 - vein quartz. The Parishholm Conglomerate is composed of 80 per cent igneous fragments, 74 per cent of them of group 1 above. Some of these rock types can be matched with Ordovician igneous rocks exposed at the surface today within 20km (12 miles) to the south, southwest and southeast, and which are old enough to have been the sources of such pebbles. Such close sources are also indicated by the angularity of the pebbles. Other igneous rock pebbles such as rhyolite cannot be matched with rocks exposed in the present Southern Uplands. Their source rocks may be buried beneath the Southern Uplands accretionary prism, subsequently obducted over them by continued plate collision. The conglomerate was probably deposited as a terrestrial alluvial fan or series of fans with their heads lying to the southeast. The sediments were deposited by sheetfloods and to a lesser extent by violent streamfloods. Rare limestone pebbles have been found in this conglomerate, 320m (350yds) west of the Ree Burn. They contain **stromatoporoids** and bryozoans, suggesting derivation from a source rock of Wenlock age.

The Parishholm Conglomerate is not present in the gradational sequence of beds of the Lesmahagow inlier, only 6.5km (4 miles) to the northwest. Correlation suggests that $\sim$ 310m (1,000ft) of beds in Lesmahagow are not represented in the Hagshaw Hills succession, and several lines of evidence suggest that this time gap is represented by a **paraconformity** at the base of the Parishholm Conglomerate. Relatively gradual uplift to produce terrestrial conditions in the Lesmahagow area was therefore probably contemporaneous with more pronounced uplift in the Hagshaw Hills area.

Cross the Douglas - Ayr road and walk along the top of the dam forming the east end of Glenbuck Loch. This loch was created in 1802 by James Finlay and Co. as a reservoir for their cotton mills down the River Ayr at Catrine. Machinery at the mills was powered by water-wheels which remained the most powerful wheels in Scotland until their demolition in 1947.

Locality 8. Dovestone Redbeds. The first beds encountered on the east shore of the loch are the Dovestone Redbeds, chocolate-coloured mudstones and siltstones. Their colour and the presence of abundant mudcracks suggest a terrestrial environment. McGiven has found that much of the Redbeds is made up of $\sim$ 25cm thick cycles, bounded below by a fine-grained sandstone, commonly rich in mud pellets, fining up through rippled and cross-stratified siltstones to mudcracked mudstone above. Such cycles probably result from deposition by successive floods, initially moving rapidly and erosively on to an exposed **playa**, and then slowly spreading out on the flat surface to give areally extensive sheets of sediment. Between floods the playa dried out, forming the mudcracked layers. Deposits such as these are probably the lateral equivalents of alluvial fans developed elsewhere.

Locality 9. The Fish Bed Formation. Continuing north along the shore of Glenbuck Loch, to a point 110m (120yds) from the dam, a 6.5m (20ft) thick light grey subgreywacke marks the base of the Fish Bed Formation (Locality 9). This Formation consists of cycles of grey-green sandstones, sometimes with sedimentary breccias at their bases, grading up into siltstone or mudstone. The rarity of mudcracks, the colour, and the lateral and vertical uniformity of the Formation suggest a more permanent body of water than was responsible for depositing the underlying or overlying Redbeds, and a lagoon or lake is envisaged. Within this Formation are two beds of finely laminated

273

siltstone which yield a rich fauna of fish. One of the beds lies immediately above the basal subgreywacke of the formation, and the other is 12m (40ft) above this. Fish can be more readily collected at Locality 12, however, but it is worth collecting briefly from the coarse micaceous siltstones in the purplish mudstones, ~ 3.1m (10ft) below the base of the overlying Redbeds proper. These contain disarticulated fragments of the eurypterid *Lanarkopterus* and of the fish *Lasanius*, as well as the calcareous tubes of the worm *Spirorbis* and fronds of a small, regularly branched organism which may be a calcareous alga. This distinctive fossil, long misidentified as the bryozoan *Glauconome*, has recently been found with other characteristic Fish Bed fossils in the Silurian of Clew Bay, Ireland (Palmer *et al.* 1989). This suggested the fault bounded Irish outcrop might be a displaced terrane that formerly adjoined the Midland Valley of Scotland inliers. Structural analysis suggests that this is not the case, implying a 500km aquatic connection between the two areas.

Above the Fish Bed Formation are the Gully Redbeds, which are almost identical to the Dovestone Redbeds, and indicate a return to the terrestrial playa conditions of those beds.

Locality 10. Hareshaw Conglomerate. Further along the shore, where the boundary wall comes down to the loch are many blocks of Hareshaw Conglomerate (Quartzite Conglomerate of Peach and Horne) fallen from the nearby exposures. Coarse grained beds of this conglomerate will be seen to be composed almost exclusively of large, well rounded quartzite pebbles. The nearest metamorphic quartzites to this area are in the Dalradian, 80km (50 miles) north, in an opposite direction to the southerly derivation indicated by the cross-stratification in the upper part of the conglomerate. Furthermore, the maximum particle size increases in typical alluvial fan style towards the source - southeastwards. McGiven has therefore suggested that the quartzite and vein quartz pebbles of this conglomerate were derived from a pre-existing conglomerate in the Southern Uplands. The explanation for this vanished source is probably the same as that given above for the Parishholm Conglomerate (Locality 7). The conglomerate was probably built up by alluvial fan sheetfloods and violent streamfloods.

A return to the transport should now be made, and vehicles left as close as is consistent with safety to the disused railway station at Inches (NS 788 284). Proceed on foot up to the exposure of Greywacke Conglomerate to the right of the path leading northwest out of

Monksfoot (Locality 11).

Locality 11. Monksfoot: Greywacke Conglomerate (NS 786 286). This conglomerate, here dipping 70° SSE on the southern limb of the Hagshaw Hills anticline, is taken as the base of the Lower Old Red Sandstone. At this locality, 88 per cent of the pebbles between 16 and 32mm diameter are of greywacke, similar in composition and grain size to greywackes of the Southern Uplands. In detail, the pebbles show a relative lack of basic fragments when compared with greywacke pebbles in the underlying two conglomerates, suggesting that Silurian rather than Ordovician greywackes were the source rock. The proportion of greywacke pebbles in this conglomerate falls towards the northwest, throughout the Midland Valley inliers. Greywackes are the least resistant to wear of all the constituents of the conglomerates, and their reduction towards the NW reflects increasing distance of transport from a SE source, as does also the increase in the proportion of disc-shaped greywacke pebbles. The conglomerate shows striking changes in thickness at right angles to its depositional strike. It reaches its maximum thickness of 460m (1,500ft) near the present locality, thinning westward to 25m (80ft) near Muirkirk and northwestward to 7.5m (25ft) near Darvel. The source of detritus for this fan-shaped body therefore lay SE of the present outcrop. Once again, the maximum size of particles increases with the thickness of the conglomerate towards the SE, confirming that the source lay in that direction. These and other properties suggest that the Greywacke Conglomerate formed an alluvial fan deposited by sheetfloods. The source was probably the obducted Southern Uplands accretionary prism.

Locality 12. Fish Bed Formation (NS 777 291). Follow the path north for 1,000m (1,100yds) until the Shiel Burn enters the Monks Water on its right (southwest) bank. Cross over Monks Water and walk 110m (120yds) along the north bank of the Shiel Burn until the head of the waterfall is reached. A further 18m (20yds) upstream from this point a NE - SW slot excavated in the left (NW) bank of the Shiel Burn marks the position of the higher of the two fish beds in the Fish Bed Formation. The bed consists of 1.2 - 1.5m (4 - 5ft) of dark grey finely laminated siltstone. Good collections of the complete fossil fish for which this region is famed may be obtained here, together with the other rarer elements of the fauna (Fig. 21.2). Large flags of the laminated siltstone should be extracted, using large chisels or crowbars,

Fig. 21.2

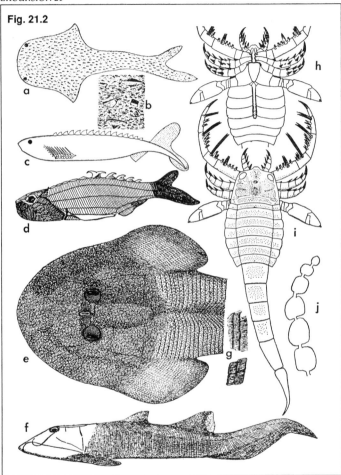

Fig. 21.2 Some of the fish (a-g), eurypterids (h, i) and plant (j) fossils that occur in the Fish Bed: all natural size unless otherwise indicated. a, b, thelodont *Lanarkia spinosa* (after Traquair), a, as it appears flattened in the rock (*Logania taiti* also occurs here - compare with Fig. 22.1b); b, detail of trunk denticles (x6); c, unarmoured anaspid *Lasanius problematicus* (after Parrington and Miles); d, armoured anaspid *Birkenia elegans* (after Stetson, Heintz and Ritchie).

and carefully split parallel to the lamination. The fossils are difficult to discern in this bed unless weathered to ochre, but immersion of the split surfaces in water improves contrast between the black fossils and their grey matrix. Specimens should be well wrapped to prevent abrasion.

The "varved" nature of the Fish Bed suggests deposition in a region of a lake where dissolved oxygen was absent and where no bottom feeders lived that could work over the sediment and disturb the lamination. Under such conditions, the abundance and perfection of preservation of the fish may be explicable by mass killing off due to rapid (?seasonal) overturning of the thermally stratified waters of the lake bringing up anaerobic waters.

The fish from this bed are some of the oldest complete fossil fish known in the world; older complete fish are known from the Jamoytius horizon, Lesmahagow (see Excursion 22). All these fish are jawless (agnathan), like the living lamprey, and characterised by poorly developed fins and by external armour. Anaspid fish (laterally compressed fish usually with elongated bony scales) from this bed are *Birkenia elegans*, which is relatively common, and the largely naked *Lasanius problematicus*, *L. armatus* and *L. sp. nov.* Ritchie. The earliest cephalaspid fish, *Ateleaspis tessellata*, occurs here; fragments of the characteristically spined trunk scales are sometimes found, but complete individuals (up to 20cm long) are very rare. Several thelodont fish also occur, and although isolated thelodont denticles had long been known from other localities these were the first completely articulated thelodonts to be discovered. The typically broad, vertically compressed thelodont head of *Logania* [*Thelodus*] *taiti* causes the front part of the fish to be preserved squashed flat on the bedding plane, whereas the laterally compressed tail becomes twisted sideways during burial so that both upper and lower lobes come to lie on the same plane. The whole body surface of thelodonts is armoured with minute tooth-like denticles, whose shape varies according to their position on the body. Around the mouth of *Logania*, for example, the

e-g, cephalaspid Ateleaspis *tessellata*, e, upper surface of head-shield; f, side view; (after Ritchie); g, spinous scales from trunk behind head and from low down on side, x2 (after Traquair), h, i, sea-scorpion Lanarkopterus *dolichoschelus*, h, under surface, showing type A (?male) genital appendage, and i, upper surface, x$^1/_2$ (after Ritchie), j. ?alga Taitia catena (after Crookall).

denticles are sub-circular, crenulated and interlocking, whereas posteriorly they become more elongate and spined (Fig. 22.1 c-e). The thelodonts *Lanarkia horrida*, *L. spinosa* and *L. spinulosa* are similar to *Logania* in body form, but their denticles are distinctive in being relatively long, hollow, conical spines (Fig. 21.2 a,b).

Remains of the up-to-60cm (2ft) long eurypterid (water-scorpion) *Lanarkopterus [Mixopterus] dolichoschelus* are not uncommon, although they are very difficult to discern. Other eurypterids also occur, but are very rare: *Parastylonurus [Stylonurus] ornatus*, *Brachyopterella ritchiei* Waterston (1979) and *Hughmilleria sp.* Fragments of the ?pod-shrimp *Dictyocaris* also occur. Crushed, carbonised and sometimes calcified spheres ~ 5mm across are colonies of the blue-green alga *Pachytheca*, which probably rolled about freely during life on the lagoon or lake floor. *Taitia [?Hormosiroidea] catena* is also thought to be algal, and fragments of other plants also occur.

The overall similarity of this fauna to the Ludlow fauna of Ringerike, Norway is remarkable, even though only one species and five genera of fish and arthropods occur in common. It suggests that both faunas were similarly related to their environment, which sedimentological criteria (Locality 9) suggest was a lagoon or lake.

If time permits, a visit can be paid to air-heave structures in the Lower Old Red Sandstone overlying the Greywacke Conglomerate. These structures can be seen in the northeast face of the now-disused railway cutting (at NS 793 281) north of Carmacoup. The cutting should be approached by the track across the field, on the north side of the A70 at Carmacoup. The structures are 82m (90yds) northwest of the point where this track meets the cutting. Such air-heave structures are thought to have been made by formerly entrapped air being forced out of sediment by a rapid rise in water level up the shore of an inland lake.

On the return journey, an archaeological diversion to Muirkirk (NS 695 272) is worthwhile. As a promoter of the Muirkirk Iron Works explained "Nothing can induce us to go into such a Desert and Inland Place as Muirkirk but the absolute Certainty of having the coal and ironstone and limestone very cheap". This attraction, coupled with the relatively inexpensive local land feus, led to the establishment in 1787 of the most important iron works in Ayrshire, and one of the earliest in Scotland. Coal and ore were readily obtained locally from the Limestone Coal Group, and later on haematite from

Auchinlongford mine, 9.7km (6 miles) to the west, was used. The furnaces were closed in 1923, but the spectacular neogothic furnace tower was only destroyed in the 1970s. Few traces of the extensive works, other than furnace slag, can now be seen. It was in this Iron Company's workshops that the first successful use of gas was made for lighting in Scotland, in the late 1790's.

Coke needed to smelt the clayband ironstones was provided by the British Tar Company after the extraction of tar, lampblack and varnish, from local coals. This company was established by Archibald Cochrane, Lord Dundonald, the pioneer of coal distillation in Scotland, and tar kilns were built at Springhill, Muirkirk in 1786. The kilns were bought in 1790 by J.L.McAdam, that "Colossus of roads". As Trevelyan has written - "Few people realise what McAdam did for this country. Had it not been for his roads the industrial revolution could not have taken place." This can be seen in microcosm at Muirkirk where the early macadamisation of the turnpikes to Ayr, Glasgow and Sanquhar enabled the transport of minerals in and of iron products out to markets. Such roads permitted the development of the iron works, and thus the creation of the village of Muirkirk, on low-cost land and minerals in a remote area, which previously would have been impossible.

The tar kilns were abandoned in 1829, but in 1931 stones from the ruined kilns were used to build a cairn to commemorate McAdam. Grassed-over foundations of thirty-four kilns may still be seen at NS 695 256). In the vicinity, too, numerous depressions in the ground mark the sites of collapsed bell-pits, sunk centuries ago to shallow coal seams in the Limestone Coal Group.

References

References are given at the end of Excursion 22 (Lesmahagow).

Excursion 22 **LESMAHAGOW**
W.D. Ian Rolfe

Theme:	Silurian arthropod and fish assemblages
Features:	Jawless fish, eurypterids (water-scorpions), pod shrimps.
Maps:	O.S. 1:63 360 Sheet 68 Biggar, Moffat and Sanquhar
	1:50 000 Sheet 71 Lanark & Upper Nithsdale
	B.G.S. 1:63 360 Sheet 23 Hamilton
Terrain:	Exposures in banks of shallow burns and slabs extending below water level; rough walking; wellington boots recommended.
Short Itinerary:	The two parts of this excursion may be covered separately, and the Shank Castle to Dunside visit abbreviated at will.
Distance and Time:	Both areas are remote from public roads, and both involve a round trip walk of one mile from the nearest vehicle-access point. A whole day is needed for both parts of the excursion - a half day at each.
Access:	Collecting is listed as a Potentially Damaging Operation (P.D.O.) by the Nature Conservancy Council at all the localities listed in this excursion. See first page of Hagshaw Hills excursion (Ex.21) for details of how to obtain the necessary permit and for local contacts that must be made. Cars should be left at Logan House (with permission - NS 739 353), at the turn off to Dunside Reservoir (NS 752 371).

Introduction

The Lesmahagow area is justly famed for its fossil arthropod and fish assemblages - some of the oldest complete fish in the world come from this area (at the *Jamoytius* horizon). Since it is difficult to trace a continuous section through the Lesmahagow succession in any one excursion, it is best to treat visits to the area as collecting expeditions, and two of the most important localities are described below. However, intending visitors will need to persuade the NCC of their good reasons for wishing to collect these rare and valuable fossils i.e. for research, teaching or museum purposes. Although these localities are 220m (700ft) apart, stratigraphically the rocks at both are thought to be of Upper Llandovery to Lower Wenlock age, and to be of marine origin. Of equal significance are the Slot Burn and Dippal Burn fish beds at higher horizons in the area (e.g. the Site of Special Scientific Interest at Slot Burn - NS 680 321), but these have been largely worked out by collectors or are otherwise difficult to collect from. The same fauna can be more conveniently collected from the fish bed in the Hagshaw Hills (Locality 12 of excursion 21).

Once permission has been obtained, to avoid disappointment the authorised collector should plan to spend a minimum of several hours at either of these localities, and should take adequate equipment for the task. "No one need dream of going fossil collecting on the banks of the Logan Water in the same manner as would be done amongst the Carboniferous rocks. It requires hard work..." as the following partial list of tools used by J.R.S. Hunter in 1872 suggests: "32 steel chisels, 2 miner's picks, 3 steel wedges, 9 hammers, 3 shovels, 3 crowbars, flask of gunpowder...sometimes we had to mourn the loss of fine specimens blown away or broken into splinters". The most important collections have been made by enthusiasts who have camped on the site, from J.R.S. Hunter who erected his tent "Siluria" at Shank Castle in 1882, through the Geological Society of Glasgow's "Camp Siluria" from 1899 to the early 1900's up to A. Ritchie in the early 1960's, and the latest camp in 1973. Many unusual fossils have been described from these localities, but new forms can still be found. Anyone collecting material suspected of being new or rare, is advised to take it to one of the major museums so that it may be recorded, and preferably deposited there for safe keeping.

There has been a recent history of illegal collecting from this area. Particular attention must therefore be paid before collecting to follow the directions given above under *Access*.

---

a. Jamoytius horizon (SSSI) (Figs. 22.1 and 22.2)

This horizon is exposed 640m (700yds) SSW of Loganhouse along both banks of the Logan Water (NS 737 346). Three exposures occur within 73m (80yds) - the central one being a 9m (30ft) cliff face capped by thick greywackes on the north side of the Logan Water. This cliff has been worked back by many collectors, including those of Camp Siluria, and it is now hazardous to remove additional material due to falling rock. More accessible exposures of the same mudstones and

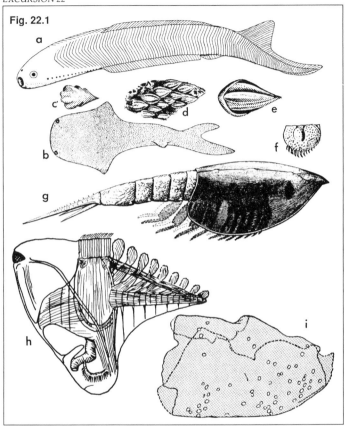

Fig. 22.1

Fig. 22.1 Some of the fossils at the *Jamoytius* horizon: two-thirds natural size unless otherwise indicated. a-e, jawless fish: a, anaspid *Jamoytius kerwoodi* (after Miles and Ritchie); b-e, *Logania* [*Thelodus*]*scotica*, b, dorsal aspect as it appears flattened in the rock, (after Traquair); c-e, details of skin denticles; c, head denticle, x24; d,e, trunk denticles; showing d, how they occur on the body, x8, e, x24 (c,e, after Gross; d, after Traquair). f, g, crustaceans; f, water-flea *Beyrichia* cf. *kloedeni,* x6 (modified from Henningsmoen); g, pod-shrimp *Ceratiocaris papilio,* (after Rolfe); h, ?sea-squirt *Ainiktozoon loganense* (after Ritchie; i, fragment of the possible crustacean *Dictyocaris* x$^{1}/_4$ (after Størmer), stipple indicates network ornament.

282

Fig. 22.2

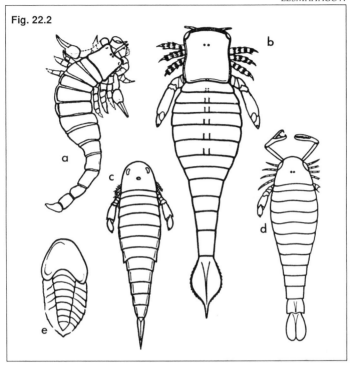

Fig. 22.2 Some of the fossil chelicerates from the *Jamoytius* horizon. a, ?aquatic scorpion *Allopalaeophonus caledonicus* x 2¹/₂ (after Petrunkevitch); b-d, eurypterids (water-scorpions, after Størmer); b, *Slimonia acuminata* x¹/₆; c, *Hughmilleria lanceolata* x¹/₂; d, *Erettopterus [Pterygotus] bilobus*, x¹/₆; e, early king crab *Cyamocephalus loganensis* x 2/3 (after Stormer).

The eurypterids are rare at this horizon, but occur more abundantly at Shank Castle, Dunside.

laminated siltstones are obtainable just upstream from this cliff, on the opposite south bank of the stream. Best results are obtained by clearing a bedding plane and peeling off large flags, which should be split as thin as possible. Contrast between fossil and matrix may be improved by immersing the flags in water.

The jawless fossil fish *Jamoytius kerwoodi* (named after the ichthyologist J.A. Moy-Thomas) is rare in these beds, and is usually seen as little more than a carbon stain on the rock: problematic material is best kept for determination in the laboratory. *Jamoytius* is the earliest anaspid fish, and its thin external skeleton (of v-shaped scales), gill basket and terminal mouth supported by cartilage, suggest that it was an ancestral lamprey (Ritchie 1968a, 1984). The only fish commonly found is *Logania* [*Thelodus*] *scotica*. It occurs as a black sheet of minute articulated denticles which originally covered the body surface (there is no internal skeleton). Calcareous concretions (usually under 5cm across) should be tapped open, since they commonly contain fossils. Frequently a soot-like powder is all that can be seen, but under magnification this can be seen to be a (? **coprolitic**) mass of disarticulated denticles of *Logania scotica*. The only other known occurrence of this fish is in Siberia, indicating E—W migration at this time, but no N—S communication with the Anglo-Welsh province. An unusual fossil in this horizon is the free swimming ?sea-squirt *Ainiktozoon loganense* (Ritchie 1985). The pod-shrimp *Ceratiocaris papilio* (Fig.22.1) is relatively plentiful (Rolfe 1962c; Rolfe and Beckett 1984), and large fragments of the net-marked, supposed pod-shrimp *Dictyocaris* occur. Such fragments are commonly pierced by circular holes up to 5mm across, which coincide in size with the suctorial mouth of *Jamoytius*. *Jamoytius* may therefore have parasitized *Dictyocaris* by rasping holes in its exoskeleton, much as the living lamprey parasitizes other fish.

The eurypterids (water-scorpions) (Fig.22.2) *Slimonia acuminata*, *Erettopterus* [*Pterygotus*] *bilobus* and *Hughmilleria* are rare, as is the water-flea *Beyrichia*. *Cyamocephalus loganensis* is the oldest synziphosure (early king crab) known (Rolfe and Beckett 1984), but only one specimen has so far been found. The ?aquatic scorpion *Allopalaeophonus caledonicus*, one of the two earliest scorpions (Kjellesvig-Waering 1986), is also known from only one specimen found, supposedly at this locality in 1883. The oldest millipede known - *Archidesmus loganensis* - has also been described from these beds, but Ritchie suggests the unique specimen may only be a plant fragment (Almond 1985). Molluscs such as *Pteronitella?*, *Euomphalopterus* (*Platyschisma*) and orthoconic nautiloids may also be found, and, very rarely, the ?plant *Taitia catena*.

b. Shank Castle to Dunside

Between Shank (or Shank's) Castle (NS 746 362) and Dunside (NS 751 371) occur greyish mudstones and laminated siltstones of the Kip Burn Formation (the *Pterygotus* Beds of Peach and Horne), dipping 20° NW. The basal beds of this Formation (Peach and Horne's *Ceratiocaris* Beds) are exposed at Shank Castle below the reservoir, where they yield the pod-shrimp *Ceratiocaris*, *Dictyocaris*, *Beyrichia*, the eurypterids *Erettopterus* [*Pterygotus*] and *Slimonia* and very rarely the fish *Logania* [*Thelodus*] and *Birkenia*. The snail *Euomphalopterus*, the conoidal fossil *Hyolithes* [= *Theca*] *forbesii* and *Lingula minima* also occur.

Approaching Dunside, higher beds are exposed as slabs forming the banks of the Logan Water. It was from these slabs that Robert Slimon made his large collection of eurypterids (now mostly in Glasgow City Museum) and specimens in many other museums throughout the world have been obtained from here. Slimon exhibited his specimens at the Old College in Glasgow during the British Association meeting of 1855, where their importance was proclaimed by Sir Roderick Murchison. The slabs yield the following rich fauna of eurypterids, the commonest being the large *Slimonia acuminata* and *Erettopterus* [*Pterygotus*] *bilobus* (? = *P. lanarkensis*); rarer forms are *Hughmilleria lanceolata*, *Stylonurella spinipes* (see Waterston 1979), *Carcinosoma scorpioides* and *Paracarcinosoma obesa* (illustrated by Rolfe 1989). Another early king crab (synziphosure), *Neolimulus falcatus*, is also known from these beds, but it too is represented by only one specimen.

References
(for Excursions 21 and 22)

ALMOND, J.E. 1985. The Silurian-Devonian fossil record of the Myriapoda. *Phil. Trans. R. Soc. Lond* **B:309**, 227-37.

BLUCK, B.J. 1983. Role of the Midland Valley of Scotland in the Caledonian orogeny. *Trans. R. Soc. Edinburgh Earth Sci.* **74**, 119-36.

_____ 1984. Pre-Carboniferous history of the Midland Valley of Scotland. *Trans. R. Soc. Edinburgh Earth Sci.* **75**, 275-95.

BUTT, J. 1967. *Industrial archaeology of Scotland.* Newton Abbot.

COCKS, L.R.M. and TOGHILL, P. 1972. The biostratigraphy of the Silurian rocks of the Girvan district, Scotland. *Q.Jl geol. Soc. Lond.*, **129**, 209-43.

DEWEY, J.F. 1971. A model for the Lower Palaeozoic evolution of the southern margin of the early Caledonides of Scotland and Ireland. *Scott. J. Geol.*, **7**, 219-40.

DORNING K.J. 1982. Early Wenlock acritarchs from the Knockgardner and Straiton Grit Formations of Knockgardner, Ayrshire. *Scott.. J. Geol.* **18**, 267-73.

HUNTER , J.R.S. 1885. Three months' tent life amongst the Silurian hills of Logan Water, Lesmahagow. *Trans. geol. Soc. Glasg.*, **7**, 272-8.

JENNINGS , J.S. 1961. The geology of the eastern part of the Lesmahagow inlier. *Univ. Edinburgh Ph.D. thesis* (unpubl.).

KJELLSVIG-WAERING, E.N. 1986 A restudy of the fossil Scorpionida of the world. *Palaeontogr. Amer.* **55**, 1- 287.

LAMONT, A. 1955. Scottish Silurian Chelicerata. *Trans. Edinb. geol. Soc.*, **16**, 200-16.

_____ 1965. Gala-Tarannon trilobites and an ostracod from the Hagshaw Hills, Lanarkshire. *Scott. J. Sci.*, **1**, 33-46.

MCGIVEN, A. 1968. Sedimentation and provenance of post-Valentian conglomerates up to and including the basal conglomerate of the Lower Old Red Sandstone in the southern part of the Midland Valley of Scotland. *Univ. of Glasgow Ph.D. thesis* (unpubl.).

MACNAIR, P. 1905. "Camp Siluria." *Trans. geol. Soc. Glasg.*, **12**, 203-13.

MOY-THOMAS, J.A. and MILES, R.S. 1971. *Palaeozoic fishes* (2nd ed.). London

PALMER,D., JOHNSTON, J.D., DOOLEY, T. and MAGUIRE, K. 1989. The Silurian of Clew Bay, Ireland: part of the Midland Valley of Scotland? *Jl geol. Soc. Lond.* **146**, 385-8.

PEACH, B.N. and HORNE, J. 1899. The Silurian rocks of Britain, vol. 1: Scotland. *Mem. geol. Surv. U.K.*

RITCHIE, A. 1963. Palaeontological studies on Scottish Silurian fish beds. *Univ. of Edinburgh Ph.D. thesis* (unpubl.).

_____ 1967. *Ateleaspis tessellata* Traquair, a non-cornuate cephalaspid from the Upper Silurian of Scotland. *J. Linn. Soc. Lond. (Zool)*, **47**, 69-81.

_____ 1968a. New evidence on *Jamoytius kerwoodi* White, an important ostracoderm from the Silurian of Lanarkshire, Scotland. *Palaeontology* **11**, 21-39.

_____ 1968b. *Lanarkopterus dolichoschelus* (Størmer) gen. nov., a mixopterid eurypterid from the Upper Silurian of the Lesmahagow and Hagshaw Hills inliers, Scotland. *Scott. J. Geol.* **4**, 317-38.

_____ 1984. Conflicting interpretations of the Silurian agnathan, *Jamoytius*. *Scott. J. Geol.* **20**, 249-56.

_____ 1985. *Ainiktozoon loganense* Scourfield, a protochordate? from the Silurian of Scotland. *Alcheringa* **9**, 117-42.

ROLFE, W.D.I. 1960. A fine air-heave structure from the Old Red Sandstone of Lanarkshire, Scotland. *Geol. Mag.*, **97**, 133-6.

_____ 1962a. The geology of the Hagshaw Hills Silurian inlier, Lanarkshire. *Trans. Edinb. geol. Soc.* **18**, 240-69.

_____ 1962b. The cuticle of some Middle Silurian ceratiocaridid Crustacea from Scotland. *Palaeontology*, **5**, 30-51.

_____ 1962c. Grosser morphology of the Scottish Silurian phyllocarid crustacean *Ceratiocaris papilio Salter In Murchison. Jour. Paleont.*, **36**, 912-32.

_____ 1989. Eurypterids. In Calder, J. (ed.) The wealth of a Nation, p. 77. National Museums of Scotland, Edinburgh.

_____ and BECKETT, E.C.M. 1984. The autecology of Silurian Xiphosurida, Scorpionida, Cirripedia and Phyllocarida. *Spec. Pap. Palaeont.* **32**, 27-37.

_____ and BURNABY, T.P. 1961. A preliminary study of the Silurian ceratiocaridids (Crustacea: Phyllocarida) of Lesmahagow, Scotland. *Breviora Mus. Comp. Zool.* **149**, 1-9.

_____ and FRITZ, M.A. 1966. Recent evidence for the age of the Hagshaw Hills Silurian inlier, Lanarkshire. *Scott. J. Geol.* **2**, 159-64.

TURNER, S. 1970. Fish help to trace continental movements. *Spectrum* **79**, 8-10.

WALTON, E.K. 1965. Lower Palaeozoic rocks, *In* Craig, G.Y. (ed.) *The Geology of Scotland*, 161-227. Edinburgh.

WATERSTON, C.D. 1962. *Pagea sturrocki* gen. et sp. nov., a new eurypterid from the Old Red Sandstone of Scotland. *Palaeontology* **5**, 137-48.

_____ 1964. Observations on pterygotid eurypterids. *Trans. R. Soc. Edinb.* **66**, 9-33.

_____ 1979. Problems of functional morphology and classification in stylonuroid eurypterids. (Chelicerata, Merostomata). *Trans. R. Soc. Edinburgh* **70**, 251-322.

WOODWARD, H. 1866-78. A monograph of the British fossil Crustacea belonging to the order Merostomata. *Palaeontogr. Soc. (Monogr.)*.

ZIEGLER, A.M. 1970. Geosynclinal development of the British Isles during the Silurian period. *Jl Geol.* **78**, 445-79.

Excursion 23 LUGAR SILL and MAUCHLINE
D. S. Weedon and W. Mykura

Themes: The picrite-teschenite Lugar sill; New Red Sandstone sediments and lavas.

Features : At Lugar, the nature and relationships of the various units within the sill - teschenite, theralite, picrite, peridotite and lugarite. At Howford Bridge, dune-bedding, millet-seed grains, pyroclastic material.

Maps:
O.S.	1: 50 000	Sheet 71 Lanark and Upper Nithsdale
B.G.S.	1: 63 360	Sheet 14 Ayr
	1: 50 000	Sheet 14E Cumnock

Terrain: The best section for examining the sill is along the banks of the Glenmuir Water. The river bank varies in steepness and difficulty of descent and it must be emphasised that great care is necessary at all times. **In certain cases, it is considered that supporting ropes are essential.**

Distance: The sill lies some 0.5 to 1.0 km east of Lugar, which itself
and Time: is about 3.0 km NE of Cumnock. The latter is 21 km (13miles) from Kilmarnock, on the A76. The total length of sill exposed is some 300 m, with 9 exposures described. With normal examination and collecting of specimens this excursion should be accomplished in about three hours.

Access: Cross the Lugar Water at the footbridge mentioned below. Cars can normally be parked at the roadside in the vicinity of the bridge; otherwise in Lugar itself. A rough track follows the south bank of the Glenmuir Water, climbing up beneath the viaduct then descending and following the river bend towards the final exposures of the section at Locality 1.

It should be noted that this section is designated an **SSSI**.

Introduction

Due mainly to the detailed investigations of G.W.Tyrrell (1917, 1948, 1952), the Lugar Sill became one of the best known and most closely studied differentiated sills in the world. It is post-Carboniferous, possibly New Red Sandstone in age, and is intruded into Passage Group and Coal Measures sediments. In addition to the exposures seen at Lugar, complete sections of the sill have been obtained in borings at Mortonmuir, about 1.6 km. (1 mile) away and at Craigston House, Lugar (Tyrrell 1948, 1952). A further boring has been made through the sill at the confluence of the Bellow Water and the Glenmuir Water (Henderson and Gibb 1987).

At Lugar, the sill is about 44 m (140 ft) thick and is composite in character. Its upper and lower units, each showing chilled margins against sandstone, consist of t**eschenite**, while the central portion consists, from above downwards, of layers of **theralite**, **picrite** and **peridotite**. The junction of the upper teschenite with theralite is sharp and the base of the latter is often separated from the picrite by a thin sheet of **lugarite** which sends veinlike offshoots into both picrite and theralite (see Geology of Central Ayrshire, fig. 16, for a generalised vertical section).

Different views have been advanced to explain the origin and mode of emplacement of the constituent layers. Tyrrell's original interpretation of the sequence of events was as follows: firstly, the intrusion of a sheet of teschenite magma; secondly, when this magma had solidified but was still hot, olivine-rich magma was injected as a thick median layer in which gravitative differentiation, involving the sinking of olivine crystals, gave rise to layers of theralite, picrite and peridotite; lastly, before the sill had cooled, the lugarite was injected as thin sheets and veins.

The Geological Survey Officers, during a subsequent re-examination of the sections in the Lugar and Glenmuir Waters obtained evidence which they interpreted as the theralite layer representing a "separately injected magma fraction" (1949, Geology of Central Aryshire p.112). In his later paper (1952), Tyrrell modified his original views and suggested (p.374) " that the arrangement of the various facies within the sill is due to gravity differentiation of a picroteschenite magma at depth, followed by the injection of the resulting fraction, and possibly much of the original magma, at higher levels in one or more successive pulses."

Henderson and Gibb (1987) obtained from drill cores a complete section through the sill. They concluded that it was formed by multiple injections of successively less-evolved teschenitic magmas followed by a larger pulse of theralitic liquid carrying abundant olivine

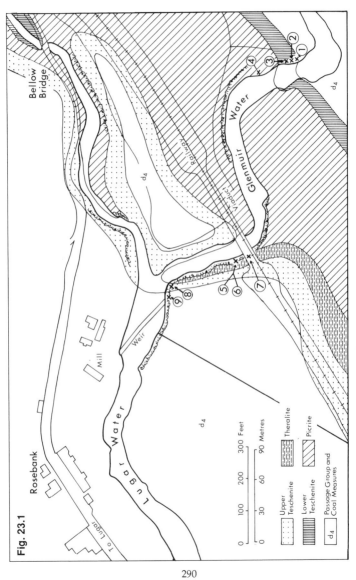

Fig. 23.1

Figure 23.1. Geological map of the Lugar Water.

Rosebank

To Lugar

Lugar Water

Mill

Weir

Bellow Bridge

ROUND

VIADUCT

Glenmuir Water

d_4

d_4

d_4

0   100   200   300 Feet

0   30   60   90 Metres

Upper Teschenite

Lower Teschenite

Teralite

Picrite

Passage Group and Coal Measures

d_4

290

phenocrysts; subsequent differentiation gave rise to the lugarite. In some aspects this modern petrological study produces a differentiation model not dissimilar from that of Tyrrell (1917), to whose pioneer work tribute is paid by the authors of this paper.

Itinerary

Cross the Lugar Water at the footbridge, some 180 m. (200 yds.) off the west of the map (Fig 23.1). Follow the south bank of the river to the site of the old weir, now largely destroyed. This track is often very heavy mud and it may be preferable to follow somewhat higher ground away from the river bank for some 300 m. and then regain the bank near Locality 9 (Fig.23.1).

The section may be examined systematically downwards through the sill starting at Locality 9: some may prefer to proceed to Locality 1 on the map, and work their way back *up* through the succession of rock units. Localities 1 to 4, shown on the east bank of the Glenmuir Water on the map, may also be examined on the opposite bank.

Locality 1. (NS 601 214) **Sandstones** underlying the sill.

Locality 2. The **Lower contact** facies of the teschenite is well exposed close to the stream at this point, but its contact with the underlying sediment is only seen in the bed of the river when the water is low.

Within 1m (3 ft) of the contact the rock is medium to fine-grained. In several specimens, bands or lenses differing in many subtle gradations of colour and texture may be seen. Thin veins of coarse flesh-coloured teschenite cutting across the schlieren are quite common.

Microscopically the rock is **holocrystalline**, generally very fine-grained, and shows numerous variations in texture and composition. The minerals present are plagioclase, augite, biotite, **analcime**, magnetite and occasional olivine.

Locality 3. The contact facies gradually merges into teschenite by increasing granularity and increased proportion of analcime. The lower contact zone is approximately 3m (10 ft) thick.

Locality 4. Peridotite. The contact between the lower teschenite and the peridotite is assumed by Tyrrell to be a sharp one, but it is not seen in the field. The peridotite, in a highly-weathered state, forms extensive outcrops in the east bank. Specimens of relatively fresh peridotite can be obtained from road cuttings near Bellow Bridge (see map); fresh specimens are unobtainable from the section along the Glenmuir Water.

Locality 5. Picrite. With decreasing olivine and increasing feldspar content the peridotite grades upward into picrite which is exposed on both banks up to the railway bridge: also in the west bank 14m (15 yds) north of the bridge.

Locality 6. Lugarite. The lugarite is intercalated near the transition between the picrite and overlying theralite. It is 1.2 m (4ft) thick at a maximum, and is intimately welded to both adjacent rocks. It also occurs as irregular, anastomosing veins ramifying through the picrite, varying in thickness from 2.5-12 cm (1 to 5 ins).

In hand specimen the rock presents a striking appearance, especially when weathered. It is **pegmatitic** and consists of a greyish-green groundmass containing analcime, **nepheline** and alteration products with abundant large prismatic crystals of black **kaersutite** (previously named barkevikite) and equidimensional crystals of black **titanaugite** and occasional whitish rectangular feldspars.

The exact position of Locality 6 is in the west bank at a point 1.2 m (4 ft) above normal winter stream-level and 14 m (15 yds) north of the bridge (viaduct).

Great care must be taken descending to this locality, and supporting ropes are considered essential.

Locality 7. Theralite. The main mass of the theralite layer, well seen at the path junction immediately underneath the viaduct, is composed of a dark-grey compact doleritic rock. The lower part of this horizon contains abundant hornblende and is slightly coarser in grain, while near the junction with the overlying teschenite the rock is veined and shot with patches of a medium-grained, light grey, analcitic variety. Neither upper nor lower facies are, however, well seen at this locality.

Locality 8. Upper teschenite. The junction between the theralite and upper teschenite layers is a sharp one but is not visible at this locality. The upper teschenite is exposed at the water's edge near Locality 8 where it exhibits both fine and coarse-grained varieties.

Locality 9. Upper contact of the sill is exposed here, fairly high in the river bank: white sandstones of the Passage Group overlying spheroidally weathering coarse teschenite. An inclusion of indurated sandstone occurs about 3.7 m (12 ft) below the contact.

The Permian Rocks, Howford Bridge.

Access: Proceed about 2 km south-eastwards from Mauchline on the A 76, turn off at (NS 513 257) on to a minor, largely disused, road forming a loop crossing the old Howford Bridge. Proceed to the bridge, which is still in good order, near which roadside parking is possible, as little traffic uses the road.

The main outcrop of New Red Sandstone rocks in the West of Scotland occurs in the Mauchline region, (Mykura 1967) where massive, brick red, dune-bedded sandstones overlie basalt lava flows with intercalated **tuffs**, sandstones and marls. The discovery of fossil plants in a thin layer of sediment between two lava flows on the north shore of the River Ayr near Stairhill (Mykura 1965), (NS 462 245) has shown that the lavas are either of Upper Stephanian (topmost Carboniferous) or Autunian (lower Permian) age (Wagner 1966).

Looking upstream from the old Howford Bridge an olivine-analcime dolerite sill can be seen in the cliff forming the north bank of the river. It contains pale-coloured "segregation" veins of analcime-syenite but is not readily accessible. Its age is uncertain, but it may well be of the same general age as the Lugar Sill. Mauchline lavas, with sedimentary intercalations, are seen at the side of the path going upstream from the sawmill at the bridge and in the river bed.

Proceed some 300 m (330 yds) back along the road to the top of the cliff section (NS 513 254), where there is good road-side parking along the road-cutting. From here a rough path descends to the river: it is steep in parts, but not dangerous if reasonable care is taken; **keep away from cliff edges.**

In this excellent cliff section the tuffs which form the top of the volcanic sequence are interleaved with and overlain by the Mauchline Sandstone. The tuff contains some wind-rounded sand grains. This is the classic section where Sir A. Geikie deduced that the lavas are of the same general age as the overlying sandstone. At reasonably low water it is possible to follow the north bank of the River Ayr downstream from this point. This "path" affords an excellent opportunity for the detailed study of the intercalated sandstones and tuffs and the overlying

Mauchline Sandstone.

The lower part of the Mauchline Sandstone is not dune-bedded. Excellent sections of dune-bedded sandstones can , however, be seen in the bright orange-red Mauchline Sandstone exposed in the cliffs along the River Ayr north of Stairhill. The best access is by the track which starts at the railway bridge across the Mauchline-Ayr road at Failford (NS 455 262).

References

HENDERSON, C. M. B. & GIBB, F.G.F. 1987. The petrology of the Lugar Sill. *Trans. R. Soc. Edinburgh:* **77**, 325-347.

MACGREGOR, A.G. 1949. *In* Geology of Central Ayrshire, *Mem. Geol. Surv. U.K.*

MYKURA, W. 1965. The age of the lower part of the New Red Sandstone in South West Scotland. *Scott. J. Geol.* **1**, 9-18.

_____ 1967. The upper Carboniferous rocks of southwest Ayrshire. *Bull. geol. Surv. Gt. Br.* **26**, 23-98 (see pp 80-82 and pp 92-93).

TYRRELL, G.W. 1917. The Picrite-Teschenite Sill of Lugar. *Q. Jl geol. Soc. Lond.* **74**, 84-131.

_____ 1948. A Boring through the Lugar Sill. *Trans. geol.Soc. Glasg.* **21**, 157-202.

_____ 1952. A second Boring through the Lugar Sill. *Trans. Edin. Geol. Soc.* **15**, 374-392.

WAGNER, R. H. 1966. On the presence of probable Upper Stephanian beds in Ayrshire, Scotland. *Scott. J. Geol.* **2**, 122-3.

Excursion 24 HEADS OF AYR
F. Whyte

Theme: A large deeply-eroded volcanic vent.

Features: Faulted contacts between Lower Old Red Sandstone lavas and Upper Old Red Sandstone sediments : also contacts between the latter group and Cementstone strata; bedded and unbedded pyroclastic rocks, cut by small intrusions of monchiquitic-basalt and analcime-basalt; Passage Group sediments and lavas; Tertiary dykes.

Maps: O.S. 1 : 50 000 Sheet 70   Ayr and Kilmarnock
                  B.G.S. 1 : 63 360 Sheet 14   Ayr
                        1 : 50 000 Sheet 14 W Ayr

Terrain: As many of the features seen on this excursion occur on wave-cut platforms within the intertidal zone, it it advisable to start when the tide is falling. Normal precautions for working on a foreshore should be observed.

Distance: The Heads of Ayr lies some 7 km (4 miles) to the SW of Ayr.
and Time: From the starting point on the shore to Longhill Point is about 3.5 km (2 miles), from which point one proceeds to Doonfoot on the A719. Normally a full day is needed to cover this excursion. It may be shortened by examining the first part as far as desired and retracing one's tracks to the starting point.

Access: Turn off the A 719 at (NS 285 178),directly south of Heads of Ayr. Keep straight on past the caravan site on the right and park along the left-hand side of the road. Proceed along the well-defined foot-path down to the shore. **(SSSI)**

Introduction

The twin headlands of the Heads of Ayr occupy about 1 km (0.6 miles) of coast and provide excellent cliff and wave-cut platform sections through a Lower Carboniferous **tuff** and agglomerate-filled vent. The western part of the vent is composed of well-bedded tuffs showing folding, which may have been caused by compression of original cone deposits into a slowly subsiding basin. Although some bedding is present in the eastern part of the vent most of it appears to

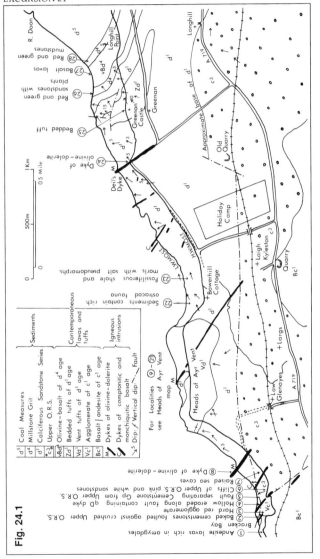

Fig. 24.1

Figure 24.1. Geological map of Heads of Ayr district.

be unbedded and may mark the site of the pipe supplying ash to the western end.

Locality 1. (Fig.24.1) . Andesite lavas rich in **amygdales** and veins of quartz, **chalcedony**, calcite, 'green earths' etc, can be seen here. The amygdales may contain agate showing a characteristic milky white outer skin; these weather out and can occasionally be collected on the shore.

Localities 2 and **5. Fault.** At these localities the fault separating Cementstone Group from Upper Old Red Sandstone can be seen. At Locality 2, the **cementstones** are baked and the sandstones of the Upper Old Red Sandstones are crushed.

Locality 3. A poorly exposed mass of hard red **agglomerate** composed mainly of blocks of Lower Old Red Sandstone lavas forms one of four vents of this age in South Ayrshire.

Locality 4. Fault and dyke. The sediments are separated from the agglomeratic lavas by a fault which has been eroded to form a distinct hollow along which runs a quartz-dolerite dyke 15 m thick.

Locality 6. Upper Old Red Sandstone. Here the cliffs are of massive mottled pink and white sandstones of Upper Old Red Sandstone age, often showing cross-stratification and containing numerous pebbly horizons. Plates of *Bothriolepis major* have been found at the base of the north end of the cliff, and one specimen of *Asterolepis* was found in the massive sandstone forming the roof of one of the sea caves.

Locality 7. Raised sea-caves. Note the line of raised sea-caves, presumably of the same age as the 12 m (40 ft.) raised beach visible at the NE end of the bay.

Locality 8. Fault and dyke. At the position where the fault (seen at localities 2 and 5) reaches the cliffs of Upper Old Red Sandstone rocks, there is a dyke of olivine-dolerite 6m (6.5 yds) thick.

East of Locality 8 there are intermittent exposures of gently-dipping cementstones, marls and thin micaceous sandstones. As the margin of the Heads of Ayr vent is approached there is a marked increase in the dip of these sediments towards the vent.

Locality 9. (Fig.24.2). **Tuff structures.** Here minor structures within the tuffs can be examined, such as cross-stratification, graded bedding, slumping and bomb-sag. Many of the fragments in the tuffs are derived from underlying Old Red Sandstone lavas. Other common

Fig. 24.2

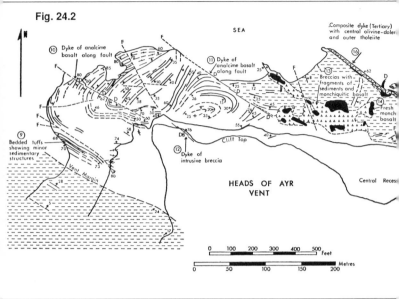

Figure 24.2. Detailed geological map of the Heads of Ayr vent.

fragments are of cementstone, fossilized wood and carbonated **peridotite**.

Localities 10 and **11. En-echelon dykes.** At both these localities thin dykes of analcime-basalt can be seen intruded 'en echelon' along faults. The dyke rocks are vesicular in part and composed of highly altered olivine and pyroxene phenocrysts in a groundmass of **analcime**, chlorite, serpentine and feldspar.

Locality 12. Breccia dyke. Here is exposed a 30 cm wide dyke of very hard intrusive breccia, material similar to that described at Locality 13.

Locality 13. Intrusive breccia. Penetrating the sediments on the shore opposite the Central Recess are irregular masses of intrusive breccia and monchiquitic-basalt. The intrusive breccia consists of angular fragments of sedimentary and volcanic rocks in a highly chloritised groundmass. There is often gradation between the breccia and the monchiquitic-basalt.

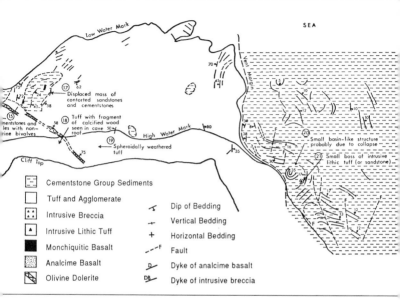

Legend:

- Cementstone Group Sediments
- Tuff and Agglomerate
- Intrusive Breccia
- Intrusive Lithic Tuff
- Monchiquitic Basalt
- Analcime Basalt
- Olivine Dolerite

- Dip of Bedding
- Vertical Bedding
- Horizontal Bedding
- Fault
- Dyke of analcime basalt
- Dyke of intrusive breccia

Locality 14. The **monchiquitic-basalt** varies in freshness from one intrusion to another. At this locality it is reasonably fresh and consists of micro-phenocrysts of olivine and augite in a groundmass of plagioclase, augite, olivine and analcime. Occasional fresh **nepheline** may be found.

Locality 15. Bivalves. The sediments on the foreshore opposite the Central Recess consist mainly of cementstone and shales in which certain horizons contain abundant non-marine bivalves.

Locality 16. Composite dyke. The Central Recess sediments and the eastern tuffs are cut by a Tertiary dyke intruded 'en echelon'. It dips steeply towards the NE and is composite, with a central olivine-dolerite and badly decomposed outer tholeiite.

Locality 17. Slumped blocks. There are three ' blocks ' of Cement-stone Group sediments within the eastern tuffs and at this locality the largest can be seen. They are slumped masses which have fallen into the vent, or blocks which have been blown upwards during vent formation.

299

Locality 18. In the cave at this locality can be seen a large angular fragment of calcified wood.

Locality 19. At a number of localities the tuffs display spheroidal weathering; here is a good example.

Locality 20. Contorted sediments. Beyond the eastern margin of the vent the sediments are contorted and fractured. The folding often occurs as small basins which suggest localised collapse of sediments over small pipes.

Locality 21. Lithic tuff. Close to one of these basins is a small outcrop of intrusive lithic tuff, comprised of quartz grains in a matrix of quartz, chlorite, **sericite** and glass.

Locality 22 (Fig.24.1). Many of the sediments in this area are visibly rich in **ostracodes.**

Locality 23. Fossils. The shales here yield small mussels, *Lingula mytiloides, Estheria striata, Spirorbis* and fish remains.

Locality 24. Deil's Dyke. The most prominent dyke cutting these sediments is the olivine-dolerite intrusion of Deil's Dyke. Near High Water Mark a branch of the dyke incorporates a strip of marly sediments, the baking resulting in the development of bands with well-marked **pisolitic** structure. Nearby is a narrow fissure-vent filled with agglomerate which extends for several metres alongside the dyke, which chills against it.

Locality 25. Greenan Castle is built on a knob of well-bedded grey-green tuff similar in fragment content to the bedded western tuffs of the Heads of Ayr vent. The cement is highly calcareous. These tuffs were probably erupted from the Heads of Ayr volcano.

Localities 26-28. Passage beds. On the foreshore north of Longhill Point rocks of the Passage Group ("Millstone Grit") are exposed. The lavas are olivine-basalts and the overlying red and green mudstones belong to the same horizon as the Ayrshire Bauxitic Clay.

References

TYRRELL, G.W. 1920. The igneous rocks of the Ayrshire Coast from Doonfoot to the Heads of Ayr. *Trans.geol. Soc. Glasg.* **16,** 339-63.

EYLES, V.A. *et al* . 1929. The igneous geology of Central Ayrshire. *Trans. geol. Soc. Glasg.* **18,** 361-87.

_____. 1949. The Geology of Central Ayrshire. *Mem. geol. Surv. U.K.*

WHYTE, F. 1964. The Heads of Ayr vent. *Trans. geol. Soc. Glasg.* **25,** 72-97.

THE GIRVAN-BALLANTRAE COMPLEX
B. J. Bluck and J. Keith Ingham

Introduction

The Girvan-Ballantrae district has always played a key rôle in our understanding of Scotland's Lower Palaeozoic history. In the past, whatever the prevailing ideas of Scottish geology of that period may have been, reference has always been made to the rocks and fossils of this region. Present day thinking, which sees southern Scotland as part of an erstwhile destructive plate margin, has drawn heavily on these rock and fossil assemblages for evidence of the nature of its margin and the processes taking place along it. Although the older Ballantrae Complex and the younger cover rocks are here described separately, they form an integrated whole; fore-arc basins, of which the Girvan cover sequence appears representative, are commonly founded on fragments of **obducted** oceanic crust such as the Ballantrae Complex.

The Ballantrae Complex

The Ballantrae rocks, although having a dark and sometimes forbidding appearance, are amongst the most varied to be found in a small region of Scotland. Not only are there unusual varieties of igneous, sedimentary and metamorphic types, but many of the rocks show evidence of having formed in widely differing régimes. Rocks which were generated at radically differing depths, sometimes as much as 50km vertical distance apart within the Earth's crust and beneath it, are now to be seen in juxtaposition on the surface and this fact implies substantial tectonic activity.

The reasons for the great variety and varied depth of provenance of this rock assemblage have a great deal to do with the tectonic régime in which it is thought to have formed. The whole complex apparently represents a fragment, or fragments, of oceanic crust and mantle which has been thrust onto a continental margin so that there are present not only rock types which were generated in the oceanic realm, but also rocks which formed during the period of thrusting. As a result of tectonic activity during the generation of the crust, as well as the thickness of the lithospheric slabs involved, we now see rock types from a range of depths.

The oceanic crust, normally the upper 6-7km of the oceanic lithosphere, forms much of the Ballantrae exposure and is believed to have formed during Arenig times (Early Ordovician, c. 493-470 Ma). There are excellent exposures of pillow lavas, lava conglomerates, **cherts** and graptoliferous black shales which formed on the sea floor and, although pillow lavas and cherts are usually thought of as deep water sediments, there is abundant evidence for a shallow water origin for at least some of them. Gabbros and **trondhjemites** which are formed in magma chambers within the crust are also present, the former commonly well foliated, having been deformed as injection took place at an active ocean ridge.

Oceanic mantle is now represented by quite large but poorly exposed tracts of **serpentinite**, amongst which there are a few exposures of the ultramafic **protolith**, usually **harzburgite**. Some of these mantle rocks may have formed at depths in excess of 40km within the lithosphere. Uplift and serpentinisation clearly took place before intrusion of the gabbro and trondhjemite during Arenig times. Although the radiometric age of the mantle material is unknown, it is assumed to be part of the dated crustal sequence.

The first major phase of obduction took place at c. 480 Ma and, during the obduction, a metamorphic sole was created with mantle rocks being brought up from depths which may be greater than 45km. Final accretion to the Midland Valley terrane was achieved by the end of Arenig time.

Thus, it is evident that the Ballantrae Complex is compound: it comprises rocks which were not all produced in the same place, either vertically or areally. Some may have been laterally transported by shears: others instigated by major thrusts which detached material from deep levels within the lithosphere. Probably during their tectonic transportation they became rotated, as shown by the palaeomagnetic data of Trench *et al.* (1988). However, the greatest interpretational difficulty lies with isolated blocks of garnet metapyroxenite which occur in **mélange-olistostrome** units. They indicate deep burial and metamorphism of ocean type crust at c. 570 Ma (Early Cambrian), a time when Scotland, or rather Hebridean Scotland, is thought of as a passive rather than a destructive Laurentian continental margin. Dempster and Bluck (1991) address this problem.

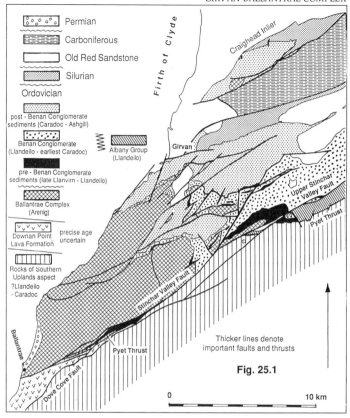

Figure 25.1. Simplified geological map of the Girvan district showing the relationships between the major rock units.

The Lower Palaeozoic cover sequence.

The Ballantrae Complex had been deformed, uplifted and had accreted to the south-eastern margin of the Midland Valley terrane as obducted sheets by Mid Ordovician (Llanvirn) times, for the Mid Ordovician to Early Silurian cover rests unconformably on an irregular, eroded Ballantrae 'basement' and is markedly transgressive northwards or northwestwards. It shows considerable overlap in

303

those directions so that the oldest beds, of Upper Llanvirn age, are exposed in the SE of the district in the Stinchar Valley area, whereas in the Craighead Inlier, to the NW of the district, a sedimentary sequence of Mid Caradoc age rests on the Ballantrae rocks (Figs 25.1, 25.2) (Ingham 1978). Late Silurian (Caledonian) movements have complicated the picture somewhat by foreshortening the original transgressive distribution pattern but the overall picture is quite clear.

One of the most striking features of the Girvan cover sequence, whether it be of Ordovician or Silurian age, is that it is rich in conglomerates dominated by a volcanic provenance and having accumulated in restricted sedimentary basins. Many of the conglomerates are coarse with large boulders often set in a matrix of volcanogenic and related sediment. Most are derived from the north or NW and have travelled no great distance. A high percentage of the clasts are of obvious local derivation, being either cobbles of Ballantrae rocks or of sedimentary rocks from the cover sequence underlying the conglomerate in question, but some high level acid plutonic clasts have no modern counterpart at outcrop and give radiometric dates which are commonly only marginally older than the conglomerates which contain them (Bluck 1983). They derive largely from a contemporary intrusive and volcanic tract, a presumed magmatic arc 'axis' of the Midland Valley terrane, which probably lay only a few kilometres north of the present Lower Palaeozoic outcrops in the Girvan district. The large regional variations in thickness of the conglomerates, commonly their limited distribution, together with sedimentological details of both the conglomerates and associated sediments, have suggested to many workers (Williams 1962; Ingham 1978; Bluck 1983; Ince 1984; Ingham and Tripp 1991) that the controls on sedimentation were essentially contemporary movements on listric basement faults which produced a sequence of basins marginal to the Midland Valley magmatic arc. It is appears therefore that the Girvan cover sequence consists essentially of a proximal fore-arc succession with regular basement faulting, producing a cyclical stratigraphy in which an initially shallow but rapidly deepening sequence is capped by a thick conglomerate, commonly channelling into the underlying sediments and this is followed by another, similar cycle.

Another important feature of the Girvan cover sequence lies in its palaeontology. Clearly such a varied sedimentary succession, deposited in a wide range of water depths, will be reflected in the

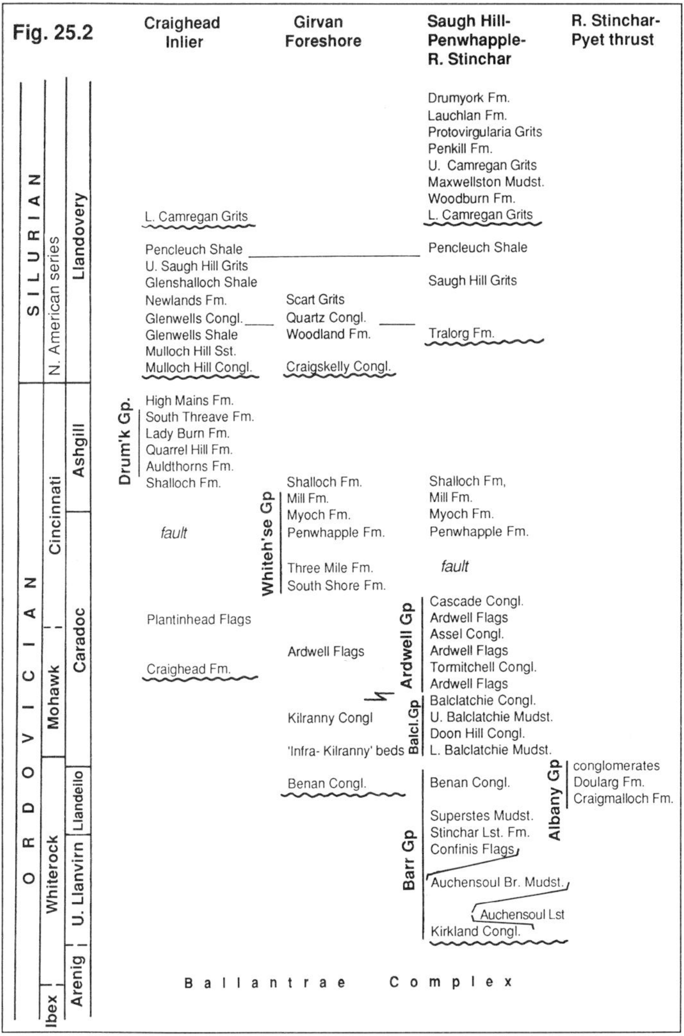

Figure 25.2. The Lower Palaeozoic successions in the Girvan district and their chronostratigraphical ages.

fossil content of its rocks. Deeper water, commonly graptolitic assemblages alternate with diverse, shallow water, shelly assemblages and there are other, bizarre facies faunas reflecting special depositional conditions. There is evidence from some parts of the succession for shallower water assemblages having been displaced, together with sediment, downslope into deeper, basinal slope environments. Most importantly, however, the shallower, inshore faunas of the Llanvirn to Late Caradoc epochs are of decidedly North American (Appalachian) aspect, so much so that it is more useful to apply a North American chronostratigraphical standard to these parts of the succession rather than the traditional Anglo-Welsh one, there being virtually nothing in common between the shelly faunas of the two areas (Fig. 25.2). Conodonts, however, have permitted a reasonably precise correlation with the Anglo-Welsh standard. This is all obviously a reflection of the Lower Palaeozoic palaeogeographical picture whereby a wide, but closing, Iapetus Ocean separated the Anglo-Welsh area (part of the Avalon terrane, then in the southern hemisphere) from southern Scotland which was peripheral to, and progressively accreting to the Laurentian palaeocontinent at much lower southern latitudes. Overall and local successional details are tabulated in Figure 25.2.

As mentioned above, the succession was finally disrupted by late, or end Silurian movements, heralded by Late Llandovery red beds. These Caledonian movements, although fairly major, appear largely to have affected only the upper crustal rocks in the Girvan area for the folding and faulting, although locally complex, is unaccompanied by cleavage. The Girvan tract was pushed progressively to the NW and some of the large-scale folds are asymmetrical in this direction with steep, sometimes vertical, NW limbs (e.g., the Byne Hill monocline). There are several major thrusts striking in the same direction as the fold axes, usually cutting the NW-facing anticlinal limbs and similarly translating the rocks north-westwards. Superimposed on this pattern is a plethora of brittle fracture conjugate faults, the dextrals essentially E-W and the sinistrals N-S. Finally, large NE-SW faults of a variety of later ages may have dextral or sinistral displacements as well as vertical throws: some of them are almost certainly rejuvenated basement faults, such as those which controlled the sedimentation patterns in the Lower Palaeozoic cover sequence (Fig. 25.1). Following some rapid erosion, a topographically varied surface was produced on which the continental deposits of the Lower Old Red Sandstone were deposited.

One day itineraries : Girvan and Ballantrae

A and B can be combined for a week-end visit.

A. **Ballantrae Complex** (B.J.Bluck)

The following localities are chosen in sequence from north to south and as they are also chosen to illustrate the origin of the ophiolite, they should be visited in conjunction with reading the introduction to the Ballantrae Complex.

1. Excursion 25, Localities 5-7: Slockenray: Hyaloclastic delta, tuffs intermixing with lavas.

2. Excursion 26, Localities 1-4: Knocklaugh: Thin metamorphic sole to the ophiolite; olistrostrome with greenschists - amphibolites.

3. Excursion 27, Localities 1-4: Bennane Lea : Cherts interfingering with mass-flow comglomerates, tuffs, fossiliferous black shales and thrust contact between cherts and serpentinite.

4. Excursion 27, Locality 6 : Downan Point : Beautiful pillow lavas in excellent exposures. Pillowed lava tubes, and many good illustrations of how pillow lavas grow.

B. **Lower Palaeozoic cover sequence** (J.K.Ingham)

All localities easily accessible by car with only a little walking.

1. Excursion 29, Locality 7: Aldons Quarry: Cover rock (including Benan Conglomerate and Stinchar Limestone) overlying spilites of the Ballantrae Volcanic Complex.

2. Excursion 30, Locality 1 : Kennedy 's Pass : Kilranny Conglomerate and Henderson's " unconformity ".

3. Excursion 30, Locality 2 : Ardwell Foreshore : "Cascade folding ".

4. Excursion 30, Localities 5-7 : Whitehouse Shore (centre) : flysch deposits, deep-water facies faunas, conjugate folding, slumping, graptolites.

5. Excursion 31, Locality 1 : Craighead Quarry : spilites of Ballantrae Complex overlain by late Ordovician limestones and mudstones with shelly fossils.

6. Excursion 31, Locality 7 : Rough Neuk Quarry : Lower Silurian shelly fossils.

C. **Girvan tour** (M.C.Keen)

Involving a walk and including some examples of Ballantrae Complex rocks, Upper Ordovician and Silurian sediments. Drive to Girvan Cemetery (NX 187 956) and park car or bus.

1. Excursion 28, Localities 2, 3 and 4 : Byne Hill (summit optional): Serpentinite, gabbro, trondhjemite and Benan Conglomerate. Return to vehicle.

2. Excursion 30, Localities 1, 2 (briefly) , 3, 4 and 6 : Kennedy 's Pass to Whitehouse shore : Kilranny conglomerate, Henderson's " unconformity ", " cascade folding ", graptolites and graded limestones.

3. Excursion 30, Localities 9 and 10 (if low tide) : Port Cardloch and Woodland Point : sinistral faulting, cross-bedding , unconformity, Silurian brachiopods and graptolites.

4. Excursion 31, Locality 7 : Rough Neuk Quarry : Mulloch Hill Sandstone, early Silurian shelly fossils.

D. **Coastal tour** (J.D.Lawson)

Mainly by car or coach : a long summer's day : probably need to select and omit according to personal interest.

1. Excursion 27, Locality 6 : Downan Point : Pillow lavas.

2. Excursion 27, Localities 1-4 : Bennane Lea : Serpentinite, cherts, tuffs, black shales with graptolites, thrust.

3. Excursion 30, Locality 1 : Kennedy 's Pass : Kilranny conglomerate and Henderson's " unconformity".

4. Excursion 30, Locality 4-6 : Whitehouse shore (but close to road): graded limestones : deep-water trilobites etc.

5. Excursion 30, Locality 10 (if tide low) : Woodland Point : Unconformity, Silurian brachiopods and graptolites.

6. Excursion 31, Locality 7 (if time permits): Rough Neuk Quarry : Mulloch Hill Sandstone, early Silurian shelly fossils.

THE BALLANTRAE COMPLEX
B.J.Bluck

Introduction

The Ballantrae Complex in SW Ayrshire has attracted a good deal of attention since the last century, when Murchison, Geikie and Bonney discussed its problematical origin. It was clear to most of these and subsequent workers that the association of **serpentinite, chert** and pillow lavas was repeatedly found in major fracture zones, and for this reason they regarded the association as significant. However, the true importance of the rocks at Ballantrae became more apparent when work in Newfoundland and Cyprus demonstrated that rocks, similar to those found at Ballantrae, were fragments of oceanic crust, and that these oceanic crustal slices had been thrust onto the continents. As the knowledge of destructive and passive margins increased it became clear that the slices of oceanic crust which had been thrust onto continental margins were a signature of typical destructive margins: and so, with the Ballantrae complex in mind, Dewey (1969) recognised for the first time the Caledonides as a destructive margin. The whole rock assemblage at Ballantrae has become increasingly important, not only because it is oceanic crust, but also because its presence here raises a number of important questions, two of which are applicable generally to rocks of this oceanic type (ophiolites).

Firstly, in what kind of oceanic setting did these rocks form ? This entails the establishment of criteria by which various types of oceanic crust can be distinguished.

Secondly, how does oceanic crust appear on land areas, when it appears that most of it is being consumed at trenches?

The excursions which follow this introduction all have a bearing on answering both of these questions.

Origin of ocean crust

Ocean crust is now known to form at two main situations: ocean ridges and marginal basins. However, crust of oceanic type may also form in hot-spots (sea mounts) or in oceanic island arcs. Most of the ocean crust now produced on the earth's surface forms at mid-ocean ridges, and this crust has a characteristic structure (Fig. 25.3) which may largely depend upon the rate at which the crust is generated.

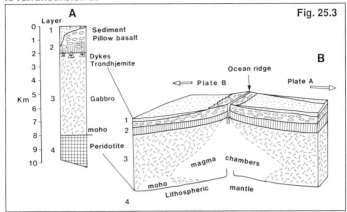

FIGURE 25.3. A. Section through typical oceanic crust. **B.** Diagram showing how oceanic crust is created in an instance of a rapidly growing plate. The peridotite of **A** belongs to the lithospheric mantle of **B**.

When this structure is compared with the rocks at Ballantrae it is clear that, with the possible exception of the sheeted dyke complex, all the rocks which are thought to be characteristic of ocean crust are present; for this reason alone it is fairly safe to assume that the Ballantrae rocks are of oceanic type (Fig. 25.4). But there are many types of oceanic crust to consider, and there has been much debate about which of these types of crust is represented by the Ballantrae Complex. The origin of the various types of crust is shown in Figure 25.5, together with their main characteristics. The most diagnostic characteristic of the various kinds of crust are seen in the layers 1 and 2: differences which might arise in the other layers of oceanic crust are not well known. Where there are faults crossing the hot ridges, deformation and metamorphism may occur whilst the oceanic crust is being formed.

Oceanic ridges are usually found in quite deep water and are characterised by fine grained sediments in layer 1: these are often produced by organisms such as **radiolarians** living within the water column and falling onto the plate surface after death. As there is little explosive activity at these depths this fine grained sediment is usually devoid of much tuff. Black shale-type deposits may comprise layer 1,

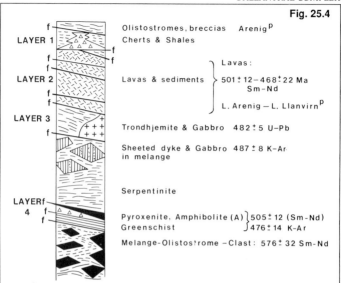

Fig. 25.4

FIGURE 25.4. Compound section through the Ballantrae Complex showing some of the absolute age determinations (the various methods used are shown by the conventional symbols K-Ar etc) and fossil ages (p). On the left of the section the various elements of the complex are interpreted in terms of a conventional ophiolite.

where the ocean floor in near a source of terrestrial sediment, as for example, where ocean crust reaches a subduction zone.

Layer 2, usually comprises basalts with a minor amount of breccia and very little evidence of explosive activity during the formation of the lavas - the water being so deep that the water pressure is too high to permit much explosive release of gas. These lavas are often pillowed but do not extend for great distances since there are low slopes at most of the positions of extrusion on the ridge and the lavas tend to chill quickly. This results in mounds of pillows locally building over the points of extrusion.

With the development of hot-spots and seamounts on the ocean plate the nature and thickness of the lava pile is changed. In this instance the lava pile grows from deep water to shallow, so that

311

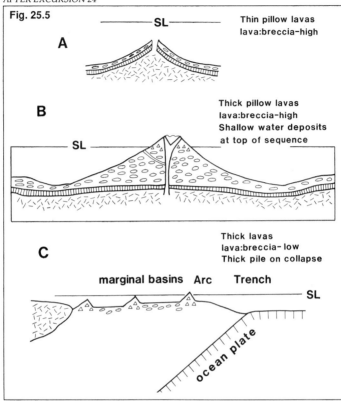

Fig. 25.5

A — Thin pillow lavas
lava:breccia–high

B — Thick pillow lavas
lava:breccia–high
Shallow water deposits
at top of sequence

C — Thick lavas
lava:breccia– low
Thick pile on collapse

marginal basins   Arc   Trench

SL

ocean plate

FIGURE 25.5. Diagram showing the various ways in which ophiolites form, together with some of the main characteristics which typifies each one. **A.** Formation at a spreading ridge; **B.** At an ocean seamount, **C.** At a marginal basin-arc. SL = sea level. The symbols are as for Figures 25.3 and 25.4.

initially the pile is dominated by pillows which lack evidence of explosive activity, to be followed at the top of the pile by a relatively thin interval of shallow water and intertidal flows and finally the subaerial flows as the cone emerges to form an island (Fig.25.5B). As these lavas are built on ocean crust which was generated at a ridge, the age of the lavas will be much younger than the age of the ocean crust, provided they formed at some distance from the ridge; and, conversely, the ages of the two will be similar if the hot spot is close to a ridge.

Marginal basins are far more complex, and whilst there are apparently many ways in which they are produced, a common way is to rift an arc to produce new oceanic crust within the rift zone (Fig. 25.6). The new oceanic crust may then grow in the usual way to create a new marginal basin terminated on the continent side by a remnant arc (RA, Fig. 25.6), and on the ocean side by the now rejuvenated active arc (Fig. 25.6). In this way there can be stretches of oceanic crust belonging to marginal basins which are divided by remnant half-arcs.

The sequences produced by this means are quite different from those produced elsewhere. Layer 1 is not now a sequence of fine grained sediments produced some distance away from source, but coarse detritus derived locally from the splitting arc (CS Fig.25.6B); however, as the marginal basin opens up so the sources become more

FIGURE 25.6. Origin and development of a marginal basin. A. Section through a developed marginal basin. B. Stages in the growth of a marginal basin. Stage 1, the splitting of an arc, Stage 2, the development of new ocean crust in the rifted arc, Stage 3, the development of a wide ocean basin. RA, remnant arc. CS = coarse sediment; FS = fine sediment.

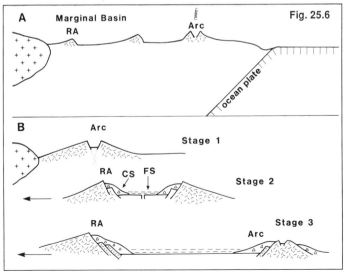

distant and the sediment finer grained (FS Fig. 25.6B). During the splitting of the arc, the foundation upon which some of the sediment has already accumulated becomes unstable and subject to extensional faulting. There are now sharp boundaries between sources and basins. The volcanogenic sediment, which accumulates as an apron around the arc, is made up of angular and (intertidally) well rounded clasts, and is displaced into deeper water as mass flows. Sediments, some of which come from the shallow-water zones are displaced towards the basin axis by slump and mass flow action. Finer grained sediment may be organically produced (e.g.cherts) in association with wind blown ash generated by explosive activity on the arc.

The arc itself comprises a great thickness of volcanogenic sediment and, to a lesser extent, lava. If the arc has been allowed to develop for a long time it becomes mature and produces acidic lavas. If, however, it is continuously rejuvenated, as when it splits to form a new marginal basin, then the arc may remain immature and produce basic lavas only. In this arc regime the volcanogenic sediments range from being subaerial to shallow water intertidal to deeper water.

There are a few critical features of the Ballantrae complex which have some bearing on the type of ocean process which might have formed it. These are as follows:

1. Cherts and black shales occur in a number of associations at Ballantrae and in terms of oceanic layering can be ascribed to layer 1 (Fig.25.3). As discussed above, of special importance are:

(a). The presence or absence of coarse grained clastic sediments; deep ocean basins are dominated by fine sediments; parts of seamounts and all of island arcs are dominated by coarse sediment (Fig.25.5). The sediments of layer 1 can be seen at Bennane Head where they are found in association with boulder-bearing conglomerates and breccias.

(b). The presence of acidic or intermediate rocks, clasts or rock fragments associated with these fine grained sediments. Ocean ridges tend to be dominated by basic rocks only, whilst hot spots may have, in addition to basic, intermediate rocks present as well. Arcs may be largely basic when youthful, but mature to produce calc-alkaline and acidic volcanic rocks. Acidic rocks fragments are associated with the cherts at Bennane Head.

(c). Whether the sediments show any signs of tectonic activity as might occur when an arc splits to form a new marginal basin i.e. aprons of mass flow deposits with much coarse sediment associated with slumped beds. These sediments can be seen at Locality 12 on Excursion 25 at Pinbain and at Locality 3 on Excursion 27 at Bennane Head. The stratigraphical associations at Pinbain are not clear as the exposure is fault bounded. Bennane Head is the critical exposure, for here is a sequence from lavas and conglomerates up into cherts, and that is the sequence one would expect where layer 2 (basalt layer of Fig.25.3) is overlain by sediments (layer 1 of Fig.25.3). So at Bennane Head it would appear that we have a clear example of layer 1 in its stratigraphical context.

2. The lava sequence is also quite critical for the identification of the origin of the ophiolite at Ballantrae. Lavas occur in at least three quite extensive blocks, the most northerly of which is the Pinbain block. The lavas and associated sediments of this block are terminated to the SE by a major fault (the Pinbain Fault seen on Excursion 25) and to the NE the unconformably overlying Girvan clastic sequence. South of Pinbain lies the Bennane Head block, which has a sequence of cherts and shale at its top (see above) and by a major fault at its base near Games Loup. The most southerly block is found in the Mains Hill-Knockdolian region: it is terminated to the south by cherts and black shales and to the north by a major fracture. A fourth block, the Aldons block is not well known. There is no contact between the lavas and the sheeted dykes and as already discussed, there is an upper contact with strata which are superficially similar to ocean layer 1 at Bennane Head.

For the lavas which can seen on Excursions 25 and 27, there are several critical lines of evidence which allow an evaluation of their origin:

1. The abundance of breccias and conglomerates characterizes shallow water volcanic processes.

2. Massive lavas can be extruded in very deep water, but where massive flows have red tops, then they are almost certainly subaerial flows.

3. Where lavas enter the sea they may produce hyalotuff deltas, the presence of which in the volcanic pile would be a certain indication of volcanicity at or above sea level.

4. Accretionary lapilli require the volcanic ejectamenta to have been through the air column: they do not form in water alone.

5. All the above points above refer to water depth, which is obvious- ly very significant. If a thick sequence of lava is built up from deep to shallow water, then it may have formed in an ocean island environment, possibly at the early stages in the growth of an island arc or (very unusually) a mid oceanic ridge. However if there is a thick sequence of lavas which are constantly extruded into shallow water, then we have to invoke subsidence at the same time as lava accumulation. This feature is common in island arcs, possible in unusual mid-ocean ridges and unlikely in oceanic islands.

Lavas are evidently important indicators in the evaluation of the evolution of an ophiolite, and they will be examined particularly in the light of the points made above.

The age of the Ballantrae Complex

With the Ballantrae Complex comprising both igneous and sedimentary rocks, dating has been carried out using both radiometric and palaeontological techniques. This has the advantage of being able to fit the radiometric into the palaeontological time-scale. The black shales which occur amongst the lavas, and those which are part of the **olistostrome** sequence, have been known for some time to contain fossils of mainly inarticulate brachiopods and graptolites. The latter are particularly useful in relative age determination and they indicate that these rocks are representative of most of the Arenig Series. Radiometric dating has been conducted on a variety of rock types using a range of methods, and with two exceptions yield ages which on the basis of world-wide data are considered to be Arenig (Fig.25.2). The exceptions are within the olistrostrome-**mélange** unit at Knockormal, where a garnet meta-pyroxenite has yielded an age of 576+-32Ma which is Cambrian; and the pillow lavas at Downan Point which have yielded younger ages of 468+-22Ma, which is roughly Llanvirn. The errors on either side of the mean in each of these determinations are large and, in the latter instance the age is not statistically different from age determinations from other pillow lavas to the north of Ballantrae (north of the Stinchar Valley). There is, however, a essential diffence between the lavas to the north and south of the Stinchar Valley; those to the north have a higher proportion of volcanogenic sediment. Downan Point is typified by massive pillow lavas with a minimum of volcanogenic sediment and this probably reflects the different regime. Indeed many workers would now place the Southern Uplands Fault along the Stinchar Valley to separate the pillows of Downan Point from the rest of the ophiolite.

From these radiometric ages and from the ages given by the faunas it is clear that the main part of the ophiolite was formed within the Arenig, between *c*.501 and *c*.476 Ma. a time-span of *c*.25 my. The age of obduction is anytime between 501-476 Ma , so it was also obducted within Arenig times. These ages imply that the oceanic crust which comprises the Ballantrae Complex was young and near to the site of its generation: wide ocean basins have oceanic crust which is often >100 Ma, since it has travelled a great distance from the ridge which created it. Thus, the diversity of the complex cannot then be explained by the great differences in its age: it has to be explained by differences within the region of its formation.

There are several papers which review the nature and origin of the Ballantrae Complex in terms of its ocean crust setting. The earliest of these are by Church and Gayer (1973), Dewey (1974), Bluck *et al* (1980) and Stone and Smellie (1988). The last is also a comprehensive guide to the complex with much new and significant information.

The significance of the Ballantrae Complex

The geological significance of the Ballantrae complex extends far beyond the region of Ballantrae. The presence of oceanic crust leads to a number of important conclusions, some of which have helped to unify a geological history over a considerable part of Scotland. The prime conclusion is that during the Arenig this part of Scotland was a destructive margin, where oceanic crust was being consumed. This further suggested that to the continent side of this margin there would have lain a volcanic arc; this, on the basis of information from the overlying Ordovician rocks (see Excursion 28 Locality 3) is thought to have lain to the NW. To the south there would have been an ocean.

The nature of the Ballantrae Complex is also highly significant. If it was produced in a marginal basin, as suggested here, then there would have been a major subduction zone to the south where dense, and probably old oceanic crust would have been consumed (marginal basins are at present seen to form where old oceanic crust is being consumed, as in the western Pacific). This in turn would suggest that there had been quite a long history of subduction in the Ballantrae region.

The North Atlantic region has a number of ophiolitic masses which are of this general age. They occur in Newfoundland, Scotland and Scandinavia (Dunning and Krogh 1985).

References

References are given after Excursion 31. However, attention should be drawn at this stage to the valuable systematic account of the Ballantrae area published by the British Geological Survey (Stone and Smellie 1988). It contains some helpful maps and photographs and should be used in conjunction with the ensuing excursion accounts.

Excursion 25   **PINBAIN BLOCK**
B.J.Bluck

Themes: 1 Examination in detail of parts of the lava sequence from Kennedy's Pass to Pinbain with a view to determining the water depth in which they were deposited.

2 Examination of the contact between the lavas and the serpentinite. The lavas formed on the surface; the serpentinite formed at depths which may have exceeded 30 km, yet are both brought to the same level at Pinbain - implying that the Pinbain fracture has a considerable throw.

3 To evaluate the significance of the olistostromes at Pinbain, and to see how they may shed light on the overall evolution of the Complex.

Features: Lavas, pillows, hyalotuff deltas, volcanic breccias, faulting, olistostromes, cherts, black shales, dykes, contemporaneous faulting, slumping, soft sediment shearing.

Maps :

	O.S.	1: 50 000	Sheet 76	Girvan
	B.G.S.	1: 50 000	Sheet 7	Girvan
		1: 25 000	Sheets NX 08, 18 and 19 (in part)	Ballantrae

Terrain: Rough shoreline with some scrambling

Time: 8 hours; recommended short itinerary, 4 hours: localities 1, 3, 4, 12, 13.

Access: Fairly low tide recommended. (Coastal **SSSI**)

Locality 1. South end of Kennedy's Pass NX (146 928): **Lavas and breccias** (Figs. 25.7, 25.8). Park cars south of Kennedy's Pass, walk 50m to the north to dark-looking rocks on the foreshore; for coaches there is a larger car park on the seaward side of the road north of Kennedy's Pass. Beneath the unconformity which divides the Ordovician clastic sequence to the north from the Ballantrae complex to the south (see Excursion 30), are a series of tough, brittle, dark grey, orange and red lavas and breccias which form the local top to the Pinbain block. The Pinbain block comprises mainly albite- bearing altered basalts (**spilites**) most of which are pillowed.

319

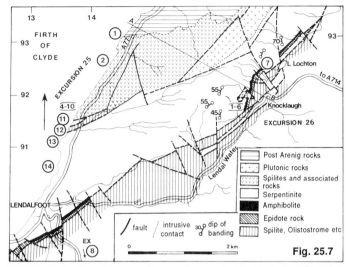

FIGURE 25.7. Simplified map of the northern part of the Ballantrae Complex, with positions of localities mentioned in Excursions 25 and 26.

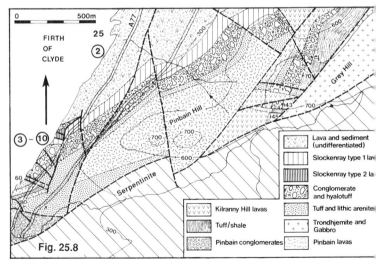

The wave-washed surfaces at this outcrop are very polished and on them the dark lavas show indistict flow banding and occasional viscous, flow-banded folding. Some of the flow-banded lavas contain quartz, which in part is secondary; but some have >60% silicon dioxide, which is considerably higher than for an average basalt. The rocks are probably a mixture of dacitic and basaltic lavas which have been considerably altered by their contact with sea water. Acidic and intermediate lavas often brecciate when extruded into water, and this is a likely reason for the intense brecciation seen here.

Locality 2. (NX 143 923): **Interfingering lavas and sediments.** This locality can be identified by the presence of an unofficial car park which is sited on the west side of the road, opposite the milestone 'Girvan 5; Ballantrae 8' (Fig.25.9). The outcrops are only barely seen at low tide. There are two types of lava exposed, the lower one is porphyritic, the upper is dark and **aphyric**. The dark lava is mainly massive, very fine grained and is partly replaced upwards (to the north) by conglomerates and breccias with a fine tuff matrix. Two thin units of pillow lava occur within these clastic rocks. Also, within the breccia unit there are layers of conglomerate, some having well rounded clasts which may be red in colour.

This locality shows the interaction between the sea and the lavas which flow into it. When lavas reach water they often brecciate, and the thick unit of breccia-conglomerate was probably produced in this way. The rounded clasts were produced during intervals when lava flowage had ceased and waves had time enough to work on the clast population before its burial. Some of these clasts are red because the lavas from which they have been derived have almost certainly been subject to sub-aerial weathering. During periods of strong lava flowage fragmentation of the lava flow takes place at the water's edge, and this may produce clasts so quickly that the waves have insufficient time to work on them and produce more rounded clasts. But if the extrusion is particulary rapid, then the lava extends beyond the water's edge and produces pillowed or massive lava flows (see Fig.25.13 for explanation). This locality shows all of these features with respect to the dark, massive lavas.

The red tops to the lavas are almost certainly the result of subaerial

---

FIGURE 25.8. Map of the Pinbain Block showng lateral extent of some of the lavas.

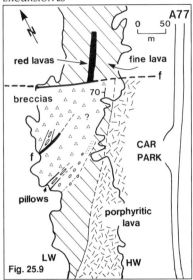

Fig. 25.9.

FIGURE 25.9. Sketch map to illustrate the geology at Locality 2, Pinbain Block. LW and HW refer to low and high water marks.

weathering, having been eroded during a period of coastal retreat. Associated with these lavas are tuffs containing accretionary lapilli (Smellie 1984).

Locality 3. Slockenray headland (NX 149 919) : **Hyalotuff deltas** (Fig.25.10). Park cars on the headland just above Slockenray Bay, at a bend in the road. Slockenray Bay is one of the most significant outcrops in the Pinbain Block. It was previously regarded as an Arenig vent, but is now thought to be a **hyalotuff** delta as it is clearly interstratified with the other lavas in the block and can be traced for some distance inland (Bluck 1981; Fig.25.8).

A detailed map of this headland is given (Fig. 25.10), where the position of the car park is marked. From the car park the following may be observed; a steeply dipping distinctly **porphyritic** lava forms the headland: beneath this lava, and in the low ground of the bay to the south is the hyalotuff deposit which underlies the lava. The contact beween the two is within the low ground beneath the southern end of the headland. The lavas are replaced to the SSW by conglomerates, and they probably wedge out in this direction. The whole sequence is upward coarsening and is terminated by the porphyritic lava.

To the north of the headland (Fig.25.11) hyalotuff deposits overlie the porphyritic lavas, and interfinger with a dark aphyric lava-type.

Locality 4. Lavas (best seen at low tide). (Fig.25.10). There are two lava types in this sequence, each of which comprises multiple flows. The main one is porphyritic with abundant **phenocrysts** >1cm long of plagioclase (now mainly albite) arranged in a swirling fashion and

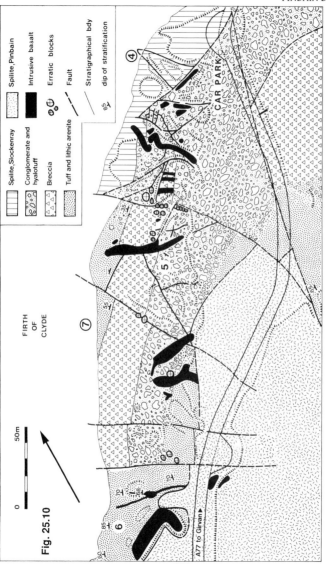

FIGURE 25.10. Map of the southern end of Slockenray. The north margin of map begins at the headland which divides this map from Figure 25.12, and the two lava types - porphyritic and dark aphyric (not subdivided in the map). They both belong to the Slockenray spilite of the caption.

suggesting alignment during turbulent viscous flow of the lava. The other is dark, aphyric and sometimes abundantly **vesicular**. This lava has also behaved in a plastic way; it has contorted margins against the porphyritic lava, which are lined with abundant vesicles left by the trapped gases; sometimes long deformed finger-like projections, and even detached irregular masses are totally enclosed in the porphyritc lava. It is clear that both lavas were extruded at the same time: at the boundary between them and (whilst they were flowing), each has injected into the other.

With Slockenray being near the contact between the two different types of lava, there must have existed on either side of this locality magma chambers each yielding a different lava. However, since both magma chambers were repeatedly producing lavas at the same time, they may have been responding to the same event-which is likely to have been structural.

Locality 5. Cross stratified hyalotuffs (Fig.25.10). These deposits comprise rounded and angular clasts of dark basalt with a texture identical to the porphyritic lavas which immediately overlie them. Some of the clasts are whole pillows, some are very angular vesiculated fragments and both contain abundant phenocrysts. The clasts range in size from >80cm to sand sized grains and have a matrix which is a brown coloured mass of chloritised volcanic glass with isolated long phenocrysts of labradorite and bytownite. Some of these crystals have been broken and then welded by the glass implying explosive activity which fragmented the grains and the rapid invasion of the broken mass by the hot lava. From the extreme angularity of many of the clasts and the pristine nature of the crystals, it is clear that this tuff has suffered the minimum of reworking since it was produced by explosive activity.

As with the tuff crystals, the clasts also contain unaltered plagiocase of labradorite-bytownite type, despite being sourced from the overlying lava which contains phenocrysts of identical shape but composed of albite.

This deposit is clearly the product of the explosive breakdown of the overlying porphyritic lava. When the lava reached the sea it disintegrated into breccia and pillows, but at the same time its surface chilled to yield abundant glassy basaltic fragments. These were then transported into deeper water where they formed a platform over which the lavas could prograde (see Figs 25.11, 25.13). The sediment

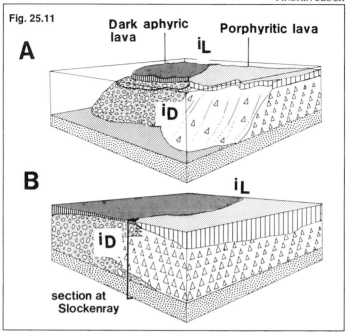

FIGURE 25.11. Explanation of the Slockenray sequence. **A.** Two lava flows, one porphyritic, the other dark aphyric, are both simultaneously extruded and flow together towards the coastline where they both build out delta cones adjacent to each other, each cone being sourced by their individual lava types. When one lava type becomes dominant the boundary between them (i_L) changes position to extend the area of the dominant flow. At the same time the delta produced by the dominant lava expands at the expense of the delta produced by the less dominant lava and the boundary between them (i_D) is affected. **B,** shows the location of the Slockenray section and the interfingering of the hyalotuff delta deposits which may have been caused by the growth of one delta at the expense of the other.

was probably laid down sometimes in a series of mass flows and sometimes as normal tractive currents. The former mechanism is evident in the abundant, poorly sorted deposits some of which have boulders strewn through the tuff; the latter is seen in the poorly developed large-scaled cross strata. By comparison with present day examples of hyalotuff deltaic deposits, sediment progradations were probably very rapid when lavas entered the sea. Pauses in sedimentation took place between periods of lava activity and are marked by the beds of clast supported (well sorted) conglomerates on the foreshore.

The breccia beds (Fig. 25.10) resemble the deposits already described, but differ in that they contain only clasts of dark aphyric lavas. These have had a provenance in the dark lavas which interfinger with the porphyritic ones at Locality 3, where evidence also suggests that both lavas were extruded at the same time. A possible explanation of this interstratification is given in Figure 25.11.

Locality 6. Graded hyalotuffs (Fig.25.10). **Graded** and ungraded beds of tuffs, some containing large clasts of vesicular lava, can be traced north into the coarse grained deposits already described. These are considered to be the deeper water, distal equivalents of the breccias and conglomerates. They sometimes have breccia bands amongst them, suggesting periods when coarse sediments by-passed the delta into deeper water, maybe as coarse-grained grain-flows. Some of the large clasts are thought to have been fragments of pumice which floated out into deeper water where they became water-logged and dropped into the regions where finer sediment was accumulating. The graded beds are probably turbidites generated in the delta region by slumping during periods of lava extrusion and rapid development of tuff.

These finer tuffs are in contact with underlying prophyritic lavas which form the floor to this sequence and make up the higher part of Pinbain Hill to the NE where they are thicker and comprise more massive flows with little interbedded tuff.

Locality 7. Red conglomerates (only at low tide; Fig. 25.10). A thin, well stratified and sometimes cross stratified conglomerate containing clasts of basalt and spilite occurs at the very top of this sedimentary sequence. The clasts are often well rounded and are either dark grey or red in colour. The red basalt clasts have almost certainly been derived from the tops of lava flows (as seen at Locality 2), having been oxidised in subareal conditions. The matrix of this conglomerate is volcanic sand with a calcite cement: the glassy tuffs which characterize most of the other rudaceous rocks are conspicuously absent.

Seemingly, the conglomerate formed during a period when lava extrusion had ceased in this particular locality and the sea was transgressing over an inactive and subsiding stack of lavas, which were being eroded at the sea margin. Clasts derived from these lavas were rounded and assembled in fairly high energy conditions, probably at the shoreline. Within this and other volcanic blocks, similar thin conglomerates with well rounded clasts can often be seen to truncate the underlying lava sequence: they probably formed on marine erosion platforms cut into lavas which were slightly tilted before or during the marine transgression. At this locality, the porphyritic lava flow appears to be eroded by such a surface beneath the conglomerate and at locality 2 the conglomerate rests on the dark lava.

Locality 8. Sediments on top of the lavas (Fig.25.12). Unless the tide is very low it is easier to return to the car park and then descend the cliff again to examine the upper part of this sequence exposed to the north of the headland. Although the lower part of the porphyritic lava sequence is massive, it is capped by a unit where large pillows of lava are enclosed in tuff. The top of the lava can be traced along the headland (Fig.25.10) and in the bays to the north (Fig.25.12). They are red in colour.

The presence of massive lava, pillowed lava and tuff can be explained by the rates of lava extrusion (see Fig.25.13). If the rate of flow is slow, then the lava will not advance seaward beyond the intertidal zone as its outer skin will be continuously converted into glass which then cools and fragments into tuff and breccia. With increasing rates of extrusion, the lava will advance beyond the intertidal zone and when the outer skin of glass forms, zones of weakness in this carapace will inflate by the pressure of the lava, much like balloons, to form pillows. If the rate of extrusion is slow enough, then the whole of the lava may be converted to pillows or pillow-like feeder tubes (Fig.29.13 B). However, if the rate of lava extrusion is quite high then only the outer margin of the complete flow becomes pillowed: the interior remains massive (Fig.25.13 C).

It is thought therefore that the massive flows at Pinbain are the product of very rapid extrusion of lava, and this outcrop at the top of the lava sequence is a record of the chilling on the outer parts of the lava flow. Above these pillows is a thick sequence of hyalotuffs and conglomerates and breccias, with mixed clasts of porhyritic and aphyric lavas. This abundance of hyalotuff, as with that below the lavas, is the produced at times of low rates of lava extrusion. The fact

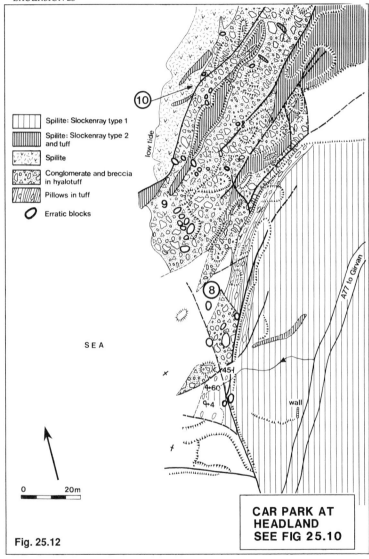

Spilite: Slockenray type 1

Spilite: Slockenray type 2 and tuff

Spilite

Conglomerate and breccia in hyalotuff

Pillows in tuff

⭕ Erratic blocks

low tide

SEA

⑩

9

⑧

45

60
9+4

A77 to Girvan

wall

0   20m

CAR PARK AT HEADLAND SEE FIG 25.10

Fig. 25.12

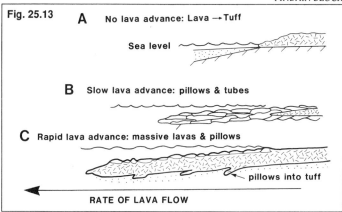

FIGURE 25.13. Explanation of the development of various lava structures and tuffs in lavas which enter the sea from the land. **A**, the lava front is moving slowly and as it enters the sea where it is rapidly chilled, all of it is converted to tuff at the shoreline. Waves and currents move the tuff offshore. If the tuffs are generated in sufficient abundance then the lavas will flow over them to build up a hyalotuff delta, as seen at Slockenray. **B**, Lava is moving sufficiently rapidly to enter into the sea, but much of its outer skin is chilled by contact with the sea water. The chilled skin is inflated by magma which is under pressure and many pillows are produced. **C**, the lava advance is rapid, so that the outer skin chills and forms pillows, either by contact with water at its top surface or by tuff at the base. However the rapidly moving interior is insulated by this pillow growth and cools to form a massive lava which cannot be chilled by contact with the sea water. The porphyritic lava at Slockenray is of this type: it is pillowed at the top and sometimes at the base, but has a thick, massive interior.

that many of the clasts are complete pillows, suggests that the lavas occasionally advanced beyond the strand line into the subtidal zone to generate pillows which then detached and rolled out in front of the migrating lava flow.

Locality 9. Lava tubes (Fig. 25.12). Thin finger-like units of aphyric

FIGURE 25.12. Map of the north of Slockenray headland, showing the sequence above the lavas. The south margin of the map is north of the car park and a key point in locating the exposures with reference to the map is the small wall on the edge of the road as marked on the map. Lava type 1 refers to the porphyritic spilite; type 2 to the aphyric.

lava occur within the hyalotuff. The origin of these is not readily apparent, but they are possibly the solidified tubes of lava which have advanced rapidly ahead of the migrating lava front and out over the platform or plinth of hyalotuff. They have mamilliferous outer chilled surfaces which may represent the incipient development of pillow buds on the skin of the lava. These features are thought to be similar to the lava tubes described from hyaloclastic deltas seen forming at the present-day.

Locality 10. Contact with the overlying porphyritic lavas (Fig.25.12). Porphyritic lavas with red and white phenocrysts are seen to rest on the hyaloclastic deposits. These lavas are massive with some zones of pillows. They represent rapid lava extrusions, probably once again at the strand-line.

Origin of the Slockenray sequence

The Slockenray sequence is considered to be the product of migration of a hyaloclastic or hyalotuff delta (Fig.25.11). There are two lava types present on the headland at Slockenray: a dark aphyric lava and a distinctive porphyritic lava. They were both extruded at the same time. This simultaneous extrusion is confirmed by the presence of dark as well as porphyritic lava clasts in the breccias and conglomerates of the hyaloclastic deltas, suggesting that the two types of lavas were hot and being broken up at the shoreline to produce their distinctive debris. In this way two cones of tuff from distinctive lava types overlapped each other and produced the interstratified sequence as seen at Slockenray.

The sequence at Slockenray is therefore significant in that it demonstrates that part, at least, of the Pinbain lava pile formed in intertidal conditions. However the whole of the Pinbain sequence is made up of lavas and breccia-conglomerates. These have been seen at Localities 1-9 and continue down the sequence to the Pinbain Fault, where they can be seen on the north outcrops of Figure 25.15. Well over 50% of the Pinbain sequence comprises volcanogenic sediment, and throughout the sequence there are clasts which are well rounded. This implies that the complete thickness of about 1.5 km was deposited in fairly shallow water, and therefore that accumulation kept pace with subsidence.

Not only at Slockenray, but also elsewhere in the Pinbain sequence, there is evidence for advances and retreat of the lava. Conglomerate

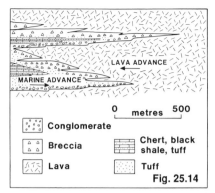

FIGURE 25.14. Explanation of the sediment-lava cycles in the Pinbain Block and elsewhere. When the rate of lava extrusion is rapid or the rate of sea-level change is slow, the lavas advance into the sea. Because of seawater-lava interactions, where the lavas break down by explosive or erosional activity, lavas are always associated with abundant breccias, often with tongues of lava entirely enclosed in breccia. However further towards the source of the lavas there are fewer breccia deposits. Shales and cherts on the other hand accumulate in deeper water and associated with them are tuffs which were deposited there either by air-fall (from explosive activity), storm deposition or turbidites.

When volcanic activity has ceased or is waning the sea transgresses over the lavas to yield well rounded conglomerates, sometimes with reddened clasts if the lavas have been subject to subaerial exposure.

This association of lava and breccia is common in nearly all the major lava sequences at Ballantrae, and in this Pinbain section massive lavas characterize Pinbain Hill; interfingers of breccias and lavas are seen on the coastal section (Localities 1-10). Transgressive conglomerates are seen at Localities 2 and 7.

with the well rounded clasts (as seen at Localities 2 and 7 for example) probably represents an initial transgression on a subsiding block of lava (Fig. 25.14). With increasing water depth the conglomerate is replaced by tuff and then by cherts, but when the lavas begin to advance again the cherts are replaced by tuffs and then by breccias and then by lavas (Fig.25.14). The cherts and tuffs associated with the deepening of the trough can be seen at the base of the sequence near the Pinbain Fault.

Locality 11. (NX 137 916): **Pinbain Fault and associated features** (Fig. 25.15 a,b,c,d,e,). The section begins at the north end of the beach to the north of Pinbain Burn (Fig.25.15). Lavas and associated sediments of the Pinbain Block strike NE-SW but are truncated at the base by the Pinbain Fault which, at the coast near Pinbain Burn is an almost E-W, 30-60 m wide fault zone. This zone contains sheared serpentinite, spilite, gabbro and a variety of other rocks. To the south of this shear

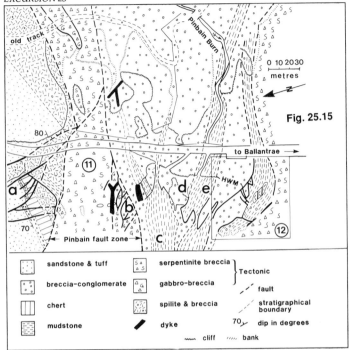

FIGURE 25.15. Plane-table map of the region near Pinbain Burn. Letters **a**, **b** etc refer to localities discussed in the text; inset is the approximate position of Figure 25.16.

belt lie the olistostromes and mass flow deposits of Pinbain.

(a). The sequence to the immediate north of the Pinbain Fault (**a** on Fig. 25.15) contains tuffs, lithic arenites, cherts and black shales which are overlain by breccias and agglomerates with accretionary lapilli. The cherts sometimes contain thin light-coloured laminae of feldspar grains; these are crystal tuffs and are probably of air-fall origin. The cherts are interstratified with thin black mudstones and shales from which, on the roadside above this exposure, Rushton *et al* (1986) have recovered fragments of trilobites, brachiopods and graptolites suggesting a Lower Arenig age. They are interstratifed with graded and ungraded beds, about 10-20 cm thick, which are probably the result of turbidity currents and grain-flows.

In terms of the fluctuating coastline shown in Figure 25.14, these beds are thought to represent the deeper water or more tranquil part of the basin. The overlying breccias are recording the seaward advance of the lavas.

(b). Exposures of a sheared gabbro-breccia faulted against a sheared serpentinite breccia which occupies most of the sandy foreshore. This breccia zone marks the position of the Pinbain Fault.

(c,d,e). The olistostromes (isolated clasts in a fine grained matrix) and breccia-conglomerates of Pinbain are exposed in the raised-beach cliff sections to the east side of the road, and are seen to interfinger with black mudstones along the middle and upper foreshore, but are almost totally replaced by black mudstones on the lower foreshore (c,d,e of Figure 25.15) and in the sub-tidal outcrops. This whole outcrop is therefore at the interfingering boundary between breccia-conglomerate / olistostromes and the black mudstones.

The boundaries between the fingers of breccia-conglomerate and the mudstones (d) of Figure 25.15) are nearly always sheared: the former may have dark zones adjacent to the black mudstones, where mud from the mudstone unit has invaded their fabric. In some instances flames of dark mudstone have penetrated into the breccia-conglomerate, thus adding further evidence for the view that the mudstone was not dewatered when the breccia-conglomerate was deposited.

A prominent outcrop at low tide at (c), Figure 25.15, comprises folded black shales made up of an early sequence of small, pyrite-bearing folds which are refolded by a later large-scale fold. The folding took place when the shale was ductile and it seems probable that both these phases of folding took place when the sediment was still plastic. In the outcrops surrounding (c), the black shales are often well exposed showing the sometimes quite intensive ductile shearing. The nature of the shearing is particularly well seen at (e) (Fig. 25.15), where siliceous beds are interstratified with cherty shale beds and light grey, silicic tuffs.

The following important points can be drawn from an examination of this outcrop:

1. The shales are made up of black and light grey tuffs which are

sheared into each other, producing a feather-like contact between the two lithologies.

2. The black shales are often tightly folded into cm scale folds, and the light grey tuffs are sometimes sheared up the cleavages, resembling flame structures.

3. Black cherty shales have either resisted deformation or have been brecciated, with mud infilling the breccia matrix.

4. Pyrite growth in the shales pre-dates the deformation in some instances, but appears to have overgrown the deformation in others.

It is concluded that the deformation in the shale sequence took place when it was unconsolidated. Clasts in the breccia-conglomerate are sometimes quite large; some of the blocks of pillow lava exceed 20 m in diameter (Locality 12; a of Fig. 25.16), forming boulders. There are clasts up to boulder size of the following types: pre-existing conglomerate, carbonates, turbidites comprising dark volcanic rich lithic arenites, various sized clasts of granite (including trondhjemite), sheared rocks rich in epidote, serpentinite, amphibolites. Some of the fine conglomerates contain clasts of blue-schist.

Locality 12. (NX 1372 9145): **Olistostromes and their contact with the serpentinite** (Fig.25.16). The olistostromes are exposed on the rock platform at (**b**) Fig.25.16, where boulders are surrounded by sheared shales. Some of the shale beds are siliceous, fairly well stratified and contain microscopic radiolaria: they are normally tougher than the unsilicified shales and have consequently resisted the otherwise pervasive shearing.

The following points are thought to be significant in an interpretation of the outcrops of sedimentary rocks described at Localities 11 & 12:

1. Large clasts were displaced into quiet waters where the shales accumulated; this in turn implies that steep slopes developed on the side of the basin in which muds formed, in order to displace repeatedly the blocks into it.

2. Considerable shearing took place during and immediately after the deposition of the sediments, shears which can now be seen in the shale-chert sequences. The shales probably acted as detachment horizons for major shears created on the basin margins: or at least during episodes of tectonic activity within the basin.

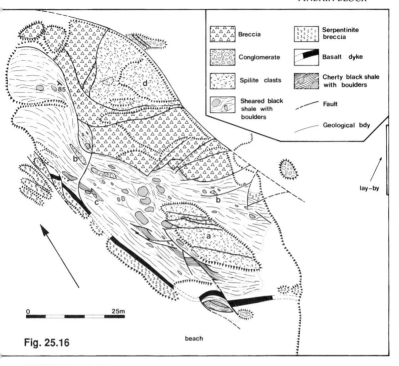

Fig. 25.16

FIGURE 25.16. Plane table map of the ground south of Pinbain Burn (see Fig. 25.15 for position).

3. The abundant tuff bands suggest that the shale basin was relatively proximal to an area of volcanic activity, but not so close that pyroclastic flows entered the basin. The considerable exposures of pillow lava may have been intruded into the wet muds of the basin but could also have been detached from cliff-like faces in older lava flows and then slid into the basin of deposition. Those clasts of pillow lava which are rounded to varying degrees, probably acquired this rounding at a shoreline and were then displaced into deeper water.

4. The source of the conglomerates comprised a wide variety of ophiolitic rocks which were formed in quite disparate environments; fragments of blue-schist from high pressure, low temperature

conditions: sepentinites from the mantle: amphibolites from fairly high temperature metamorphic regimes: and trondhjemites, gabbros and dolerites from quite high in the oceanic lithosphere. Some rocks were already deformed by the time they entered the conglomerate. All this implies that a great deal of the ophiolite, including rocks which have a provenance deep within the lithosphere and the mantle such as blue-schists, amphibolite and serpentinite, were exposed at the time, and had all been mixed before arriving at the basin of sedimentation.

Since black shale sedimentation accompanied tuff accumulation, it is reasonable to assume that the basin opened during extension accompanied by volcanicity and that the conglomerates are associated with normal rather than compressional faults. The faults probably detached within the black shale and chert horizons, causing the intense ductile-style deformation there. The acidic-intermediate tuffs together with the pillow lavas, indicate accumulation in a submarine to subareal volcanic regime and the presence of ophiolitic debris and the absence of terrigenous detritus suggest a volcanic complex founded on pre-existing oceanic crust.

The whole exposure at Pinbain is terminated in the south by a prominent dyke (Fig.25.16), possibly of Tertiary age, south of which there is a sandy beach with a few exposures of breccias and serpentinite, seen only at low-tide. The breccias which outcrop for a few metres to the immediate south of the dyke (Fig.25.16) are associated with sheared black shales and sheared blocks of ophiolitic rock and at this point probably constitute a mélange. To the south of the breccia there is a wide outcrop of normal serpentinite, which makes up most of the low ground extending to Lendalfoot.

There is clearly major displacement between the serpentinite and the breccia- olistostrome sequence, as each formed at totally different crustal levels. The sediments formed on the surface; the serpentinite has been brought up from depths exceeding 10 km. The timing of the juxtaposing of these two lithological units is uncertain: the serpentinite may have been uplifted before the deposition of the sedimentary units so providing a source for the conglomerates.

These sediments are not typical of layer1, ocean basin sediments in the ocean crust sequence. They are clearly deposited in basins where there was a copious supply of coarse clastic sediment. For this reason they are not thought to be associated with an ocean ridge, although it

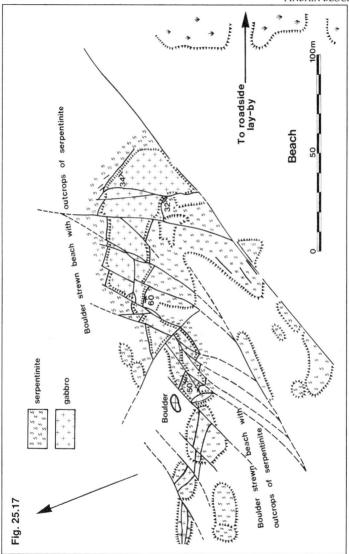

FIGURE 25.17. Plane-table map of Bonney's Dyke.

337

is possible that they are part of a fracture-zone sequence; also they are not likely to have formed as part of a hot-spot, as the composition of the conglomerates indicates a source which included metamorphic rocks and serpentinite which are not found in hot-spot oceanic islands; but in all details they resemble the sediments produced during arc-rifting and marginal basin formation (see Introduction).

Locality 13. Bonney's Dyke (NX 1347 9113): **Gabbro pegmatite** (Fig.25.17). Bonney's Dyke was named by Balsillie (1932) after the famous petrologist T.G.Bonney. The feature is not a dyke but a steeply dipping, sill-like sheet intruded into serpentinite, comprising a coarse gabbro pegmatite of altered diallage and feldspar, most of the latter being replaced by white prehnite and pectolite. The following points should be noted: the sheet thins towards the west: it is sinistrally shifted by a number of faults and as such provides an excellent strain marker within the serpentinite: it has a hydrogrossular northern margin and contains rafts of serpentinite. The serpentinite to the immediate south of the sheet contains large crystals of diallage: to the immediate north is a norite with enstatite crystals enclosed in plagioclase; the norite is only visible at low tide.

Locality 14. Albite diabase sheets and rodingite. The serpentinite to the south of Bonney's Dyke is intruded by many diabase sheets which can be examined at most tides along the shoreline to Lendalfoot (see Balsillie 1932). These sheets are mostly altered but detailed work on their chemistry and mineralogy has now demonstrated that there are at least two types of sheets present (Holub *et al* 1984); group 1 have mainly amphibole and plagioclase and a provenance in a depleted mantle source; group 2 have clinopyroxene and plagioclase present, and a source in a less depleted mantle. Group 1 sheets were intruded during elevated temperature, possibly when the serpentinite-peridotite was at greenschist facies; group 2 were intruded into colder rocks. Both have been, in places, altered to a white massive hydrogarnet rock (**rodingite**) and both therefore were intruded during the period of serpentinization.

Many of these intrusions are pod-like. It is often possible to trace chilled margins over entire exposed surfaces. The sheets have large xenoliths of serpentinite within them and may have a very irregular, flame-like contact with the serpentinite which encloses them.

References are given after Excursion 31.

Excursion 26   KNOCKLAUGH
B.J.Bluck

Theme: The metamorphic sole produced beneath the ophiolite during its emplacement (obduction); some of the ultra-mafic rocks of the overlying ophiolite; the dykes which cut these metamorphic rocks.

Features: Metamorphism, mylonites, greenschists, amphibolites, garnet-metapyroxenite, olistostromes, dykes, pyroxenites, serpentinites.

Maps:

O.S.	1: 50 000	Sheet 76	Girvan
O.S.	1: 25 000	Sheet NX 19	
B.G.S.	1: 50 000	Sheet 7	Girvan
	1: 25 000	Sheets NX 08, 18 and part of 19	Ballantrae

Terrain: Moderately rough open ground, excursion begins with a steep walk.

Distance and Time: 2 km : 4 hours walking.

Access: Permission should be requested from Knocklaugh Farm.

Short Itinerary: stops 1-6

Introduction

The base of the northerly **serpentinite** belt runs from near the coast at Carleton Port, south of Lendalfoot to roughly the base of Cairn Hill, NE of Loch Lochton (Fig 25.7). In places this contact is marked by a metamorphic **aureole** comprising a zone of structurally bounded slices of rocks with highly contrasting metamorphic grade. The zone is not always well exposed and has often been totally cut out by a fracture which brings serpentinite in contact with **spilite** and **olistostrome** (Figs 25.7,26.1). This can be seen in the vicinity of Knocklaugh, on the NE and SW margins of Figure 26.1.

The component rocks which make up the aureole vary in thickness along strike. Here the amphibolites are well exposed and quite thick but elsewhere, as near the coast, the epidote mylonite rock is thick. Garnet metapyroxenite is particularly well exposed in this locality but is so thin everywhere that **it should not be collected.**

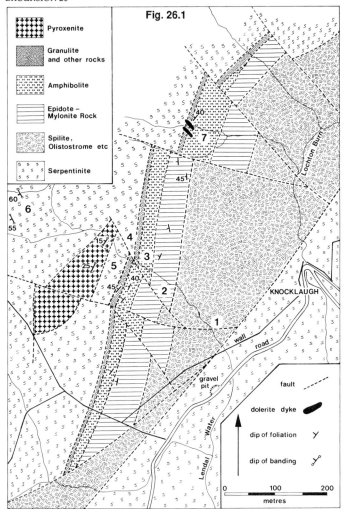

FIGURE 26.1. Map of the metamorphic sole at Knocklaugh, Excursion 26.

Locality 1. (NX 1692 9183): **Olistostromes** (Fig. 26.1). At the base of the waterfall sheared black shale is faulted against sheared serpentinite. The black shales have yielded graptolites to Peach and Horne (1899), and form part of a thick unit which comprises most of the immediate hillside. These black shales have thin graded beds of lithic-arenite and large clasts of basic and ultra-basic rock, carbonates and other sedimentary rocks. The graded beds comprise mainly grains of basic volcanic rock implying a source in a basic volcanic terrane. This unit, which is widespread in the ground to the SE of the serpentinite contact zone, is an olistostrome formed when large clasts roll or are otherwise displaced into an area where finer-grained sediments are accumulating. This type of deposit is typically generated near areas of submarine tectonic activity.

Commonly, at the top of the olistostrome unit where it is in contact with the metamorphic zone there are spilitic lavas which are often greater than 30 m thick. These have not been mapped as a separate unit although one interpretation of the metamorphic sole would require that they should be (see below). Within the ground covered by the map (Fig. 26.1) there are places where the metamorphic aureole is in contact with shale.

Locality 2. Banded epidote-mylonite rock (Fig.26.1). Banded epidote **mylonitic** rock, grey-green in colour is exposed in a small waterfall and adjacent banks. The rock has in many places a classical mylonitic texture with coarse augen of epidote, albite and quartz. Small-scale folds are associated with the augen, and larger scale folds are up 30 cm in amplitude. The epidote rock is composed of actinolitic-hornblende, chlorite, albite **porphyroblasts**, epidote (sometimes as porphyroblasts) and mica. They are seen elsewhere to interleave with sheared shales and **phyllites** and no doubt are partly derived from them; but some of the epidote rocks have the chemistry of basalts, suggesting that they had a basaltic **protolith**.

Locality 3. Amphibolite (Fig.26.1). Amphibolite, sometimes with excellent foliation, forms small exposures in the river banks and scattered over the hillside. The foliation generally dips to the NW but there is sufficient regional and local variation to suggest that there have been episodes of subsequent refolding which may be both ductile and brittle (see Spray and Williams (1980). Folded amphibolite is also fairly well seen at Locality 7. Garnets up to 20 mm in diameter occur in this amphibolite. The amphibolite is seen outside this area to interleave with the epidote rock and Spray and Williams (1980) have further subdivided the amphibolite into a lower, and an upper, the latter distinguished by having fairly abundant garnets. The amphibolites have a chemistry suggesting a protolith in basaltic rocks. The temperature-pressure regime under which the amphibolites formed is thought to be a minimum of 7kb and 850 °C. This pressure is equivalent to a depth of burial of 21 km.

Locality 4. Serpentinite and garnet metapyroxenite (Fig.26.1). Sheared, tough, platy tremolite-bearing serpentinite outcrops in this and many other sections along strike. These rocks are replaced upstream by unsheared, banded serpentinite which represents the sheared base of that segment of the oceanic lithosphere which was involved in the obduction event. A few metres upstream from this point is the outcrop of the garnet metapyroxenite, although there are only a few scattered small blocks now to be seen. This rock is thought to have formed under pressures greater than 10 kb (= >30km of burial depth) and temperatures of about 900 °C (Treloar *et al* 1980).

Altogether the rocks exposed at Localities 2-4 represent the sheared slices of the metamorphic sole to the ophiolite.

Locality 5. Pyroxenite (Fig.26.1). This bold feature on the hillside to the NW comprises altered pyroxenite. It has a pod-like outcrop, is bounded by shears and is probably a structurally detached block caught up during the obduction of the serpentinite and incorporated into it. The rock is an olivine websterite with evidence of banding produced by tectonic granulation.

Locality 6. Serpentinite (Fig.26.1). Serpentinite, which forms much of the high ground in this area, is exposed at a variety of places. It is a fairly tough foliated rock with foliations being almost N-S and striking into the zone of metamorphism at the base of the serpentinite. This discordant foliation is probably the result of tectonic overthrusting and rotation of an original foliation which may have been produced in the mantle during the movement of the oceanic plate away from the ridge where it developed. The original ultra-mafic rock was mainly a lherzolite comprising olivine, enstatite, diopside and picotite. However, plagioclase-bearing ultramafic rocks associated with these lherzolites would certainly not have formed in the same pressure-temperature regime. This evidence together with the granulation of

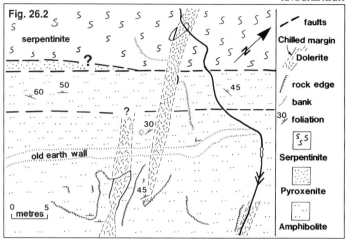

FIGURE 26.2. Detailed map showing the relationship between the dykes and the metamorphic sole at Knocklaugh (see Locality 7).

the ultramafic rocks suggest structural interleaving within the serpentinite.

Locality 7. Dykes cutting aureole (Figs 26. 1 & 2). Returning now to the metamorphic sole it is possible at this locality (Fig. 26.2) to study the rocks of the thermal aureole cut by dykes of the type seen along the coast (Excursion 25 Locality 14) and also at Carleton Bridge. The dykes are porphyritic and have distinct chilled margins against the amphibolite and serpentinite into which they intrude. In outcrop they clearly cut across the metamorphic zones with no displacement, thus indicating that both the development of the zones and their reduction in width were accomplished before dyke intrusion. It is also clear that the serpentinite was fairly cold at the time of dyke intrusion. Chemical and mineralogical analyses of these dykes indicate that they belong to the second phase of intrusion as identified by Holub *et al* (1984). At this locality it is possible to see some well developed banding and preferred mineral growth in the amphibolite and also some metre-scaled folds. The amphiboles from this locality yielded ages of 476+-14 Ma which represent the cooling time of the amphibolite during its obduction.

343

Here, as elsewhere along the outcrop, there is a zone of sheared tremolitic serpentinite between the outcrop of amphibolite and the meta-pyroxenite. The serpentinite and metapyroxenite may belong to the late stage history of the thermal aureole, being emplaced during the time when the originally much thicker aureole was being sheared down to the thin representative now present. The metapyroxenite at this locality has a cooling age of 505+-11 Ma.

From this position it is possible to see Grey Hill and the tops of Byne and Mains Hill to the NW. These are gabbros, diorites and trondhjemites which have intruded into the serpentinite. To the SE lie the lavas of Aldons, the southern serpentinite and pods of sheeted dykes of Millenderdale and Fell Hill and beyond that the higher hills of the Southern Uplands.

There are some paradoxes concerning this thermal aureole which need discussion.

1. In most metamorphic complexes, where there has been no tectonic inversion, the pressure-temperature path increases downwards in the sequence. This example records the reverse of this: the rocks indicate a pressure-temperature decrease down section from the serpentinite to the black shales and olistostromes.

FIGURE 26.3. Possible explanation of the metamorphic sole to the ophiolite. **A** an arc, because of changes in the location and sense of subduction, is driven towards the source of the plate which created it. In colliding with the underriding plate it underplates onto it the high pressure rocks belonging to this oceanic plate (**B**). But only fragments of this plate are accreted to the sole of the arc (**C**).

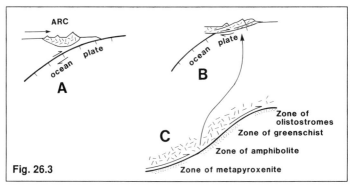

Fig. 26.3

2. In a distance of <100m the metamorphic grade changes from low grade, graptolitic shales to high grade metapyroxenite. This change in metamorphic grade, would normally have taken place over vertical distances of >30km, so that the boundaries between the various lithological units here must be greatly compressed. The faults which bound each of the metamorphic slices are therefore considered to have substantial throws.

3. One interpretation suggests that as the oceanic pile was being thrust onto the continental edge, shear planes developed within the ocean lithosphere and detached slices of lithosphere from differing levels along the subducting plate brought them together as a condensed sequence within the aureole (Fig. 26.3 B). These slices were then attached to the upward moving hot plate and became the metamorphic sole to the ophiolite.

4. The protolith to the amphibolite and garnet meta-pyroxenite is mafic rock similar to that found in layer 2 of the oceanic crust. If the P-T conditions of formation of these rocks require that they come from > 20-30 km depth, then how can layer 2 occur that deep in the

FIGURE 26.4. General map of the Carleton Hill - Knockormal area, Locality 8.

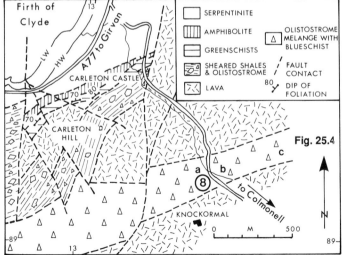

lithosphere? The obvious solution is to have it descend down a subduction zone and then become detached as outlined in Figure 26.3 B. There are, however, many other ways of effecting the obduction, and these can be followed up in the literature.

Return to the road and travel west to Lendalfoot. At Lendalfoot turn left at the A77 and then immediate left again to take the narrow road south towards Garnaburn, which is NW of Colmonell. After passing Carleton Castle and Little Carleton stop at the first cattle grid where there is a stretch of broad open marshy ground. Park south of the cattle grid. The exposures form the high northern edge to the low ground.

Locality 8. (NX1375 8890). **Blue-schist, pyroxenite and wehrlite** (Figs. 26.4, 26.5). The whole of this poorly exposed ground is characterized by blocks of granulites, lavas, limestones, cherts, granites, blue-schist, pyroxenites, serpentinites and wehrlites. In some instances these blocks are clearly in a highly deformed and mylonitic matrix; in others they are associated with less deformed black shales. It therefore seems reasonable to interpret the unit in which the blue-schist occurs as a mélange into which a wide variety of different rock-types have been emplaced.

. Blue-schist is exposed in the river section to the west (**a**) and in the field to the east are crags of blue-schist (**b**), and some 200m to the east of these are further blocks of pyroxenite and wehrlite (**c**) Fig. 26.5.

References are given after Excursion 31

FIGURE 26.5. Detailed map showing the locations of the outcrops discussed (Locality 8).

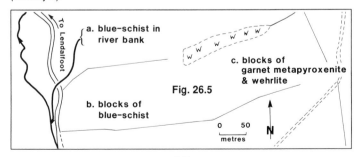

Excursion 27 BENNANE HEAD TO DOWNAN POINT
B.J.Bluck

Themes :   Accretion of a thick sequence of lavas and sediments; types of lava and associated sedimentation; sedimentation of cherts and conglomerates and their significance; the structural significance of the contacts between the lavas and the serpentinite which bound both the north and south margins, but are examined only in the south.

Features: Sedimentation of cherts, slumping, tuff-beds and their significance; recognition of various volcanogenic features; evaluation of the tectonic regimes of sediment accretion and the origin of the ophiolite.

Maps: O.S.   1: 50 000   Sheet 76   Girvan
   B.G.S.   1: 50 000   Sheet 7   Girvan
      1: 25 000   Sheets NX 08,
         18 and 19 (in part) Ballantrae

Terrain: Rough walking along foreshore, walking on cliff edge past headlands; **slippery and sometimes difficult rocks to cover.**

Distance   Distance 2 km. The less agile should visit localities 1-4.
and Time: 4-6 hours.

Access: Although all the localities are on the foreshore and are part of a coastal **SSSI** access is mostly via private roads or over private land.

> It is vital therefore, that the rights of the owners
> should be respected.

These include Melville (Bennane Lea and Meikle Bennane), Shanklin (Little Bennane) and Melville (Troax). Otherwise access may be refused to these most significant and instructive geological localities. See details under particular localities.

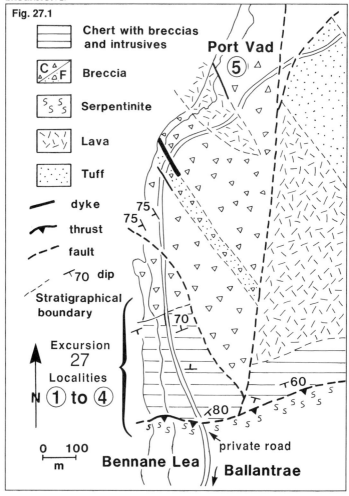

Fig. 27.1

Chert with breccias and intrusives

Breccia

Serpentinite

Lava

Tuff

dyke

thrust

fault

70 dip

Stratigraphical boundary

Excursion 27 Localities ① to ④

N

0   100
m

Port Vad ⑤

Bennane Lea

private road

Ballantrae

FIGURE 27.1. Simplified map of Bennane Head. In the breccia symbol, C refers to coarse, F refers to fine grain size. (Note that the A77 road has been rerouted to the east of Bennane Hill and reaches the coast at the south of this map.)

Some important problems raised by the Bennane Head section

There are four important points raised by this section which have considerable bearing on the origin of the Ballantrae Complex as a whole.

1.   The origin of the sedimentary pile which sits above the lava sequence. In particular, was it of shallow or deep water origin? Was it deep but close to a source in shallow water? Was it deposited in a tectonically stable or unstable regime? Is it conventional layer 1 of the ocean crust - if not, what is it?

2.   The nature of the volcanogenic pile; did it form in deep or shallow water and what is the importance of water depth anyway? Are the lavas and the sediments they produce all basic in composition? Is this sequence conventional layer 2 of oceanic crust?

3. If these aspects of the section (1,2 above) are different from conventional oceanic crust, what is the significance of that difference?

4. What is the nature of the contact beween high level **spilitic** lavas and mantle-depth **serpentinite**; and when did that juxtaposit-ioning occur?

The exposures on this excursion are very good, confused in places by faulting, but in general contacts are clear even if their interpret-ation is not. There is evidence for structural repetition of parts of the sequence (Stone and Rushton 1983) so it may not be as thick as previously supposed (Bluck and Halliday 1981). Some of the lavas from this block have been analysed for their chemistry by Wilkinson and Cann (1974), Lewis and Bloxam (1977) and Thirlwall and Bluck (1984) and all agree that chemically they resemble ocean island type basalts.

Locality 1. (NX 0921 8599) **Contacts beween Triassic sandstones and Arenig serpentinite; serpentinite and doleritic and tuff rocks belonging to the Bennane Head sequence** (Figs. 27.1,27.3). The coastal road shown on Figure 27.1 is now private although it is assumed that well-behaved groups will be allowed to **walk** along it to Locality 5. The A77 road has been rerouted east of Bennane Hill and joins the old road at Bennane Lea where a lay-by is to be constructed. **Vehicles must be parked south of the cattle grid and well away from the cottages and their access routes.** Go onto the beach via a track which leads to a sand pit just south of Bennane Burn. Localities 1, 2, 3 and 4 can be studied by keeping entirely west of the road. Note the small monument to 'Snib', a bank clerk from Dundee, who finally settled for a life free of income tax and other boring attributes of modern living. He adopted a cave in the cherts as his home. Snib, a man suspicious of what he assumed to be 'authority', had many very articulate discussions with this writer about what he could do with the subject of geology and where he could put the plane table set-up used to draw Figure 27.3.

The southern margin of the Bennane Head Block is bounded by a fault dipping at a fairly low angle to the south which brings volcanic rocks and cherts in contact with the southern serpentinite (Fig.27.3). Much of the foreshore and the raised beach platform farther to the south is underlain by Triassic red beds which along the raised beach cliff and at Ballantrae comprise breccias of serpentinite and other local rocks. The raised beach cliff is therefore a little more complicated than it seems at first sight: it is at or near to an old boundary of a Triassic basin. When there is little sand on the beach, as in winter, it is possible to trace out the contact between the Triassic rocks and the serpentinite. The Triassic sediments are red sandstones and shales; the sandstones often showing rippling which is particularly clear in section where they show-up as small scaled cross strata.

The serpentinite at this point is red stained and forms the southernmost of the dark rocks. It is thrust over the volcanic rocks of the Bennane Head sequence, which youngs towards the south. The trace of the reverse fault is marked by a band of carbonate breccias and mineralisation and it is a thrust of some magnitude: it places mantle lithologies over the superficial sediment of the ocean basin - a depth difference of 10's of km. However the serpentinite may have been emplaced at high levels in several stages; indeed by comparison with present-day marginal basins the serpentinite could have been brought up structurally even at the time of **chert** sedimentation; there are clasts of carbonate rock which contain chrome spinel (Bailey and McCallien 1957).

The dolerite-tuff may have been intruded into the chert at quite high levels as this would account for the development of associated tuffs and breccias. However, the contact between dolerite and chert on the coast does not have the kind of pepperite mixtures of both lithologies which characterises intrusions into wet sediment. This may be due to the nature of the chert or may indicate that the chert was indurated at the time of intrusion.

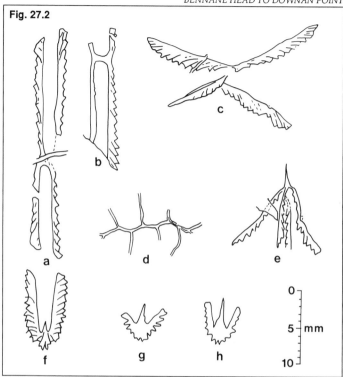

Fig. 27.2

FIGURE 27.2. Graptolites recovered from the Bennane Head sequence by Stone and Rushton (1983). **a,b.** *Tetragraptus approximatus,* **c.** *Tetragraptus reclinatus reclinatus.* **d.** *Sigmagraptus praecursor,* **e.** *Tetragraptus fruticosus,* **f.** *Isograptus caduceus,* **g, h.** *Pseudoisograptus dumosus*

Locality 2. Folded cherts (Fig. 27.3). Below the dolerite-tuff there are red bedded cherts interstratified with coarse-grained, buff-coloured tuffs. Both these lithologies are deformed by a series of slump folds in which the limbs of the folds are thinned and the axes considerably thickened. The tuff bands comprise angular sand sized grains of a variety of volcanic rock fragments including acidic, intermediate and basic, together with some angular clear quartz. The cherts have small circular holes, often filled with fibrous silica, which are sections of

351

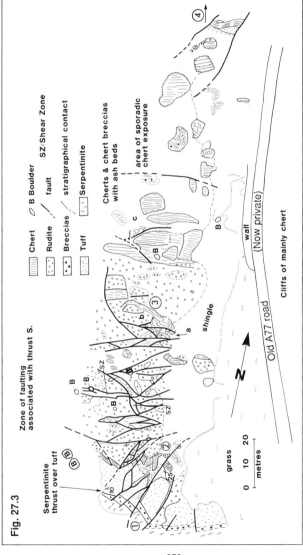

Fig. 27.3.

Zone of faulting associated with thrust S.

Serpentinite thrust over tuff

	Chert			B Boulder	SZ-Shear Zone
	Rudite			fault
	Breccias			stratigraphical contact
	Tuff			Serpentinite

Cherts & chert breccias with ash beds

area of sporadic chert exposure

wall (Now private)

Old A77 road

Cliffs of mainly chert

grass

0 10 20

metres

N

shingle

FIGURE 27.3. Detailed plane-table map of the contact beween the serpentinite and the dolerite-tuff and chert; the cherts and conglomerates and associated rocks, N of Bennane Lea.

radiolaria. Some of the coarser cherts have numerous, partly **chloritized** glass shards and angular grains of clear quartz.

The tuff bands show flame-structures, some of which inject the axial planes of the folds; other bands in differing parts of the outcrop here and at Locality 3 show extensional faults cutting them but with the tuffs thinned along the fault planes (Fig. 27.3). All these features attest to the syn-sedimentary origin of the extensional and compressional features and have probably formed at different positions in the slumped sheet (Fig 27.3).

The cherts are followed by breccias and conglomerates which have clasts of volcanic (including acidic) rocks which form the main component, together with a pink coloured, coarse grained igneous rock, limestones of uncertain origin, clasts of dark coloured and red coloured chert. These clasts are often angular but some are very well rounded. They have clear, sharp erosive contacts with the underlying cherts; but the conglomerate-chert contact is often marked by contortion in the cherts and the incorporation of breccias and conglomerates into the slumps.

Locality 3. Deformed cherts and interstratified, interfingering rudites (Fig.27.3). There are a number of important features to examine at this locality. The contact between chert and overlying conglomerate-breccia is marked by abundant deformation (**a**). The conglomerate has no visible bedding and has large rafted blocks of chert within it. The cherts within the blocks are folded, suggesting either that the conglomerate was deposited by a mass flow which displaced some of the soft cherts, or that both the emplacement of the conglomerate and the slumping of the chert were produced by the same mechanism, such as a seismic shock or a grossly oversteepened surface of sedimentation. In any event the tectonic regime in which this sediment accumulated is unstable and close to an abundant supply of coarse grained sediment.

Massive chert is seen to interfinger with the conglomerate (**b**), with once again the disruption of the cherts at the contact. As at locality (**a**) the cherts are overfolded with a vergence towards the east and in this direction the conglomerates of the shore are replaced by the cherts in the raised-beach cliff. Mapping at low-tide and in the shallow waters to the west has shown that there is an almost entire boulder-bearing conglomerate to the west which is replaced by cherts to the east, and the shore section is along the interfingering zone between the two.

At (c) is a beautifully exposed fold, although there may be divergent opinions as to its origin. There are beds in the fold which appear to have been plastically deformed; but the main fold itself may be a late brittle feature.

Locality 4. (NX 0912 8618), **Black and red cherts, black shales and breccias with clasts having a range of compositions** (Fig.27. 2,3). On the rocky foreshore platform, near the most northerly of the high chert stacks, the red chert sequence rests on breccias and green-gray tuffs with abundant volcanic clasts. At this locality (Fig.27.3) there are excellent extensional features, such as **boudinage** in the tuffs and some fine glass shards in some of the cherts. In addition, there are very fine breccias with basic and acidic volcanic fragments; tuffs (**lithic-arenites**) with abundant quartz, feldspar, and basic-acid rock fragments; black cherts and interstratified black shales.

The black shales have yielded graptolites which indicated to Stone and Rushton (1983) a mid-Arenig age. These graptolites include *Tetragraptus fruticosus, Sigmagraptus praecursor, Didymograptus extensus and D.* cf. *protomurchisoni.* The first two graptolites are illustrated in Figure 27.2.

The breccias and lavas are some 300 m thick and can be traced as far as Port Vad, Locality 5, where they rest on spilitic pillow lavas. They represent a mixture of breccias and conglomerates which contain both reddened and dark grey coloured clasts: some are poorly sorted with boulder-sized clasts randomly scattered through them; others are well stratified with rounded clasts in a distinctive white calcite cement. Some beds are dominated by accretionary lapilli enclosed in hyalotuff, and these must represent very shallow-water accumulations. It is clear that this section represents the sediment accumulating on the periphery of a volcanic centre. When the rate of lava eruption was high, basic lavas reached well out into the adjacent sea bed and developed extensive pillow basalts. These may have been accompanied by mass flow deposits comprising volcanogenic breccias; and during periods of intermediate and acidic volcanic activity volcanogenic sediment would have been produced in the marine realm whatever the rate of lava extrusion. At times when the rate of volcanic activity was low, the sediment underwent recycling during a transgression of the sea with the result that well rounded clasts accumulated in well stratified conglomerates (Fig.25.14). The reddened colouration of some of the clasts may well be the result of subaerial weathering (as discussed in Excursion 25).

Locality 5. Port Vad (NX 0927 8695) **Spilitic pillow lavas and associated tuffs** (Fig. 27.1). Port Vad may be reached (on foot only) from the south after studying localities 1 and 4 by rejoining the private road north of the northernmost gate and walking for less than a kilometre to a point where the road cuts through solid rock. It is then possible to descend, **with great care**, into Port Vad. Coming from the north, park vehicles in the prominent car park (NX 100 875) above Balcreuchan Port and follow the old road southwards to the point above Port Vad. At this locality some excellent exposures of pillows and associated sediments are to be seen. The pillows are relatively undeformed, and show the interpillow carbonate growth typical of Downan Point, Locality 6 and some have tuff within the inter-pillow spaces. At the south side of Port Vad it is possible to trace these pillowed beds into the overlying tuffs and breccias, although there is much faulting here and some splendid examples of sheared pillows.

To the north of this locality there is a thick sequence of interstratified pillows, conglomerate-breccias and tuffs. Stone and Rushton (1983) demonstrated repetition within the lava within this sequence and cautioned against unconditionally assuming the lava sequences to be thick.

Significance of the Bennane Head sequence

The Bennane Head sequence illustrates a number of important features which have relevance to the interpretation of the whole ophiolite. The section from the red cherts through the breccias to the pillow lavas at Port Vad is comparable with a section through the layers 1 and 2 of normal oceanic crust, where sediments cover the lavas produced at the spreading ridge. But there are significant differences:

1.   The cherts interfinger with boulder bearing breccias and conglomerates, and the cherts are themselves often highly contorted. This suggests that the cherts formed in or close to a zone of much tectonic instability where the slope of the floor on or near which they accumulated changed radically to allow mass flows to enter the basin and the cherts to slide.

2. There is also much significance in the presence of tuff bands with acid-basic lithologies, layers of crystal tuff and the presence of glass

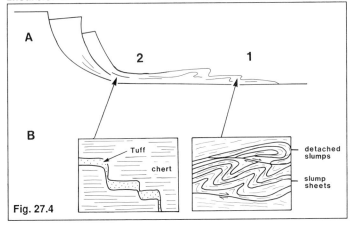

FIGURE 27.4. Diagram showing in **A** the structures typical of the cherts south of Bennane Head. The folds, with associated injection features, were probably formed at position 1; the extensional structures probably formed in position 2. **B** shows the structures which may occur when a large scale slump takes place.

shards within the cherts. These features, together with clasts within the interstratified conglomerates and breccias which are acid to basic in composition, all point to much contemporaneous volcanic activity. Volcanic activity of the kind which produces large volumes of tuff is not a characteristic of most mid-ocean ridges, neither is acidic volcanic activity normally associated with ocean ridges, which are dominantly totally basic in character. This volcanic activity took place during the periods of instability which produced the slumping: the instability was probably caused by faulting and the faulting probably took place in an extensional regime.

3. The great thickness of breccia and conglomerate occurring below the cherts implies that volcanic activity persisted over a considerable period of time. The record here is dominated by rudaceous rocks; lavas form <10% of the record. The presence of well rounded clasts in this sequence also implies shallow water depths and the presence of mass flows, a fairly copious supply of volcanogenic sediment. Indeed the whole sequence through Bennane Head, from Bennane Bridge to

Games Loup, comprises an alternation of breccias, conglomerates, tuffs and lavas. Although faulting and the repetition of strata make estimates of the thickness of this sequence difficult, there is at least 2 km of such lithologies there.

Any hypothesis for the origin of these sequences must therefore account for a thickness of fairly shallow water lava related activity, the presence of contemporaneous acidic volcanic activity towards the top of the pile, general tectonic instability, particularly during the sedimentation of the cherts, and the fairly rapid change in facies from coarse volcanic detritus to fine grained chert.

Of the three possible ways of producing oceanic crust, the sequence at Bennane Head does not resemble the crust of a mid-oceanic ridge, although a possible exception may be the crust found in Iceland which sits astride the Mid-Atlantic ridge. Oceanic islands show a trend from deep water at the base to shallow at the top, and this trend is not seen at Bennane Head. Island arcs, and in particular the basins which lie within or alongside them, have abundant acidic volcanic activity, an abundance of volcanogenic sediments, rapid facies changes from the ground bordering the volcanoes to the deeper basins, and much instability produced not only by the volcanic eruptions but also by the structural fragmentation of the arc during periods of marginal basin formation (see Figure 25.5). It is therefore concluded that the Bennane Head sections represent the basement (Port Vad and the ground to the north) and the rift facies (breccias and cherts of the upper part of the sequence) of a splitting arc. The doleritic intrusive-extrusive unit at the top of the sequence is thought to represent a shallow sill intruded into this extensional regime.

Locality 6. North of Downan Point (NX 0748 8100): **Pillow lavas, showing clear examples of how they are formed, lava caves and the relationship between massive and pillowed lavas** (Fig 27.5). Take the A77 road south from Ballantrae. Shortly after crossing the bridge over the River Stinchar branch off to the right along the road through Garleffin. Cars and minibuses can take the next turn right, near a bungalow, and drive through Kinniegar. Turn right down a rough track c. 300m SW of Kinniegar and drive towards the storm beach. Although the route is private, geologists are at present allowed to open (and close) the gate and park near to the old cottage. Coaches, however, should discharge passengers at the T- junction beyond Garleffin and then proceed south-westwards to the cemetery where

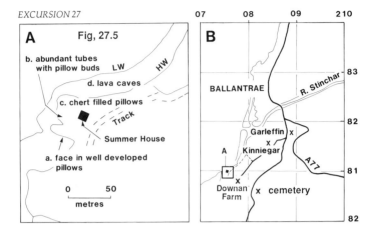

FIGURE 27.5. Maps showing the location of the pillows north of Downan Point, Locality 6. **A**, detailed map, LW, low water and HW high water marks; **B**, general map of the region.

there is ample parking space. From here, the driver can watch the party returning from the shore and meet them at the drop-off point. **Vehicles must not be parked at or near Downan Farm** unless prior written permission has been obtained from Mr. E. MacIntyre, Downan Farm, Ballantrae, Ayrshire KA26 OPB.

Follow the path on foot to the headland c.100 m to the south and stop at the gravel beach south of the stream (Fig.27.5). The north face of the headland is a magnificent exposures of pillow lavas and their geometry can be seen in some detail.

Pillow lavas are magnificently exposed along this coastline to as far south as Dove Cove. The age of these pillows has been the subject of some controversy. Lewis and Bloxam (1977) thought they were Caradoc in age. Thirlwall and Bluck (1984) obtained an age of 468 Ma with a rather large error of 22Ma, which taken at face value would be roughly Caradoc. The chemistry of these lavas has been studied by Wilkinson and Cann (1974), Lewis and Bloxam (1977) and Thirlwall and Bluck (1984) all of whom found that they resembled the chemistry of ocean islands.

On the intertidal, well washed exposures it is possible to see some fine details of the pillows. They have green chloritic rims which are the result of the alteration of glassy chilled margins (Fig.27.6 A **a**). Young

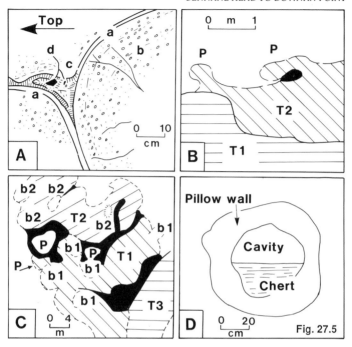

FIGURE 27.6 A, sketch showing the details of some of the pillows. The outer surface (**a**) is chilled, and can rarely be seen as a glass; mostly it is glass which has been almost totally replaced by chlorite, thus giving many of the pillows a green external colour. The interior of the pillow often has vesicles (**b**) which may be in radiating trails or in concentric lines which are preferentially developed towards the top of the pillows. The spaces beween the pillows are often filled with a fibrous calcite (**c**) and the centre of the pores may be filled with chert (**d**). **B,** illustrates two tubes T1 and T2 in section, with the lavas flowing from the right. T1 has provided the relief over which T2 has flowed; P are the two pillow-buds (incipient pillows) developed on the top of T2, and one pillow probably flopped over after it was inflated. The dark area is unfilled space. **C** is a plan sketch of the base of a sequence of pillow lavas. T1, T2 and T3 are the bases of three tubes. T1, 2 in particular have grown many pillow-buds b1 and b2, and some pillows (P). The dark areas are pore-space fillings which occur between the tubes and pillows. **D,** a section through a pillow which, when inflated did not fill with lava. It was subsequently partly filled with chert.

pillows wrap around older giving a clear indication of younging to the west, and the abundant vesicles, sometimes arranged concentrically with the pillow outline, are concentrated near their the top margins (Fig. 27.6 A **b**). Interpillow spaces are filled with calcite, and only rarely do these show a geopetal infilling (Fig. 27.6 A **c**).

Moving to the north, and on the north side of a small indentation of the sea, (**b**), Figure 27.5 A, there are thin bands of dark chert and tuff amongst the pillows showing a clear NE-SW strike. At this locality it is possible to see a whole range of important attributes of this sequence. Although in section the pillows have a roughly circular outline, examination of faces which are in the strike of the beds reveal them to range in shape from long tubes with many pillow buds on them (Fig.27.6 B **T1,T2**) to irregular flat bottomed masses with many tubes and buds coming off them (Fig.27.6 B **P;**27.6 C). It is readily apparent that the first face visited showing the classical pillow shapes gives a false impression of their real shape.

Some pillows at this locality have hollow centres now partly filled with stratified chert (Fig. 27.6 D). These must have been inflated with lava and then drained to leave a space subsequently to be filled with the chert.

From these localities it is possible to speculate on the origin of the pillow pile. The almost spherical pillows are produced from the buds which appear on the lava tubes. These buds grow by the lava pressure forcing out the tube wall at points of weakness or points where there is a greater pressure in the tube. They inflate to a size where they are unstable and then roll off. The lava tubes grow along the floor, sometimes climbing over pre-existing tubes and sometimes filling the inter-tube spaces, all the time budding and breaking up into separate tubes. In this way the pillow lava pile grows upwards.

A little to the north, at (**d**), (Fig. 27.5), there are larger lava caves, where up to 2m wide holes in the lava, now partly filled with stratified lava and tuff, probably represent the routeways for lava through horizontal conduits in the lava pile. There is much alteration along these small lava caves and it is probable that much gas escaped along here during the later degassing phases of the lava pile.

There are numerous exposures of pillow lavas and massive spilite to the south of this locality, and many of these are worth examination for the insights they give into the growth of lava piles of this type. However some 200m to the south of locality 6 there are excellent exposures showing the development of pillow tubes off a massive lava (see Fig. 25.13). In this instance the rate of lava extrusion was so great that it did not break down into tubes except at the edges where it was easily chilled. The relationships between the various types of pillows, tubes and massive lavas are illustrated in Figure 25.13.

The lava flows of Downan Point differ from those studied at Pinbain (Excursion 25) and at Bennane Head (Excursion 26) in having comparatively little volcanogenic clastic rock present. This implies that the environment of extrusion was different and an obvious factor in this respect is the water depth. The Downan point lavas were probably extruded in deeper water than most of the lavas in the Ballantrae Complex. They may well be much younger than the Ballantrae Lavas, and many geologists now put the Southern Uplands Fault along the river Stinchar, so making Downan Point part of the Southern Uplands.

References are given after Excursion 31.

THE ORIGIN OF THE BALLANTRAE COMPLEX
Conclusions for excursions 25-27
B.J.Bluck

The origin of the Ballantrae Complex has been debated by several workers (Dewey 1974; Church and Gayer 1973; Bluck et al, 1980; Barrett et al, 1981; Stone 1984). There are several lines of evidence which are critical to the understanding of the Ballantrae Complex and solving the problem of its origin:

1. The nature of the sediments which make up the top layer of the **ophiolite**, equivalent to layer 1 of normal ocean crust, as produced in the large ocean basins. These are seen at Pinbain (Excursion 25) and Bennane Head (Excursion 26): and the make-up of Bennane Head in particular is significant in that it differs from normal layer 1 of the crust in the following ways:

(a). Although the cherts and black shales are well bedded, both contain the remnants of volcanic activity in the form of glass shards and lithic fragments of acidic and intermediate volcanic rock. Sometimes thin breccias of volcanogenic origin are interstratified with the cherts. All of this implies that the basin in which the chert formed was close to an active acidic volcanic complex and received some of the ash blown out by the eruptions. Ash would be incorporated into layer 1 of the deep oceans at hot spots which produce ocean islands, or where the mid-ocean spreading ridge has grown sub-aerially, but in these instances most of the ash would be basic in composition.

(b). The cherts and black shales are very commonly slumped i.e. they have been deformed by submarine sliding when they were still unconsolidated. This repeated slumping, seen at Benanne Head and Pinbain, implies deposition on either some reasonably steep slope or a shallow slope which was affected by tectonic activity, setting the sediment pile in motion. This is not a characteristic feature of deep oceanic sediment: slopes are normally very shallow in the deep abyssal plains where chert sequences of this thickness are normally found. However, in the deep ocean steep slopes and instability may be generated near ridges and transform faults.

(c). The cherts and black shales are interbedded with conglomerates and breccias, some of which are boulder-bearing. Some of the clasts are well rounded and may have spent some time in fluvial transportation or have been abraded by wave activity whilst in shallow coastal regimes. When the whole sequence is mapped out both at Bennane Head and Pinbain, it can be clearly seen that the cherts and black shales pass rapidly into laterally equivalent thick sequences of rudite. This type of relationship is not characteristic of normal oceanic crust, is not usual at spreading ridges and is uncommon at transform faults. It is, in contrast, found in basins produced by arc splitting where new ocean crust is being formed. Here there are many normal faults over which substantial piles of arc-derived (acid-basic) sediments are draped. Steep surfaces upon which sediment accumulates are common, and many are rendered unstable by the continual fault activity which extends the basin. During this time there is extensive deformation of newly laid sediment.

2. The characteristics of the lavas equivalent to layer 2. There are a number of important points here:

(a). Layer 2 of oceanic crust produced at the major ocean ridges is characterized by an abundance of massive and pillowed lava; breccias and conglomerates account for <10% of the rock record. The presence of abundant breccias and tuffs throughout these lava sequences is evidence of explosive eruption of the lavas, and that in turn implies that they were continuously erupted in shallow water.

(b). A shallow water origin is also demonstrated by the presence of well-rounded lava clasts (Excursion 27); hyaloclastic deltas (which are intertidal, Excursion 25) and subaerial lava flows with reddened tops. The repetition of such features through the stratigraphic column suggests subsidence *during lava extrusion* which is not a common feature of ocean ridges or oceanic islands. Lavas created at oceanic ridges generally undergo subsidence after extrusion has stopped and when the lithosphere is cooling and moving away from the ridge. Ocean islands on the other hand build up from deep water to shallow, so the base of the pile should be dominated by massive and pillowed flows and the top by shallow water volcanic activity.

(c). Although there is repetition by faulting which tends apparently to thicken the section, the lavas are nevertheless very thick. Normal oceanic crust is < 1.5 km thick, and oceanic islands can produce extremely thick lavas.

(d). Breccias and lava flows of intermediate-acid type occur at the top of both the Pinbain and Bennane Head lava sequences. This type of lava is not typical of oceanic spreading centres, but is commonly found in magmatic arcs.

(e). Much work has been done on present-day oceanic lavas with a view to correlating their chemistry with the tectonic setting of their extrusion. For present-day basaltic lavas major element discriminant plots are very useful in indicating the tectonic settings in the oceanic realm. When these techniques are applied to the lavas at Ballantrae they fall into a wide variety of geochemical fields typical of oceanic islands (hot-spots), marginal basins, oceanic ridges and island arcs (Wilkinson and Cann 1974; Thirlwall and Bluck 1984). Although the validity of using these geochemical plots for ancient oceanic crust has been questioned, for recent environments of ocean crust formation those basalts formed in island arcs and marginal basins show the greatest degree of diversity in chemistry.

3. Evidence from the age dating and the obduction.

It is clear from the age determinations carried out on the ophiolite that it is of Ordovician age and was generated and obducted within the Arenig epoch. It was therefore not old crust at the time of obduction but young. Young crust tends to be thin and hotter than old, yet the metamorphic rocks at the sole of the ophiolite are required to have been buried by at least 30 km of rock (see Excursion 26). If the ophiolite were to be an arc-marginal basin assemblage which has collided with a subduction zone, then the thickness of the crust, its age and the age of obduction can easily be accounted for as shown in Figure 26.3.

Ophiolites with similar characteristics and roughly similar age to the Ballantrae Complex have been found in Newfoundland and SW along the Appalachians (Dunning and Krogh 1985). Ophiolites of this age have also been found in Scandinavia, and their widespread occurrence at this time suggests a long destructive margin to the northern continent of Laurentia (see Introduction). In most of these instances a marginal basin origin has been proposed for the ophiolites, and we may therefore infer that the oceanic crust being consumed at that time was quite old.

There is evidence within the Ballantrae Complex and elsewhere for a long history of subduction. There is a meta-pyroxenite block within the mélange at Knockormal which has yielded an age of 576 +- 32 Ma. On most time-scales this date is Cambrian, and the composition of the block suggests its **protolith** to be basalt. If this is so, then it is probable that oceanic crust, older than 576 Ma was somewhere being consumed. Of course this event may not have taken place at Ballantrae; the block could have been tectonically transported from some distance. However, in the dating of island arc type andesitic and rhyolitic fragments from the Southern Uplands, Kelley and Bluck, (1989) found them to have ages of 560 Ma and 630 Ma respectively— again pointing to the presence of Cambrian subduction. Dempster and Bluck (1991) have shown that an ophiolite along the Highland Border zone was thrust onto the continent at about 537 Ma., and they further discuss the implications of these ages.

Excursion 28 DOW HILL, BYNE HILL and ARDMILLAN BRAES

B. J. Bluck and J. Keith Ingham

Themes:	To examine intrusive rocks and their relationships within the Ballantrae Volcanic Complex; in particular to examine the contact between the intrusive gabbroic rocks and the serpentinite; to trace the transition between gabbro and trondhjemite and to examine the conglomerates (Benan Conglomerate) which form part of the summit of Byne Hill and the summit of Dow Hill; to examine part of the fossiliferous cover sequence above the Benan Conglomerate - the 'Infra-Kilranny' greywackes and mudstones (Balclatchie Group) of the western flanks of Byne Hill and on Dow Hill and to examine the fossiliferous lowest Ardwell Flags at Ardmillan Braes.
Features:	Serpentinite, rodingite, trondhjemite, diorite, chilled margins, conglomerates, mass flows, greywackes, mudstones, trilobites, brachiopods, deep water faunules.
Maps:	O.S. 1:25 000 Sheet 490 (NS10 NX19) Girvan
	1:50 000 Sheet 76 Girvan
	B.G.S. 1:50 000 Sheet 7 Girvan
Terrain:	Rough walking, steep hillside, scrambling in places.
Distance and Time:	About 9 km ,5.6 miles (maximum), 4-5 hours, depending on time spent at each locality.
Access:	Cars and buses should be parked alongside Girvan Cemetery, just off the Newton Stewart road (A714) to the south of Girvan.

Locality 1. Dow Hill (NX 192 960): Benan Conglomerate, fossiliferous Balclatchie mudstones (Fig. 28.1b).

From Girvan Cemetery, the isolated, near conical Dow Hill can be seen a short distance to the east. Access is obtained by crossing the main road, negotiating a field gate beyond which can be seen an underpass beneath the railway line leading down into Girvan. Beyond this a short climb will lead you to the exposures around the summit of the hill.

Dow Hill is composed largely of Middle Ordovician Benan

Conglomerate (essentially Llandeilo in age) which has been offset by **sinistral** wrench faulting from the main outcrop of Byne Hill (Fig. 28.1b). Exposures are extensive on and around the summit and detailed mapping shows the outcrop to be traversed by a number of small sinistral wrench faults. The succession youngs towards the NW and the beds dip quite steeply in this direction. The Benan Conglomerate here is thought to rest unconformably on **serpentinite** (Ballantrae Complex) but no exposures are available between the summit of the hill and the major Craiglea Fault which follows the line of the sharp valley immediately to the SE.

In a number of places along the NW face of the summit the conglomerate can be seen passing into the finer-grained sandy beds at the base of the so-called 'Infra-Kilranny' unit (part of the Balclatchie Group of early Caradoc age) but a rather larger than usual sinistral wrench fault brings back mudstones a little higher in this unit to crop out in a well marked excavation by the fence on the southern side of the summit. The Benan Conglomerate is described and characterized under Locality 4. The overlying mudstones seen in the exposure mentioned above have been excavated over many years and there are extensive samples from this classical locality in a number of museum collections. The fauna is a relatively low diversity one and reflects an offshore environment in which the sea bed had foundered somewhat. Inarticulate brachiopods are relatively common but the well preserved trilobites are what usually attract collectors to this locality. The most common species by far is the blind raphiophorid *Lonchodomas maccallumi* (Fig. 30.9) but other forms can usually be found with a little diligence. This is the type locality for the strange trinucleid *Reedolithus subradiatus*, the genus being known from rocks of almost the same age in eastern Canada and Norway. The bizarre remopleuridid *Teratorhynchus bicornis* can also be found, together with two or three other, largely pelagic forms (see Tripp 1980a).

Locality 2. Byne Hill : Benan Conglomerate, serpentinised harzburgite. (Fig 28. 1b).

From Dow Hill, return to Girvan Cemetery and follow the track down to Daltippan farmyard. From this track a splendid view of the Benan Conglomerate outcrop forming the steep NW face of Byne Hill can be seen. The beds are dipping steeply seawards and the outcrop is cut by a number of small sinistral and dextral wrench faults. Follow the track through the farmyard beyond which it climbs and twists

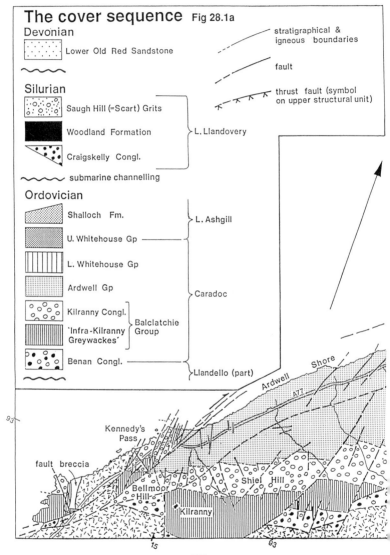

The cover sequence Fig 28.1a

Devonian

Lower Old Red Sandstone

Silurian

Saugh Hill (=Scart) Grits
Woodland Formation
Craigskelly Congl.

L. Llandovery

~~~~ submarine channelling

Ordovician

Shalloch Fm.   L. Ashgill

U. Whitehouse Gp

L. Whitehouse Gp

Ardwell Gp   Caradoc

Kilranny Congl.
'Infra-Kilranny Greywackes'   Balclatchie Group

Benan Congl.   Llandeilo (part)

stratigraphical & igneous boundaries

fault

thrust fault (symbol on upper structural unit)

Ardwell   Shore

A77

Kennedy's Pass

fault breccia

Bellmoor Hill

Kilranny

Shiel Hill

368

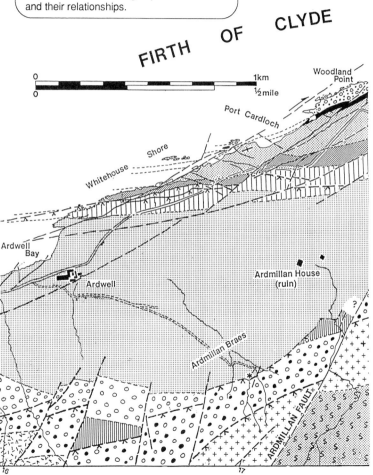

Figure 28.1. a,b A panoramic geological map from Kennedy's Pass to Girvan showing the disposition of the main groups and formations and their relationships.

FIRTH OF CLYDE

Woodland Point

Port Cardloch

Shore

Whitehouse

Ardwell Bay

Ardwell

Ardmillan House (ruin)

Ardmillan Braes

ARDMILLAN FAULT

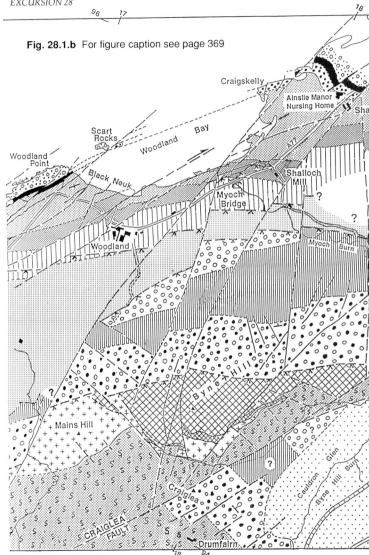

Fig. 28.1.b For figure caption see page 369

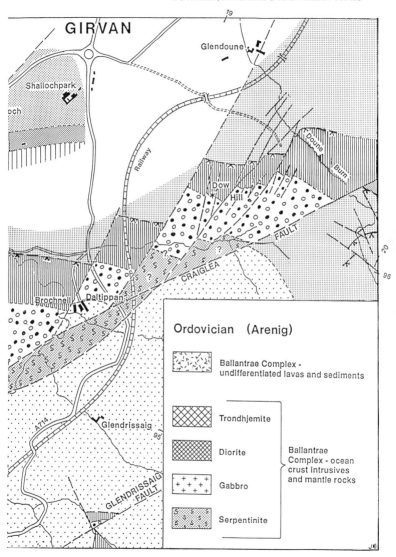

Ordovician (Arenig)

Ballantrae Complex - undifferentiated lavas and sediments

Trondhjemite

Diorite

Gabbro

Serpentinite

Ballantrae Complex - ocean crust intrusives and mantle rocks

towards the north-eastern bluff of Byne Hill where Benan Conglomerate can be seen at outcrop for some distance. The stream below Byne Hill here, immediately to the east and draining north from Cauldron Glen, contains a number of exposures of sheared serpentinite (Ballantrae Complex), caught up along the large Craiglea Fault (Fig. 28.1b). Continue following the path leading to Drumfairn Farm at Craiglea along the steep flank of Byne Hill above Balaclava Wood. Part way along this path, on the bank to the right and opposite a row of trees above the Craiglea Fault negative feature, is an exposure of serpentinised **harzburgite**. This represents upper mantle material, originally beneath oceanic crust, and now caught up within the Ballantrae Complex. Its significance in terms of the large scale crustal movements which must have been taking place in Early Ordovician, and perhaps earlier, times, is very important.

At the point where this path curves sharply SE to cross a small stream (at NX1833 9466), leave the track, climbing up somewhat to continue along and above the wall alongside the foot of Byne Hill. This wall follows approximately the boundary between serpentinite and gabbro, which is about 20-30m to the west. Continue until the wall turns sharply WSW.

Locality 3. (NX 181 944). **Junction between the gabbro-trondhjemite intrusion and the serpentinite** (Figs 28.1b, 28.2). The low ground here and in the burn immediately to the east is made up of serpentinite and the main gabbro mass of this part of Byne Hill has chilled against the serpentinite to give a vertical wall of doleritic rock at (**a**). Tracing away from this margin up the hill the rock becomes coarser grained and gabbroic. Cutting this vertical wall, and also cutting the serpentinite within this outcrop are white dykes a few tens of centimetres thick. These are dykes of hydrogrossular garnet (**rodingite**), which are fairly abundant along the coast (Excursion 25) and in the main mass of the northern serpentinite inland. This vertical contact between gabbro and serpentinite is displaced by a vertical NNE-SSW trending fracture immediately to the west and makes a clear feature. A similar and parallel fracture truncates the outcrop to the east and brings in serpentinite in the lower ground.

Ascend to the summit of Byne Hill and as one ascends examine the rocks with care for the presence of incoming quartz. They show a fairly gradual transition between gabbro-diorite-**trondhjemite**. The

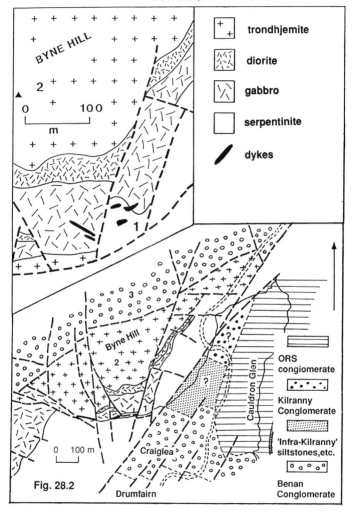

Figure 28.2. A detailed geological map of the southern end of Byne Hill (see also Fig. 28. 1).

trondhjemite is distinctive; it is pale pink in colour, rich in quartz and foliated.

Locality 4. Byne Hill summit (NX 178 945) : **Trondhjemite; a spectacular view of the Firth of Clyde and the local geology** (Fig. 28.1b). There are abundant exposures at and around the summit of Byne Hill and it is from this locality that **zircons** have been extracted from the rock which date it at 482±5 Ma, this being an Early Ordovician (Arenig) age. Trondhjemites and associated gabbros and diorites are thought to have formed either in the magma chamber beneath ocean ridges or by some fractionation process which takes place after the plate has moved off the ridge. In any case, the trondhjemite, being silica rich, normally accumulates at the top of the magmatic sequence so that here it is associated with the sheeted dyke complex and the lava pile (Fig. 25.1). With respect to these outcrops (Localities 3 & 4) a number of points are worth making:

1. The gabbroic rocks associated with the trondhjemite are chilled against serpentinite, and are therefore associated with mantle rocks deeper in the magmatic pile than rocks towards the top.

2. Although there is much evidence for structural jumbling within the serpentinite, discussions in Excursion 26 conclude that the **protolith** to the serpentinite crystallised at depths greater than 25km. The trondhjemite on the other hand is a high level intrusion, so it is clear that the serpentinite was uplifted prior to the intrusion of the gabbro-trondhjemite complex. However, the timing of the intrusion of this complex in relation to the timing of **obduction** is unclear. The ages (and their errors) of both the trondhjemite at 482±5 Ma and of the amphibolite in the metamorphic zone beneath the serpentinite at 476±14 Ma overlap so much that they are of no help. However it is clear from the chemistry of the trondhjemite mass that during its generation it saw no continental crust, so a genesis in a fully oceanic realm is evident.

3. Although the contact between serpentinite and gabbro is now almost vertical, if the gabbro-trondhjemite sequence was intruded before the folding of the obduction zone (?post cover sequence folding) then it would need to be untilted by the amount of dip of the metamorphic sole. This sole dips towards the NW at c. 45° so that the Byne Hill-Grey Hill intrusion, when untilted around the pole to this dip would then turn out to be a northerly dipping sheet rather than a

small, vertical pluton. Similar rotation of the folded cover sequence at Byne Hill, to which the intrusions form a monoclinal core, produces similar results.

From the summit of Byne Hill a good deal of the local geology together with its regional context can be seen. To the west, in the Firth of Clyde, lies the Tertiary volcanic plug of Ailsa Craig. This is an **arfvedsonite** microgranite which has been used extensively in the past for the manufacture of curling stones. Beyond this, on a fine day, it is possible to see Kintyre (Late Proterozoic Dalradian metamorphic rocks of the Grampian terrane) and to the NW the Isle of Arran. Along the coast to the SW lies Kennedy's Pass which exposes, among other things, the Kilranny Conglomerate of the Lower Palaeozoic cover sequence (beginning of Excursion 30) and beyond that the coast of Antrim. Almost due west on the foreshore is Woodland Point, where the Lower Silurian rests unconformably on the Ordovician. To the left of it lie the long, straight sectors of the Whitehouse and beyond that the Ardwell foreshores with their spectacular and varied Mid-Late Ordovician sequences. To the right of Woodland Point lies the Myoch foreshore, also a particularly important Late Ordovician site: beyond that to the north lies the upstanding Craigskelly rock and the adjacent foreshore, mostly Silurian. The entire cover sequence seen along the foreshore from this vantage point has near vertical dips and youngs seawards, thus emphasising the essentially monoclinal structure of this entire coastal tract. To the north and NE lies the Upper Palaeozoic cover of the Midland Valley of Scotland, the long, low hill immediately to the north of the Girvan Valley (Craighead Inlier - Excursion 31) being the most northerly place where the Ordovician cover sequence overlaps the obducted Ballantrae Complex 'basement'.

Locality 5. Benan Conglomerate with a variety of igneous clasts (Fig. 28.1b). The Benan Conglomerate is well exposed along the north-westerly ridge of Byne Hill. It is a massive, boulder-bearing conglomerate of Llandeilo-earliest Caradoc age, with clasts of various granites and porphyries, together with a variety of basic igneous rocks which are thought to have their provenance in the underlying Ballantrae Complex. There are only a small number of clasts of metamorphic rock and these are mainly quartz rich. The composition and ages of the granite boulders have been studied in detail. Most of the granites are hornblende-bearing, high level intrusions and have

Rb-Sr whole rock mineral ages which range from 559±20 - 466±13 Ma: one has a Pb-Pb age of 475±3 Ma (Longman *et al.* 1979). Some of these dates are only a little older than the chronometric age assigned to the chronostratigraphical date of the conglomerate itself. This conglomerate was probably deposited on a foundering sea floor as part of a fan-delta complex (Ince 1984) which drained a major plutonic-volcanic arc. As many of the clasts are boulder sized, the immediate source was not distal; and as the palaeoflow for the conglomerate is from the north, then a plutonic-volcanic arc within the Midland Valley is suggested as being present at this time. It was evidently an uplifted area in which the plutons were being unroofed rapidly by erosion. The Benan Conglomerate in the Byne Hill area is estimated to be less than 200 m in thickness. This contrasts strongly with areas to the SE, just north of the Stinchar Valley (Excursion 26), where it is substantially thicker.

Locality 6. SW side of Byne Hill: Benan Conglomerate and 'Infra-Kilranny' greywackes (Fig.28.1b). Descend the hill along strike to the SW to the wall. Following it around the foot of the hill toward the NW the outcrop of the Benan Conglomerate, striking over from the western crest of Byne Hill, is traversed and a number of exposures of the typical lithology are visible on the lower flanks. Further along, as one progressively descends, still following the wall, a number of exposures of fine, weathered sandstone or greywacke is seen above it. These constitute basal beds of the 'Infra-Kilranny' greywackes (Balclatchie Group) which overlie the Benan Conglomerate and form the lower slopes to Byne Hill on the seaward side. A search through this material for only a few minutes will yield trilobite debris belonging largely to the genera *Remopleurides* and *Calyptaulax* , together with a variety of brachiopods. Complete trilobites are not unknown.

Locality 7. Ardmillan Braes (NX169 938) : Basal Ardwell Flags, trilobites, brachiopods, thrust, Benan Conglomerate (Fig. 28.1a). From the SW side of Byne Hill the itinerary is optional. Either, one can proceed down the hill towards the foreshore at Woodland Farm (Black Neuk) and pick up Excursion 30 at Locality 11, or one can proceed southwards for a brisk moorland walk of about 1.5 km, aiming for the small streams surrounded by extensive gorse bushes beyond Ardmillan Burn above the wall behind Ardwell Farm. This gorse covered moorland site is known as Ardmillan Braes and was, at the beginning of this century, a favourite picnic and collecting spot for members of the famous Gray family from Edinburgh whose world famous collections are now largely housed in the Natural History Museum in London.

There are three small streams at this site. The middle one has the critical section: it is now deeply embedded in gorse bushes but perseverance will be rewarding. A small 'waterfall', usually dry, identifies the locality and there is abundant evidence of collecting activities. The most profitable rock is the weathered kind from the top of the section on the south side of the stream from which with diligence and a small, deftly used hammer a wide variety of brachiopods, including *Rostricellula ardmillanensis*, and trilobites, many complete, can be obtained. Again, as on Byne Hill, *Remopleurides* and *Calyptaulax* predominate but otherwise quite rare forms such as *Hemiarges* and *Isotelus* can be found (see Williams 1962; Tripp 1980a).

The locality can further be identified by an exposure above the north bank a short distance above the 'waterfall'. Here a small bluff of Benan Conglomerate has been thrust over strongly sheared shale.

From this locality proceed down the slope, negotiate the wall and then follow the track down to the coastal road at Ardwell Farm. A number of exposures of steeply dipping, typical Ardwell Flags will be seen on the way. At Ardwell Farm, Excursion 30 can be picked up at Locality 3 and if all, or part, of this excursion is followed it is only a short walk along the lane from Shalloch Mill, near Myoch Bridge (Locality 11) to where cars may previously have been parked by Girvan cemetery near Daltippen Farm.

References are given at the end of Excursion 31.

Excursion 29   UPPER STINCHAR VALLEY AND ADJACENT AREAS
J. Keith Ingham

Themes: To examine elements of the Lower Palaeozoic cover sequence and faunas of the Girvan district, particularly its oldest part in the Stinchar Valley. To contrast some of the shallower water facies and faunas preserved in the Barr Group on the north side of the valley with some of the deeper water facies represented in the partly equivalent Albany Group to the south of the valley.

Features: Balclatchie Mudstone and Balclatchie Conglomerate at Balclatchie Bridge; Kirkland Conglomerate, Auchensoul Bridge Mudstone, Confinis Flags, Stinchar Limestone, Superstes Mudstone and Benan Conglomerate in, and to the north of, the Stinchar Valley; Doularg Formation (Albany Group) south of the Stinchar Valley; trilobites, brachiopods and other fossils; evidence of basement faulting controlling facies distribution; conglomerates in successive fan delta cycles of a trangressive proximal fore-arc régime.

Maps: O.S.   1 : 25 000   Sheet NX 29 / 39   Barr
                      1 : 50 000   Sheet 76 Girvan
              B.G.S. 1 : 50 000   Sheet 7   Girvan

Terrain: Some rough moorland walking and scrambling (short distances).

Distance and Time: About 12 km, mostly by car, from the first to the last locality, taking perhaps 5-6 hours depending on the time spent at each locality.

Access: This excursion is really only practicable by car or similar vehicle. Adequate parking facilities are available throughout but a tight hairpin bend on the B734 Barr-Pinmore road near its junction with the A714 makes any vehicle larger than a minibus impracticable. The excursion is best followed in the order given partly because the hairpin bend is much easier to negotiate downhill from the E and also because of access angles from the rather narrow B734.

Locality 1. Balclatchie Bridge (NX 256 969) **: Balclatchie Mudstone and Balclatchie Conglomerate, trilobites, brachiopods** (Fig.25.1). Leave Girvan northwards on the A77, passing under the railway bridge. Almost immediately, take the B734, on the right, to Old Dailly, a distance of about 4 km. At Old Dailly take the first road uphill to the right (still the B734) which leads to Barr. At the top of this initial hill, another small road from Old Dailly joins from the left and shortly thereafter the road forks. The right hand, unclassified road leads to Tormitchell, Pinmore and Pinwherry, crossing the valley of Penwhapple Burn. Follow the left hand road (still the B734) to Barr and continue for a distance of about 3 km. The narrow, tree-choked gorge incised into the fairly featureless moorland area some distance to the right of the road indicates the course of Penwhapple Burn. Over much of its length it is a dark, dank and dismal place which, unfortunately, some local farmers have tended to use for farm refuse for many years. It is difficult of access, with very steep sides and is dangerous in places, not least because of virtually invisible strands of rusty barbed wire. It tends to be visited only by particularly keen geologists and palaeontologists and for the reasons mentioned above most of it has not been included in the formal excursion itinerary. Nevertheless, nearly continuous exposures there reveal a much faulted and thrust, largely inverted sequence, dipping to the SE, of Ordovician and Silurian rocks, among which the Ardwell Group, Lower and Upper Whitehouse groups and Shalloch Formation, are represented.

As stated above, after about 3 km of the moorland tract of the B734 has been followed, the road crosses Penwhapple Burn at Balclatchie Bridge. A short distance before this is reached, a fenced pumping station on the right, opposite Penwhapple reservoir (invisible on the uphill side of the road) is the most convenient place to park (NX 256 969).

The succession hereabouts is much faulted and the beds, although locally overturned, young consistently to the NW. Scattered exposures over the fence on the uphill side of the road are of Balclatchie Mudstones, as are the much more extensive exposures in the adjacent section of Penwhapple Burn. Upstream, the mudstones pass down into a thick conglomerate. Originally thought to be the Benan Conglomerate, careful mapping (Williams 1962) has revealed this to be a quite separate local conglomerate tongue (one of several) almost at the base of the Balclatchie Group, named the Doon Hill

Conglomerate. Downstream, the mudstones pass up into another such conglomerate tongue, the Balclatchie Conglomerate, above which are siltstones and mudstones of the Ardwell Group. Large fossil collections have been made in the past from the Balclatchie Mudstones hereabouts and from the matrix of the Balclatchie Conglomerate (see Williams 1962, Tripp 1980a). Deeper water forms predominate in the mudstone facies and the fauna is comparable with that from the mudstones at Dow Hill (Excursion 28, Locality 1) with which it broadly correlates. Some elements, particularly from the Balclatchie Conglomerate are transported shallower water forms and suggest the relatively rapid deposition of such conglomerates down a palaeoslope from shallower water environments. Apart from a very few deeper water trilobites from the mudstone facies, the vast majority of the fauna is profoundly North American (Appalachian) in aspect and the beds correlate essentially with part of the Edinburg Limestone and its deeper water shaley facies in Virginia and Tennessee. Both sequences contain a number of common species of both trilobites and brachiopods.

Locality 2. Brockloch (NX 256 951) : **Confinis Flags, upper Stinchar Limestone, Superstes Mudstone, basal Benan Conglomerate, brachiopods, trilobites, 'Chazy' facies** (Fig.25.1) Cross Balclatchie Bridge and continue along the B734 towards Barr for a little over 2 km watching out for a farm track leading off to the right to Brockloch Farm. After about 1 km, this track leads to an old limekiln and a group of four small quarries. The succession here consists, in outline, of honeycomb-weathered, pale green, calcareous, pebbly sandstones and siltsones, seen in the third quarry, which have yielded brachiopods suggesting their equivalence to the Confinis Flags of the Stinchar Valley to the south (Locality 6), followed by rubbly blue-grey and grey-green limestones (Stinchar Limestone), passing up into grey-green siltsones and mudstones (Superstes Mudstone equivalent), in turn followed by calcareous conglomerate (Benan Conglomerate). The whole sequence here (Fig. 29.1) is mappable southwestwards for a distance of over 2 km towards Dupin Farm. Its disposition is along the north-western flank of the Benan Syncline in the core of which is the thickest development of the Benan Conglomerate in the whole Girvan district. The occurrence of small partly faulted areas of serpentinite (Ballantrae Complex) near the quarries suggests that the Kirkland Conglomerate, so well developed at the base of the Barr Group over much of the upper Stinchar Valley (see Localities 4 & 5),

Fig. 29.1

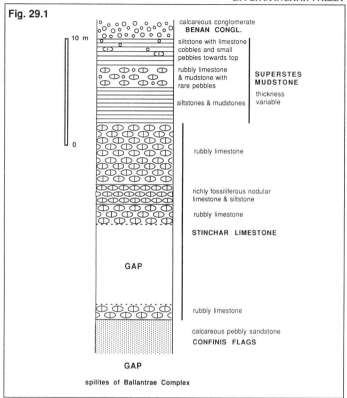

Figure 29.1. Generalised succession in the Brockloch area.

is not represented here. To the NW of the quarries, the succession is thrust over another tract of Benan Conglomerate (Dupin Thrust) and, less than 1 km across strike to the NW around Pinmery and Tormitchell, the Stinchar Limestone and associated beds are repeated before again being substantially thrust over the Balclatchie and Ardwell groups (Tormitchell Thrust).

One of the members in the limestone succession in the quarries (Fig. 29.1) is particularly fossiliferous and, although containing some trilobites (Tripp 1979), has yielded a rich brachiopod fauna (Williams

381

1962) containing a number of species which are conspecific with forms from the Pratt Ferry and Little Oak formations of Alabama, indicating that the Barr Group broadly correlates with the upper Whiterockian Series (shallow water Chazy facies) of eastern N. America. This equates essentially with the upper Llanvirn and Llandeilo Series of southern Britain.

Some of the rubbly limestones in these quarries have been brecciated and occasionally the fragments show signs of abrasion and therefore transport. Many fit together like a jigsaw puzzle but are now set in an anastomosing network of mudstone veins. The feature has been ascribed to "tremor brecciation" (Williams 1962, p.14; see also Henderson 1935, p.492). Submarine earthquakes must have been a common occurrence during Ordovician and Silurian times in the Girvan district for evidence of this kind is frequently seen.

The lower part of the Benan Conglomerate here is worthy of note. Parts of it are best described as pebbly limestone and some sections show a profusion of limestone clasts which must have been scoured up from local Stinchar Limestone substrate as the first debris-loaded currents came in from the north or NW. One limestone clast has been discovered here, however, which is quite foreign to the Girvan District. The rock is undeformed and yielded fossils, again of North American type, which indicate an earliest Canadian [= early Tremadoc], i.e. earliest Ordovician, age (Rushton & Tripp 1979). It was transported from the north and presumably originated in the northern part of the Midland Valley of Scotland from whence other Early Ordovician shallow water carbonates are known (see Ingham *et al.* 1986, p. 482). At Girvan during Early Ordovician times, the rocks of the Ballantrae Complex were being generated and accreted to the Midland Valley terrane from an oceanic or marginal setting and in the Central Highlands (Grampian terrane) the climax deformation and metamorphism of the Dalradian rocks (Grampian event) was still underway. This single clast therefore tells us a great deal about the subsurface geology of the northern part of the Midland Valley terrane and of its distinctiveness in Early Ordovician times. Higher up the succession the Benan Conglomerate assumes its typical lithology with its profusion of igneous clasts (see Excursion 28 , Locality 5).

Locality 3. Plantation Burn, E of Doularg Farm, S side of the Stinchar Valley (NX 269 928) : **Doularg Formation of the Albany Group, trilobites, brachiopods, 'Whiterock' facies** (25.1, 29.2 - 29.6). Proceed back to the road (B734) and follow it down into the village of Barr. Immediately after the road bears sharply left into the village it crosses the River Stinchar and follows its tributary, the Water of Gregg, on the right. A little further along the main street a narrow bridge takes the B734 sharply to the right over the stream. Follow this road out of Barr for rather more than 1 km. You will shortly pass Alton Albany Farm on the right. The road skirts the partly tree-lined lower slopes of Doularg Hill and for some distance keeps very much to the floor of the Stinchar Valley. If you reach Doularg Farm on your left, you have gone too far!

Watch out for a wooded stream descending steeply to the road from the left, to the left of which is a gate. The road is a little wider here and it is possible to park quite safely although the surface can be rather muddy. Negotiate this gate and then another one a short distance beyond it and climb the hill for about 0.5 km keeping fairly close to the wall bounding the stream to your right. After crossing a drainage gully, eventually you will see a step-type wooden stile over the wall, both of which have seen better days and in front of them is a relatively new mesh wire fence (Fig. 29.3). Negotiate the wall at this point and follow it for a short distance, making your way through a cluster of gorse bushes. Beyond these you will see a fence coming in from the right. You need proceed no further.

The succession in the Plantation Burn is a critical one for it is unlike the 'standard' Barr Group succession on the north side of the Stinchar Valley and it contains beds which constitute the most south-easterly (i.e., across strike), richly fossiliferous rocks in the Girvan district. The rocks seen here are the finer grained calcareous silts and mudstones of the Albany Group — broadly a lateral equivalent of the Barr Group to the north. The Albany Group consists largely of a fairly thick succession of greywackes, silts and conglomerates and in this section, although sometimes slightly overturned, the beds young largely to the NW. The finer grained calcareous beds exposed at this locality constitute the Doularg Formation, the disposition of the various members of which are shown in Figures 29.3, 29.4. It was thought that they represent the 'down slope' tailings of the Stinchar Limestone and associated beds on the northern side of the Stinchar Valley but this is

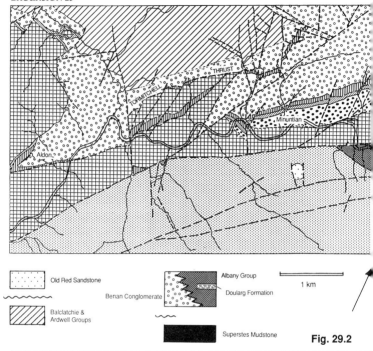

Old Red Sandstone

Benan Conglomerate

Balclatchie &
Ardwell Groups

Albany Group

Doularg Formation

1 km

Supestes Mudstone

Fig. 29.2

Figure 29.2. A geological map of the upper Stinchar Valley.

now known not to be the case for there are good faunal reasons to
believe that they are the time equivalents of some part of the Benan
Conglomerate - a little younger than the Superstes Mudstone
Formation and a little older than the Balclatchie Group (Ingham &
Tripp 1991 and Figs 29.5, 29.6).

The lowest fossiliferous unit within the Doularg Formation is the
Gorse Member, a calcareous mudstone containing small decalcified
carbonate nodules. It is exposed in two small bluffs close to the fence,
in the gorse bushes on the east side of, and overlooking, the stream.
The fossils from the nodules here are small and fragile, consisting of
internal and external moulds largely of trilobites and brachiopods;
they have been listed and described (Williams 1962, Tripp 1965,

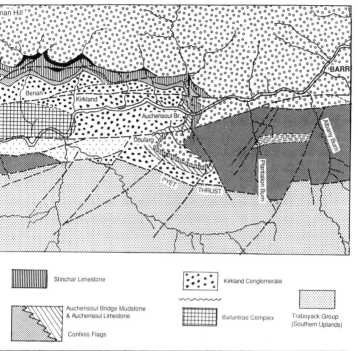

Stinchar Limestone	Kirkland Conglomerate	
Auchensoul Bridge Mudstone & Auchensoul Limestone	Ballantrae Complex	Traboyack Group (Southern Uplands)
Confinis Flags		

Ingham & Tripp 1991). The fauna is very large and diverse. Amongst the trilobites, it is dominated by *Lonchodomas pernix*, *Bumastoides? scoticus*, *Dimeropyge hystrix*, *Sphaerexochus* cf. *arcuatus*, *Encrinuroides obesus* and, above all, the pliomerid *Quinquecosta williamsi*. (Fig. 30.7) The latter genus is known only from the Stinchar Valley at Girvan. The assemblage falls broadly within the fairly shallow water illaenid-cheirurid association but the relative abundance of *Lonchodomas* and *Dimeropyge* suggest a rather offshore, outer shelf environment such as has been well documented for rocks of similar age and fauna in the Mackenzie Mountains of western Canada (Chatterton & Ludvigsen 1976, Ludvigsen 1978).

Following the Gorse Member is the Jubilation Member, exposed sporadically downstream for about 20 m but best examined in and around a small excavation on the west bank of Plantation Burn below

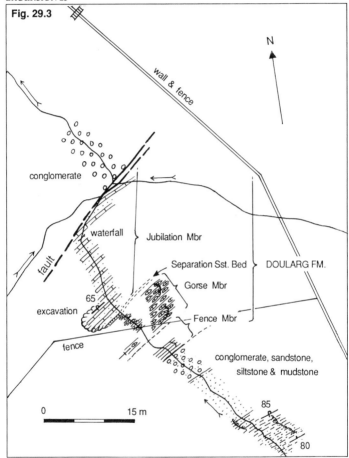

Figure 29.3. A detailed locality map of the Doularg Formation and its members in the Plantation Burn, east of Doularg Farm.

the fence. A little preparation of the site may be necessary but the lithology can clearly be seen to consist of calcareous mudstones and fine siltstones in which the carbonate concentrations occur in well-defined seams. The beds here dip upstream and are inverted. The

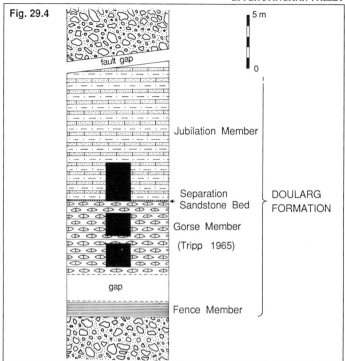

Figure 29.4. The succession in the Plantation Burn, east of Doularg Farm.

fauna is again a large one and collecting is best attempted from the weathered rock (internal and external moulds). Brachiopods are relatively few, the most common one being *Ptychoglyptus* cf. *virginiensis* but the trilobite fauna is dominated by four or five common forms — *Nileus teres, Pteraspis* sp., *Bronteopsis matutina, Sphaerexochus lanei* and the spectacular encrinurid *Cybelurus expansa* ; complete specimens are fairly frequent. (Fig. 30.7) The association is widely known from the Middle Ordovician in a deeper water 'slope' facies commonly associated with the periphery of the N American (Laurentian) palaeocontinent and its outboard arcs. It has often been referred to as the typical 'Whiterock' association and the Jubilation Member occurrence is probably the youngest one known, of upper Whiterockian

387

[= Llandeilo] age.

Between the Gorse Member and the Jubilation Member is a thin (15 cm) decalcified sandstone, the "Separation Sandstone Bed". It is not now exposed but was originally seen well down at the left hand margin of the excavation. It is interesting in that the sparse fauna collected from it is intermediate between that from the Gorse and Jubilation members.

Quite clearly, the Doularg Formation as a whole records a deepening (transgressive) event and this probably relates to basement foundering probably along a fault line just to the north, approximating to the present line of the large Upper Stinchar Valley Fault.

About 15 m downstream of the excavation is a small waterfall over rather sheared Jubilation Member rocks and the stream turns sharply to the right, following the line of a fault which is exposed above the next sharp bend in the stream. Beyond this, conglomerates are seen which are believed to be higher in the succession and which are probably the lateral equivalent of some higher part of the Benan Conglomerate to the north of the Stinchar Valley.

The view to the north and NW across the Stinchar Valley reveals something of the disposition of the various formations of the Barr Group developed in that direction. The main mass of Benan Hill is, as might be supposed, formed of a very thick Benan Conglomerate sequence disposed in the core of a broad syncline whose axis, plunging north-eastwards roughly parallels the Stinchar Valley. The northern slopes of the valley reveal features formed by the underlying formations, particularly that of the Stinchar Limestone which makes a positive, scarp-like feature descending into the valley towards the NE. Lower units appear on the valley slopes progressively to the SW and the prominent 'bump' made by the basal Kirkland Conglomerate can be seen some distance to the west, above Benan Farm (Locality 5).

Locality 4. River Stinchar at Auchensoul Bridge (NX 259 929) : **Kirkland Conglomerate, Auchensoul Bridge Mudstone, trilobites, brachiopods** (Figs 29.2, 29.5, 29.6). Return to the road and continue westwards for a short distance watching out for the River Stinchar approaching the road from the right. Stop by the footbridge leading to Auchensoul Farm. Cross it and at reasonably low water extensive low exposures will be seen in and adjacent to the river.

Here, three lithological units are seen. The dip is to the east and the lowest unit, the purple-tinged Kirkland Conglomerate is exposed for

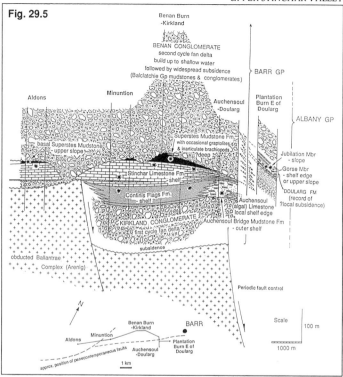

Figure 29.5. Local correlation within the Barr and Albany groups in the upper Stinchar Valley, showing depositional environments.

about 40 m upstream of the bridge and consists of the uppermost 16 m or so of the formation. It is capped by a brecciated pale blue limestone, the fragments being set in a calcareous siltstone. This is taken as the basal unit of the Auchensoul Bridge Mudstone Formation (see Ince 1984), previously referred to the Auchensoul Limestone of Williams (1962). After an exposure gap covering several metres of strata the succession continues with about 15 m of largely calcareous strata, basically blue-grey or maroon mudstones and siltstones but with limestone lenses and bands (NX 246 924). Fossils are best extracted from the limestone lenses where they are decalcified. The

389

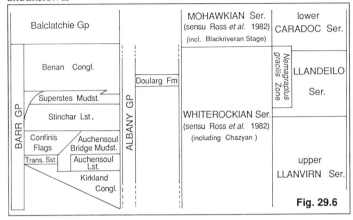

Figure 29.6. Chronostratigraphical correlation of the upper Stinchar Valley successions.

brachiopod *Valcourea confinis* is known throughout the succession here and indicates that the Auchensoul Bridge Mudstone Formations the lateral equivalent of part of the Confinis Flags Formation, more typically developed towards the west.

The trilobites known from the Auchensoul Bridge Mudstone have been described by Tripp (1979 - as Auchensoul Limestone fossils, see also Ingham & Tripp 1991, fig. 4). *Remopleurides ateuchetos* and *Isotelus* sp. are the most common forms.

Locality 5. Benan Burn: Kirkland Conglomerate, Confinis Flags, Stinchar Limestone, Superstes Mudstone, Benan Conglomerate, brachiopods, trilobites, other fossils (Figs 29.2, 29.5, 29.6). Continue westwards for about 1.5 km along the B734 and take the access road to the right leading to Kirkland and Benan farms, crossing the River Stinchar near Kirkland Farm (NX 246 924). The tributary flowing down to the Stinchar from the north here is Kirkland Burn and not Benan Burn as it is labelled on the O.S. 1:50 000 map. Continue along the track to Benan Farm (NX 240 920) and park after first seeking permission from the farm owners. A track leads into Benan Burn which again flows from the north and deeply dissects the flank of Benan Hill. There are extensive exposures hereabouts of the Kirkland Conglomerate Formation, particularly on the hillside between Benan and Kirkland burns and it is estimated that the minimum thickness of the formation must be in the order of 260 m. Although the base is not seen, regional mapping suggest that it rests unconformably on the Ballantrae Complex. It is a massive purple and grey conglomerate commonly reddish-weathering and contains pebbles and cobbles of Ballantrae rocks and also acid igneous types not known from the Ballantrae Complex. Derivation was from the north or NW. The Kirkland Conglomerate forms the first fan-delta cycle of Ince (1984) (see also Ingham & Tripp 1991, fig. 3).

In Benan Burn some 15 m of this lithology is seen followed by about 7 m of rubbly weathering, cross-bedded, calcareous sandstone with occasional large pebbles. This unit forms part of the "Transitional Sandstone" of Ince (1984) and it is followed by the Confinis Flags Formation. Although in this section there is an exposure break covering about 35m of succession, typical Confinis Flags Formation is then exposed in the stream and along the paths. About 45 m of purplish-brown weathering, fine calcareous sandstone is seen. Weathering effects occasionally give the rock a slightly honeycombed appeerence. Small pebbles are sometimes found. Fossils occur throughout and are dominated by a shallow water trilobite-brachiopod association. The relatively common Appalachian brachiopod *Valcourea confinis* gives the formation its old, well-established name. Although the shelly fauna is N American in its affinities, conodont studies have shown conclusively that this part of the Girvan succession is, in Anglo-Welsh terms, of late Llanvirn age (Bergström 1990).

Further along the valley, the lower beds of the Stinchar Limestone are encountered. They consist of rubbly, grey muddy limestones with some greenish mudstones and weather with a honeycombed surface and a yellowish-brown colour. Brachiopods and the alga *Girvanella* can be found. The Stinchar Limestone succession is complicated in this section by some faulting but overall the thickness appears to be in the order of 60m. The higher beds, beyond the confluence with a tributary from the north, become more thinly bedded and 'platy'. Although still honeycombed and weathering to a bright yellowish tint, the highest Stinchar Limestone here is richly fossiliferous, the largely trilobite and brachiopod fauna occurring as friable moulds. The described fauna from this horizon at a variety of localities in the Stinchar Valley is considerable (Williams 1962, Tripp 1967): again it is a shallow water, platformal assemblage of N. American aspect. Conodont biostratigraphy (Bergström 1990) indicates that the Llanvirn-Llandeilo boundary of the Anglo-Welsh chronostratigraphical scheme falls within the Stinchar Limestone.

Further upstream, in both Benan Burn and its tributary, scattered exposures of the Superstes Mudstone Formation are seen, estimated to be some 40m thick here: the rock is a finely-bedded alternation of dark, greenish, nodular weathering, graded siltstone and mudstone. Fossils are few, consisting mostly of occasional inarticulate brachiopods and poorly preserved graptolites including the eponymous *Didymograptus superstes* . A much deeper water environment is indicated and it has been suggested that the successional changes are due to contemporaneous faulting along lines to the north or NW of the immediate area (Fig. 29.5, see also Ingham & Tripp 1991, fig.3).

Above the Superstes Mudstone Formation lies the Benan Conglomerate constituting Ince's (1984) second fan delta cycle. This formation is particularly thick in this area and, although its lowest beds are seen to interdigitate with the underlying mudstones in the Benan Burn-Kirkland Burn area, to the NE and, particularly to the SW of Benan Burn, the conglomerate channels down through the Superstes Mudstone to rest on the Stinchar Limestone. Four or five kilometres to the SW it has scoured to the level of the Ballantrae Complex and is thus clearly disposed in at least two broad channels. The lithological characteristics are typical of the whole area (see Excursion 28, Locality 5).

Locality 6. Minuntian Quarry (NX 220 911) : **Confinis Flags Formation, lower and middle Stinchar Limestone, trilobites, brachiopods** (Figs 29.2, 29.5, 29.6). Return to the main road (B734) and proceed for a little more than 2 km, taking the service road to the right to Minuntian Farm. Ask permission at the farm for access to the old quarry which lies, together with its ruined kiln, less than 0.5 km west of the farm on the flank of the hillside and is reached by a path along the upper part of a field beyond the farm. The final part of the track leads obliquely up the bank to the old quarry entrance and exposures here of the upper part of the Confinis Flags Formation (see Locality 5) have yielded a particularly extensive trilobite and brachiopod fauna (Tripp 1962, Williams 1962). The brownish rock is largely decalcified and the fossils comprise rather friable internal and external moulds. Soft wrapping materials are essential.

At the mouth to the quarry, which is quite small, the abrupt change to typical Stinchar Limestone is seen (Fig. 29.2). Most of the rock is unweathered and fossils are not easily extracted but cross-sections through the large gastropod *Maclurea* can be found. Fairly high on the back wall of the quarry (not very high, but **take care**), the rock is locally deeply decalcified and exquisite but very friable fossil moulds can be collected. Again the fauna is a large, relatively shallow water assemblage, dominantly of trilobites. The most common species encountered are *Remopleurides vulgaris*, *Ceraurinella* aff. *magnilobata* and *Hemiarges inghami*, the latter species (a lichid) being unknown from any other locality but closely resembling a species of about the same age from the Mackenzie district of western Canada (Tripp 1979; Chatterton and Ludvigsen 1976) .

Locality 7. Aldons Quarry (NX 198 896) : **Ballantrae Complex, pebbly facies of the upper Confinis Flags-lower Stinchar Limestone, algal Stinchar Limestone, basal Superstes Mudstone, Benan Conglomerate, trilobites, brachiopods, other fossils** (Figs 29.2, 29.5, 29.6). Return to the main road (B734) and continue south-westwards for about 3 km to its junction with the A714 Girvan-Barrhill road, carefully negotiating the tight hairpin bend prior to crossing the R. Stinchar at the road junction. Turn left (south) and continue for less that 0.25 km. Park at the roadside layby. A short distance further down the road, a steep track to the right services Aldons Cottage and a small church and continues to the extensive old quarry workings. Ask permission for access at the cottage. Follow the rough track up over the brow and along to the main, northern, quarry (a short walk), passing to the right of the two old limekilns. As the quarry is reached, its floor, at least initially, will be seen to be something of a quagmire. Keep to the bank to the left of this.

The succession revealed in and adjacent to the quarry at this locality is highly instuctive in that it reveals, not only the short distance successional changes in this part of the Stinchar Valley but is suggestive of the sedimentation controls. The beds dip to the ESE and are disposed on the south-eastern flanks of a major Girvan structure known as the Aldons anticline. The local structure is more complicated for, towards the smaller, south eastern quarry, the dip reverses forming a plunging syncline which is then truncated by a shear zone bringing in Ballantrae rocks. In the main quarry area, however, the succession is relatively straightforward and is dominated by limestones. The lower beds are exposed at and beyond the northwestern side of the quarry where, in this direction, the base to the succession can be worked out. Here spilites belonging to the Ballantrae Complex are overlain unconformably by a thin, dark green basal conglomerate, about 1.5 m thick, the angular pebbles consisting virtually entirely of spilite, followed by about 17 m of dark green pebbly sandstones. Grey, cobbly limestones with green sandy partings then come in, only about 1.5 m thick, followed by another 1.5 m of cobbly and pebbly limestone. This is the most clastic-rich part of the succession and not only do the limestone cobbles consist of algal nodules (*Girvanella*) and other organic debris but virtually all the pebbles and shell fragments are coated with growths of this alga. Following this are some 6 m of cobbly *Girvanella* limestone with green mudstone surrounds and about 28 m of pale, creamy-weathering, nodular and platy limestone, again very rich in *Girvanella* growths and this is capped by over 12 m of grey, thinly-bedded, platy limestones and calcareous mudstones before the next distinctive lithology is encountered on the south-eastern wall of the main quarry. A large shelly fauna has been collected from the upper beds, particularly where it is weathered (e.g. Tripp 1967) and it is typical of the platy upper Stinchar Limestone of other localities in the Stinchar Valley. What is particularly notable, however, is that there is no trace of either the very thick Kirkland Conglomerate or the typical Confinis Flags Formation (see Localities 5 & 6), both of which are present only a few kilometres away to the NE. The pebbly basal beds at Aldons are probably equivalent to the lower part of the Stinchar Limestone and some upper part of the Confinis Flags Formation elsewhere. It is clear that there is profound, short distance overlap here and the most likely explanation is of contemporaneous basement faulting between Aldons and Minuntian.

On the SE wall of the main quarry, immediately above the typical upper Stinchar Limestone there are less than 2 m of sheared mudstones with calcareous nodules before typical Benan Conglomerate is seen. The best exposures of these mudstones are now unfortunately concealed beneath two large slipped blocks of Benan Conglomerate, immediately to the right of the main Benan outcrop. Again, a substantial shelly fauna has been described from the weathered nodules (Williams 1962, Tripp 1976) which is similar in many respects to that known from the Jubilation Member of the Doularg Formation (Albany Group)(see Locality 3) and is indicative of deepening marine conditions, again probably brought about by contemporaneous basement faulting. These beds constitute the transitional basal part of the Superstes Mudstone Formation. Shearing in these higher beds is related to slight thrusting, brought about by the local folding of competent and incompetent strata at the base of the Benan Conglomerate but not much succession can have been cut out and the Benan Conglomerate here seems to have channelled through almost the entire Superstes Mudstone. Not far to the north of the quarry, the Benan is seen to have transgressed the entire Stinchar succession and for some distance it rests directly on the spilites of the Ballantrae Volcanic Complex. This major channelling overstep has already been referred to above (Locality 5).

Return to the main road (A714) and turn left (northwards). Girvan is reached after a drive of about 9 km.

References are given after Excursion 31

Excursion 30 GIRVAN FORESHORE
J. Keith Ingham

Themes: Mid Ordovician -Early Silurian fore-arc sequences of the Girvan foreshore (Kennedy's Pass to Craigskelly area). To examine a variety of lithological units and their relationships, largely in stratigraphical sequence, in order to elucidate the cyclical and essentially fault-controlled environments of deposition. Opportunities for collecting fossil associations, not just of stratigraphical significance, will emphasise the importance of some associations in the understanding of palaeo-environments.

Features: Sediments and sedimentary environments ranging from shallow to extremely deep water, including shallow water carbonates, clastics, proximal and distal turbidites, submarine fans, slump-controlled sequences, significant stratigraphical relationships, environmentally and stratigraphically significant faunas, all typical of fore-arc basin and marginal régimes.

Maps: O.S.   1:25 000   Sheet NX19   Girvan
                      1:50 000   Sheet 76   Girvan
             B.G.S. 1:50 000   Sheet 7   Girvan

Terrain: Rocky shoreline, locally rough.

Distance and Time: c. 5 km. 6-8 hours, depending on the amount of time spent at particular localities.

Access: Low tide essential, particularly in the middle and later part of the excursion. **(SSSI)**

Locality 1. Kennedy's Pass (NX 149 933) **: Kilranny Conglomerate and Henderson's 'unconformity'** (Figs 28.1a, 30.1).   Parking is available in layby on seaward side of headland.

Extensive, much faulted exposures of the Kilranny Conglomerate (Balclatchie Group - early Caradoc) are well-exposed below and beside the road. Minor faulting is much in evidence and a large **dextral fault** crosses the foreshore in the bay immediately to the north. The conglomerate consists for the most part of clasts of volcanic and intrusive rocks of a variety of sizes, some of the largest being a distinctive pink granite. Some were derived from the Arenig Ballantrae

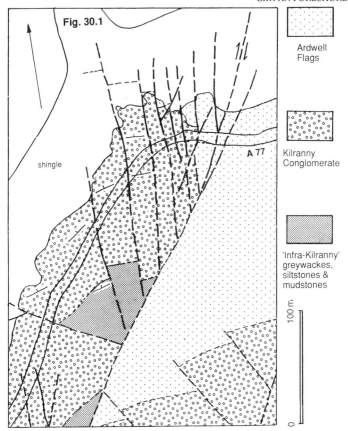

Figure 30.1. Detailed geological map of the area around Kennedy's Pass.

Complex, others from an acid igneous complex. The conglomerate was generally deposited fairly rapidly on a subsiding sea floor (probably fault controlled) but there are many framework beds. On the north side of the headland below the road and between two small faults the relationship between the Kilranny Conglomerate and the overlying Ardwell Flags can be seen (the so-called Henderson's unconformity). Examination of this junction, together with regional

397

mapping data, reveals it to be a channel fill whereby an erosional channel on the upper surface of the conglomerate has been progressively filled by the thinly bedded silts of the basal Ardwell Flags Formation.

Across the road, a few metres to the south is a cutting through Kilranny Conglomerate which exposes its base. Underlying the formation are the so-called 'Infra-Kilranny Greywackes' (Williams1962) - also belonging to the Balclatchie Group - consisting of shales, siltstones and fine greywackes, overlying the Benan Conglomerate (the basal formation in this tract). Occasional brachiopods and trilobites can be found here in these beds and at other localities inland.

Locality 2. Ardwell Foreshore: Ardwell Flags, 'Cascade' folding (Fig. 28.1a). Walk north-eastwards along the foreshore towards Ardwell Bay (about 1 km of fairly rough going) or drive and park at the layby about halfway along the Ardwell foreshore, progressively ascending a thick succession of Ardwell Flags. These beds comprise an alternation of fine, laminated sandstone with ripples, alternating with thin, grey mudstones. Magnificent exposures of 'cascade folding' can be seen which have been interpreted variously as a late Caledonian fold phase (Williams 1959) or as penecontemporaneous slumping of partly lithified sediment. The succession youngs obliquely seawards and in order to appreciate the second, more likely, alternative one has to rotate the entire block in one's mind to the 'horizontal' in order to appreciate that the sediment may have been transported down-slope from the NW. Towards the middle and north-eastern section of the foreshore a number of good exposures of contemporaneous sedimentary breccias and small-scale slumping will be discovered (some iron-stained): they are best seen when wet. The beds are folded and brecciated in a complex way so that cohesive strata can be seen to pass into brecciated beds. All this speaks of the considerable instability of the environment of deposition. Fossils are relatively uncommon in this part of the succession and are dominated by graptolites and orthocone nautiloids. Examples of the former, of Caradoc age, can sometimes be obtained from the small disused quarry behind and a little to the south of Ardwell Farm.

Locality 3. Ardwell Bay - north-west side (beginning of the Whitehouse foreshore) (NX 158 943) : **Uppermost Ardwell Flags with graptolites** (Fig. 28.1a). Parking is available adjacent to Ardwell Farm.

This is the point at which visitors who have followed the itinerary ending with the Ardmillan Braes lower Ardwell Flags fossil locality (Excursion 28, Locality 6) will come down to the road via the track at Ardwell Farm and can pick up this itinerary if they so wish. The first exposures, on the seaward side of Ardwell Bay, are only available at low tide. They constitute the very topmost beds of the Ardwell Flags Formation and are rather folded, being largely caught between branches of the large dextral fault running out to sea from Kennedy's Pass (see Locality 1). Here the beds consist of dark shales and even-textured sandstones. The former yield graptolites - largely *Orthograptus* and other diplograptids diagnostic of the late Caradoc *Dicranograptus clingani* Biozone (Fig. 32.3).

Locality 4. Whitehouse shore (south): Lower Whitehouse Group - South Shore Formation (limestone flysch) (Fig. 28.1a). The aforementioned strata are followed sharply by a limestone **flysch** unit - the South Shore Formation at the base of the Lower Whitehouse Group. These beds are locally similarly folded and faulted and consist of alternations of graded detrital limestones and grey and green shales in a major, upward fining sequence: the basal unit is particularly coarse. The basal elements of each graded unit were deposited in fairly proximal turbidity currents from the NW - some of the units are multiple and show every member of the **Bouma Sequence**. Clear exposures are best seen for about a hundred metres fairly close to the road where small bluffs stick up through the sand. Some of these outcrops show beds which comprise two turbidites. These are produced when one turbidity current runs over another as the first one was still depositing its sediment. Across the foreshore along strike to the SW the rocks are largely covered with barnacles and seaweed. Fossil shelly debris, transported from an outer platformal environment has been collected from the coarse bases of the graded units but it is difficult to come by and quite dangerous to extract. **The rock is hard and goggles are essential.** Trilobite, brachiopod and coral fragments are the most usual finds. Of the former, the late Caradoc *Tretaspis ceriodes* (species group) is typical. This is an outer **neritic** trilobite of widespread distribution, being known from Scandinavia, northern England, the Welsh Borderland and even western China. Its presence at Girvan indicates that the geographical barriers (i.e. Iapetus Ocean), which had, until late Caradoc times, controlled profoundly the distribution of shallower water faunas, were beginning to break down. Upwards

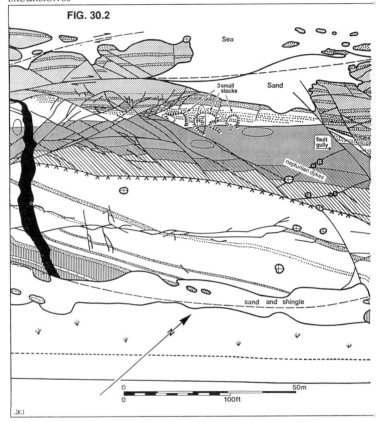

Figure 30.2. Detailed geological map of the central part of the Whitehouse Shore.

from this level, the essentially North American aspect of the Girvan neritic faunas, becomes less and less evident.

Locality 5. Whitehouse shore (centre): Lower Whitehouse Group - Three Mile Formation (distal sandstone flysch), thrust foreshortening of stratigraphical succession (Figs 28.1a , 30.2). A lay-by is available here (NX 165 947).

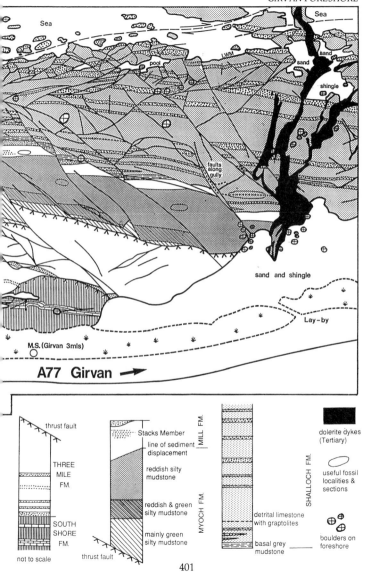

Sea

Sea

LWM

pool

sand

sand

shingle

faults
along
gully

sand and shingle

Lay-by

M.S. (Girvan 3mls)

A77 Girvan ➞

thrust fault

THREE
MILE
FM.

SOUTH
SHORE
FM.

not to scale

Stacks Member

line of sediment
displacement

reddish silty
mudstone

reddish & green
silty mudstone

mainly green
silty mudstone

thrust fault

MILL FM.

MYOCH FM.

SHALLOCH FM.

detrital limestone
with graptolites

basal grey
mudstone

dolerite dykes
(Tertiary)

useful fossil
localities &
sections

boulders on
foreshore

401

Within the Lower Whitehouse Group the South Shore Formation is followed by the Three Mile Formation - also nearly vertical and younging seawards. This is a distal turbidite sequence and is much less calcareous than the underlying formation. For the most part the unit consists of alternations of shales with thin yet very persistent sandstone beds which stand out sharply - a 'ribbon' rock. Two or three of the sandstones are rather thicker and provide useful marker horizons. There are no fossils known from this formation.

For structural reasons, the third and terminal formation of the Lower Whitehouse Group (the graptolitic Penwhapple Formation - lower *Pleurograptus linearis* Biozone) is not exposed on the Whitehouse foreshore. A strike-oriented thrust or reverse fault cuts out perhaps 200m of strata here. The Lower Whitehouse Group has effectively been thrust (seawards) over the Upper Whitehouse Group. A prominent gully along the line of this fault follows the seaward margin of the Three Mile Formation (Fig. 30.2).

Locality 6. Whitehouse foreshore (centre): Upper Whitehouse Group - Myoch Formation, deep water facies faunas, sandstone dykes, conjugate faulting (Figs 28.1a, 30.2). There are two formations in the Upper Whitehouse Group - the Myoch Formation and the Mill Formation. The former is distinctive and consists largely of red and green silty mudstones. There is a sandstone unit near the base but this is only locally seen to the SW at low water mark because of the reverse faulting mentioned above (Locality 5). In the middle sector of the foreshore the lowest beds of the Myoch Formation consists of greenish silty mudstones followed by reddish and greenish banded beds, these in turn being followed by dominantly reddish beds. It is from the upper part of the latter unit that, with patience, a substantial and strange fauna can be extracted. The fauna consists largely of trilobites and constitutes what is known as the cyclopygid **biofacies**. Although there are benthic elements, much of the fauna was pelagic. Typical, blind, benthic elements are *Dionide* and the trinucleids *Novaspis* and *Nankinolithus*. Pelagic elements include the all-seeing cyclopygids *Cyclopyge, Symphysops, Degamella* (two species), *Novakella, Microparia, Psilacella* and *Ellipsotaphrus* together with *Telephina, Bohemilla* and the eyeless *Raphiophorus* and a host of others, some rare (Fig. 30.7). This indigenous fauna represents an Ordovician deep water assemblage and is known from a variety of levels throughout the Ordovician. It is most typical of southern Britain, central Europe and Asia. Here, at

Girvan, it is found on the subtropical fringes of the North American palaeocontinent of Laurentia and reflects the widespread distribution of deep sea, colder water and ocean-going faunas. Brachiopods are relatively rare and are tiny. They also constitute a peculiar assemblage - the so-called *Foliomena* Community, believed to be the the the deepest water brachiopod association. For the dark, deep sea bed to accommodate benthic elements calls for the water to have been oxygenated and this is reflected in the colour of the beds — largely due to iron oxide. It is believed that these reddish siltstones of the Myoch Formation comprise the overbank 'fines' of submarine channels building up a deep water fan deriving from the west or NW perhaps near the lower ends of submarine canyons. The age is at about the boundary between the Caradoc and the Ashgill Series.

Other features which can be observed in these beds locally on the Whitehouse foreshore include sandstone dykes - sand which has been winnowed by bottom currents into deep fissures in partly consolidated sediment - an indication of submarine disturbances.

Another notable feature of much of the central tract of the Whitehouse foreshore is the conjugate (brittle fracture) faulting displayed there. Approximately N-S faults usually have sinistral displacements, whereas E-W ones are dextral. There is a substantial vertical component in all of them which can be calculated with some precision locally, particularly where the near vertical beds are also affected by the somewhat earlier thrusting. Nevertheless, this phase of faulting reflects the final brittle displacements of the beds after the formation of the Byne Hill monocline in late Silurian times, the whole tract having been pushed towards the NW. Although locally both sinistral and dextral faults can be seen together (Fig. 30.2), it is more usual to find one or other set predominating.

Locality 7. Whitehouse shore (centre - small sea stacks): Upper Whitehouse Group - Mill Formation, stratigraphical gap due to mass sediment movement, slumping, channelling, transported deep water facies faunas, graptolites (Figs 28.1a, 30.2). The junction between the Myoch and Mill Formations is very sharp and detailed comparisons with the succession nearer Girvan at Myoch Bay suggest that part of the succession is missing here. The nature of the junction is best seen in a rock pool between the first and second of three small sea stacks situated at about the middle of the Whitehouse Shore. Here, profound mixing of partly consolidated sediment testifies to the large scale movement of substantial tracts of sediment perhaps under the influence of contemporaneous earthquake shocks.

The Mill Formation on the Whitehouse Shore is divisible into two members - a lower laminated and largely shaley unit and an upper unit dominated by sandstones and siltstones. Both members are best seen on and around the three small sea stacks mentioned above. The lower member of grey and green banded silty shales yields graptolites indicative of the low Ashgill *Dicellograptus complanatus* Biozone (Williams 1987)(see also Fig. 32.4). Some thin seams contain a cyclopygid biofacies trilobite fauna very similar to the one already referred to in the Myoch Formation (Locality 6) but this time the remains have been transported. Some new forms appear, not known from earlier beds, such as *Dindymene* and *Aethidionide,* the latter only otherwise known from China! It is from this unit that the famous Gray Collection of Upper Whitehouse fossils, now housed in the Natural History Museum, was obtained. The upper, sandy member also yields occasional fossils but is best examined for its cross-bedded sandstone units consisting of comminuted shelly debris (westerly derivation) and its slumped beds, seen best on the seaward side of the middle small stack. At this locality the Upper Whitehouse Group terminates with a thick channel-fill sandstone bed seen just beyond the stacks at about low water mark. Above it is a widespread bed of unfossiliferous, leaden-grey mudstone about a metre or so thick which forms the basal bed of the overlying Shalloch Formation.

Locality 8. Whitehouse shore (centre to north): Shalloch Formation, graptolites, Tertiary dykes (Figs 28.1a, 30.2). Dextral faulting trending roughly E-W is responsible for the progressive 'stepping back' of the Shalloch Formation adjacent to the layby on the Whitehouse Shore and this formation then occupies the rest of the foreshore and round into the next bay to the NE - Port Cardloch (Locality 9). The formation is a sandstone flysch sequence consisting of rapidly alternating, fairly thick beds of sandstone and shale. Fossils are few (the old name for the formation was the 'Barren Flagstones') but graptolites from a thin fine-grained detrital carbonate rock about nine metres from the base again indicate the *D. complanatus* Biozone (see Fig. 32.4). Substantially higher up the succession the mid Ashgill *D. anceps* Biozone has been recognised (Toghill 1970). Other, rare detrital carbonates have yielded shelly debris typical of the lower - middle Ashgill.

Adjacent to the Whitehouse shore layby, one of several dolerite

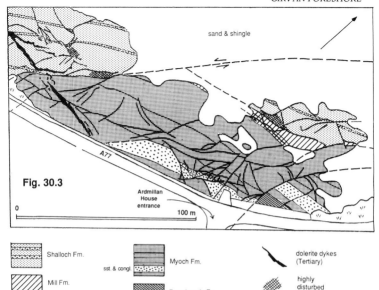

Figure 30.3. Detailed geological map of the foreshore at Port Cardloch.

dykes which cross the foreshore can be examined. The form of this particular one is complex and the multiple branches of it have enclosed tracts of Upper Whitehouse and Shalloch strata. The beds show evidence of baking. The age of the dykes is Tertiary and they constitute part of the Arran swarm.

Locality 9. Port Cardloch (NX 167 949) **: Whitehouse Group** (Figs 28.1a, 30.3). Parking is available by the gatehouse. In this bay at the north-eastern end of the Whitehouse Shore, the Upper Whitehouse Group makes an appearance again and is typically developed but the near basal sandy beds are much better seen than on the Whitehouse Shore, the large thrust fault having 'moved somewhat inland' at this locality (Fig. 28.1a). These thick beds of sandstone, very obviously faulted sinistrally near the road, opposite the gatehouse, are locally cross-bedded and contain frequent shale clasts. They represent migrating channel fill sands at or near the initiation of construction of the deep water submarine fan which dominates the the Myoch

Fig. 30.4

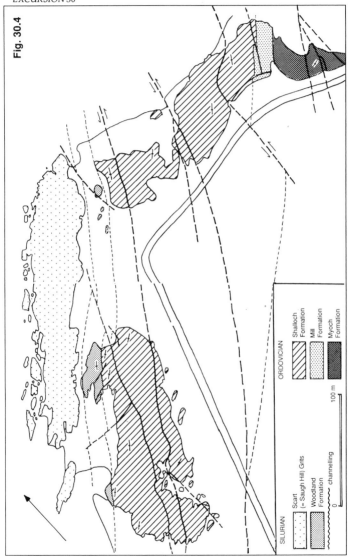

Figure 30.4. Simplified geological map of Woodland Point.

SILURIAN

Scart
(= Saugh Hill) Grits

Woodland
Formation

channelling

ORDOVICIAN

Shalloch
Formation

Mill
Formation

Myoch
Formation

0   100 m

Formation of the Upper Whitehouse Group.

Locality 10.   Woodland Point: Shalloch Formation, Silurian Formations with deep submarine channelling at the base

(Figs 28.1a,b, 30.4).   A short walk along the foreshore northwards from Port Cardloch leads to the promontory known as Woodland Point. Initially, on its south side, exposures of the Upper Whitehouse Group are poor and variable, depending on the migrating beach sand cover, but seawards a substantial and much faulted Shalloch Formation sequence dominates the foreshore. This deep water flysch-type succession can be correlated, bed for bed, with the Whitehouse Shore exposures (Locality 8). On Woodland Point itself, rocks of different type and age are encountered but a low tide here is essential for seeing the successional details and relationships. The latter can best be worked out on the southern side of the Point where the regularly bedded sandstones and shales of the early mid Ashgill Shalloch Formation are overlain unconformably by calcareous sandstones (locally coarse) of the basal Woodland Formation. These contain pentamerid brachiopods and are of Early Silurian (Early Llandovery) age. The unconformity is angular (about 8°) and overstep is towards the south. This unconformity is not believed to represent a period of uplift and subaerial erosion but a time of deep Silurian submarine channelling into Ordovician fault blocks (Fig. 30.5). This is partly reflected by the extreme variability of the Lower Silurian rocks over short distances (Locality 12).A substantial part of the Ashgill Series is missing here as compared with the succession seen in the Craighead Inlier (Excursion 31).

Seawards, the calcareous sandstones become increasingly muddy, with bands of purer carbonate rock, and the fossils more frequent (*Pentamerus, Stricklandia, Leptaena*), with some of the brachiopods in their original growth positions. Above these, and just before the rocky headland, thinly bedded shales at the top of the Woodland Formation are seen in places beneath the beach sand. The shales exhibit evidence of slumping and contain Lower Llandovery graptolites (*Monograptus cyphus* Biozone)(see also Fig. 32.8).

The rocky headland consists entirely of coarse clastic rocks constituting the Lower Llandovery Scart [=Saugh Hill] Formation. This largely conglomeratic unit contains, besides the usual igneous clasts and shale flakes, a particularly high proportion of quartz pebbles. The deposit is believed to have accumulated rapidly on a

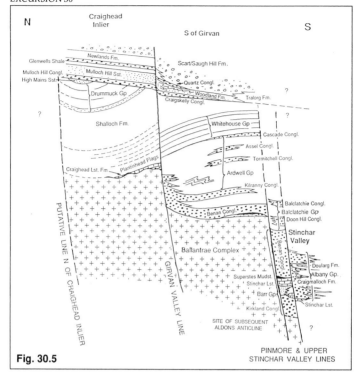

Figure 30.5 . Stratigraphical sketch section, illustrating the nature of the sub-Silurian unconformity in the Girvan district, which is believed to reflect submarine channelling across pre-Silurian fault blocks: basement faulting has not only controlled Ordovician sedimentation but the effects continue into the Silurian.

subsiding sea floor and overall the entire Llandovery succession here is of a cyclical nature, beginning with moderately shallow water sands progressing to slumped graptolitic shales, followed by the even deeper water Scart clastics - a situation reminiscent of parts of the underlying Ordovician sequence. This indicates that the proximal fore-arc régime which began in the Girvan area in Late Llanvirn times continued into the Silurian some 30 million years later.

Locality 11. Black Neuk to Myoch Bridge area: Shalloch Formation, Lower Whitehouse Group - Penwhapple Formation, graptolites, Upper Whitehouse Group - Myoch and Mill Formations (full development), graptolites, trilobites, channel fills, mud clast conglomerates, evidence of mass sediment transport from shallow into deep water (Figs 28.1b, 30.4, 30.6). Parking is available by pulling off the road, immediately before the field, a short distance to the north of Myoch Bridge (NX 179 958) .

A walk from the north side of Woodland Point along the rocky foreshore known as Black Neuk takes one down the succession again over typical Shalloch Formation flysch facies. A striking lithological change as one approaches the bay is indicative of the top of the Upper Whitehouse Group (Mill Formation). The succession abruptly becomes shaley and the 1m thick leaden grey mudstone at the base of the Shalloch Formation is well-exposed but here there is no channel-fill sandstone beneath it. Instead, a thick greenish grey shale unit, sparsely fossiliferous (largely graptolites) forms the topmost unit of the Mill Formation — thicker and much more shaley here than on the Whitehouse Shore (Locality 6). The lower units of the Upper Whitehouse Group (Myoch Formation) are only sporadically exposed below the curve of the main road.

The largely sandy beach between Black Neuk and the rocky foreshore of the Myoch Bridge area (c. 0.5 km to the NE) conceals some faulting, for the exposures near the bridge incorporate both Lower and Upper Whitehouse Group sediments. A large isolated outcrop sticking up though the lower beach is entirely Shalloch Formation.

The Lower Whitehouse Group, although severely deformed, is dominantly shaley and constitutes part of the Penwhapple Formation at the summit of the Group. In Myoch Burn, a short distance upstream from the road, dark shales with occasional sandstones yield graptolites indicative of the *Pleurograptus linearis* Biozone — a zone which crosses the Caradoc-Ashgill boundary. Here part of the lower, Caradoc, portion of the zone is represented.

The geology of the Myoch Foreshore is extremely complex both successionally and structurally (Fig. 30.6) but the area is significant in exposing the most complete Upper Whitehouse sequence known and rock units are preserved here which have no equivalents on the Whitehouse Shore owing to the contemporaneous mass sediment transport there (Locality 6). A full Myoch Formation succession is

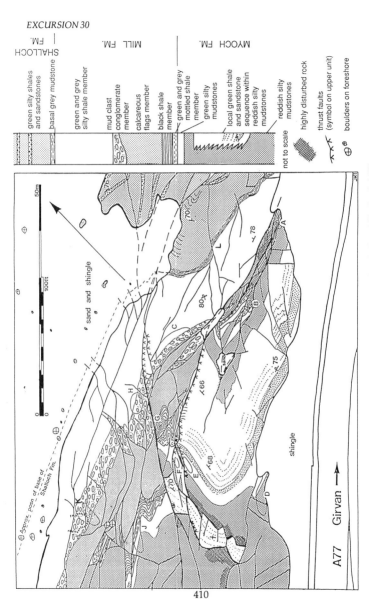

Figure 30.6. Detailed geological map of part of the foreshore at Myoch Bay (Shalloch Mill).

exposed, beginning with the basal sandstones and mudstone-matrix conglomerates, seen near the bridge, passing up into the typical greenish and reddish silty mudstones containing fossils of the deep water cyclopygid biofacies, as elsewhere (e.g. Localities 11D, E, F and J). However the succession nearest the road differs from that in the central part of the Whitehouse Shore in that the reddish mudstone contains a substantial sandstone/shale channel fill unit disposed in a plunging syncline (Fig. 30.6) with the reddish beds reappearing in the core. The seaward side of this syncline is truncated by a thrust belt beyond which a typical Myoch Formation sequence contains no such unit, reflecting its extremely localised occurrence.

Above the Myoch Formation, only the uppermost shale member of the Mill Formation has an equivalent on the Whitehouse shore where it rests abruptly on the red mudstones (Locality 6). Important members within the Mill Formation of the Myoch Foreshore are the thin graptolitic shale near the base and the mudstone conglomerate some metres higher in the succession. The former, much affected by strike faulting, yields abundant graptolites at several levels (Localities 11A, B and G). *Dicellograptus complanatus, D. gravis* and *Orthograptus* of the *calcaratus* species group are common. The fauna is considered to represent a level close to the boundary between the *Pleurograptus linearis* and *Dicellograptus complanatus* biozones (Williams 1987). As lowest Ashgill strata in Scandinavia are known to correlate with the highest part of the *Pleurograptus linearis* biozone and, inland at Girvan (Penwhapple Burn), an horizon within the Myoch Formation has yielded highest Caradoc trilobites of Scandinavian aspect, the Caradoc-Ashgill boundary must lie within the upper part of the reddish silty mudstones of the Myoch Formation, i.e., within the upper part of the *Pleurograptus linearis* Biozone.

The aforementioned mudstone conglomerate member of the Upper Whitehouse Group is well exposed on the Myoch foreshore (Figs 30.6) and is a most interesting deposit. Where it first appears, not far from the sea wall (Locality 11C), it is less than 1m thick but as it is traced across the foreshore (across several faults and thrusts) it expands in thickness considerably and yet is not present in the succession as seen across the bay to the south at Black Neuk. It is evidently a channel fill deposit and consists for the most part of a grey calcareous mudstone matrix containing a wide variety of clasts. Most of the latter are of deformed grey and green mudstone or siltstone flakes which were evidently ripped up from the local sea floor as this mass slide deposit was emplaced in the deep water environment indicated by much of the Upper Whitehouse succession. There are also limestone clasts and occasional igneous pebbles transported, like the matrix, from a much shallower, platformal, situation. Only one small group of igneous pebbles is known (Fig. 30.6, Locality 11C). **Please do not remove them.** The overall lithology of this unit can be seen best in a small embayment about half-way along its main outcrop near low water (Locality 11K). The fauna available from the matrix reflects the platformal origin and consists of a diverse assemblage of trilobites, brachiopods and gastropods. Of the former, the trinucleid *Tretaspis* cf. *hadelandica convergens* is particularly significant, for it first appears elsewhere (northern England, Wales) at the beginning of the Ashgill Series (Pusgillian Stage) as does its associate, the brachiopod *Skenidioides greenoughi*. The brachiopods *Onniella* and *Orthambonites* are also common, the whole assemblage reflecting the much more cosmopolitan nature of the outer neritic faunas at this level than hitherto, but one trilobite, the trinucleid *Cryptolithus latus latus*, is a North American form and its presence reflects the continuing Laurentian influence. It is known particularly from Locality 11H. In the British Isles this trilobite is only otherwise known from Pomeroy in Northern Ireland.

Above the mud clast conglomerate member of the Mill Formation there follows some 16m of predominantly greyish green silty shale with occasional graptolites (*Dicellograptus complanatus* Biozone), equivalent in part to the thinner shaley and sandy sequence forming the summit of the Upper Whitehouse Group on the small sea stacks in the central tract of the Whitehouse foreshore (Locality 7). Comparison shows that a substantial part of the Mill Formation present on the Myoch foreshore is not represented at the latter locality. Thus the Upper Whitehouse succession of the Myoch tract is the most complete one known.

Following the terminal shaley unit of the Upper Whitehouse Group the c.1m thick leaden grey mudstone at the base of the Shalloch Formation is well displayed in the deep, curved gully scoured out by the sea (Locality 11L). Beyond this, a low rocky platform of typical and

Figure 30.7. A selection of trilobites and brachiopods from various horizons in the Ordovician strata of the Girvan district.

Fig. 30.7

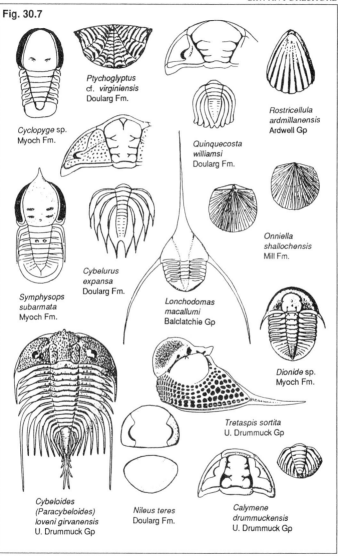

Cyclopyge sp.
Myoch Fm.

Ptychoglyptus
cf. *virginiensis*
Doularg Fm.

Rostricellula
ardmillanensis
Ardwell Gp

Quinquecosta
williamsi
Doularg Fm.

Onniella
shallochensis
Mill Fm.

Symphysops
subarmata
Myoch Fm.

Cybelurus
expansa
Doularg Fm.

Lonchodomas
macallumi
Balclatchie Gp

Dionide sp.
Myoch Fm.

Tretaspis sortita
U. Drummuck Gp

Cybeloides
(Paracybeloides)
loveni girvanensis
U. Drummuck Gp

Nileus teres
Doularg Fm.

Calymene
drummuckensis
U. Drummuck Gp

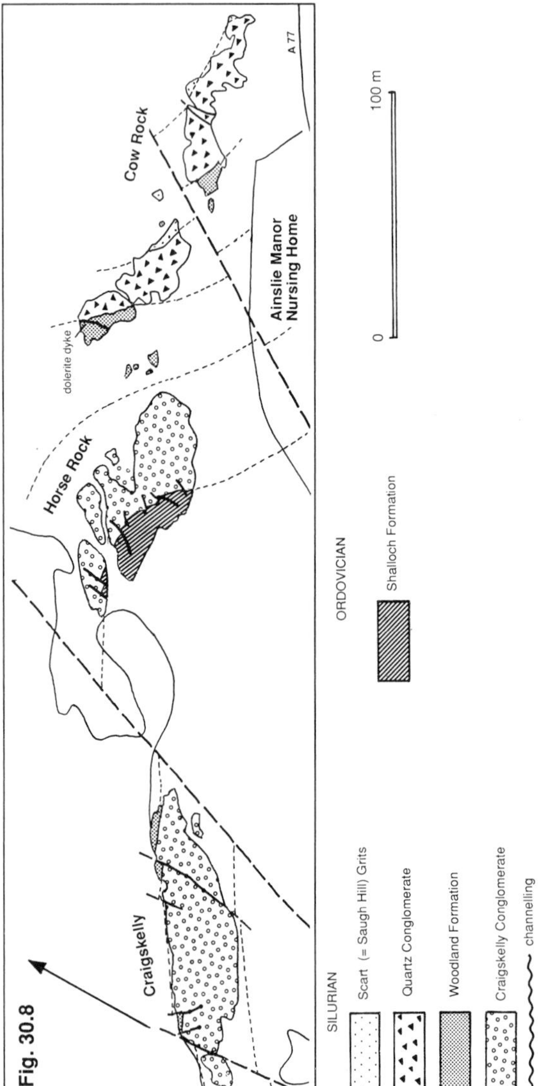

Figure 30.8. Detailed map of the geology around Craigskelly: the strata are almost vertical so that outcrop widths reflect thicknesses.

rather faulted Shalloch Formation is seen before sand cover obliterates most of the succession, apart from the large, low, rocky tract a short distance to the north.

Locality 12. Craigskelly area (NX 180 961)**, adjacent to Ainslie Manor Nursing Home (site of former Haven Hotel): Shalloch Formation, Lower Silurian succession, channel fill Craigskelly Conglomerate, Woodland Formation, shelly fossils, graptolites, Scart Formation, rapid substrate loading and deformation** (Figs 28.1b, 30.8). Parking is available, with toilet facilities, in the large car park a short distance to the north on the outskirts of Girvan.

The largely sandy foreshore between the Myoch outcrops and the Craigskelly area certainly conceals the thickest development of the low Ashgill Shalloch Formation in the whole Girvan foreshore tract. It also conceals a section of the major sinistral fault traceable from the upper reaches of Ardmillan Burn which crosses the foreshore a short distance to the south of Myoch Bridge and again in the Craigskelly area.

The large, rocky bluff projecting through the beach is Craigskelly itself which, together with the much lower, but extensive Horse Rock to the landward side, are composed of the Craigskelly Conglomerate Formation of Lower Llandovery age. The two outcrops are substantially offset and help define the position of the Ardmillan Burn Fault mentioned above. On the Horse Rock outcrops the conglomerate is seen to rest with a small angular unconformity on the underlying sandstone/shale sequence of the Shalloch Formation. Many other small faults can be traced but the relationship is clear. The Craigskelly Formation is some 40m thick, consists largely of acid igneous clasts derived from a volcanic/plutonic arc no great distance to the north, together with debris from the Ballantrae Volcanic Complex and younger Ordovician sediments. It is therefore not unlike many of the conglomerates in the Middle to Upper Ordovician part of the Girvan sequence and probably reflects a similar proximal fore-arc fault-controlled origin. It is very limited in its distribution for it is not present at the base of the Silurian sequence at Woodland Point across the bay to the SW. In fact the last vestige of it can be seen (by boat) on the landward of the two small islands (Scart Rocks) to the north of Woodland Point (see Fig. 30.4). It is evidently disposed in the form of a broad channel fill which has scoured down deeply into the underlying tilted Ordovician rocks (see also Fig. 30.5).

To the north, above the Craigskelly Conglomerate of the Horse Rock, the Woodland Formation is seen as at Woodland Point but the lower beds are not well exposed, being best seen in small outcrops jutting through the sand between the Horse Rock and the Cow Rock. These beds are rather more calcareous here than on Woodland Point and contain corals and trilobites as well as the usual brachiopods.

The upper, shaley part of the Woodland Formation is next seen on the southern flanks of the Cow Rock and adjacent faulted exposures but graptolites are rare. The beds are strongly folded and abruptly truncated above by the next clastic unit, the so-called Quartz Conglomerate. Again, this is another very local deposit at the base of the Scart [=Saugh Hill] Formation. It is a distinctive unit, consisting largely of small clasts of vein quartz and some shale flakes set in a sandy matrix. Examination of the available sections which are extensive, particularly at low tide, reveals that this conglomerate has locally injected the underlying shale unit and in places has peeled off substantial slabs of the shale which must have been only partly lithified at the time. The folding pattern in the underlying shale in which the folds fan out over the extent of the available outcrops indicates that they too are directly related to the abrupt deposition of the Quartz Conglomerate. This relationship again indicates an extremely active environment of deposition in which contemporaneous faulting, not far to the north, was triggering mass debris flows which then locally disrupted the not yet fully consolidated substrate.

At low tide on the seaward exposures of the shale/Quartz Conglomerate outcrop extensive exposures of a Tertiary dolerite dyke with chilled margins can be seen.

A short distance to the north the Cow Rock, the last few exposures of typical Scart Formation (as at Woodland Point) project through the sand at the beginning of the expanse of Girvan town Beach.

References are given after Excursion 31

Excursion 31   THE CRAIGHEAD INLIER
J. Keith Ingham

Themes: To examine parts of the Lower Palaeozoic cover sequence and faunas of the Craighead Inlier, near Girvan, to contrast the shallow water facies of the upper Ardwell Group with the more distal facies examined in Excursion 30, and to examine some later Ordovician formations not known elsewhere together with some succeeding Silurian rocks.

Features: Craighead Limestone, Kiln Mudstone and Sericoidea Mudstone at Craighead Quarry; Shalloch Formation and formations of the Lower Drummuck Group on Quarrel Hill; formations of the Upper Drummuck Group in Lady Burn; the late Ordovician High Mains Sandstone Formation; the Early Silurian Mulloch Hill Conglomerate and Mulloch Hill Sandstone formations, the Glenwells Shale and the Newlands Formation; trilobites, brachiopods and other fossils; shallow water and succeeding unstable slope sedimentation of a continuing transgressive proximal fore-arc régime.

Maps:
O.S.   1 : 25 000   Sheet NS 20/30 Maybole (south) and Dailly
O.S.   1 : 50 000   Sheet 76   Girvan
B.G.S. 1 : 50 000   Sheet 14 W   Ayr

Terrain: Some rough moorland walking and scrambling, with short car journeys between.

Distance and Time: About 20 km (12.5 miles), largely driving, from the first to the last locality, taking perhaps 6-7 hours depending on the time spent at each locality.

Access: This excursion is really only practicable by car or similar small vehicle. With nothing larger than a minibus there is adequate parking throughout. Permission is needed for some localities, as indicated in the text.

Introduction

The Craighead Inlier is an area of Ordovician and Silurian rocks isolated from the main expanse of the Girvan Lower Palaeozoic tract and is situated a few kilometres NE of Girvan on the northern side of the Girvan Valley. The inlier is about 12 km long but only reaches about 2 km wide at the most (see Fig.25.1). Structurally it consists of a simple anticline plunging towards the NE. The north-western limb has quite shallow dips and the Lower Palaeozoic rocks are overlain unconformably by Lower Old Red Sandstone with some volcanic and intrusive rocks but the south-eastern side, flanking the Girvan Valley, is more complex with steep dips and a marginal fault belt of post Carboniferous age - the Kerse Loch Fault, which brings down Old Red Sandstone and Carboniferous rocks in the Girvan Valley, including coal-bearing strata, once mined. Almost certainly this fault line approximates to the position of a putative basement fracture of much earlier, mid Ordovician date.

The oldest rocks, belonging to the Ballantrae Complex, are confined to the south-western portion of the inlier around Craighead Hill and these are overlain unconformably largely by a shallow water facies of the upper Ardwell Group (the Craighead Limestone Formation) on their south-eastern flanks, adjacent to the Kerse Loch Fault - a particularly striking exposition of the profound overlap of the Girvan cover sequence in a north-westerly direction. An oblique, ENE-WSW fault, bounding Craighead Hill on its northern side, is responsible for the absence at outcrop of any representative of the Whitehouse Group in the inlier because, to the north and NE of this fault, the core of the Craighead anticline exposes only the upper part of the Shalloch Formation. Unlike the foreshore sequence south of Girvan where basal Silurian channel-fill conglomerates rest on a scoured Shalloch Formation foundation (Excursion 30, Locality 12), younger late Ordovician (Ashgill) formations are preserved in the Craighead Inlier and thus the stratigraphical break at the base of the Silurian sequence is far less pronounced. These higher Ordovician and Silurian formations successively arch around, with some faulting, the nose of the north-eastwards plunging anticline so that younger formations appear progressively in that direction. The topographically low, extreme north-eastern part of the inlier is very poorly exposed.

Locality 1. Craighead Quarry (NS 234 014) : **Ballantrae Complex, Craighead Limestone Formation (various shallow water facies), Kiln Mudstone Member, Sericoidea Mudstone Member, Plantinhead Formation, trilobites, brachiopods, other fossils, unconformity over complex topographical foundation (Fig. 25.1).**

Leave Girvan, driving northwards along the A77 for about 1 km, passing the roundabout at the junction with the B734, and take the next turning to the right just after crossing the Water of Girvan (B741). This road follows the northern side of the Girvan Valley. Continue for about 5 km noting that you will cross the Glasgow railway line three times. About 0.5 km after the third crossing, which will take you to the northern side of the line, you will see Craighead Quarry on your left with a minor road at Low Craighead Farm leading towards it. Take this road for a short distance. An old quarry access track leaves the road sharply to the left and leads up towards the old ruined quarry plant. This is the most convenient place to park. This is a Nature Conservancy Council Site of Special Scientific Interest (**SSSI**) but there are no access problems at the time of writing.

The geology of Craighead quarry is complicated by faulting, hardly surprising in view of its proximity to the Kerse Loch Fault. Nevertheless, the general upwards succession is towards the east with Ballantrae **spilites** and **cherts** to the west of the quarry. The mid Ordovician erosional surface on which the Craighead Limestone Formation rests is evidently highly irregular for there are striking facies changes, and not only in the basal beds, over very short distances. From the vantage point of the old quarry plant, the extreme western slopes of the main quarry expose the lowest beds, with the underlying Ballantrae rocks (spilites and cherts) largely beyond the quarry margin. The beds dip generally and irregularly towards the east and consist of spilitic conglomerates and green sandstones, variably calcareous, passing laterally and vertically into rubbly and sometimes pebbly limestones. Yet on the facing wall of the main quarry is a very evident and striking topographic high of Ballantrae rocks - a 'window' of spilites - truncated behind by a fault. Resting on this high are massive limestones which on close inspection are revealed to consist of slightly pinkish and greenish brecciated algal rocks consisting very largely of *Girvanella* (see Williams 1962). The algal masses were obviously brecciated by vigorous current action and in all probability formed in extremely shallow water above the wave base. In other parts of the quarry and through the narrow passage leading to the back quarry, other lithologies are seen including limestones which have evidently slumped down slopes and sometimes containing uprooted and rolled coral masses, relatively well-bedded limestones rich in crinoid debris and occasionally mudstone lenticles

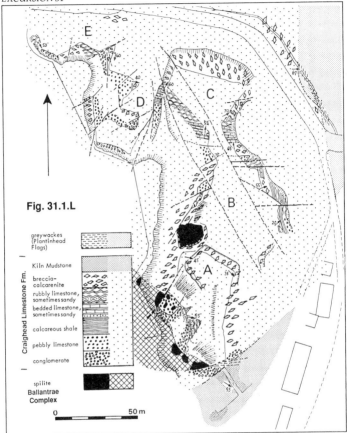

Figure 31.1. Geological map of the area around Craighead Quarry.

and beds yielding faunas reflecting even deeper depositional environments. The submarine topography at the time of the Craighead transgression here was evidently very irregular indeed. One of the deeper water mudstone lenses is a relatively thin unit between bedded limestones and is exposed above the now rather overgrown ramp leading down the eastern side of the main quarry. It is known as the

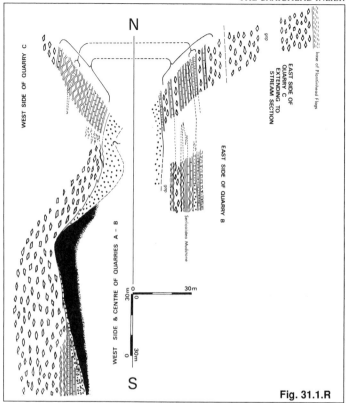

Fig. 31.1.R

Sericoidea Mudstone Member, named after a small strophomenoid brachiopod. It has yielded a moderately rich and important fauna of brachiopods (Williams 1962), trilobites (Tripp 1980b) and graptolites (Rickards *in* Tripp 1980b) indicating the basal part of the *Dicranograptus clingani* Biozone (mid Caradoc). The fauna allows a precise correlation with a level some distance above the middle part of the off shore, perhaps basinal facies, of the Ardwell Group south of Girvan.

Another, more substantial mudstone member, known from measured section evidence in other small quarries to the SW, to interdigitate in the massive bedded limestones of the higher part of

421

the Craighead Formation, is best exposed near the narrow south western cutting into the main quarry by the old, ruined kiln. This, the Kiln Mudstone Member contains large numbers of small, calcareous concretions, commonly decalcified, which have yielded a very large trilobite-brachiopod fauna (Tripp 1954, 1980a, Williams 1962). The exposure has been much collected and this has undercut a high brick retaining wall.

> Further sampling should be done with the greatest care.

At this mid Caradoc level the Craighead Formation shelly faunas have a very strong Appalachian aspect and relatively rare fossils from the limestone of the quarries have permitted a correlation with the basal Shermanian Stage of eastern N. America.

To the east of the back quarry, in the stream section at the other side of the minor road, the highest Craighead limestones are overlain by fine graded greywackes - the basal Plantinhead Flags Formation much more typical of the Ardwell Group lithologies south of Girvan. Occasional graptolites confirm the correlation. This part of the succession suggests a rapid foundering of the area at this level, probably due to contemporaneous activity along one or more basement fractures somewhere to the north or NW of the Craighead Inlier.

Locality 2. Quarrel Hill area (NS 250 022) : Shalloch Formation, Lower Drummuck Group, Auldthorns Formation, Quarrel Hill Formation, trilobites, brachiopods, gastropods, bivalves, other fossils, mud-flow stratigraphy (Fig. 31.2). Return to the B741 at Low Craighead Farm and turn left, driving to the NE for about 3 km. Shortly after crossing the railway line again, a minor road appears on the left. It is not easy to see as you approach it as the junction is very acute and you will have to turn very sharply into it and will probably have to make more than one attempt. Follow this rather twisting road for about 2 km, past Glenlochrie Farm and up the hill to Farden Farm (NS 250 027). Park by the roadside.

Seek permission at Farden Farm to walk along the southern flank of Quarrel Hill, ENE of the farm, following closely above Glenmard Plantation and aiming for the old ruins of Auldthorns about1 km away. Until 1977, in Glenmard Wood, 0.5 km ESE of Farden Farm a spectacular quarry section through much of the Ashgill Lower Drummuck Group yielded not only beautifully preserved fossil

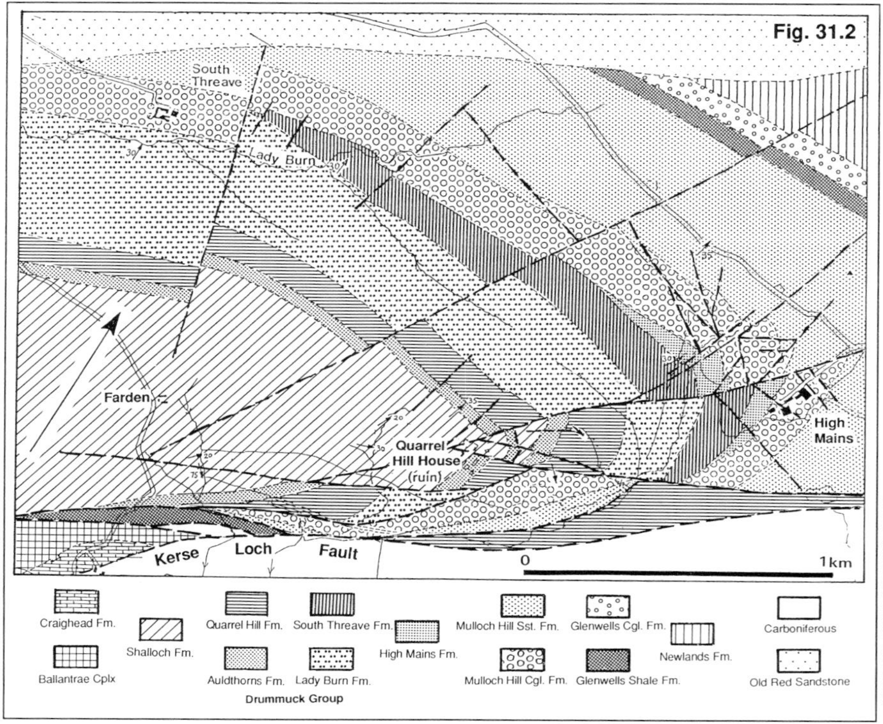

Figure 31.2. Geological map of the central sector of the Craighead Inlier.

423

assemblages including trilobites, brachiopods, gastropods and bivalves, but showed conclusively that a great deal of the succession there (Quarrel Hill Formation) consists of a series of mass mud flows which had accumulated on an unstable slope, originating in a neritic environment and ending in a rather deeper water one. Many of the fossils showed evidence of of having rolled, as a coating on fist-sized mud balls and there were also two very large, disrupted calcareous blocks in a slumped mudstone matrix. The quarry had been opened by the Forestry Commission some years earlier to provide bottomings for the tracks in the plantation. The great importance of this section became widely known and the regional Forestry Commission manager guaranteed to keep it open and available. Due to unfortunate circumstances and a new regional manager, the quarry was filled, graded and replanted without warning and hardly a trace of this vital section is now visible. Other published localities in the immediate vicinity were also lost (see Harper 1982).

Continue along above Glenmard Wood until an un-named burn is reached. Here, typical Shalloch Formation sandstones and shales will be seen dipping generally south-eastwards (see Excursion 30 Localities 10-12). A short distance further to the ENE the ruins of Auldthorns and Quarrel Hill House will be reached. This ground is rather faulted and lies on the axis of the Craighead anticline but a distinctive suite of lithologies makes a number of scarp features showing some fault repetition. To the NW of the ruins the geology is rather more simple and a clear scarp feature can be followed in a roughly E-W direction. This is formed by the sandy and sometimes conglomeratic Auldthorns Formation which forms the lowest division of the Lower Drummuck Group. It is divided into two members beginning with a lower Escarpment Member consisting of thickly-bedded medium to coarse-grained sandstones with some pebbly horizons. Fossils, largely broken brachiopods and trilobites are found in a few thin horizons and indicate a mid Ashgill, Cautleyan age. The upper, East Brow Member consists of a rapid alternation of fine to medium-grained sandstones and mudstones containing much the same fauna in thin seams in the sandstones but in a much more comminuted state (Harper 1982). In the mid 1970's a deep excavation was undertaken at the base of the main scarp to reveal the lower boundary of the Auldthorns Formation. It was seen to rest with a sharp base on a typical Shalloch Formation succession (see above).

A walk of not more than 0.5 km further to the ENE will bring you to a small stream draining the east flank of Quarrel Hill in which are a number of small, largely mudstone exposures fully documented by Harper (1982). They comprise the Quarrel Hill Formation, the upper unit of the Lower Drummuck Group. Large, late Cautleyan shelly faunas are known from this section dominated, amongst the trilobites by *Cryptolithus latus latus* and a species of *Tretaspis*. Many brachiopods, gastropods, bivalves and echinoderms are also known. The discontinuous section, now virtually the only one available, cannot match the one previously exposed in the now infilled Glenmard Quarry mentioned above and clear evidence of mass sediment movement cannot be documented in such relatively small exposures.

Locality 3. Lady Burn (Threave Glen) and South Threave (NS 243 037): **Upper Drummuck Group, Lady Burn Formation, South Threave Formation - including the famous Lady Burn Starfish Beds, Mulloch Hill Conglomerate, trilobites, brachiopods, gastropods, bivalves, starfish and other echinoderms, other fossils, mudflow stratigraphy, transported assemblages** (Figs. 31.3, 31.4). Return to Farden Farm and drive north-westwards for about 1.5 km to Drummuck Farm. The road then swings to the right into Threave Glen, crosses Lady Burn and then climbs back out of the valley to the left. A short distance further along, an access drive leading to South Threave Farm leaves to the right. Take it and drive for about 1 km to the farm where you should park (NS 244 036). Seek permission at the farm for access to the upper part of Threave Glen which will usually be given readily (this is a much visited and internationally famous locality and the farmer knows all about it).

The section in Lady Burn adjacent to and upstream of South Threave Farm reveals most of the divisions of the Upper Drummuck Group, of late mid Ashgill (Rawtheyan) age, followed by an unconformable basal Silurian sequence. The section is largely a near-strike section with the beds dipping northwards (Fig. 31.3) and is hardly affected by faulting. One small fault crosses the valley about 300 m east of the farm with a downthrow to the west. This brings the base of the Lower Silurian Mulloch Hill Conglomerate close to Lady Burn just E of the farm and a small largely overgrown quarry helps to fix its position.

In and adjacent to Lady Burn behind the Farm are exposures high in the Lady Burn Mudstone Formation, which, particularly near the

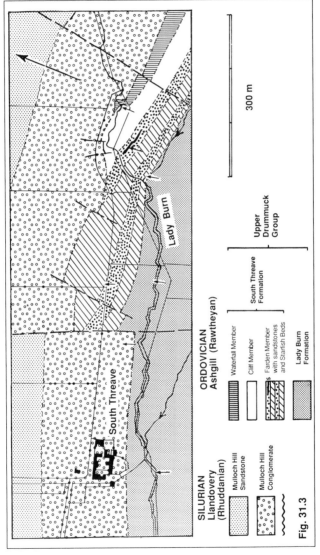

Figure 31.3. Detailed geological map of the area adjacent to Lady Burn (Threave Glen) (after Harper 1982).

Fig. 31.4

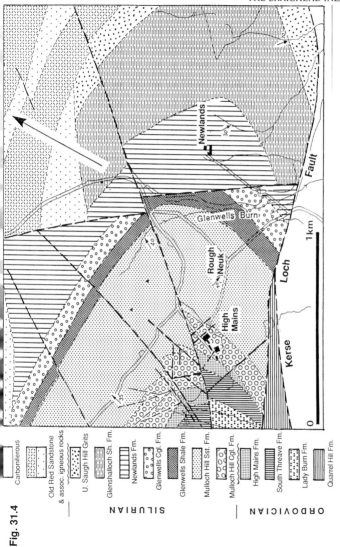

Carboniferous

Old Red Sandstone & assoc. igneous rocks

U. Saugh Hill Grits

Glenshalloch Sh. Fm.

Newlands Fm.

Glenwells Cgl. Fm.

Glenwells Shale Fm.

Mulloch Hill Sst. Fm.

Mulloch Hill Cgl. Fm.

High Mains Fm.

South Threave Fm.

Lady Burn Fm.

Quarrel Hill Fm.

SILURIAN

ORDOVICIAN

Newlands

Glenwells Burn

Rough Neuk

High Mains

Kerse Loch

Fault

0   1 km

Figure 31.4. Geological map of part of the north-eastern sector of the Craighead Anticline.

confluence of the small stream draining from the ESE have yielded rich trilobite faunas, beautifully preserved as internal and external moulds. A relatively common form is *Calymene (sensu lato) drummuckensis* as is *Cybeloides (Paracybeloides) loveni girvanensis* (see Fig. 30.7 and Ingham 1968, 1974; Kielan-Jaworowska *et al.* 1991). The Lady Burn Formation is seen sporadically for a further 400 m or so of the Lady Burn section the highest beds being seen in the next small stream flowing into Lady Burn from the ESE. Fossils are not common at every exposure but some yield small dalmanellid and other brachiopods, small gastropods, ctenodontid bivalves and hyolithids. Lithologically the poorly bedded Lady Burn Mudstone Formation resembles parts of the underlying Quarrel Hill Formation (Lower Drummuck Group) and it may be that similar mass sediment transport may be involved at some levels.

Above the Lady Burn Formation is the South Threave Formation which is divided into three members. The lithologies present suggest a return to conditions more typical of the Lower Drummuck Quarrel Hill Formation. The basal Farden Member consists of well-bedded silty mudstones with many sandstone lenses throughout. Towards the top of the member lie the world-famous Lady Burn Starfish Beds which have yielded enormous fossil assemblages to many collectors for more than a century. The largest collections, made by the Gray family, and now housed in the Natural History Museum in South Kensington, were made through extensive quarrying operations and much partly overgrown debris can still be seen on the steep east bank of Lady Burn a few metres south of where a wall crosses the stream. Other substantial collections (Begg, Lamont) are housed in the Hunterian Museum at Glasgow University. More recent deep excavations on top of the bank have produced a great deal more spectacular material. A wide range of phyla is represented in the fauna. Trilobites, commonly complete, brachiopods, gastropods, bivalves, hyolithids, starfish, echinoids, cystoids and other echinoderms and allied forms together with calcareous algae (receptaculitids) and a host of other forms are all equally abundant in the probably discontinuous horizons in the hard sandstone beds. Without further major excavation, material is only readily available from the abundant debris littering the site. Although some revision of small parts of the fauna have been undertaken (e.g. Owens 1973, Lane 1971, Harper 1984, 1989, Hughes *et al.* 1975, Ingham & Tripp - in prep.), the primary reference is still the monograph series produced by Reed (1903-6, 1914, 1917, 1931, 1935), and in many short papers. The faunal diversity is staggering and seems to represent more than one palaeo-environment. It is now widely believed that the accumulation is at least partly due to mass transport down an unstable slope and rapid burial of live organisms from a number of ecosystems.

The second member of the South Threave Formation is the Cliff Member, best exposed in the small cliff, stream bed and banks of Lady Burn, north of the wall. The bluish nodular mudstones yield relatively few brachiopods, but enrolled trilobites are not uncommon, particularly *Paraproetus girvanensis* and *Tretaspis sortita*. Commonly the fossils are arranged concentrically in what were probably originally mud balls, suggesting a similar transport and burial régime to that characteristic of parts of the Lower Drummuck Group Quarrel Hill Mudstone Formation (see Locality 2).

About 100 m east of the sharp bend in Lady Burn, north of the wall, the third, Waterfall Member of the South Threave Formation is seen in part. It consists of a few metres of poorly fossiliferous, well-bedded, greenish silty mudstones exposed for a short distance below the small waterfall. Above this member in this section lies the basal Silurian Mulloch Hill Conglomerate Formation (see Locality 4). Its base is unconformable and it rapidly oversteps the members of the South Threave Formation in a westerly direction so that near South Threave Farm it rests on the Lady Burn Formation (see above).

Locality 4. The Kirk Hill road (NS 260 042): **Mulloch Hill Conglomerate and Mulloch Hill Sandstone formations, brachiopods, trilobites** (Figs. 25.1, 31.4). Return to the minor road via the South Threave access drive and turn right. Continue for less than 0.5 km to a minor cross-roads and turn right again. This minor road, sometimes known as the Craigens or Kirk Hill road serves North Threave and East Threave Farms and you should follow it for about 1.5 km at which point it turns sharply to the right just after East Threave Farm. It then follows closely beneath Craigens Hill and Kirk Hill which lie to the north. After less than 1 km, two or three very small, old building stone excavations will be met with on the left. This stretch of road is a convenient place to stop in order to take in something of the local geology.

The small 'quarries' mentioned above expose part of the pink-stained and slightly ochreous-weathering Mulloch Hill Sandstone

Formation, of Early Silurian, Early Llandovery (Rhuddanian) age. Trilobites and brachiopods are relatively common, the former including *Calymene, Encrinurus* and *Acernaspis* (Fig. 31.6). The exposures are fully documented in Howells (1982). To the south of the road, the rugged, hilly ground comprises the much-faulted, basal Silurian formation, the Mulloch Hill Conglomerate, which underlies the Mulloch Hill Sandstone. This badly faulted ground occurs where the conglomerate is folded around the nose of the Craighead anticline (Fig. 31.4). Cocks & Toghill (1973) renamed the conglomerate the Lady Burn Formation to avoid confusion with the overlying sandstone unit but without realising that a Lady Burn Formation already existed in the Upper Drummuck Group. A short walk across to any of the exposures of the conglomerate will show that its characters are very similar to those of the Craigskelly Conglomerate, of similar stratigraphical position in the Girvan foreshore sector to the SW (Excursion 30, Locality 12). It also probably represents a channel fill and may be part of an Early Silurian fan-delta cycle not unlike those documented for the mid Ordovician in the Stinchar Valley (Excursion 29).

Locality 5. High Mains (NS 267 039) : **High Mains Sandstone Formation, brachiopods, trilobites, other fossils** (Figs. 31.4, 31.5). Continue a very short distance along the road and take the access track to the right leading to High Mains Farm. Seek permission to visit the excavation, made in the mid 1970's, c. 90m west of the farm buildings (Harper 1981).

The High Mains Sandstone Formation is the youngest Ordovician Formation in the entire Girvan district. It rests on the Waterfall Member of the South Threave Formation (Locality 3) and is preserved only in the faulted nose of the Craighead anticline, being rapidly overstepped in a westerly and south-westerly direction on both limbs of the fold. Exposures are limited but the excavation west of High Mains farmhouse, mentioned above (Locs H1 & H2 of Harper 1981, Owen 1986), should provide blocks of typical, fossiliferous material. Brachiopods are the most abundant fossils in this brown-weathering sandstone and are dominated by *Hirnantia sagittifera*, *Eostropheodonta* aff.*hirnantensis* and *Hindella crassa incipiens.*

Trilobites are less common but comprise a relict American assemblage of *Achatella, Flexicalymene, Isotelus* and others (Harper 1981, Owen

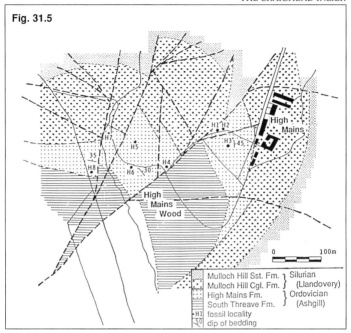

Figure 31.5. Detailed geological map around High Mains Farm
(after Harper 1981).

1986). Crinoid columnals are locally very common on certain bedding-planes. It is a particularly interesting assemblage as the brachiopods are typical of the widely-known end Ordovician *Hirnantia* fauna, largely of late Ashgill, Hirnantian age, known also from the Anglo-Welsh area and from locations as far apart as China and maritime eastern N. America. The fauna is believed to represent one of a number of closely-related, colder water ecosystems which became almost globally distributed with the onset of the well-documented late Ordovician south polar glaciation centred on Saharan Africa. The concomitant eustatic sea level lowering may well explain the undoubted shallow water facies represented by the High Mains fauna.

Locality 6. Glenwells Burn (NS 271 043) : **Mulloch Hill Sandstone Formation, Glenwells Shale Formation, Glenwells Conglomerate)** (Fig. 31.4). Return via the access track to the Craigens or Kirkhill road and turn right. After less than 0.5 km, the road crosses the upper reaches of Glenwells Burn. Park by the side of the road (271 045).

The fine, sandy and silty beds exposed by the side of Glenwells Burn, upstream of the road, represent the top of the Mulloch Hill Sandstone, near its transition to the overlying Glenwells Shale Formation. This occupies the slack ground to the north, but fossiliferous exposures can only be found some distance further down the burn where they have yielded graptolites typical of the *Coronograptus cyphus* Biozone (Early Llandovery, i.e. Rhuddanian, age). A deepening régime is evident here, strongly reminiscent of the Mid Ordovician Kirkland Conglomerate-Superstes Mudstone sequence in the Stinchar Valley. In fact, the brachiopod association from the highest beds assigned to the Mulloch Hill Sandstone here is indicative of a rather deeper water environment of deposition than that from the main mass of the formation (see Locality 7, below). As in the case of the Middle Ordovician sequence in the Stinchar Valley, the graptolitic shale unit is capped by a conglomerate - the Glenwells Conglomerate - seen on Kirk Hill, to the north of the road. It forms a basal unit to the cycle continuing with the Mid Llandovery (i.e. Aeronian) Newlands Formation (Locality 8).

Locality 7. Rough Neuk Quarry (NS 271 040) : **Mulloch Hill Sandstone Formation, brachiopods, trilobites, other fossils, shallow water Early Silurian assemblage** (Fig. 31.4). Continue for a very short distance and take the minor road leading off sharply to the right. Follow this road for 0.5 km obliquely down the hill, again crossing Glenwells Burn until a right-angled bend is reached. An old, ruined cottage on the corner is now represented only by the remains of the foundations. Park off the road in the angle opposite the cottage remains. Rough Neuk Quarry will be seen a short distance into the woods to the west. New forest growth following replanting may make it rather less evident but nevertheless follow the old, very rough and sometimes muddy track into the wood for about 50 m and bear off to the right up into the quarry.

The rock here is a well-bedded calcareous sandstone packed with fossil remains on some bedding planes. At exposure, the rock is usually decalcified and brownish weathering and the fossil shell material is leached out leaving both external and internal moulds of the various fossil organisms. If collections are being made, remember that both moulds should be kept in such circumstances, i.e. even the 'hole' that the fossil came out of as this is the only mould that retains the impression of the true external surface of the organism. Fresher rock, commonly seen in the core of a block, is grey and retains the original whitish fossil shell material. It is difficult to extract fossils from such rock.

Brachiopods are by far the most abundant fossils, the most significant being *Dalmanella* sp., *Mendacella mullockiensis* and *Hyattidina* ? *[Cryptothyrella] angustifrons* : these are taken as indicative of the shallow water *Cryptothyrella* brachiopod community (see Cocks & Toghill 1973). Strophomenoid and pentamerid brachiopods also occur. Trilobites are rarer but application will usually be rewarded by remains assignable to *Calymene ubiquitosa*, the phacopid *Acernaspis* cf. *elliptifrons* and perhaps the illaenid *Bumastus*. Streptelasmatid rugose corals are quite common as is the calcareous alga *Mastopora fava* again indicating a shallow water environment well within the photic zone. Gastropods and bivalves are also known. An horizon low in the quarry succession has recently yielded abundant remains of asteroids and crinoids. The whole association is regarded as representing a quite shallow water inshore ecosystem in which the shelly remains have been winnowed into local shell bank accumulations by bottom currents. The shoreline at the time of deposition of this formation cannot have been very far away to the north or NW (Fig. 31.6).

Locality 8. Newlands Farm (NS 276 044) : Newlands Formation, trilobites, brachiopods, other fossils, deeper water Early Silurian platformal assemblage (Fig. 31.4). Return to the road and drive down the hill for less than 0.5 km until the next farm access track to Newlands Farm will be seen on the left. This track is rather rough, twists a little where it crosses Glenwells Burn and will need to be taken carefully. Continue to the farm and park. Seek permission for access to the famous Newlands exposures. This will usually be given readily and directions indicated. Negotiate the gate immediately to the left of and down the side of the farm house and cross the field towards the NE almost following the contour of the slope, if anything climbing very slightly. At the far side of the field negotiate the fence by one of the trees there and you will find a small burn, sometimes dry, set in a small but steep-sided valley with a number of exposures on the far

433

Fig. 31.6

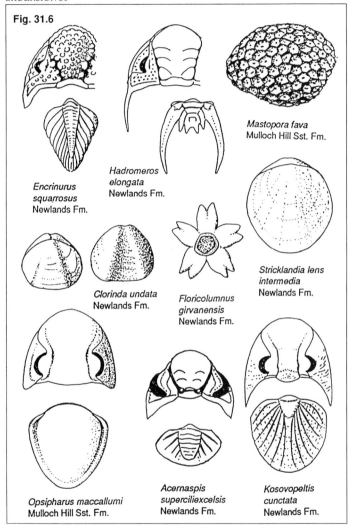

Encrinurus
squarrosus
Newlands Fm.

Hadromeros
elongata
Newlands Fm.

Mastopora fava
Mulloch Hill Sst. Fm.

Clorinda undata
Newlands Fm.

Floricolumnus
girvanensis
Newlands Fm.

Stricklandia lens
intermedia
Newlands Fm.

Opsipharus maccallumi
Mulloch Hill Sst. Fm.

Acernaspis
superciliexcelsis
Newlands Fm.

Kosovopeltis
cunctata
Newlands Fm.

Figure 31.6. A selection of trilobites and other fossils from various horizons in the Silurian strata of the Girvan district.

bank {NS 278 046}.

This is the classical and well-known 'Newlands' locality and the Newlands Formation is of Lower Silurian, Middle Llandovery (Aeronian) age. The rock in the exposures, when unweathered, is a hard, massive, blue-grey calcareous siltstone from which fossils are difficult to see, let alone extract, but fortunately much of it is deeply weathered here and it has been converted largely into a softer, ochreous brown rock in which the beautifully preserved fossil moulds are very obvious as they are coated with a bright yellow residue. Again, both internal and external moulds should be kept if collections are being made (see Locality 7). Trilobites are rather more common than brachiopods here and a number of species can usually be collected in a fairly short time. *Acernaspis superciliexcelsis*, *Encrinurus squarrosus*, *Calymene ubiquitosus*, *Kosovopeltis cunctata* and *Hadromeros elongatus* are usually the forms found with greatest regularity. The entire trilobite fauna has recently been thoroughly documented by Howells (1982). Of the brachiopods, the pentamerids *Clorinda undata* and *Stricklandia lens intermedia* are probably the most frequently found forms but several other species occur. The association indicates a deeper water, more offshore environment than the Lower Llandovery Mulloch Hill Sandsone (Locality 7)(see Cocks and Toghill 1973) but still within the photic zone as indicated by the occasional occurrence of the calcareous alga *Mastopora fava*. Corals are rarer than in the Mulloch Hill Sandstone but the strange-looking star-shaped crinoid columnal *Floricolumnus girvanensis* is quite common (see Donovan & Clark 1992) (Fig. 31.6).

Return to the farm and drive back to the minor road. Turn left and follow the road down the hill for less than 1 km to the road junction at the old coal mining settlement of Wallacetown. Turn right and follow this road which, although unclassified around Wallacetown, soon becomes confluent with the B741 and leads back to the A77 trunk road just north of Girvan, a distance of about 9 or 10 km.

BAILEY, E.B., and McCALLIEN, W.J. 1957. The Ballantrae serpentinite, Ayrshire. *Trans. Edinb. Geol. Soc.* **17,** 33-53.

BALSILLIE, D. 1932. The Ballantrae Igneous complex, south Ayrshire. *Geol. Mag.* **69,** 107-131.

BERGSTROM, S. M. 1990. Biostratigraphic and biogeographic significance of Middle and Upper Ordovician conodonts in the Girvan succession, south-west Scotland. *Courier Forsch.-Inst. Senckenberg.,* **118,** 1-43, 4 pls.

BLOXAM T.W and ALLEN, J.B. 1960. Glaucophane schist, eclogite and associated rocks from Knockormal in the Girvan-Ballantrae Complex, south Ayrshire. *Trans. R. Soc. Edinb.* **64,** 1-27.

BLUCK, B.J. 1982. Hyalotuff deltaic deposits in the Ballantrae ophiolite of S.W. Scotland: evidence for the crustal position of the lava sequence. *Trans R. Soc. Edinb. Earth Sci.* **72,** 217-228.

_____ 1983. Rôle of the Midland Valley of Scotland in the Caledonian Orogeny. *Trans. R. Soc. Edinburgh: Earth Sciences,* **74,** 119-136.

_____ 1985. The Scottish paratectonic Caledonides. *Scott .J. Geol.* **21,** 437-464.

_____ and HALLIDAY, A.N. 1981. Comment and reply on age and origin of the Ballantrae ophiolite and its significance to the Caledonian Orogeny and the Ordovician time-scale. *Geology,* **10,** 331-333.

_____ HALLIDAY, A.N., AFTALION, M., and MACINTYRE, R.M. 1980. Age and origin of the Ballantrae Complex and its significance to the Caledonian orogeny and the Ordovician time scale . *Geology* **8,** 492-495.

CHATTERTON, B. D. E and LUDVIGSEN, R. 1976. Silicified Middle Ordovician trilobites from the South Nahanni River area, District of Mackenzie, Canada. *Palaeontogr., Abt. A,* **167,** 77-119, pls 9-24.

CHURCH, W.R. and GAYER, R.A. 1973. The Ballantrae ophiolite. *Geol. Mag.* **110,** 497-510.

COCKS, L. R. M. and TOGHILL, P. 1973. The biostratigraphy of the Silurian rocks of the Girvan district, Scotland. *J. Geol. Soc. London,* **129,** 209-243.

DEMPSTER, T.J. and BLUCK, B.J. 1991. The age and tectonic significance of the Bute amphibolite, Highland Border Complex, Scotland. *Geol. Mag.* **128,** 77-80.

DEWEY, J.F. 1969. Evolution of the Appalachian/Caledonian orogen. *Nature* **222,** 124-129.

_____ 1974. The geology of the southern terminations of the Caledonides, *in* Nairn, A, (ed) *The ocean basins and their margins. Vol. 2 The North Atlantic.* 205-231. New York

DONOVAN, S. K. and CLARK, N. D. L. 1992. Unusual crinoid columnals from the Llandovery of England and Wales. *Palaeontology* **35** (in press).

DUNNING, G.R. and KROGH, T.E. 1985. Geochronology of ophiolites of the Newfoundland Appalachians. *Canadian Journ. Earth. Sci.* **22,** 1659-1670.

HARPER, D. A. T. 1981. The stratigraphy and faunas of the Upper Ordovician

High Mains Formation of the Girvan district. *Scott. J. Geol.*, **17**, 247-255.

_____ 1982. The stratigraphy of the Drummuck Group (Ashgill), Girvan. *Geol. J.*, **17**, 251-277.

_____ 1984. Brachiopods from the upper Ardmillan succession (Ordovician) of the Girvan district, Scotland. Part I. *Palaeontogr. Soc. [Monogr.], London.* 1-78, pls 1-11.

_____ 1989. Brachiopods from the upper Ardmillan succession (Ordovician) of the Girvan district, Scotland. Part 2. *Palaeontogr. Soc. [Monogr.], London.* 79-128, pls 12-22.

HENDERSON, S. M. K. 1935. Ordovician submarine disturbances in the Girvan district. *Trans. R. Soc. Edinburgh*, **58**, 487-509, 4 pls.

HOWELLS, Y. 1982. Scottish Silurian trilobites. *Palaeontogr. Soc. [Monogr.], London.* 1-76, 15 pls.

HOLUB, F.V., KLAPOVA, H. BLUCK, B.J. and BOWES, D.R. 1984. Petrology and geochemistry of post-obduction dykes of the Ballantrae complex, SW Scotland. *Trans R.Soc. Edinb. Earth Sci.* **75**, 211-223.

HUGHES, C. P., INGHAM, J. K. and ADDISON, R. 1975. The morphology, classification and evolution of the Trinucleidae (Trilobita). *Phil. Trans. R. Soc. London, B*, **272**, 537-604.

INCE, D.M. 1984. Sedimentation and tectonism in the middle Ordovician of the Girvan district, SW Scotland. *Trans R.Soc.Edinb. Earth Sci.* **75**, 225-237.

INGHAM J. K. 1968. British and Swedish Ordovician species of *Cybeloides* (Trilobita). *Scott. J. Geol.*, **4**, 300-316, 2 pls.

_____ 1974. The Upper Ordovician trilobites from the Cautley and Dent districts of Westmorland and Yorkshire . Part 2. *Palaeontogr. Soc.[monogr.]* , 59-87, pls 10-18.

_____ 1978. Geology of a continental margin 2: middle and late Ordovician transgression, Girvan. *In* Bowes D. R. and Leake, B. E. (eds) Crustal evolution in northwestern Britain and adjacent regions. *Geol. J. Special Issue* **10**, 163-176.

_____ , CURRY, G. B. and Williams, A. 1986. Early Ordovician Dounans Limestone fauna, Highland Border Complex, Scotland. *Trans. R. Soc. Edinburgh: Earth Sciences*, **76** (4) (for 1985, publ. Feb.1986). 481-513.

_____ and TRIPP, R. P. 1991. The trilobite fauna of the Middle Ordovician Doularg Formation of the Girvan district, Scotland, and its palaeoenvironmental significance. *Trans. R. Soc. Edinburgh: Earth Sciences*, **82**, 27-54.

KELLEY, S. and BLUCK, B.J. 1989. Detrital mineral ages from the Southern Uplands using ^{40}A - ^{39}A laser probe. *J. Geol. Soc. Lond.* **146**, 401-404.

KIELAN - JAWOROWSKA, Z., BERGSTROM, J. and AHLBERG, P. 1991. Cheirurina (Trilobita) from the Upper Ordovician of Vastergotland and other regions of Sweden. *Geol. Foren. ; Stockholm Forhandl.*, **113**, 219-244.

LANE, P. D. 1971. British Cheiruridae (Trilobita). *Palaeontogr. Soc. [Monogr.], London.* 1-95, 16 pls.

LEWIS, A.D and BLOXAM, T.W. 1977. Petrotectonic environments of the Girvan-Ballantrae lavas from rare-earth element distributions. *Scott. J. Geol.* **13**,

211-222.

LONGMAN, C.D., BLUCK, B.J. and VAN BREEMEN, O. 1979. Ordovician conglomerates and the evolution of the Midland Valley. *Nature*, **280**, 578-581.

LUDVIGSEN, R. 1978. Middle Ordovician trilobite biofacies, southern Mackenzie Mountains. *In* Stelck, C. R. and Chatterton, B. D. E. [eds] Western and Arctic Canadian biostratigraphy. *Geol Assoc. Can., Spec. Pap.* **18.**

OWEN, A. W. 1986. The uppermost (Hirnantian) trilobites of Girvan, SW Scotland with a review of coeval trilobite faunas. *Trans. R. Soc. Edinburgh: Earth Sciences,* **77**, 231-239.

OWENS, R. M. 1973. British Ordovician and Silurian Proetidae (Trilobita). *Palaeontogr. Soc. [Monogr.], London* . 1-98, 15 pls.

PEACH, B.N. and HORNE, J. 1899. The Silurian rocks of Britain,1: Scotland *Mem Geol.Surv. U.K.*

REED, F. R. C. 1903-6. The Lower Palaeozoic trilobites of the Girvan district, Ayrshire. *Palaeontogr. Soc. [Monogr.], London*. Pt 1 (1903), 1-48, pls 1-6, Pt 2 (1904), 49-96, pls 7-13, Pt 3 (1906), 97-186, pls 14-20.

_____ 1914. The Lower Palaeozoic trilobites of Girvan. Supplement. *Palaeontogr. Soc. [Monogr.], London.* 1-56, 8 pls.

_____ 1917. The Ordovician and Silurian brachiopods of the Girvan district. *Trans. R. Soc. Edinburgh,* **51**, 795-998, 24 pls.

_____ 1931. The Lower Palaeozoic trilobites of Girvan. Supplement No 2. *Palaeontogr. Soc. [Monogr.], London.* 1-30.

_____ 1935. The Lower Palaeozoic trilobites of Girvan. Supplement No 3. *Palaeontogr. Soc. [Monogr.], London.* 1-64, 4 pls.

RUSHTON, A. W. A. and TRIPP,R. P. 1979. A fossiliferous lower Canadian (Tremadoc) boulder from the Benan Conglomerate of the Girvan district. *Scott. J. Geol.,* **15**, 321-327.

_____ , STONE, P., SMELLIE, J.L. and TUNNICLIFF, S.P. 1986. An early Arenig age for the Pinbain sequence of the Ballantrae Complex. *Scott. J. Geol.* **22**, 41-54.

SMELLIE, J.L. 1984. Accretionary lapilli and highly vesiculated pumice in the Ballantrae ophiolite complex: ashfall products from subaerial eruptions. *Rep.Br. Geol. Surv.* **16**, 36-40.

SPRAY, J.G. and WILLIAMS, G.D. 1980. The sub-ophiolite metamorphic rocks of the Ballantrae igneous complex, SW Scotland. *J.Geol. Soc.Lond.* **137**, 359-368.

STONE, P. 1984. Constraints on genetic models for the Ballantrae complex, SW Scotland. *Trans. R.Soc.Edinb. Earth Sci.* **75**, 189-191.

_____ ,and RUSHTON, A.W.A. 1983. Graptolite faunas from the Ballantrae ophiolite complex and their structural implications. *Scott. J. Geol.* **19** 297-310.

_____ , and SMELLIE, J.L. 1988. *Classical areas of British geology: The Ballan-trae area: a description of the solid geology of parts of 1:25 000 sheets NX 08, 18 and 19.* (London: HMSO for British Geological Survey.) B.G.S.

THIRLWALL, M.F. and BLUCK, B.J. 1984. Sr-Nd isotope and geological evidence that the Ballantrae "ophiolite", SW Scotland is polygenetic. in Gass,

I.G., Lippard, S.J., and Shelton, A.W. (eds) *Ophiolites and oceanic lithosphere*. *Spec. Pub. Geol. Soc. Lond*. No **13**, 215-230.

TOGHILL, P. 1970. Highest Ordovician (Hartfell Shales) graptolite faunas from the Moffat area, south Scotland. *Bull. Brit. Mus. nat. Hist. (Geol.)*, **19**, 1-26, 16 pls.

TRELOAR, P.J., BLUCK,B.J., BOWES, D.R. and DUDEK,A. 1980. Hornblende-garnet metapyroxenite beneath serpentinite in the Ballantrae complex of S.W.Scotland, and its bearing on the depth of provenance of obducted ocean lithosphere. *Trans. R. Soc. Edinb. Earth Sci*. **71**, 201-212.

TRENCH, A., BLUCK, B. J. and WATTS D. R. 1988. Palaeomagnetic studies within the Ballantrae Ophiolite; southwest Scotland: magnetotectonic and regional tectonic implications. *Earth and Planetary Science Letters*, **90**, 431-448.

TRIPP, R. P. 1954. Caradocian trilobites from mudstones at Craighead Quarry, near Girvan, Ayrshire. *Trans. R. Soc. Edinburgh*, **62**, 655-693, 4 pls.

_____ 1962. Trilobites from the *confinis* Flags (Ordovician) of the Girvan district, Ayrshire. *Trans. R. Soc. Edinburgh*, **65**, 1-40, 4 pls.

_____ 1965. Trilobites of the Albany division (Ordovician) of the Girvan district, Ayrshire. *Palaeontology*, **8**, 577-603, pls 80-83.

_____ 1967. Trilobites of the upper Stinchar Limestone (Ordovician) of the Girvan district, Ayrshire. *Trans. R. Soc. Edinburgh*, **67**, 43-93, 6 pls.

_____ 1976. Trilobites from the basal *superstes* Mudstones (Ordovician) at Aldons Quarry, near Girvan, Ayrshire. *Trans. R. Soc. Edinburgh*, **69**, 369-423, 7 pls.

_____ 1979. Trilobites from the Ordovician Auchensoul and Stinchar Limestones of the Girvan district, Strathclyde. *Palaeontology*, **22**, 37-40, pls 37-40.

_____ 1980a. Trilobites from the Ordovician Balclatchie and lower Ardwell groups of the Girvan district, Scotland. *Trans. R. Soc. Edinburgh: Earth Sciences*, **71**, 147-157, 1 pl.

_____ 1980b. Trilobites from the Ordovician Ardwell Group of the Craighead Inlier, Girvan district, Scotland. *Trans. R. Soc. Edinburgh: Earth Sciences*, **71**, 123-145, 4 pls.

WILLIAMS, A. 1959. A structural history of the Girvan district,SW Ayrshire. *Trans. R. Soc. Edinburgh*, **63**, 629-667.

_____ 1962. The Barr and lower Ardmillan Series (Caradoc) of the Girvan District, south-west Ayshire, with description of the Brachiopoda. *Mem. Geol. Soc. London*, **3**, 1-267, 25 pls.

WILLIAMS, S. H. 1987. Upper Ordovician graptolites from the *D. complanatus* Zone of the Moffat and Girvan districts and their significance for correlation. *Scott. J. Geol.* **23**, 65-92.

WILKINSON, J.M. and CANN, J.R. 1974. Trace elements and tectonic relationships of basaltic rocks in the Ballantrae igneous complex, Ayrshire. *Geol Mag.* **111**, 35-41.

Excursion 32 DOB'S LINN
S. Henry Williams and James D. Lawson

Themes: Upper Ordovician and Lower Silurian graptolites and the
international stratotype section of the Ordovician-Silurian
boundary.

Features: Fossils: black shales: metabentonites: faults: inverted strata:
landslip.

Maps: O.S.   1 : 50 000   Sheet 79   Hawick & Eskdale
B.G.S. 1 : 63 360   Sheet 16   Moffat
1 : 50 000   Sheet 16E Ettrick (drift)

Terrain: Steep grassy and scree-covered slopes plus a few narrow
stream crossings. Care should be taken on unstable,
slippery rock if venturing up to the higher localities.

Distance   A short walk (approximately 1 km): 2 hours minimum on
and Time: exposure.

Access: Dob's Linn is on National Trust land and is also part of the
Moffat Hills **SSSI**. Although collection of a few specimens,
particularly from scree, poses no problem, permission
should be sought before extracting large amounts of
material.

Historical background

The name "Dob's Linn" is derived from a 17th Century covenanter
named Dobson, who used a ledge by the waterfall in the Linn Branch
to hide from government forces. Graptolites were first recorded from
Dob's Linn over one hundred years ago, although the earliest
publications describing species from the Moffat Shale Group paid
little or no attention to their potential stratigraphic importance.
Furthermore, despite attempts by several eminent scientists of the
day, the structurally complex region of the Southern Uplands still
defied satisfactory geological interpretation. In 1864 Charles Lapworth
was offered a teaching post connected with the Episcopal Church at
Galashiels. He had no formal geological training, but soon developed
an interest in the local geology of the Southern Uplands. Over the
following years he mapped large tracts of land, and made detailed
collections of graptolites from the Moffat Shale at a number of critical
localities. The classic summary of Lapworth's work was published in

1878; in this article he established beyond doubt the precise, ordered change in graptolite assemblages through the sequence of black and grey shales, and demonstrated unequivocally the value of graptolites in understanding the geology of a complex succession of Lower Palaeozoic strata. Lapworth's work in southern Scotland, both in the Moffat region and at Girvan, received widespread recognition: in 1875 he was appointed Assistant Master at Madras College, St. Andrews; then in 1881 was elected to the Chair of Geology at Mason College, Birmingham, which subsequently became the University of Birmingham.

Most of Lapworth's new species were first described by Elles and Wood (1901-18), whose work he supervised. Following this major publication, no taxonomic or stratigraphic work was done at Dob's Linn for half a century, with the exception of Davies (1929) who included material from the locality in his revision of certain Upper Ordovician and Lower Silurian graptolites.

The dearth of publications was broken by Packham in 1962, who utilised specimens from the Birkhill Shale in an evolutionary study of Lower Silurian diplograptids. Following this, Toghill published several papers listing revised zonal assemblages for the Birkhill Shale (1968 a & b), and giving taxonomic descriptions and illustrations of graptolites from the top Lower Hartfell Shale and Upper Hartfell Shale (1970). Following several years of critical study, Ingham published a completely new geological map of Dob's Linn in 1979. Ingham's mapping permitted intensive collecting of the graptolite fauna from continuous sections: a series of papers was published by Williams which included taxonomic descriptions of the late Ordovician and earliest Silurian faunas, and biostratigraphic revision of the top Lower Hartfell to basal Birkhill Shale (Williams 1982a, 1982b, 1983; Williams and Ingham 1987). This work confirmed Lapworth's faith in graptolites as a critical biostratigraphic tool, and resulted in more precise definition of the zonal boundaries.

Geological setting

Dob's Linn lies within the central part of the Southern Uplands. This region is dominated by a monotonous series of mostly Silurian **greywackes** referred to the Gala Greywacke. These are underlain by the Upper Ordovician and Lower Silurian Moffat Shale Group, which is exposed in a series of elongate, E-W faulted inliers formed by imbricate thrusting. Owing to the relatively soft nature of the shale, the inliers normally form steep-sided gorges, the most spectacular in the Moffat region being those at Hartfell Spa and Craigmichan Scaurs. Although slightly less impressive, the section at Dob's Linn preserves the most complete succession through the Moffat Shale, and is more readily accessible than the other inliers. Strangely, the base of the Moffat Shale is nowhere seen in the central Southern Uplands, although older strata, including Lower Ordovician **cherts** and pillow lavas, are exposed to the north.

The Moffat Shale Group is composed of a black shale-dominated sequence, now generally considered to have been deposited within the Iapetus Ocean which separated England and Wales from Scotland during the Ordovician before closing in the Silurian. It is interesting to note that shales, greywackes and graptolites almost identical to those of the Southern Uplands are found in central Newfoundland in eastern Canada, providing evidence that the two areas were once in close proximity before the opening of the present day Atlantic during the Mesozoic.

The Moffat Shale Group is divided into four formations: the Glenkiln Shale, Lower Hartfell Shale, Upper Hartfell Shale and Birkhill Shale. The Glenkiln Shale is composed of an unknown thickness of pale grey and black, commonly siliceous, shales and cherts. At Dob's Linn the formation is poorly exposed and generally unfossiliferous, even the black shales rarely yielding identifiable graptolites. Better, more fossiliferous sections are present at Glenkiln Burn and Craigmichan Scaurs. The lower part of the Glenkiln Shale belongs to the Llandeilo-Caradoc *Nemagraptus gracilis* Zone, while the upper part has traditionally been assigned to the *Climacograptus peltifer* Zone. Many graptolite workers now consider it doubtful whether this second zone may be distinguished faunally from the following *Climacograptus wilsoni* Zone of the Lower Hartfell Shale, and the two are often combined into one *Diplograptus multidens* Zone in the U.K. outside of southern Scotland. The Glenkiln Shale apparently passes gradationally into the almost continuously black Lower Hartfell Shale, which yields a far more abundant graptolite fauna and is over 20 m thick. The amount of chert decreases upwards thoughout the unit which is made up predominantly of black shale in the top 5 m. Following the *C.wilsoni* Zone, the *Dicranograptus clingani* and *Pleurograptus linearis* zones are represented, the Caradoc-Ashgill boundary probably falling within the latter.

The overlying Upper Hartfell Shale is composed mainly of non-graptolitic, pale grey-green shales and mudstones 28 m thick. Its lower boundary is marked by a transitional 3 cm interval of alternating pale grey and black shale laminae. Three groups of graptolitic black shale bands occur within the formation, named the Complanatus, Anceps and Extraordinarius Bands after their diagnostic zonal assemblages, indicative of the *Dicellograptus complanatus, Dicellograptus anceps*, and *Climacograptus extraordinarius* zones respectively. The *D. anceps* Zone has been divided recently into two subzones, namely the *Dicellograptus complexus* and *Paraorthograptus pacificus* subzones, which have proved useful in international correlation. The 43 m of Birkhill Shale is composed almost entirely of black, continuously graptolitic shale and mudstone in the lower part. The shales become progressively siltier, less fissile and paler towards the top of the formation, culminating in a transition to coarse turbidites of the overlying Gala Greywacke Group. The lowest part of the Birkhill Shale belongs to the uppermost Ordovician *Glyptograptus persculptus* Zone, while the base of the *Parakidograptus acuminatus* Zone of the earliest Silurian falls at 1.6 m above the boundary with the Upper Hartfell Shale. The significance of this boundary is discussed in the next section. The remainder of the Birkhill Shale is divided into a number of graptolite zones, the boundary with the Gala Greywacke falling within the *Rastrites maximus* Zone.

The Ordovician-Silurian Boundary Stratotype

The Ordovician System was introduced by Lapworth in 1879, in a successful attempt to solve the mid-19th Century debate between Sedgwick and Murchison; Lapworth established his stratigraphy primarily through the use of graptolites. During the 1960's it was recognised that despite most systems of the Geological Time Scale having been in international use for the past century, none had been properly defined.

In order to rectify this situation, the International Union of Geological Sciences (IUGS) established a Commission on Stratigraphy, who in turn set up a number of working groups to study the system boundaries and make recommendations regarding an international stratotype section for each. It was considered that any boundary stratotype should include an unbroken, continuously fossiliferous section across the relevant interval, have ease of access and the potential for palaeomagnetic, geochemical and radiometric studies. Once a stratotype had been decided, an imaginary "golden spike" would be placed at the exact horizon and locality marking the defined, internationally-accepted boundary. The Ordovician-Silurian Boundary Working Group was established in 1974 to formally define the stratigraphic level and boundary stratotype location for the base of the Silurian System. During the next decade it received over fifty reports from geologists around the world (see Cocks and Rickards 1988); following much discussion, the choice for stratotype was narrowed down to two sections, namely Anticosti Island in eastern Canada, with a boundary based on **conodonts**, and Dob's Linn in southern Scotland, with a boundary defined using graptolites. Although both were well studied, richly fossiliferous and relatively complete, neither section provided a perfect candidate for the boundary stratotype. The succession on Anticosti Island is an essentially undeformed, shallow-marine limestone sequence rich in shelly macrofossils (e.g. trilobites and brachiopods) and conodonts, but with few graptolites. Dob's Linn is an oceanic shale sequence rich in graptolites, but with only rare examples of other fossils, and is structurally complex. Objections to choosing Dob's Linn as stratotype included the sparsity of non-graptolitic faunas (with only rare conodonts, trilobites and inarticulate brachiopods), and inadequacy for palaeomagnetic studies, while those against Anticosti Island included the likely presence of undetected breaks in a shallow marine sequence and difficulty of precise correlation with many Ordovician-Silurian boundary sequences. Following a series of formal ballots, Dob's Linn was finally ratified as the stratotype by the IUGS in 1985.

The Ordovician-Silurian boundary had historically been considered to lie at the base of the Birkhill Shale. This was, however, considered to be an unsuitable horizon at which to place a chronostratigraphic boundary, owing to a lithological change from unfossiliferous grey mudstone to graptolitic black shale and lack of major evolution in the graptolite fauna. The "golden spike" was thus placed at the base of the *P. acuminatus* Zone, 1.6 m above the base of the Birkhill Shale in the Linn Branch section. This horizon is recognised by the first occurrence of *Akidograptus ascensus* and associated species, an event which may be correlated accurately in many sections around the world. A summary paper on Dob's Linn as stratotype was published by Williams (1988).

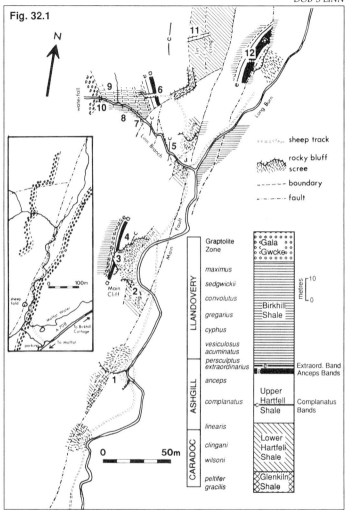

Figure 32.1. Locality map and geological succession of Dob's Linn (after Williams 1980, fig. 1).

Itinerary

To get to Dob's Linn, travel to Moffat via the A74, then take the A708 Selkirk road from the town centre. The road travels along the side of the glaciated and U-shaped valley of the Moffat Water; the present small stream is a misfit which meanders around the broad valley floor, sometimes splitting and rejoining to give a braided pattern. There are also hanging valleys, the most famous and spectacular being at the Grey Mare's Tail with its lofty waterfall. Proceed 1 km beyond the Grey Mare's Tail car park, which is 16 km (10 miles) from Moffat, to a double lay-by on the left-hand side of the road, (NT 196 154) from where the gorge in black shale and greywacke is clearly visible. If time allows, it is worth making a "pilgrimage" to Birkhill Cottage, another 0.5 km (500 yds) further at the highest point of the road. This is where Lapworth stayed during his fieldwork, and a plaque commemorating his work has been erected on the cottage wall.

From the lay-by, follow the poorly-defined sheep track into the bottom of the valley, then northwards for about 150 m (Fig.32 1). The first black shale scree slope traversed is derived from faulted Birkhill Shale.

Locality 1. Glenkiln Shale. Proceed to a small but prominent bluff which the track crosses after dividing; just to the left of this, under a thin cover of scree, is the only fair-sized exposure of Glenkiln Shale at Dob's Linn. It is not, however, recommended to stop here before visiting the other localities, as graptolites are difficult to find and poorly preserved due to the rather pale, cherty lithology. It might be worth collecting from this stop after seeing the other outcrops, when specimens of *Dicellograptus, Dicranograptus, Climacograptus* and *Orthograptus* may be found (Fig 32. 2).

Locality 2. Main Cliff : Lower Hartfell Shale. The first recommended stop is at the Main Cliff. Before studying the shales in detail, follow the track over to the right-hand bank of the stream and look across at the exposure, largely hidden by scree on the lower slopes. Note how the black Lower Hartfell Shale at the base, and Birkhill Shale at the top are separated by the paler grey Upper Hartfell Shale. At this locality the strata are dipping at about 45^0 and are the correct way up, while at all other parts of Dob's Linn the strata are dipping at a high angle and are inverted. The explanation is that the whole of the Main Cliff

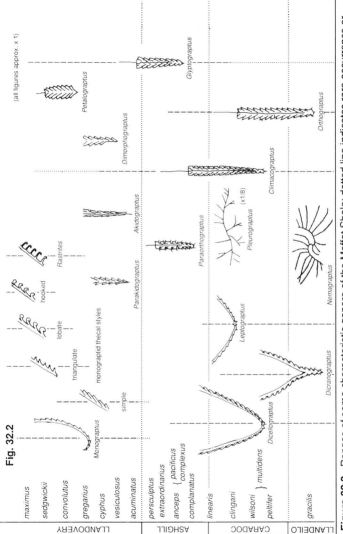

Figure 32.2. Ranges of some characteristic genera of the Moffat Shale: dotted line indicates rare occurrence or range recorded from elsewhere (after Williams 1980, fig. 2). All drawings approximately ×1 unless otherwise stated.

447

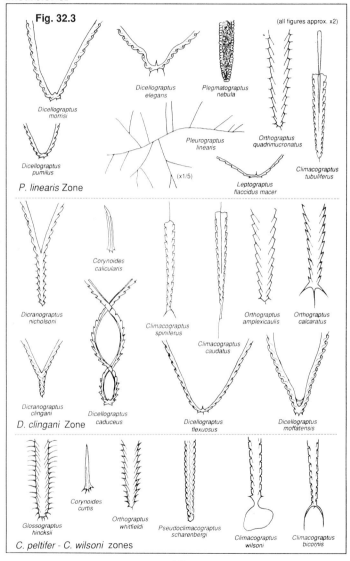

Fig. 32.3

(all figures approx. x2)

P. linearis Zone

Dicellograptus morrisi

Dicellograptus pumilus

Dicellograptus elegans

Plegmatograptus nebula

Pleurograptus linearis (x1/5)

Leptograptus flaccidus macer

Orthograptus quadrimucronatus

Climacograptus tubuliferus

D. clingani Zone

Dicranograptus nicholsoni

Dicranograptus clingani

Corynoides calicularis

Dicellograptus caduceus

Climacograptus spiniferus

Climacograptus caudatus

Dicellograptus flexuosus

Orthograptus amplexicaulis

Orthograptus calcaratus

Dicellograptus moffatensis

C. peltifer - C. wilsoni zones

Glossograptus hincksii

Corynoides curtis

Orthograptus whitfieldi

Pseudoclimacograptus scharenbergi

Climacograptus wilsoni

Climacograptus bicornis

448

slumped and rotated during the Pleistocene; it is not a tectonic feature as assumed by early workers. The succession is heavily faulted, so detailed measured sections may only be constructed with extreme care. Now proceed to the lowest bluff just above the stream. This belongs to the *Dicranograptus clingani* Zone of the Lower Hartfell Shale and contains a fauna including *Dicellograptus* (*D. caduceus, D. flexuosus, D. moffatensis*), *Dicranograptus* (*D. clingani, D. nicholsoni, D. ramosus,*), *Climacograptus* (*C. caudatus, C. spiniferus*), *Orthograptus* (*O. amplexicaulis, O. calcaratus*) and the strange graptolite genus *Corynoides* (*C. calicularis*). (Fig. 32. 3).

Just above this is a second, slightly hollowed-out exposure.This belongs to the upper part of the *Pleurograptus linearis* Zone, and contains *P.linearis, Leptograptus* (*L. capillaris, L. flaccidus macer,*) *Dicellograptus* (*D. carruthersi, D. elegans, D. morrisi, D. pumilus*), *Climacograptus* (*C. mohawkensis, C. tubuliferus*) *Orthograptus* (*O. amplexicaulis, O. calcaratus basilicus, O. pauperatus, O. quadrimucronatus*) and *Plegmatograptus nebula,* but no *Dicranograptus* or *Corynoides* (Fig. 32.4).

Locality 3. Main Cliff: Anceps Bands. Climb the scree to the exposure of black shale and cream **metabentonites** in the top of the Upper Hartfell Shale. These are the five groups of Anceps Bands of the *Dicellograptus anceps* Zone, numbered A to E, and contain abundant *Dicellograptus* (*D. anceps, D. complexus, D. minor*), *Climacograptus* (*C. latus, C. longispinus supernus, C. miserabilis*), *Orthograptus* (*O. abbreviatus, O. fastigatus*) and *Pseudoplegmatograptus craticulus.* The three upper groups of bands C to E additionally contain *Paraorthograptus pacificus,* while the top band E yields rare specimens of *Dicellograptus ornatus* and *Climacograptus ? extraordinarius* (Fig. 32. 4.). These and other species have permitted the division of the *D. anceps* Zone into a lower *Dicellograptus complexus* Subzone (Bands A and B) and an upper *Paraorthograptus pacificus* Subzone (Bands C to E). This allows accurate correlation of this part of the succession with that of the Soviet Union, North America, China and Australia. The occurrence of metabentonites indicates the presence of volcanic activity during deposition of the shales. The top Anceps Bands are repeated by strike faulting before the Birkhill Shale is entered. Only the *Glyptograptus persculptus* and *Parakidograptus acuminatus* zones are easily accessible on the Main

Figure 32.3. Schematic figures illustrating some of the characteristic Upper Ordovician graptolites found at Dob's Linn.

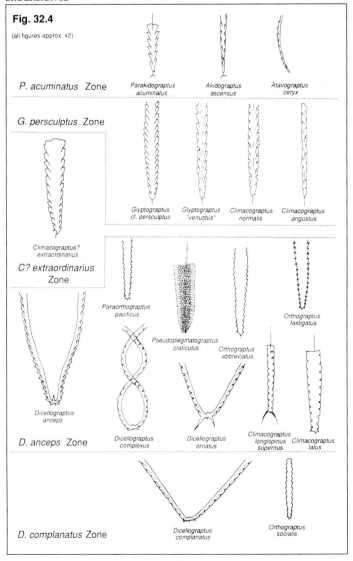

Fig. 32.4

(all figures approx. x2)

P. acuminatus Zone

Parakidograptus acuminatus

Akidograptus ascensus

Atavograptus ceryx

G. persculptus Zone

Glyptograptus cf. *persculptus*

Glyptograptus "*venustus*"

Climacograptus normalis

Climacograptus angustus

Climacograptus? extraordinarius

C? extraordinarius Zone

Paraorthograptus pacificus

Pseudoplegmatograptus craticulus

Orthograptus abbreviatus

Orthograptus fastigatus

Dicellograptus anceps

D. anceps Zone

Dicellograptus complexus

Dicellograptus ornatus

Climacograptus longispinus supernus

Climacograptus latus

D. complanatus Zone

Dicellograptus complanatus

Orthograptus socialis

450

Cliff.

The basal 1.6 m. of Birkhill Shale belong to the latest Ordovician *G. persculptus* Zone. It yields a low-density fauna consisting entirely of diplograptids, including *Glyptograptus* (*G. avitus, G.* cf. *persculptus* "*G. venustus*"), and *Climacograptus* (*C. angustus, C. normalis*), but no *Dicellograptus* or any of the other genera present in the *D. anceps* Zone (Fig. 32. 2). The following basal Silurian *P. acuminatus* Zone contains a similar fauna to that of the *G.persculptus* Zone, but is distinguished by the incoming of *Akidograptus ascensus, Parakidograptus acuminatus* and the earliest monograptid (*Atavograptus ceryx*). (Fig. 32.4).

Locality 4. Main Cliff : Complanatus Bands. Now cross the scree of the Main Cliff without descending to the bottom. If a little time is spent, it should be possible to find the two black Complanatus Bands of the *Dicellograptus complanatus* Zone, bounded by pale grey shale. These contain *Dicellograptus* (*D. complanatus, D. minor*), *Climacograptus* (*C. miserabilis , C. tubiliferus* and *Orthograptus socialis* (Fig. 32. 4), together with a relatively common inarticulate brachiopod *Barbatulella lacunosa* in both the black and grey shale. The bands are seen more easily in the Linn Branch (Locality 5), but at that locality are almost impossible to collect.

Locality 5. Proceed to where the main stream divides and turn into the left hand tributary, the Linn Branch. The first exposures of black shale in the hollow on the left bank of the stream belong to the *D. clingani* and *P. linearis* zones and contain similar faunas to those seen at Locality 2. Just upstream from this, the two Complanatus Bands seen at Locality 4 may be observed at the back of an excavation in the stream bank. These should not, however, be collected owing to their **very limited outcrop**.

Locality 6. Climb up the track to the trench visible from the junction of the Linn Branch and Long Burn (see Fig. 32.5). This Linn Branch trench is the least tectonically disturbed section through the top of the Upper Hartfell Shale and basal Birkhill Shale, and is the stratotype section for the Ordovician-Silurian boundary (Fig. 32.6). The Anceps Bands contain the same fauna described from Locality 3. Midway between the top Anceps Band and the base of the Birkhill Shale

Figure 32.4. Schematic figures illustrating some of the characteristic Upper Ordovician and Lower Silurian graptolites found at Dob's Linn.

451

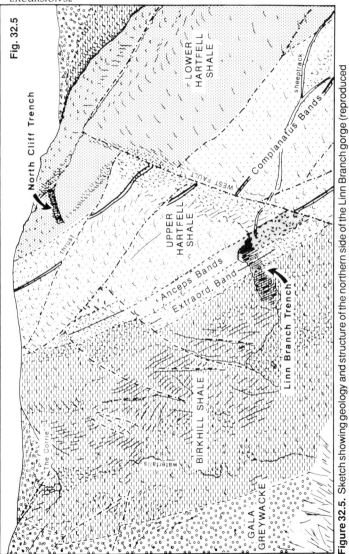

Figure 32.5. Sketch showing geology and structure of the northern side of the Linn Branch gorge (reproduced from Williams 1988, fig. 3, by permission of the Trustees of the British Museum, Natural History).

(remember that the strata are inverted and young upstream) is a narrow dark brown band. Rare diplograptids occur on one lamina of this Extraordinarius Band, including *Climacograptus? extraordinarius* (Fig.32.4), indicating the *Climacograptus? extraordinarius* Zone; no other graptolites are present. The late Ordovician graptolite mass extinction, which almost resulted in the complete extinction of the group, therefore occurred sometime between the deposition of Anceps Band E and of the Extraordinarius Band. Just below the Extraordinarius Band, in a conchoidally-fracturing calcareous mudstone, rare fragments of a blind mucronaspid trilobite have been found. The lack of eyes presumably indicates a mode of life in deep water below the photic zone. Following along the trench upstream, the basal Birkhill Shale is encountered, beginning in the *G. persculptus* Zone. The base of the *P. acuminatus* Zone, marking the "golden spike" for the Ordovician-Silurian boundary, occurs at 1.6 m above the base of the Birkhill Shale, with a faunal assemblage as described for Locality 3. The full thickness of the *P. acuminatus* Zone (about 5 m of black shale with thin metabentonites or "claystones") occurs here and should be searched thoroughly for the small and slender proximal ends of the zone fossil (Fig. 32. 4.). The *Cystograptus vesiculous* Zone follows, but is only 1.3 m thick and difficult to distinguish; it is worth looking for the zone index fossil (Fig. 32. 8), but otherwise this interval is best considered with the *Coronograptus cyphus* Zone and studied in the stream below. The general evolutionary changes in the Silurian graptolite fauna discussed here and in localities 7 to 10 are summarised in Figure 32. 2, while some of the most characteristic species are shown in Figures 32. 8 and 32.9. A more detailed stratigraphical description of the Lower Silurian interval with species ranges is provided by Toghill (1968a, 1968b).

Locality 7. cyphus Zone. The Linn Branch burn provides a continuous section from the *P. acuminatus* to *R. maximus* zones, but most zonal boundaries are not easily recognisable. It is wisest, therefore, to collect from the central body of each zone at the numbered localities (Figure 32.7).

The graptolite assemblages from Locality 7 in the *C. cyphus* Zone (7.3 m of black shale) display the general characteristics of the *C. vesiculosus - C. cyphus* interval, i.e. the common occurrence of monograptids with simple thecae (e.g. *C.cyphus*) and some with gently sigmoid thecae (e.g. *Atavograptus atavus,*. The distinctive

453

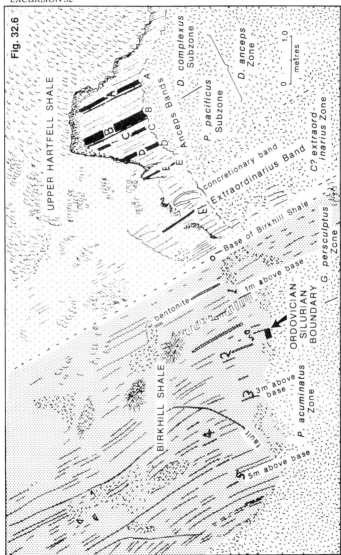

Figure 32.6. Sketch of Linn Branch trench (reproduced from Williams 1988, fig. 4, by permission of the Trustees of the British Museum, Natural History).

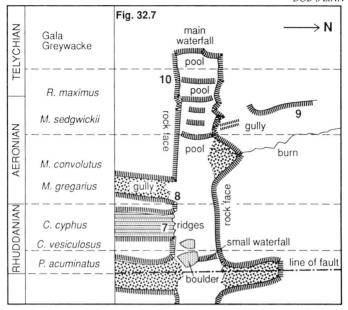

Figure 32.7. Geological sketch map showing localities and approximate positions of Lower Silurian graptolite zones in the sides and stream bed of the Linn Branch burn.

dimorphograptids with their short uniserial portion occur at this level but are not easy to find, although examples of the diplograptid genus *Climacograptus* are relatively common.

Locality 8. gregarius and convolutus Zones. The general characteristics of the middle Llandovery *Coronograptus gregarius* and *Monograptus convolutus* zones can be discussed together in terms of their general characteristics. The *C. gregarius* Zone comprises 7.9 m of black shale with thick nodular claystones and is best collected at Locality 9. The *M. convolutus* Zone is 5.35 m thick, and is represented by two intervals of richly fossiliferous black shale separated by barren grey mudstones; it can be seen at Locality 10 and on the opposite side of the gully. Monograptids with triangulate thecae (e.g. *Monograptus triangulatus* in the *C. gregarius* Zone, and *M. convolutus* in the *M.*

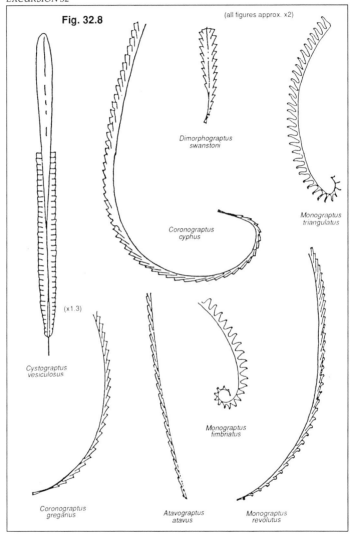

Fig. 32.8

(all figures approx. x2)

Dimorphograptus swanstoni

Monograptus triangulatus

Coronograptus cyphus

(x1.3)

Cystograptus vesiculosus

Monograptus fimbriatus

Coronograptus gregarius

Atavograptus atavus

Monograptus revolutus

Figure 32.8. Illustrations of some characterisitic Lower Silurian graptolites found at Dob's Linn (adapted from Webb *et al.* in press).

convolutus Zone) become common in these strata. *Petalograptus* appears at this level and is relatively abundant on some bedding planes. At the base of the *M. convolutus* Zone, monograptids with lobate thecae (e.g. *Monograptus lobiferus* and *M. clingani*) appear and are fairly common. *Climacograptus* specimens are noticeably rarer than in previous zones, (Fig. 32. 9).

Locality 9. sedgwickii and **maximus Zones.** The youngest characteristic graptolitic interval present at Dob's Linn comprises the *Monograptus sedwickii* and *Rastrites maximus* zones. The *M. sedwickii* Zone is 8.4m thick, with 2 m of black shale sandwiched between lower and upper units of barren, grey mudstones. The *R. maximus* Zone is 6.55 m thick, composed mostly of grey mudstones and fine greywackes with a number of fossiliferous black shale bands. Locality 9 in the *M. sedwickii* Zone shows the main characteristics of this division. Monograptids with hooked thecae (mostly *M. sedwickii)* become common, although triangulate forms still occur in the basal layers and monograptids with simple thecae (e.g. *Pristiograptus regularis*) persist (Fig. 32.9).

Locality 10. Gala Greywacke. Here the gradational transition from the Birkhill Shale to the Gala Greywacke occurs. It falls within the *R. maximus* Zone, the black shale bands yielding hooked, triangulate and simple monograptids, together with species of *Rastrites* which have long, isolate thecae.

Locality 11. North Cliff trench : Lower Hartfell Shale. If time and energy allow, it is worth visiting the final two localities, although care must be exercised on the rather steep slopes. Locality 11 may be reached by climbing up the scree-filled gully on the down-stream side of the Linn Branch trench, or via the scree and grass-covered slopes above the junction of the Linn Branch and Long Burn (see Fig. 32.5). The North Cliff trench exposes the only unfaulted section through the *P. linearis* and top *D. clingani* zones, with faunal assemblages as described for Locality 2. The boundary between the two zones is approximately marked by the line of a possible old trench excavated along strike.

Locality 12. Long Burn : Anceps Bands. This is another trench cut through the Anceps Bands, and is situated above a scree slope in the Long Burn. At this locality the succession is more than twice as thick as that in the Linn Branch (Locality 6). This apparently rapid change

Fig. 32.9

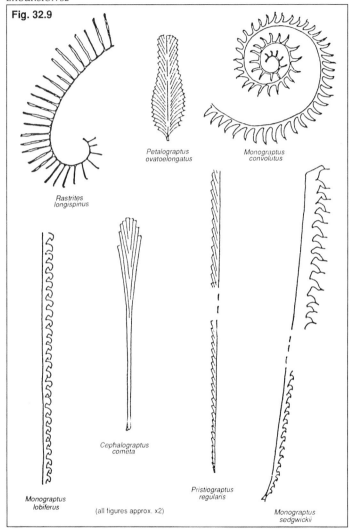

Rastrites
longispinus

Petalograptus
ovatoelongatus

Monograptus
convolutus

Monograptus
lobiferus

Cephalograptus
cometa

Pristiograptus
regularis

Monograptus
sedgwickii

(all figures approx. x2)

Figure 32.9. Illustrations of some characterisitic Lower Silurian graptolites found at Dob's Linn (adapted from Webb *et al.* in press).

in depositional thickness is more easily understood when realising that the localities are separated by a major thrust (the Main Fault, see Fig. 32.1), and were probably deposited tens or even hundreds of kilometres apart. The greater thickness of graptolitic shale means that scree-scramblers visiting this locality will be rewarded by a more abundant and better preserved *D.anceps* Zone fauna than at Localities 3 and 6.

Identification of characteristic graptolite species

Graptolites were originally colonial, planktonic animals, which belonged to the invertebrate phylum Hemichordata. Their organic external skeletons, originally a series of tubes, are all that remain of the original animal. Identification of graptolites relies on:

1. The overall form of the complete fossil (rhabdosome), including features such as number of branches (stipes), stipe attitude, width, etc.
2. The nature of early development of the colony (seen at the proximal, normally spinose, end).
3. The outline and spacing of the tubes (thecae).

In earlier publications, much emphasis was placed on the overall form and thecal outline when identifying genera. It is now believed that these features are often unreliable, partly because they are frequently affected by deformation caused during flattening of the cylindrical thecae, and partly because of tectonic stretching. More emphasis is therefore placed on proximal development, including position of thecae, nature of spines, etc. Unfortunately, such features are often difficult to observe in flattened, deformed specimens as normally found at Dob's Linn and in other black shale sequences, and many genera are currently being revised.

When identifying graptolite species, first look for overall form and distinctive proximal features, then finally check the thecal outlines. Remember that graptolite colonies grew continuously by budding, and while large specimens might have several hundred thecae, others may have died after growing only three or four, or with only the conical sicula present (which housed the first individual). Also be careful not to identify a single, broken-off stipe of a *Dicellograptus* as a *Monograptus*, and watch out for two or more rhabdosomes overlapping to give the false appearance of a different graptolites (e.g. two *Monograptus* stipes resembling a *Dicellograptus*). Good luck!

Dob's Linn for the amateur geologist

The amateur geologist should not be discouraged by the detailed biostratigraphy of the foregoing account, or by the difficulties encountered when identifying graptolites. Although not perhaps the most prepossessing of fossils, graptolites have proved to be of world-wide importance in establishing contemporaneity of strata in the older Palaeozoic rocks owing to their rapid evolution and diversification. Many of the species and zones at Dob's Linn can be recognised over much of the world; particularly close comparisons have been made recently with China, Siberia and Newfoundland.

Many sections yield graptolites slowly and reluctantly, but at Dob's Linn you cannot fail to find them in abundance and variety. Remember, however, that most professional geologists need to send their specimens to a very limited number of experts for accurate identification of species. Nevertheless, it is not difficult to recognise the more distinctive genera and the main thecal types of monograptids; a knowledge of these enables one to instantly distinguish between Ordovician rocks of Llandeilo, Caradoc and Ashgill age, and Silurian strata belonging to various divisions of the Llandovery Series (see Fig. 32.2). These cover a time span of about 30 million years in just over 90 m (300 feet) of strata - 100 000 years for every foot you cover!

Most of the specimens you find will not be readily identifiable because of fragmentation, distortion or poor preservation. Look for specimens which are as large as possible but still show the early stages (sicula and proximal thecae), and use an elementary text book.

Refer to the foregoing account and start at Locality 2 at the base of the Main Cliff in the Lower Hartfell Shale. The graptolites tend to occur in bands with differing species components, so examine the black shales layer by layer. The abundant diplograptids can mostly be identified as *Orthograptus* or *Climacograptus*, but are not helpful unless identified to species level. The stratigraphically significant genera are, unfortunately, less common and reward patient search.

These Caradoc rocks are characterised the world over by the presence of slender, gently or strongly curved, two-branched *Leptograptus*, the slender but stiff *Pleurograptus* with side branches, the V-shaped *Dicellograptus*, and the Y-shaped *Dicranograptus*. The latter genus is easier to find at the more precarious Locality 11.

Ascend the Main Cliff to Locality 3, or move to Locality 6 above the Linn Branch to collect from the Anceps Bands in the Upper Hartfell

Shale. Although the fauna at this level is dominated by *Climacograptus* and *Orthograptus* , specimens of *Dicellograptus* with complex thecae are not uncommon (mostly *D.anceps*). *D.complanatus* with more simple thecae can be found at Locality 3. These rocks belong to the Ashgill Series at the top of the Ordovician; although *Dicellograptus* has persisted. *Dicranograptus* and *Leptograptus* have disappeared; again a world-wide pattern.

At Locality 6, study the Ordovician-Silurian boundary. Note that it is not now taken in the formerly accepted position at the base of the Birkhill Shale where continuous black shale deposition began, but 1.6 m above where *Akidograptus ascensus* and *Parakidograptus acuminatus* appear; reasons for this change are discussed earlier in the text. Now descend to the stream and collect from the *C. cyphus* Zone at Locality 7 (Fig. 32.7). Note the common occurrence of monograptids with simple thecae. Search for the rarer dimorphograptids characteristic of this level. Diplograptids are still common.

On both sides of the gully at Locality 8, collect from the *C. gregarius* Zone which yields an abundant and varied fauna. Monograptids with triangulate thecae are now common in addition to the simple forms. Isolate forms (*Rastrites*) and the distinctive *Petalograptus* are less common and need to be looked for carefully. Lobate monograptids appear in the higher layers. The small ridge with bedding planes exposed at Locality 9 is within the *M. sedgwickii* Zone, notable for the appearance of hooked monograptids, particularly the zone fossil. The transition from the Birkhill Shale into the overlying Gala Greywacke is visible at Locality 10.

Acknowledgements

Figures 32.5 and 32.6 are reproduced from Williams (1988), (British Museum (Natural History) publication), while Figures 32.8 and 32.9 of Silurian graptolites are based on illustrations in Webb, Rushton and White (British Geological Survey publication, in press). We thank these individuals and organisations for their permission to employ diagrams in the excursion guide. S.H.W.'s study of the late Ordovician and early Silurian graptolites was made for a Ph.D. thesis at Glasgow University, supervised by J.K. Ingham and supported financially by NERC.

References

BARNES, C.R. and WILLIAMS, S.H. 1990. The Ordovician-Silurian boundary. *In* BRIGGS, D.E.G. and CROWTHER, P.R. (eds.). *Palaeobiology: a synthesis.*. Blackwell, U.K.

DAVIES, K.A. 1929. Notes on the graptolite faunas of the Upper Ordovician and Lower Silurian. *Geol.Mag.* , **66,** 1-27.

ELLES, G.L. and WOOD, E.M.R. 1901-18. A monograph of British graptolites. *Palaeontogr. Soc. (Monogr.)* clxxi & 539 p, 52 pls.

INGHAM, J.K. 1979. The Moffat area. *In* BASSETT, M.G. *et al. Guidebook to field meeting,* Great Britain, March 30-April 11, 1979 , 42-46. Subcommission on Silurian Stratigraphy, Ordovician-Silurian Boundary Working Group, IUGS.

LAPWORTH, C. 1878. The Moffat Series. *Q.J. geol. Soc. Lond.* **34,** 240-346.

LAPWORTH, C. 1879. On the tripartite classification of the Lower Palaeozoic rocks. *Geol. Mag.* **6,** 1-15.

PACKHAM, G.H. 1962. Some diplograptids from the British Lower Silurian. Palaeontology **5,** 498-526.

TOGHILL, P. 1968. The graptolite assemblages and zones of the Birkhill Shales (Lower Silurian) at Dobb's Linn. *Palaeontology,* **11,** 654-668.

TOGHILL, P. 1968b. The stratigraphical relationships of the earliest Monograptidae and the Dimorphograptidae. *Geol. Mag.* **105 ,** 46-51.

TOGHILL, P. 1970. Highest Ordovician (Hartfell Shales) graptolite faunas from the Moffat area, south Scotland. *Bull. Br. Mus. nat. Hist. (Geol)* **19 ,** 1-26, 16 pl.

WEBB, B., RUSHTON, A.W.A and WHITE, D.E. (in press). Classical areas of British geology. Moffatdale and the Upper Ettrick Valley. British Geological Survey, London, H.M.S.O.

WILLIAMS, S.H., 1980. An excursion guide to Dob's Linn. *Proc. geol. Soc. Glasgow* **121/122 ,** 13-18.

WILLIAMS, S.H., 1982a. The late Ordovician graptolite fauna of the Anceps Bands at Dob's Linn, southern Scotland. *Geol. et Palaeontol.,* **16,** 29-56.

WILLIAMS, S.H., 1982b. Upper Ordovician graptolites from the top Lower Hartfell Shale Formation (*D. clingani* and *P. linearis* zones) near Moffat, southern Scotland. *Trans. Roy. Soc. Edinb.: Earth Sciences* **72 ,** 229-255.

WILLIAMS, S.H., 1983. The Ordovician-Silurian graptolite fauna of Dob's Linn, southern Scotland. *Palaeontology* **26,** 605-639.

WILLIAMS, S.H., 1987. Stratigraphy and graptolite fauna of the *D. complanatus* Zone in Scotland. *Scott. Jl. Geol.* **23,** 65-92.

WILLIAMS, S.H., 1988. Dob's Linn - the Ordovician-Silurian boundary stratotype. *In* COCKS, L.R.M. and RICKARDS, R.B. (eds.). The Ordovician-Silurian boundary. *Bull. Br. Mus., nat. Hist. (Geol.)* **43,** 17-30.

Excursion 33 QUATERNARY
W.Graham Jardine

Introduction

Until comparatively recently, the Quaternary "Ice Age" was frequently regarded as a time of continuous glaciation of the British Isles. Research over the last 25-30 years has shown such a concept to be incorrect. To date, at least six major cold intervals, alternating with major temperate intervals, have been distinguished in the British Quaternary stratigraphical record. The last three major cold intervals are represented by glacial deposits in parts of Britain north of the Bristol Channel - Thames Estuary isthmus, so that demonstrably the Quaternary Period (Sub-era of some authorities) included at least three "ice ages". Also, in keeping with terrestrial evidence of multiple-rather than mono-glaciation, cores of Quaternary sediments from the Atlantic and Pacific Oceans have revealed a series of more than twenty alternating cold and temperate **Isotopic Stages** (some of these being major climatic intervals, and some minor). In the Glasgow district, the visible effects of glaciation - both erosive and depositional - are believed to be due to ice masses that originated in the SW Highlands (and perhaps to a lesser extent in the Renfrewshire uplands) and had their greatest effect during the last major cold interval. This interval is thought to have commenced approximately either 125 or 70 thousand years ago (depending on the authority quoted and the evidence that is accepted) and to have lasted until about ten thousand years ago (Price 1983; Sutherland 1984; Jardine 1986).

Important effects of the alternation of major cold and temperate climatic phases were world-wide changes in sea level and regional changes in land level. These changes accompanied, and were due to, the growth and decay of enormous ice sheets approximately contemporaneously in North America, Fennoscandia and northern Britain: global sea level was at least 100m lower than its present level during intervals of glaciation, and approximated to its present level during interglacial intervals; in a severely-glaciated area the landmass was depressed appreciably during glaciations by the weight of superincumbent ice, whence rebound of the landmass occurred in the intervening interglacial intervals. The combined effects of global changes of sea level and regional changes of land level produced in the Glasgow area, in the course of the last thirteen thousand years or so, a series of tilted marine shorelines: these now stand at various heights above present sea level due to differential land uplift having continued after sea level had approximately attained equilibrium.

A number of secondary recessions and advances of ice fronts, corresponding respectively with milder and more severe climatic intervals within the last major glaciation, occurred in western central Scotland. During the milder climatic phases (known as "interstadials") sub-arctic type vegetation and animals occupied parts of the region outside the static or receding ice fronts. When conditions again became more severe and the ice readvanced (during a "stadial"), remnants of flora and fauna were occasionally buried by the advancing ice and its deposits. A few of the interstadial deposits have been fortuitously preserved in the Glasgow area, and have been temporarily exposed in excavations during the last 150 years or so.

A summary of the sequence of events in the Glasgow district during the Quaternary Period is given in Table 33.1.

a. Erosive effects of glaciation

In the Glasgow district, as in other parts of western Scotland, the relative importance of erosion by ice in the course of the Quaternary period and denudation by river action during the immediately preceding Tertiary time interval in determining the configuration of the present land surface is still an unsolved problem (*cf.* Jardine 1986, pp. 28-30). Many geomorphologists would agree with George (1955, p. 302) that 'The local effects of glaciation in the modification of landscape ... are no more than the final touches given to the pre-Glacial landforms by ice; and ... compared with the radical transformations that took place during the 50 or 60 million years of Tertiary times, the changes in surface grain arising through the coming and going of glaciers and ice-sheets during the past half-million years or so are more spectacular than fundamental'. Despite this claim, since Linton (1951) suggested that many major valleys were produced by 'diffluent' Quaternary ice that caused watershed breaching, there has been a nagging doubt concerning the relative erosive efficacy of river action and ice action.

Allowing for this doubt, and accepting that the configuration of the landscape of the Glasgow district as the product of glacier erosion is the cumulative result of multiple- rather than mono-glaciation, several good examples of both large-scale and small-scale glacial erosion may

Table 33.1				
Age/Stage	Minor Climatic Divisions	Ice Advances	Text para.	Deposits of the Glasgow District
FLANDRIAN			v	Lower group raised marine/estuarine deposits and shore-lines bordering the River Clyde and its estuary
───── 10,000 radiocarbon years before present ─────				
DEVENSIAN (cold) Last Glaciation	Loch Lomond Stadial	Loch Lomond Readvance	iv	End-morainic deposits, Loch Lomond and Lake of Menteith areas
───── *c.* 11,000 years B.P. ─────				
	Windermere Interstadial		iii	Upper group of marine/estuarine deposits and shore-lines:Paisley, Renfrew, western and central Glasgow
───── *c.* 13,000 years B.P. ─────				
	Dimlington Stadial	Main Devensian ice advance (c. 25,000 to 14,000 years B.P.)	ii	Tills (boulder clays) of Glasgow and environs
	Un-named and undefined stadials and interstadials		i	sands, gravels and tills, of uncertain ages, filling the buried channels underlying the Rivers Clyde, Cart and Leven.

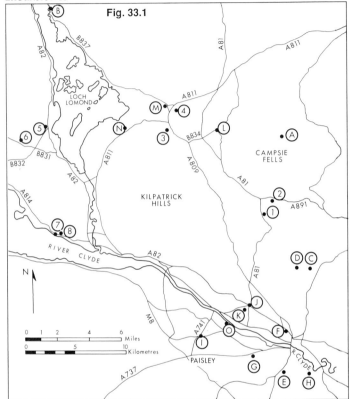

Figure 33.1.
Location map for Excursion 33. The localities denoted by numbers are those included in the excursion. Other localities mentioned in the text are denoted by capital letters.

be recognised. The most impressive examples of the former are the overdeepened basin of the Firth of Clyde between the islands of Arran and Bute (rockhead at -320m O.D.) and the depths of the basins of the northern part of Loch Lomond (to *c.* -170m O.D.) compared with the depth of the southern part of the loch (to *c.* -10m O.D.). Further examples of large-scale erosion are the so-called 'buried channels' that are cut in

466

solid rock to depths as low as -75m O.D below the Rivers Clyde, Kelvin and Leven (and to a lesser extent the River Cart). The origin of these channels is controversial, but excavation by subglacial meltwater streams under hydrostatic pressure, rather than by glacier ice, probably was an important process involved in their formation (Jardine 1986, pp.31-32). Another frequently cited example of marked glacial erosion is the deepening of the WNW-ESE oriented valley between Strathblane and Lennoxtown; especially when the Campsie Fells are covered with a thin sprinkling of snow, the tributary valley of Fin Glen is seen to 'hang' above the main valley. To the south of Strathblane, much smaller ice-scooped hollows, including that now occupied by Loch Ardinning (Locality 1, NS 564 780, Fig. 33.1), also testify to the erosive action of the Quaternary ice, and suggest its WNW-ESE passage over the area. Corries on the northern face of the Campsie Fells, especially the impressive Corrie of Balglass (Locality A, NS 589 850), provide evidence of cirque erosion.

Small-scale effects of glacial erosion are more difficult to find, mainly since much of the solid rock is covered by at least a thin veneer of Quaternary deposits (see below). Near the NW end of Loch Ardinning, however, striations are developed, even if only poorly, on the upper surface of the quartz conglomerate that is exposed in the nearby quarry. In contrast, 40km to the north of Glasgow, on the eastern shore of Loch Lomond 50m to the east of Rowardennan pier (Locality B, NS 358 986), excellent examples of glacial striae are to be seen on an ice-smoothed **roche moutonnée** of quartz mica schist. The striations are oriented N-S, at right angles to the foliation of the schist. The small hill named Dunglass (Locality 2, NS 575 789), located on the floor of the valley between Strathblane and Lennoxtown, combines the effects of ice erosion and deposition, its western end being (mainly) the crag, and its eastern end the corresponding tail, of a crag-and-tail ice- moulded landform.

b. Quaternary deposits

The Quaternary deposits of the Glasgow district comprise sediments laid down by ice and its meltwaters in the course of glaciation and deglaciation, together with sediments deposited by marine waters, by the River Clyde and its tributaries and by other terrestrial agents during interstadial intervals and after the ice had finally melted. Broadly, the Quaternary sedimentary succession is that shown in the right-hand column of Table 33.1.

(i) The types and sequences of deposits filling the buried channels that underlie the Rivers Clyde and Kelvin are uncertain, being known mainly from occasional temporary exposures of the uppermost sediments and from borehole data recorded by drillers rather than geologists (Clough *et al.* 1925; Menzies 1981; Browne and McMillan 1985). The buried channels appear to contain beds of mainly water-laid (? glaciofluvial) sands and gravels, together with occasional layers or lenses of till. The uppermost sand and gravel deposits are almost certainly Devensian in age, since fossils of this age have been found in them (see next paragraph). Many of the other deposits, both tills and water-laid sediments, may also date from the Devensian glacial age. In the 1960s and 1970s, deposits in the vicinity of the buried channel that underlies the River Kelvin were exposed extensively in commercial sand and gravel pits within the burgh of Bishopbriggs. Sections on the site of the former Cawdor golf course (Locality C, NS 610 721) and in the Wilderness pit (Locality D, NS 600 722), together with borehole records (Browne and McMillan 1985, fig. 11), indicated that 3-7m of red till rest on a thick sequence of gravel and sand layers. The gravels comprise pebbles mainly of quartzite, vein quartz, **schistose grit** and basalt - all durable, but non-local, rock or mineral clasts - with occasional locally-derived white/yellow sandstone. The sands are mainly of quartz grains with sporadic concentrations of small coal fragments. Stratification in both the gravels and sands is horizontal for the most part, but occasional cross-stratification and cut-and-fill structures do occur. From time to time fossil ice wedges and involutions were exposed in the working faces in the gravels, indicating periglacial frost action after deposition of the gravels but before deposition of the overlying cover of red till (Galloway 1961).

In 1963, there was found in the sands directly below the uppermost gravels of the former Wilderness pit (Locality D, NS 600 722), a bone of the woolly rhinoceros, *Coelodonta antiquitatis* (Blumenbach), dated 27,550 +1370/-1680 years B.P. (before present) by radiocarbon assay (Rolfe 1966). Until recently, it was considered possible that the age of the bone is greater than the age of the gravels in which it was contained. The discovery in 1986, however, of a well-authenticated interstadial site at Sourlie (NS 336 414), near Irvine, Cunninghame District, with a possible time range of c. 33,500 - 29,000 years B.P. established by radiocarbon dating of plant debris, a reindeer antler and carbonaceous silt/clay underlain and overlain by thick till deposits, suggests that the Wilderness bone and gravels are contemporaneous. More significantly, the combined evidence from Sourlie and Wilderness is strongly indicative of interstadial conditions in at least low-lying parts of Scotland during the period *c*. 33,500 - 26,000 years B.P. (Jardine *et al*. 1988).

Two other examples of interstadial fossiliferous deposits are known from the Glasgow district. In 1937 the remains of bones of the reindeer, *Rangifer tarandus* Linné, were found in SE Glasgow near Queen's Park (Locality E, at approximately NS 588 618) in water-laid sands and gravels that were overlain by up to 20m of till forming a drumlin (Macgregor & Ritchie 1940). The age of the reindeer bones is unknown, but the overlying till almost certainly dates from the (Late Devensian) main phase of the last major cold interval in Britain (Dimlington Stadial, Table 33.1), a phase that is thought to have had its glacial climax in northern Britain around 20,000 - 18,000 years B.P. and perhaps lasted from c. 25,000 - 14,000 years B.P. It is possible, but by no means certain, that the interstadial deposits at Queen's Park and those in which the dated bone was found at the Wilderness pit, Bishopbriggs, are of approximately the same age and that they represent the same interstadial interlude within the last major cold interval. The Queen's Park section is no longer exposed, but the reindeer remains from it are preserved in the Glasgow Art Gallery and Museum at Kelvingrove.

In the 1850s, part of the beam of a reindeer antler was found in a thin succession of stratified deposits near Croftamie, Dunbartonshire, in the (former) railway cutting (Locality 3, NS 473 860) a few metres north-east of the point where the minor road between Croftamie and Kilmaronock Church intersects the cutting (Jack 1877). The stratified deposits were overlain by shelly till of the Loch Lomond Stadial (see below). More recently, felted organic detritus obtained from approximately the same horizon as the reindeer antler was dated 10,560 ± 160 years B.P. (Rose 1981; Rose *et al*. 1988). The recent records also show that the stratified deposits are underlain by up to 1.5m of till that is attributed to deposition during the Dimlington Stadial. The deposits containing the reindeer antler and dated organic detritus at Croftamie, therefore, represent a later interstadial (Windermere Interstadial, Table 33.1) than the interstadial or interstadials represented by the ossiferous deposits at Wilderness and Queen's Park. The antler from Croftamie is now in the Royal Museum of Scotland, Edinburgh.

(ii) Most of the low hills on which central and western Glasgow is built are glacial **drumlins** consisting of grey till (boulder clay) with a mainly silty mud and sandy silt matrix, derived largely from local Carboniferous shales and sandstones (Abd-alla 1988, p.77 and p.263). Embedded in the matrix are s.ones of variable size up to boulders about one metre in diameter. The stones, which frequently bear striations, are dominantly of the same local rocks as the matrix, but occasional erratic quartz schists and schistose grits (from NW of the Highland Boundary Fault), Carboniferous basalts (? from the Kilpatrick Hills) and Devonian (ORS) sandstones (? from the vicinity of Dumbarton) occur. Opportunity to examine the nature and characteristics of the till is provided occasionally in temporary excavations within the city. The drumlins, of which Garnethill (Locality F, NS 582 661) and the large hill within Bellahouston Park (Locality G, NS 549 638) are good morphological examples, are streamlined ground morainic forms, and the grey till is a **lodgement till** of the last major ice sheet that moved over the Glasgow area (in a WNW-ESE direction during the Dimlington Stadial). In central Glasgow (e.g. within the precincts of the University of Strathclyde) the uppermost two or three metres of the grey till are strongly weathered to a rusty brown colour.

In NW Glasgow and adjacent parts of Dunbartonshire there occurs a red till that is distinctly different in appearance and nature from the grey till of central Glasgow. The red till has a dominantly silty sand matrix, derived mainly from Devonian (ORS) sandstone fragments (Abd-alla 1988, p.77 and p.263). The stone content is dominantly of Highland quartzite and schistose grit, ORS rock fragments and Carboniferous lavas, but occasional small fragments of local Carboniferous shale and white/yellow sandstone occur (*cf.* Menzies 1981). The thickness of the till increases in a north-westerly direction, from about 1m or less near a SW-NE oriented line extending approximately from Partick railway station (NS 556 664) to Possil Loch (NS 585 698), to several metres or tens of metres in Bearsden and Milngavie District. Although only occasional small temporary exposures of the red till are now to be seen, in the 1960s and 1970s extensive exposures at Cawdor (Locality C, NS 610 721) and Wilderness (Locality D, NS 600 722) showed that about 3-7m of red till (rather stonier here than 1km to the west, where it also is thicker) rest on stratified gravels and sands in the vicinity of the Kelvin buried channel (see above).

The nature and mode of origin of the red till and its relationships with the grey till were subjects of debate in the late 1960s and early 1970s (e.g. Jardine 1968; Sissons 1968). It is now generally agreed that the two tills are lodgement deposits of a single ice advance (during the Dimlington Stadial), differences in the characteristics of the tills, including colour, being due to derivation from different source rocks (see above; Menzies 1981; Browne and McMillan 1985). There still remain, however, a few puzzling aspects of the relationships between the tills. For example, it has long been known that there is a 3-4km wide zone, immediately to the NW of the 'feather edge' of the red till (see above), within which both the grey and red tills are present and where, in places, the red till rests on grey till. Recently, grain-size, clay mineralogical and geochemical analyses of the matrices of the two tills (Abd-alla 1988, pp. 476-477) confirmed earlier field observations by Jardine (1968) that at a few locations within this zone a thin cover of red till rests on weathered rather than fresh grey till. This poses a problem, since such evidence suggests that at least a short period of exposure of the grey till occurred at these locations before the red till was deposited on the grey till. A possible sequence of events is as follows:

1) The main advance of the Late Devensian ice sheet deposited grey lodgement till in the central Glasgow area, red lodgement till in NW Glasgow and Dunbartonshire and red-on-grey lodgement till in the zone mentioned above.

2) During general recession of the ice front from east to west, there was a short period of stillstand of the front in the vicinity of sites within the zone where red till now rests on weathered grey till. At these sites, grey till was exposed beyond the ice front, or perhaps in hollows in the ice near the front.

3) Following alteration of 'fresh' grey till to weathered grey till at these sites, thin covers of red till were deposited as flow till on top of the weathered grey till.

Such an explanation is in keeping with the thickness of the red till that rests on weathered grey till at these sites being less than two metres.

In addition to the grey and red tills described above, there are other distinctive tills occurring over limited areas within the Glasgow district. They are exposed occasionally, as in the Toryglen area (Locality H, NS 600 618), where a bright orange red till, probably derived from soft red sandstones of the (locally) underlying Barren Red Measures, occurred in an excavation in 1965 (see also Clough *et al*. 1925, pp. 223-227).

(iii) In western and central Glasgow, and also in the neighbourhood of Renfrew and Paisley, marine and brackish-water Late Devensian sediments occupy the low ground (up to 25m or 41m above O.D., depending on the author quoted: Rose 1975, p. 20; Sissons 1976, p.128; Browne *in* Jardine 1980, p.13; Browne *et al*. 1983) (Fig. 33.2). The sediments concerned, deposited during the Windermere Interstadial (Table 1), are part of the well-known *Clyde Beds* . They are exposed

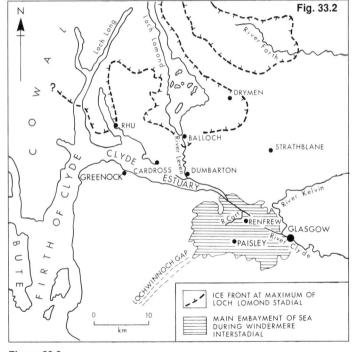

Figure 33.2.
Map of the area to the NW of Glasgow, showing locations mentioned in the text of marine deposits of the Windermere Interstadial and on the Loch Lomond Stadial; adapted from Jardine 1986, figure 3.

occasionally in artificial excavations; a small natural cliff at Geilston, Cardross (Locality 7, NS 341 777), is poorly exposed now compared with its condition when described by Rose (*in* Jardine 1980, pp. 25-27). Broadly, the marine and brackish-water sediments consist of two units (*cf.* Peacock 1975, p. 46; 1981, pp. 225-226), the lower comprising laminated clays, silts and sands, commonly <1m in thickness but 2-3m in places, the upper comprising fossiliferous clays and silty sands (with locally-abundant remains of large bivalves, e.g. *Arctica islandica*, and with foraminifers and ostracodes), commonly >5m in thickness.

The marine waters perhaps penetrated the Paisley-Glasgow area around 13,000 years B.P. (Browne *et al.* 1977; *cf.* Peacock 1989), initially either by a sinuous channel through the narrow Lochwinnoch Gap (Peacock 1971), or by Greenock along the line of the present estuary of the Clyde (Sissons 1974, p. 330). By *c.*11,700 years B.P. the sea had penetrated the Vale of Leven from Dumbarton to Balloch and extended into the Loch Lomond basin (Fig. 33.2). Opportunities to examine the Late Devensian marine and associated estuarine deposits are infrequent. Because of this, the sequence shown in an exceptionally fine former section at Junction 27 on the M8 motorway near Paisley (Locality I, NS 495 657) is recorded in Figure 33.3 (see also Aspen & Jardine 1968). Some compensation for the scarcity of sedimentary exposures is afforded by traces of former shoreline features dating from the same general episode when, in relative terms, sea level stood higher than at present. Some of the best examples occur near Anniesland

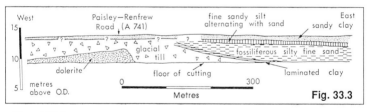

Figure 33.3.
Composite W-E section formerly exposed at Junction 27 on the M8 motorway near Paisley, showing a roche moutonnée (of dolerite) overlain by till which, in turn, is overlain by laminated clay and fossiliferous marine sediments (Clyde Beds) deposited during the Windermere Interstadial. The overlying layer of fine sandy silt alternating with sand probably represents land conditions. The conditions under which the uppermost bed, of sandy clay, accumulated are uncertain. Adapted from Aspen & Jardine 1968, Figure 1.

Cross (Locality J, Fig. 33.1) where two abrupt rises along the length of Bearsden Road, at Glencoe Street (NS 546 689) and at Sutcliffe Road (NS 547 690), with intervening terrace, mark former shorelines in this area. Similar terraces and sand- or gravel-covered till slopes, although less well defined, are detectable in the Jordanhill area (Locality K), *e.g.* in Chamberlain Road (at NS 541 682), Jordanhill Drive (at NS 541 684) and Seggielea Road (at NS 539 685).

(iv)   The Dimlington Stadial, in the course of which the main Devensian glaciation of northern Britain took place, was followed by the Windermere Interstadial (Table 33.1). During this fairly short-lived (*c.* 13,000 - 11,000 years B.P.) temperate interval the ice melted rapidly, and the whole of Britain may have been clear of ice by 12,500 years B.P. Around 11,000 years B.P., conditions became colder both on land in NW Britain and in the Atlantic Ocean and neighbouring sea lochs of western Scotland including the Firth and Estuary of the Clyde. In the course of the ensuing Loch Lomond Stadial (broadly from 11,000 - 10,000 years B.P.), glacier ice reappeared in many parts of western Scotland, especially in the Loch Lomond basin (hence the name given to the Stadial) and adjacent valleys. End morainic and associated glaciofluvial deposits dating from this time were formerly well exposed at Rhu Point (NS 265 840), but now are only poorly exposed on rare occasions. A detailed account of their characteristics is given by Rose (*in* Jardine 1980, pp. 31-37).

Deposits of the Loch Lomond Stadial do not occur within the city of Glasgow itself. Indeed, the nearest these deposits are to be found is 25km from the city centre in the neighbourhood of the villages of Killearn (Locality L, NS 523 861) and Drymen (Locality M, NS 474 886). This is because this late phase of glacier advance was not powerful enough to carry ice far beyond the vicinity of the Highland Boundary Fault. In 1970, pipe-line excavations at NS 430 865 (Locality N), in the vicinity of Gartocharn village, revealed characteristic Loch Lomond Stadial ground-morainic till, with small shell fragments embedded in the till. A typical, though small, end-morainic ridge produced by the same ice advance is to be seen on Highfields Muir (Locality 6, NS 323 857) to the north of the B831 road (*cf.* Rose *in* Jardine 1980, pp. 37-39). The ridge is readily recognisable since recently a metalled but non-surfaced private road has been constructed along its crest. Meltwater deposits laid down near the ice margin have been extracted extensively from time to time in a sand and gravel pit near Drymen (Drumbeg,

Locality 4, NS 483 880). The nature and quality of exposure varies as work progresses. The sediments occasionally exhibit structures typical of glacial meltwater deposits: unconformities, top-set and fore-set bedding, cut-and-fill structures, alternation of thick sand beds and thinner gravel layers. In addition, these deposits have yielded shell fragments (of marine molluscs that inhabited the Loch Lomond basin during the immediately preceding Windermere Interstadial, but which were carried out to the Drymen area by ice and meltwaters during the Loch Lomond Stadial) radiocarbon dated at 11,700 ± 170 years B.P. (Sissons 1967). Between Balloch and Luss on the western side of Loch Lomond, a discontinuous, narrow, sinuous ridge of gravel, occurring a few tens of metres east of Duchlage farm (NS 350 871) and SSW of Muirland School (Locality 5, NS 348 867), is an **esker** formed by the meltwaters of the ice that occupied the Loch Lomond basin.

(v)   Flandrian marine and fluviatile deposits occupy the very low ground bordering the River Clyde and its estuary. The sediments vary in nature and composition, in places being silts or fine sands (? fossil tidal-flats) where they occupy wide flat tracts, *e.g.* between Shieldhall (Locality O, NS 532 664) and Renfrew Cross (NS 507 676), or in places being gravels and sands (fossil beach deposits now forming raised surfaces some 8-10m above O.D.), as between Dumbarton and Cardross (Locality 8, NS 354 767). In several places the Flandrian raised coastal deposits are backed by low cliffs cut in solid rock or in till. Good examples of cliffs, cut in Old Red Sandstone rocks, occur between Dumbarton and Cardross, at Locality 8.

Itinerary

Themes: A variety of Quaternary landforms and erosive features, and a more limited number of Quaternary deposits, in the area to the NW of Glasgow city centre.

Features: Crag-and-tail, drumlins, dry valley, end-moraine, esker, Flandrian raised beach, beach, former marine embayment, former marine shoreline, former sea cliffs, glacial striations (striae), glacially-deepened valley, 'hanging valley', ice-scooped hollow, position of buried channel; Clyde Beds deposits; glacial meltwater deposits; shelly till.

Maps:	O.S.	1 : 50 000	Sheet 56 Inveraray & Loch Lomond
			Sheet 57 Stirling & The Trossachs
			Sheet 63 Firth of Clyde
			Sheet 64 Glasgow
	B.G.S.	1 : 63 360	Sheet 30 Glasgow (Drift)

Terrain: Road or easy track, except at Locality 7 (which is optional), where the track is muddy and a stream has to be forded on foot. An easily negotiated fence has to be climbed at Locality 3 (which is also optional).

Distance and Time: Approximately 95 km (60 mls) round trip by car from University of Glasgow.
Short walks to exposures. Total time, 6-7 hours.

Short itineraries: Slightly shorter itineraries, each of around 4-5 hours duration, would be to
  (a) Localities 1, 2, 3 and 4, or
  (b) Localities 5, 6, 7 and 8.

Access: Many of the stops are made for the purpose of observing landforms from a distance and, therefore, present no access problems. Access at Locality 4, a working pit, is discussed below.

Starting at the University of Glasgow Department of Geology & Applied Geology, which is sited at the SW margin of the Hillhead drumlin, proceed to the northern end of Byres Road. The route from thence, westwards along Great Western Road (and therefore opposite in direction from ice flow during the Dimlington Stadial; Table 33.1), undulates gently over the low till-based ground between the Dowanhill and Kelvindale drumlins as far as Bingham's Pond (beside the Pond Hotel), where it drops for a distance of 200-300m into what was a marine embayment during the Windermere Interstadial, *c.*13,000-11,000 years B.P. A low till-cored rise is next crossed until, at Anniesland Cross (Locality J), Great Western Road again drops to lower ground underlain, *e.g.* in the High School playing fields to the SW of the Cross, by marine *Clyde Beds* deposits.

From Anniesland Cross follow Bearsden Road (A806) through the Temple area, noting in passing that the road rises abruptly at Glencoe Street (NS 546 689) and again at Sutcliffe Road (NS 547 690) as it crosses two former late-Quaternary marine shoreline positions. Having crossed the Forth & Clyde Canal, Bearsden Road rises rapidly to near the southern entrance to the University of Glasgow Garscube Estate, from whence, as far as Canniesburn Toll, it cuts athwart the eastern ends of a series of W-E oriented till-formed hills in what is known as Switchback Road.

At Canniesburn Toll, the A81, Milngavie Road, should be followed, but before this is done it may be worth reflecting that concealed several tens of metres below the ground surface near the Toll is the southern boundary of the buried channel of a former course of the River Kelvin. The northern boundary of the same channel is located about 1.5km from the Toll. It underlies Milngavie Road 300-400m north of Hillfoot Station, although no trace of its presence is betrayed by the surface features that occur in this area, mainly the W-E oriented Kilmardinny and Boclair drumlin-like hills.

Locality 1. Loch Ardinning (NS 564 780) (Fig.33.1). The A81 route to Strathblane skirts the eastern side of the town of Milngavie and, having passed Craigmaddie Reservoir on the left, winds through an area where drumlins may be seen on the right around Baldernock, before the road straightens between Craigmaddie House and Loch Ardinning (Locality 1), where the first major stop should be made in the lay-by on the right (eastern) side of the road c.100m south of the loch. The summit of the conglomerate crags in the quarry immediately to the north of Loch Ardinning provides an excellent viewpoint for the observation of a number of physical features that testify to the WNW-ESE passage of glacier ice over the surrounding area during at least one of the major cold intervals of the Quaternary period. To the south, Loch Ardinning in the immediate foreground occupies an ice-scooped hollow, whilst in the distance may be seen the large drumlin field on which much of the city of Glasgow and its environs are built. On the top surface of the conglomerate itself, poorly developed glacial striations occasionally may be observed; the quality of the striae has deteriorated recently, probably because of excessive recreational activity in the form of unauthorised motor-cycle 'scrambling'. To the north is the glacially-deepened valley that extends from Strathblane to Lennoxtown, with the tributary valley of Fin Glen 'hanging' above it on the southern face of the Campsie Fells. Far off to the NW may be seen the isolated peak of Ben Lomond which, although covered completely by ice in the course of the 'main' Devensian glaciation (*i.e.* Dimlington Stadial; Table 33.1), stood high above separate lobes of ice to its west and east during the later Loch Lomond Stadial.

Locality 2. Dunglass (NS 575 789). Leaving Loch Ardinning, the A81 route continues down the hairpin bend immediately south of Strathblane. It is at this bend that the first glimpse of the 'crag-and tail' feature represented by the intrusive mass of Dunglass (Locality 2) is to be seen but, if a more prolonged view is desired, a short digression from the main route should be made eastwards along the A891 to a point near the entrance to Ballagan House. From such a location, the steeper solid-rock 'crag' at the western end and the streamlined 'tail' of glacially-deposited debris at the eastern end of the hill show up well, although it must be said that the feature as a whole is not a perfect example of its kind.

To reach the next major stop, at Drumbeg pit (Locality 4, NS 483 880), the A81 should be followed from Strathblane for about 8.5km to the crossing of the A81 and B834, where a left turn into the B834, and thence westwards across the Blane Water, leads to the junction of the B834 with the A809. Here a right turn should be made NW along the A809 towards the village of Croftamie.

Locality 3. Croftamie (NS 473 860). If desired, a brief digression may be made to the left (west) as the village of Croftamie is entered, into a minor road signposted 'Pirniehall', to visit the former railway cutting crossed by the road from Croftamie to Kilmaronock Church. Here shelly till of the Loch Lomond Stadial has been found to rest on a very thin layer of fossiliferous interstadial deposits which, in turn, rest on up to 1.5m of till that is attributed to the Dimlington Stadial. The cutting is now largely overgrown but, 10-15m from the south-western side of the road and on the southern bank of the cutting, there is a small exposure of the red-coloured till of the Loch Lomond Stadial. Small fragments of shells can occasionally be found in the till. To gain access to the exposures in the cutting a low wire fence has to be straddled. There is parking space for one vehicle near the cutting, where a private farm road joins the public road.

Locality 4. Drumbeg pit (NS 483 880) **(Sunday visits preferred).** From Croftamie, the entrance to the Drumbeg pit is reached by first travelling northwards along the A809 to its junction with the A811, about 150m south of the graceful red sandstone bridge that spans the Endrick Water. From the junction, ignoring the various side roads that lead off on the left, the A811 should be followed for about 1.6km to the point where a narrow road, signposted 'Gartness' on the left of the A811 but leading off on the right of the A811, is reached. Follow this road for about 800m to the entrance to Drumbeg pit, which is alongside the (signposted) entrance to Drumbeg farm. **Visitors to the site should drive down into the pit to park**. They must **not** leave their vehicles near the entrance to the site or on the access roads. **Trucks must not be obstructed**.

This is a working pit, in operation from Monday to Friday and on Saturday mornings. During working hours, permission to examine the faces should be sought from the site foreman, normally to be found in the office at the weighbridge. Permission to visit the pit outside working hours must be obtained in advance from John Wilson, Ardgowan Estate Office, Inverkip, telephone number 0475 521656, as agent for the owner. Neither the owner nor the operator can accept responsibility for the safety of any visitor. To comply with safety regulations, **hard-hats must be worn** while on the site, and working faces must not be approached closely because of the risk of their collapse. Wellington boots are recommended as footwear.

The stratified sediments exposed in the Drumbeg pit are part of a complex of morainic and meltwater deposits that accumulated at several locations close to the southern margin of the lobe of ice that occupied the Lomond basin during the Loch Lomond Stadial (*c.* 11,00-10,000 years B.P.). The sediments exposed in the pit vary as work progresses, but thicker layers of sand and thinner layers of gravel may be seen. The sediments occasionally exhibit structures typical of glacial meltwater deposits: unconformities, top-set and fore-set bedding and cut-and-fill structures. Shell fragments are found occasionally within these deposits (see section **iv** of the text above).

Locality 5. Muirland School (NS 348 867). The route from Drumbeg pit to Locality 5 takes the Quaternary geologist back to the T-junction of the A811 and A809 south of Drymen. From thence, the A811 should be followed southwestwards towards Balloch, attention being paid, on the right (western) side of the road *c.* 2.5km beyond the village of Gartocharn, to the deep dry valley that extends for several hundreds of metres parallel to the road. The channel is thought to have been cut by glacial meltwaters that were flowing from approximately north to south, either sub-glacially or close to the margin of the ice lobe that occupied the Lomond basin during the Loch Lomond Stadial.

In Balloch, signposts showing the route to Luss and Crianlarich should be followed. These take the traveller, via two major roundabouts, to the new northward-leading A82 road, which should be followed for 6-7km to a point near Duchlage Farm (NS 350 871), where care should be taken to turn left on to the old B832 road rather than the newer road a short distance north of the B832. Vehicle parking is not easy on the B832, but it may be possible near Muirland School (Locality 5, NS 348 867). The purpose in stopping here is to examine at close quarters the narrow sinuous ridge of gravel that occurs discontinuously near the western margin of Loch Lomond in this area. This esker, formed by the meltwaters of ice that occupied the Loch Lomond basin, is seen well as a prominent ridge a few tens of metres east of Duchlage Farm, and a similar distance SSW of Muirland School. Occasionally the stratified nature of the gravel is to be seen in small exposures.

Locality 6. Highfields Muir (NS 323 857). About 2km south of Muirland School, the B832 meets the B831 at a crossroads. Turning right, the B831, leading towards Glen Fruin, should be followed for *c.*1.5km to the point near where a track on the left (SW) side of the road leads to Inverlauren farm and, on the right beyond a gate, a recently-metalled but non-surfaced private road leads northeastwards on to Highfields Muir (Locality 6, NS 323 857). There is limited parking on the NE side of the B831. The private road has been constructed on a small, but typical, end-morainic ridge, which was produced at the margin of the Loch Lomond Stadial ice lobe. The ridge extends for several kilometres to the north of the B831 as a narrow 'ribbon' oriented approximately SW-NE, parallel to the previous part of the route along the B832. In the autumn, vegetational variations make the ridge especially conspicuous and, after leaving Muirland School, its presence may be noted on this basis on the way to Highfields Muir. The approximate altitude of the ridge, at around 125m above the present water level in Loch Lomond but at a level well below the crest of the hill that the ridge flanks, is a useful reminder that, although ice occupied the Lomond basin during the Loch Lomond Stadial, there were large areas of the surrounding higher ground that contemporaneously were ice-free. In such areas, severe frost action was in progress at that time (*c.* 11,000-10,000 years B.P.).

Locality 7 . Geilston (NS 341 777) . The best route from Highfields Muir to the next potential stop, at Geilston (Locality 7) near Cardross, is by returning on the B831 to its junction with the B832 and thereafter taking the B832 road southwards into Helensburgh. The Geilston stop is recommended to only the keenest and ablest-bodied Quaternary geologists, since the exposure at this Locality has deteriorated greatly since it was described in detail by Rose (in Jardine 1980), and access to the site is not easy if the water is high. Wellingtons (or better, waders) are recommended. This, however, is one of the few localities, or perhaps the only locality, in the Glasgow district where Clyde Beds are (semi-)permanently exposed. From Helensburgh, the A814 coast road should be followed eastwards to Geilston, at the western end of the village of Cardross. As soon as the built-up area is entered a stone-built hall (resembling a church) will be seen set back about 25m from the left (northern) side of the road. It is preferable to park vehicles in the small lay-by on the other (southern) side of the road. Very close to this parking place, the Geilston Burn flows under the A814. The site is located on the eastern bank of the Burn *c*.150m south of the A814. The geologically most interesting route to the site is to walk southwards on a footpath that enters a narrow wood to the west of the bridge over the Geilston Burn. The path leads down to the low ground of the Flandrian raised beach. By skirting fields located on the sands and gravels of the raised beach it is possible to reach the western bank of the lower reaches of the Geilston Burn. A faintly-defined footpath leads northwards upstream, but at some point the burn has to be crossed to arrive at the site described in detail by Rose (in Jardine 1980, pp. 25-29). The site is best visited when vegetation is at its minimum. The Clyde Beds consist of sticky grey clays containing fragile marine fossils of bivalves (*Arctica* and *Mytilus*) and gastropods. A spade may be necessary for excavation. Lodgement till and beach gravels are also exposed.

Locality 8. 500m east of Cardross (NS 354 767). The final scheduled stop is located *c*. 500m east of the eastern end of the village of Cardross (Locality 8). Vehicles can be parked off the A814 on the left (northern) side of the road where a farm road joins the A814 about half way along a stretch of the main road that is bordered on the left by fields backed by red sandstone cliffs. The cliffs, together with a rock platform at their foot (a platform which is now covered with stratified sand and gravel deposits), probably are the equivalents of similar features that are thought by many authors to be the products of severe shore erosion during the Loch Lomond Stadial, by combination of frost riving and marine action. An alternative suggestion is that initial formation of the cliff and rock platform pre-dated the Loch Lomond Stadial, and the sea re-occupied a former position of the marine shoreline during the Loch Lomond Stadial (cf. Jardine 1986, p.37). The sand and gravel sediments resting on the platform are thought to date from a time later than the time(s) of formation of the platform, being deposited around 7,000-6,000 years B.P., when the culmination of the Flandrian marine transgression again led to the former shoreline position being re-occupied by the early **Holocene** sea. Since then, isostatic uplift of the land has led to the sand and gravel shore-zone sediments (together with the underlying platform and adjacent cliff) being raised to their present position, a few metres above present mean sea level (equivalent to Ordnance Datum, O.D.).

Return to the starting point via Dumbarton and the A82, which passes through Anniesland Cross. Note at Dumbarton that, whereas the River Leven now flows on the western side of Dumbarton Rock, at some (unknown) time during its Quaternary history it flowed on the eastern side of the Rock; the buried channel (to -68m O.D. or lower, Jardine 1986, p.31) is located on that side.

References

ABD-ALLA, M. A. A. 1988. Mineralogical and geochemical studies of tills in south-western Scotland. *Univ. Glasgow Ph. D. thesis* (unpubl.).

ASPEN, P. & JARDINE, W. G. 1968. A temporary exposure of Quaternary deposits at Renfrew, near Glasgow. *Proc. geol. Soc. Glasgow* **109**, 35-37.

BROWNE, M. A. E., HARKNESS, D. D., PEACOCK, J. D. & WARD, R. G. 1977. The date of deglaciation of the Paisley-Renfrew area. *Scott. J. Geol.* **13**, 301-303.

_____ & MCMILLAN, A. A. 1985. The tills of central Scotland in their stratigraphical context. *In* Forde, M. C. (ed) *Construction in glacial tills and boulder clays* 11-24. Edinburgh: Engineering Technics Press.

_____ , MCMILLAN, A. A. & GRAHAM, D. K. 1983. A late-Devensian marine and non-marine sequence near Dumbarton, Strathclyde. *Scott. J. Geol.* **19**, 229-234.

CLOUGH, C. T. *et al.* (eight authors) 1925. The geology of the Glasgow district (2nd edition). *Mem. Geol. Surv. U.K.*

GALLOWAY, R. W. 1961. Periglacial phenomena in Scotland. *Geogr. Ann.* **43**, 348-353.

GEORGE, T. N. 1955. British Tertiary landscape evolution. *Sci. Prog. Lond.* **43**, 291-307.

JACK, R. L. 1877. Notes on a till or boulder clay with broken shells, in the lower valley of the River Endrick, near Loch Lomond, and its relation to certain other glacial deposits. *Trans. Geol. Soc.of Glasgow* **5**, 1-25.

JARDINE, W. G. 1968. The 'Perth' readvance. *Scott. J. Geol.* **4**, 185-186.

_____ (ed) 1980. *Glasgow Region: Field Guide.* Cambridge: Quaternary Research Association.

_____ 1986. The geological and geomorphological setting of the Estuary and Firth of Clyde. *Proc. R. Soc. Edinburgh* **90B**, 25-41.

_____ , et al. (six authors) 1988. A late Middle Devensian interstadial site at Sourlie, near Irvine, Strathclyde. *Scott. J. Geol.* **24**, 288-295.

LINTON, D. L. 1951. Watershed breaching by ice in Scotland. *Trans. Inst. Br. Geogr.* **15**, 1-16.

MACGREGOR, M. & RITCHIE, J. 1940. Early glacial remains of reindeer from the Glasgow district. *Proc. R. Soc. Edinburgh.* **60**, 322-332.

MENZIES, J. 1981. Investigations into the Quaternary deposits and bedrock topography of central Glasgow. *Scott. J. Geol.* **17**, 155-168.

PEACOCK, J. D. 1971. Marine shell radiocarbon dates and the chronology of deglaciation in western Scotland. *Nature , Physical Science,* **230**, 43-45.

_____ 1975. Scottish late- and post-glacial marine deposits. *In* Gemmell, A. M. D. (ed) *Quaternary studies in North East Scotland,* 45-48. Aberdeen: University of Aberdeen.

_____ 1981. Scottish late-glacial marine deposits and their environmental significance. *In* NEALE, J. & FLENLEY, J. (eds) *The Quaternary in Britain,* 222-236. Oxford: Pergamon Press.

_____ 1989. Marine molluscs and late Quaternary environmental studies with particular reference to the late-glacial period in northwest Europe: a review. *Quaternary Sci. Rev.* **8**, 179-192.

PRICE, R. J. 1983. *Scotland's environment during the last 30,000 years.* Edinburgh: Scottish Academic Press.

ROLFE, W. D. I. 1966. Woolly rhinoceros from the Scottish Pleistocene. *Scott. J. Geol.* **2**, 253-257.

ROSE, J. 1975. Raised beach gravels and ice wedge casts at Old Kilpatrick, near Glasgow. *Scott. J. Geol.* **11**, 15-21.

_____ 1981. Field guide to the Quaternary geology of the south-eastern part of the Loch Lomond basin. *Proc. geol. Soc. Glasgow,* Sessions **122/123**,12-18.

_____ , LOWE, J. J. & SWITSUR, R. 1988. A radiocarbon date on plant detritus beneath till from the type area of the Loch Lomond Readvance. *Scott. J. Geol.* **24**, 113-124.

SISSONS, J. B. 1967. Glacial stages and radiocarbon dates in Scotland. *Scott. J. Geol.* **3**, 375-381.

_____ 1968. The 'Perth' readvance. *Scott. J. Geol.* **4**, 186-187.

_____ 1974. The Quaternary in Scotland: a review. *Scott. J. Geol.* **10**, 311-337.

_____ 1976. *The Geomorphology of the British Isles: Scotland.* London: Methuen.

SUTHERLAND, D. G. 1984. The Quaternary deposits and landforms of Scotland and the neighbouring shelves: a review. *Quaternary Sci. Rev.* **3**, 157-254.

GLOSSARY

Acritarch. Single-celled, organic-walled microplankton, probably algae, characterised by varied sculpture, some being spiny, others smooth. They are predominantly Palaeozoic, and are widely used in correlation.

Agglomerate. A coarse-grained rock made up of material ejected during a volcanic eruption.

Amygdales. Vesicles and cavities in lavas which are infilled with secondary minerals.

Anaerobic. A term indicating a condition in which oxygen is absent.

Analcime. A mineral, generally white in colour, a hydrous silicate of sodium and aluminium.

Antiform. A structural term denoting that a fold closes upward in strata for which the stratigraphic sequence is not known.

Aphyric. A texture of igneous rocks where the crystals are of uniform size.

Arfvedsonite. A mineral; a sodium, magnesian, aluminium silicate, deep-green to black in colour, often found as aggregates of long, prismatic crystals. Arfvedsonite and other soda-rich amphiboles occur in silica-poor igneous rocks, such as nepheline- syenites.

Arkose. An arenaceous sedimentary rock, rich in feldspar, usually close to its source material.

Aureole. (metamorphic) The heat modified area of rock surrounding a once hot igneous intrusion.

Axial planar. Parallel to a surface which contains the fold hinges in successive layers within a fold. In a symmetrical fold it bisects the angle between the limbs of the fold.

Barkevikite. See Kaersutite.

Barytes. A mineral, barium sulphate, quite dense and generally white in colour.

Bauxite. A fine-grained, soft sedimentary rock rich in hydrated alumina. Grey-brown in colour, it is produced by weathering of certain rocks in tropical conditions.

Bedding-cleavage intersection lineation. A fine striation lineation on bedding planes or a faint colour striping or compositional banding on slaty cleavage planes, resulting from the intersection of slaty cleavage with bedding.

Biofacies. A rock unit which contains an assemblage of fossil features reflecting the conditions of origin of the rock.

Biogenic. Produced by organic means.

Biostratigraphy. A branch of Geology dealing with the sequence and correlation of rocks by the use of fossils.

Bioturbation. A process whereby animals moving or resting on or in sediment produce structures there.

Blaes. A grey-blue somewhat carbonaceous shale or mudstone.

Bole. Red argillaceous horizons found on top of basalt lava flows, indicative of extrusion and weathering in a tropical climate.

Bostonite. An intermediate igneous dyke rock, often porphyritic, whose groundmass comprises mainly flow-oriented orthoclase laths.

Boudinage. A structure resulting from deformation whereby a competent layer enclosed in less competent rocks is extended or broken at regular intervals into a series of isolated segments.

Bouma sequence. An idealised section through a **turbidite** deposit comprising from top to bottom (E) mud (D) mud and silt (C) small-scale cross-bedding (B) planar laminations and (A) a massive unit sometimes showing graded bedding. Members may well be missing, but those present are in the correct order.

Bowlingite. A secondary mineral derived from the hydrothermal alteration of olivine. It is of variable composition and is frequently found together with the alteration products iddingsite and serpentine.

Brockram. A sedimentary rock made up of coarse angular fragments (breccia) specifically of New Red Sandstone age.

Buchite. A metamorphic rock formed by partial or complete melting (vitrification) under high temperature contact metamorphic conditions (pyrometamorphism) of shale or shaley-sandstone, either in place or as xenoliths. Cordierite is commonly developed within the vitrified rock.

Caliche. See **Cornstone**

Cementstone. A sedimentary rock, an argillaceous dolomitic limestone.

Chalcedony. A mineral composed of finely crystalline and amorphous silica. It is usually light coloured with a waxy appearance.

Chert. An opaque, dark-coloured variety of chalcedony (see above), usually occurring in massive or stratified form among sedimentary rocks.

Chitinozoa. Fossils of uncertain affinity, but may be egg cases of extinct worms.

Chlorite. A mineral, a hydrous silicate with aluminium, magnesium and iron. Usually greenish in colour and greasy to touch.

Cirri. Flexible appendages attached to the stem of a crinoid.

Clastic. Sediments composed of broken fragments of pre-existing rocks.

Cobbles. Rounded rock fragments which are coarser than pebbles and finer than boulders, i.e. between 64 and 256 mm.

Conodonts. Microscopic (< 2mm) phosphatic tooth-like structures: widespread in marine sediments of Cambrian to Jurassic age: important stratigraphically; considered by some to be related to primitive vertebrates.

Coprolite. Fossilised excreta.

Coralla. The calcareous skeletons of corals.

Cordierite. A primary metamorphic mineral formed in high grade hornfelses, surrounding igneous intrusions, at high temperatures and relatively low pressures. It is an alumino-silicate containing magnesian and iron, blue in colour. It may also occur in some regional metamorphic rocks.

Cordierite-buchite. See buchite.

Cornstone. A rock, a concretionary limestone resembling a desert-type soil, where groundwater saturated with calcium carbonate is brought to the surface by capillary action during a desiccation period.

Corundum. A mineral, an oxide of aluminium, extremely hard and often crystallising with a barrel-like shape.

Crag and tail. A landform produced by moving ice meeting a solid rock obstruction (the crag), passing over and around the obstruction, and leaving a tapering mass of unconsolidated debris (the tail) on the 'downstream' side of the obstruction.

Crenulation cleavage. A regular, often closely-spaced, planar fabric in micaceous rocks formed by the microfolding or plication of a pre-existing cleavage.

Crenulation lineation. An alignment of small plications (on a mm or smaller scale) seen on bedding or cleavage surfaces, which commonly results from the intersection of a crenulation cleavage with these surfaces.

Crinanite. A medium-grained igneous rock which is a variety of analcime-bearing dolerite: *cf* teschenite.

Cross strata. Sets of strata which are inclined to the general stratification of the beds. They dip in the local direction of fluid flow at the time the beds were laid down.

Cumbraite. An igneous dyke rock composed of phenocrysts of calcium-rich plagioclase feldspar in a groundmass of other minerals and glass. The rock is very dark in colour.

Cuprite. A mineral, red oxide of copper, found in the upper oxidised zones of copper lodes.

Curvilinear. Applied to folds, this term denotes that the fold hinges have a curved form in 3-D, varying in both amount and direction of plunge.

Cuvettes. Basins of deposition, particularly those which existed in the Old Red Sandstone.

Dalmeny (basalt). An igneous rock with microphenocrysts of olivine, augite and plagioclase, in a fine-grained groundmass.

Dextral fault. A term which refers to a strike slip fault where the ground on the other side of the fault from the observer has moved to the right.

Diachronism. A term referring to a situation where a rock unit systematically changes its age as it is traced out laterally.

Diagenesis. The chemical, physical and biological changes undergone by a sediment during its transformation into rock.

Disharmonic. Refers to folds which do not have a consistent wavelength and amplitude, and show abrupt changes in profile where they affect different layers in a sequence.

Drumlin. A hill of till (boulder clay), whale-backed in shape, and elongate in the direction of ice movement.

Druse (drusy). A term referring to a rock cavity into which well formed crystals have grown.

Dunsapie (basalt). An igneous rock with macrophenocrysts of plagioclase, augite and olivine in a finer-grained groundmass.

Esker. A long winding ridge of sand and gravel deposited by glacial meltwater streams underneath or within the ice-mass.

Essexite. A variety of alkali gabbro, notable for its prominant augite phenocrysts.

Facies. Part of a sedimentary rock unit, characterised by lithological and fossil features which differentiate it from other parts of the unit, and reflect the enviroment of origin.

Facing. A term used in structural geology, referring to the orientation of the structure. A fold faces in the direction along the axial plane of a fold, at right angles to the hinge, in which the beds become younger.

Fanglomerate. An alluvial fan conglomerate deposit which has become fossilised,

Felsite. An igneous rock, light-coloured and extremely fine-grained with a chemical composition similar to a granite.

Fenestrate. With small window-like openings between branches, in a net-like arrangement.

Fireclay. A fine-grained sedimentary rock, usually grey and friable and low in alkalis. It often contains fossil plant roots, commonly occurring beneath a coal seam. It is a fossil soil.

Flexural (fold). A fold in which the rock deformation has been produced by movement along planes of weakness.

Fluorite. A mineral, calcium fluoride, often found as cubes.

Flow banding. A texture occurring in some fine-grained igneous rocks, usually granitic in composition, and due to viscous flow segregation or streaking of the constituents of the magma.

Flute cast. Bulbous cast (generally in sandstone) of an erosion hollow (generally in mudstone). This is found most frequently in **turbidite** deposits, where sands infill the fluted' surfaces of muds.

Flysch. A thick marine sedimentary sequence, essentially comprising shales and greywacke sandstones deposited from turbidity currents. Origin considered from erosion of rapidly rising fold mountains and then itself becoming folded: a syngenetic deposit. (A term originally restricted to the Swiss Alps).

Foliation. A structure of metamorphic rocks where minerals in the rock have been either segregated into bands or have acquired some degree of common orientation: a combination of compositional layering and schistosity.

Foraminifera. Small unicellular animals.

Geopetal. A term referring to a cavity (generally quite small), the lower part of which is filled with sediment (sometimes layered); and the upper part of which is filled with mineral growths. The flat top of the sediment is parallel to the horizontal at the time of formation and can therefore be used as a 'way-up' structure.

Geosyncline. A major structural downwarp in the Earth's crust which has been infilled with sediment.

Graben. A block of ground which has been downthrown between two parallel faults, (cf. **Horst**).

Graded bedding. A structure referring to beds or layers in rocks which show a gradation in grain size from bottom to top (often coarse at base and fine at top).

Grainstone. A carbonate rock composed of sand-sized particles which are in contact and which support one another.

Greywacke. A sedimentary rock, a poorly sorted sandstone made up of quartz, feldspar and rock fragments.

Groove cast. Elongate ridge on the base of a bed (generally sandstone) which is the cast of an elongate hollow in the underlying rock (generally mudstone).

Hard ground. Sea bed sediment which is lithified to form a hardened surface. It implies a gap in sedimentation.

Harzburgite. An ultrabasic rock (peridotite) composed essentially of olivine and orthopyroxene.

Hatchettite. A naturally occurring hydrocarbon mineral, found as a soft, yellow-white translucent paraffin wax in crevices of septarian concretions, and in geodes. Also known as mountain tallow, or mineral adipocere, it is named after the chemist C. Hatchett.

Hawaiite. A volcanic igneous rock somewhat richer in alkalis and silica than alkali-basalt. It is a member of the series alkali-basalt, hawaiite, mugearite, benmoreite, soda-trachyte.

Heulandite. A reddish brown hydrated silicate mineral containing aluminium, calcium and sodium: it is a member of the zeolite family of minerals. It is a characteristic mineral of amygdales in basalt where it is associated with stilbite.

Hillhouse (basalt). An igneous rock with microphenocrysts of olivine and augite in a finer-grained groundmass, itself rich in augite.

Holocene. The Holocene Epoch is the last part of geological time, spanning the interval from 10,000 radiocarbon years B.P. (Before Present) to the present day, 1950 A.D. being 'Present' in the radiocarbon timescale.

Holocrystalline. A texture of igneous rocks, where the rock is entirely crystalline.

Hornfels. A metamorphic rock produced by thermal metamorphism of fine-grained rocks usually of sedimentary origin.

Horst. An area which has been upthrown between two parallel faults (cf **Graben**).

Hyalotuff. A deposit formed from the extrusion of lava into water or wet sediments and its consequent shattering into glassy fragments.

Ice wedges. Wedge shaped masses of sediment occupying hollows once filled by ice.

Isotopic Stages. Quaternary time intervals (of unequal length), established on the basis of variations in the relative abundance of the two isotopes of oxygen, O16 and O18, in the world's oceans during the Quaternary period.

Iddingsite. A mineral, a hydrated silicate of iron and magnesium.

Involution. A form of contortion in sediments, which are often synclinally or vertically folded.

Isograd. A line on a map joining points of equal grade of metamorphism.

Isopach. A line on a map joining points where the intervals between two stated reference planes bounding rocks are equal. In this way the thickness distribution of a rock unit can be represented.

Jasper. A mineral, often red/yellow in colour, comprising very fine crystalline silica.

Jedburgh (basalt). An igneous rock with microphenocrysts of plagioclase (labradorite) feldspar in a finer grained groundmass

Kaersutite. A mineral belonging to the amphibole (hornblende) group. Dark (brown/black) in colour: previously known as barkevikite.

Keratophyre. An igneous rock, an albite (plagioclase feldspar) bearing trachyte or rhyolite.

Kink bands. Angular, asymmetric minor folds which occur in linear zones and are commonly from conjugate sets.

Larvikite. A coarse-grained igneous rock of syenitic composition comprising mainly anorthoclase feldspar showing blue iridescence (schiller structure). The ferro-magnesian minerals occur in patches, made up of titanaugite, ferro-olivine, biotite, apatite and magnetite. A commonly used ornamental stone.

Listric faults. Curved normal faults in which the the fault surface is concave upwards. A succession of such faults may develop within the hanging wall as 'rollover antiforms'.

Lithic sandstone. A sedimentary rock, sandstone, which is partly made up of rock fragments.

Lithosome. An accumulation of sediments deposited under uniform physiochemical conditions.

Load cast. A sedimentary structure, generally bulbous and rounded, formed when sand (usually) founders and injects into the underlying strata (usually mud).

Lodgement till. An unsorted mixture of sediment which has been deposited at the base of an ice sheet or glacier.

Lugarite. An igneous rock comprising kaersutite and titanaugite in a grey-green matrix which is made up largely of nepheline.

Malachite. A mineral, green copper carbonate, which occurs as a secondary mineral in the weathered zone of copper deposits and is usually banded. It is often associated with azurite, (blue copper carbonate).

Mandibles. Jaw parts of arthropods.

Markle (basalt). An igneous rock with large crystals (macrophenocrysts) of plagioclase feldspar (labradorite) in a finer grained groundmass.

Marl. A sedimentary rock, a calcareous mudstone.

Mélange. A heterogeneous rock type in which a variety of exotic rock clasts are contained in a pervasively foliated fine-grained matrix.

Mesoscopic structure. A structure seen at the scale of an outcrop (between microscopic and megascopic) : Greek *mesos* : intermediate.

Metabentonite. An altered bentonite, which is a clay deposit formed from the devitrification of volcanic ashes of glassy composition.

Metaquartzite. A metamorphic rock: a quartzite formed by metamorphic recrystallization.

Microlite. Small, needle-like incipient crystal, found in glassy igneous rocks.

Microlithon. One of the elements of a spaced cleavage. It consists of narrow slices of rock, generally a few mm thick, which are separated by cleavage planes and preserve the earlier mineralogy and tectonic fabric (often crenulated) of the rock.

Microperthite-adamellite. Microperthite is a fine intergrowth of various feldspars: (albite or oligoclase into orthoclase or microcline); and an Adamellite is a granitic rock in which plagioclase feldspar (albite/oligoclase) and potash feldspar (orthoclase) are present in roughly equal amount.

Microphyric. A texture in which the phenocrysts are small.

Millerite. A brass-coloured mineral generally occurring as fine hairlike crystals. A nickel sulphide, NiS.

Moraine. The accumulations of materials which have been transported and deposited by ice.

Monchiquite. A soda-rich igneous rock comprising phenocrysts of biotite, hornblende, augite and olivine in an analcime-rich groundmass. Typically, feldspar is absent.

Microphenocryst. A small crystal present in a groundmass of even finer crystals.

Mugearite (basalt). An igneous rock, with small crystals of olivine and soda-rich plagioclase (oligoclase) in a finer grained groundmass.

Mullite. A mineral, aluminium silicate, forms prismatic crystals, resulting from high grade metamorphism of argillaceous rocks.

Nappe. A geological structure, a fold with the axial plane horizontal or nearly so. In this volume, the term refers to a flat-lying fold of regional dimensions.

Natrolite. A white hydrated silicate mineral containing aluminium and sodium, a member of the zeolite family of minerals. It occurs in vesicles, cavities and amygdales in basaltic rocks, being deposited from hydrothermal solutions.

Nepheline. A mineral, alkali aluminium silicate. Occurs as small glassy crystals, or as interstitial material in the groundmass of undersaturated igneous rocks (eg. **theralite**).

Neritic zone. The shallow-sea environment from low water down to 200m (100 fathoms).

Obduction. The large scale thrusting of oceanic crust onto a continental margin.

Olistostrome. A massive and chaotic conglomerate which accumulated in deep water as a result of large-scale slumping.

Oolitic. A texture referring to ooliths, which are small spherical concentrically layered grains, <2 mm. in diameter. They occur typically in certain limestones, hence oolitic limestone.

Ophiolite. An association of basic and ultrabasic igneous rocks consisting of basaltic pillow-lavas, dolerite dykes, gabbros and peridotites (serpentinites), together with pelagic sediments (eg. radiolarian cherts). They probably represent segments of oceanic crust obducted on to a continent by Plate collisions.

Ophitic. Texture of basic igneous rocks, where large plates of augite enclose earlier-formed, well shaped, smaller crystals of plagioclase feldspar.

Ossicles. The calcified skeletal units, especially stem units, of crinoids.

Ostracode. A microfossil belonging to the arthropod group.

Palaeokarst. A topography formed on limestone, by solution, at some time before the present.

Palaeocurrents. The direction of flow taken by currents of former times, as they deposited sediments.

Paraconformity. A term referring to an unconformity where there is no visible discordance between the beds on either side of the break.

Paragenetic sequence. The order in which minerals are deposited.

Pegmatite. An igneous rock, very coarse grained, often associated with granite and usually occurring as a segregation vein or dyke.

Pelite. A rock, argillaceous, now used almost exclusively by metamorphic petrologists to describe the fine grained sedimentary rock before its metamorphism.

Peridotite. An igneous rock composed largely or entirely of olivine, together with other ferro-magnesian minerals and devoid of feldspar.

Phenocryst. Refers to any large, well formed crystal, which occurs in a finer grained groundmass in an igneous rock.

Phyllite. A metamorphic rock, resulting from regional metamorphism of an argillaceous sedimentary rock. A fine-grained rock with a silky sheen, which is intermediate in appearance and physical properties between slate and mica schist.

Picrite. An igneous rock, in which ferro-magnesian minerals such as olivine, augite and hornblende predominate.

Pisolite. A rock made up of pisoliths, which are spherical, concentrically layered grains 3-6 mm. in diameter (cf. **oolite**).

Playa. A flat,clay surfaced inter-montane basin.

Pod-shrimp. Oldest and most primitive of higher crustaceans (shrimps and lobsters), characterised by a large, laterally compressed carapace, or head-shield, enveloping the front regions of the body, an extra, seventh abdominal segment, and with a trifid tail-piece instead of a tail-fan.

Porphyritic. A texture of igneous rocks, describing large often well-shaped crystals in a finer grained groundmass.

Porphyroblast. Large, often well formed crystals which have grown in rocks during metamorphism.

Prehnite. A silicate mineral containing calcium and aluminium, it occurs in amygdales in basalts in association with other zeolite minerals.It is pale green in colour and occurs in botryoidal masses with a radiating fibrous structure.

Pressure solution. A process by which grain boundaries at right angles to the local principal compression direction are preferentially dissolved and the material (usually quartz and calcite) is either redeposited locally or removed from the rock via the pore fluid.

Prod and skip casts. Structures which are the casts of impact marks produced by suspended components in a current (eg. empty shells) as they impinge on the underlying bed.

Protolith. An original lithology which has been converted by metamorphism or metasomatism into a different, secondary rock type.

Provenance. A place of origin, in particular the area or region from which the constituents of a sedimentary rock facies were derived.

Psammite. A metamorphosed feldspathic sandstone with a low mica content.

Quartz feldspar porphyry. An acid igneous dyke rock composed of large quartz and feldspar crystals in a finer groundmass.

Quartz fibre lineation. Lineation comprising fibres of optically continuous quartz which have grown parallel to the local extension direction in the rock.

Ramp. The transgressive portion of a thrust where it changes stratigraphic level.

Radiolaria. Small marine planktonic organisms with silica tests.

Red bole. See Bole.

Rhyolite. An acid igneous rock, very fine grained and often displaying flow banded structures.

Roche moutonnée. An asymmetrical rock mound with a smooth slope on one side and a rough slope on the other. It is caused by ice erosion, the ice moving towards the rough slope.

Rodingite. Altered dolerite dyke, comprising augite with schiller structure and garnet.

Sanidine. A mineral, a high temperature variety of potassium/sodium feldspar.

Schistose grit. A metamorphosed clay-rich coarse-grained sandstone that resembles a schist in its foliated appearance but is coarser-grained than most schists.

Sclerosponge. A sponge with a layered calcareous skeleton.

Scolecodont. A part of the jaw apparatus of marine worms.

Scoriaceous. A texture of lavas or pyroclastic rocks which is typified by irregular vesicular cavities.

Seat earth. A bed of rock underlying a coal seam, representing an old soil that supported the vegetation from which the coal was formed.

Septarian. A structure developed in some concretions consisting of an irregular polygonal system of internal cracks, which are usually occupied by calcite or other secondary minerals.

Sericite. A mineral, a very fine grained form of mica, resulting often from the alteration of another mineral.

Serpentine. A mineral, hydrous magnesium silicate, usually green in colour. The rock, serpentinite, is often referred to as serpentine: it is the altered product of an ultrabasic rock (eg. pyroxenite).

Sinistral fault. A term which refers to a strike-slip fault where the ground on the other side of the fault from the observer has moved to the left.

Slaty cleavage. A pervasive fine-grained cleavage (or plane of splitting) developed in low-grade metamorphic rocks, and especially in mudrocks.

Slickensides. A polished rock surface, frequently striated with linear grooves and ridges, found on fault planes caused by the movement of adjacent blocks.

Slickenside lineation. Lineation, either mechanical in origin or due to the growth of quartz or calcite fibres, found on a slickenside.

Sole markings. A group of structures which commonly occur at the bases (soles) of turbidites. (See **Flute cast** and **Groove cast**).

Spaced cleavage. A cleavage in metamorphic rocks which consists of alternating light coloured (quartz-rich) stripes and thinner, dark-coloured (mica and chlorite) domains.

Sphaerosiderite. A mineral, iron carbonate, in spherical grains with radiating fibres.

Spilite. An igneous rock of basaltic type, but rich in albite and chlorite, the latter derived from the alteration of ferromagnesian minerals. Spilites are generally, but not necessarily, found in pillow lavas.

Spinel. A mineral, magnesium aluminate, commonly occurring as small octohedra.

Stretching lineation. A metamorphic term defining very fine discontinuous and streaky-looking lineation found on cleavage planes, which results from the elongation or 'stretching' of small rock particles parallel to the X-direction of the strain elipsoid during deformation.

Strontianite. A pale-green mineral, strontium carbonate.

Stromatoporoids. Palaeozoic fossils which belong to the same group as corals, with which they show some similarity.

Stylolitic. An irregular, interlocking surface, resembling a zig-zag line in cross section. It is produced by pressure solution along cracks in limestones.

Subgreywacke. The commonest type of sandstone, intermediate in composition between greywacke and orthoquartzite, containing less than 75% quartz, more than 25% of unstable fragments (feldspar and rock) and less than 15% detrital clay matrix.

Synform. A structural term denoting that a fold closes downwards in strata for which the stratigraphic sequence is not known.

Terrigenous. Refers to rocks which have either been formed of material eroded from the land, or deposited on the land.

Teschenite. An igneous rock of gabbroic type containing analcime.

Theralite. An igneous rock of gabbroic type containing nepheline.

Titanaugite. A mineral, a titanium-rich variety of augite.

Tholeiite (basalt). An igneous rock saturated or slightly oversaturated with silica, hence is olivine free and may contain intersertal quartz in the groundmass.

Thomsonite. A snow-white hydrated silicate mineral containing aluminium, calcium and sodium: it is a member of the zeolite family of minerals. It commonly occurs in cavities in basaltic rocks, being deposited from hydrothermal solutions.

Thrust duplex. A schuppen or imbricate structure with lower and upper bounding thrusts.

Torbanite. A sedimentary rock, resembling an oil shale, and apart from the argillaceous material consists of carbonaceous material of algal origin.

Tourmaline. A mineral, composed of a complex borosilicate of aluminium. It occurs normally as black prismatic crystals.

Trachyte. A fine-grained igneous rock, intermediate in composition but may contain a little quartz. Usually light in colour and characterised by the alignment of small feldspar laths (hence " trachytic texture").

Trachybasalt. An igneous rock, basalt, in which the alkali and calc-alkali feldspars are present in roughly equal amounts.

Transposition. The rotation of a pre-existing surface (bedding or foliation) into an orientation approximately parallel to the axial plane of folds; it is achieved by such processes as extreme flattening, development of axial plane foliation and segmentation of marker beds or layers.

Tridymite. A mineral, the stable form of silica between 870 and 1470 C; colourless to white.

Trondhjemite. An igneous rock of granodioritic composition but potash-feldspar free, soda-feldspar rich and usually very low in ferro-magnesian minerals.

Tuff. A rock, formed of consolidated volcanic ash, finer grained than an agglomerate.

Turbidite. A rock which was formed from material deposited by a turbidity current, that is a flow of dense sediment and water, typically occurring on the continental slopes.

Vergence. The direction in which the next major antiformal fold is located, as deduced from the apparent sense of rotation shown by minor folds of the same age found on the limbs of the structure.

Vesicles. Small spherical or elipsoidal cavities in an igneous rock, formed by escaping gases.

Vesicular. Containing vesicles.

White trap. A carbonated dyke rock, originally basaltic in most cases.

Xenocryst. A crystal in an igneous rock, larger than the groundmass, but unlike a phenocryst it has not grown from the magma, but rather has been incorporated into the melt from elsewhere. It often displays corrosion around its margins.

Xenolith. An inclusion of pre-existing rock into some igneous rock.

Zeolites. A group of minerals, hydrated silicates of calcium and aluminium. They often occur as secondary minerals filling cavities and joint spaces.

Zircon. A mineral, zirconium silicate, an important ore for zirconium, hafnium and thorium. Found as an accessory mineral in the more acid igneous rocks; also as a detrital mineral. Some varieties are used as gemstones.